CREATIVE MICROWAVE CUISINE

MARTY KLINZMAN and SHIRLEY GUY

CREATIVE MICROWAVE CUISINE

NH
NEW
HOLLAND

This edition first published in the UK in 1992 by
New Holland (Publishers) Ltd
37 Connaught Street, London W2 2AZ

ISBN 1 85368 083 4 (hbk)
ISBN 1 85368 174 1 (pbk)

Editors: Valerie Fourie and Alison Leach
Designer: Joan Sutton
Cover designer: Neville Poulter
Illustrator: Bruce Snaddon
Phototypeset by Sparhams
Reproduced, printed and bound in Singapore by Tien Wah Press (Pte) Ltd

CONTENTS

FOREWORD

Every day more and more cooks are discovering the advantages of microwave cooking and realizing the method's versatility and convenience. These modern cooks are always on the lookout for a microwave companion which will supply the best practical information as well as provide a wealth of creative ideas. So we decided that it was time to compile a really comprehensive guide to microwave cookery to help all microwave cooks make the most of their ovens.

The Complete Microwave Cookbook contains some 350 of our recipes, including lots of exciting new dishes and a number of old favourites. The book is packed with everything you need to know to create a wide range of wholesome family fare, elaborate menus for special occasions and easy-to-prepare snacks. We have also included in each section a host of hints and tips to help you achieve the very best results. The colour photographs, which illustrate almost every recipe, will assist you in the often difficult task of deciding which dish to prepare as well as providing lots of fresh ideas for presentation and serving.

Whether you are new to microwave cookery or an 'old hand', this book is for you. We hope that you will enjoy cooking from it, that it will enable you to produce innumerable memorable meals and that it will inspire you to be ever more adventurous when experimenting with your microwave.

Marty Klingman   Shirley Guy

Sausage and Pepper Frittata

100%, 50% .... 11 minutes

90 g (3 oz) sausagemeat
60 ml (4 tbsp) chopped green
  pepper
4 eggs
salt and black pepper
15 ml (1 tbsp) oil
15 g (½ oz) butter
60 g (2 oz) Gruyère cheese, grated

Crumble sausagemeat into a bowl
and microwave on 100% for
2 minutes, stirring once. Drain off
excess fat and combine with green
pepper, eggs, salt and black
pepper, mixing well.
   Microwave oil and butter in a
pie dish for 45 seconds. Tip dish
to coat evenly, then add egg
mixture and microwave on 70%
for 5 minutes. Sprinkle with
grated cheese and microwave for
1-3 minutes more, or until egg
mixture has just set. Cut in
wedges to serve.
Serves 2.

Eggs Poached in Cream

100%, 50% .... 3½ minutes

125 ml (4 fl oz) single cream
salt and black pepper
pinch of garlic salt
pinch of paprika
30 g (1 oz) butter
4 eggs
paprika and parsley to garnish

Season cream with salt, black
pepper, garlic salt and paprika
and whip until thick but not stiff.
Divide butter between four
ramekin dishes, microwave for
1 minute on 100%, then brush
melted butter around each dish.
Gently break an egg into each
ramekin and prick each yolk twice
with a thin skewer. Spoon cream
over, sprinkle with paprika and
microwave on 50% for
2-2½ minutes. Allow to stand for
1 minute before serving. Garnish
with paprika and parsley.
Serves 4.

Baked Grapefruit

100% .... 3 minutes

1 large grapefruit
30 ml (2 tbsp) apple juice
30 ml (2 tbsp) soft brown sugar
pinch of ground cinnamon

Cut grapefruit in half, remove pips and cut around each section to loosen. Place halves in individual bowls and spoon apple juice over. Mix sugar and cinnamon together and sprinkle on top of grapefruit halves. Microwave on 100% for 2-3 minutes. Serve immediately. (If necessary, rotate grapefruit halves a quarter turn after half the cooking time has elapsed.) Serves 2.

Variation
For a delicious starter to a special brunch, replace apple juice with sherry or white rum.

French Toast

100% .... 7½ minutes

2 eggs
45 ml (3 tbsp) milk
pinch of salt
few drops of vanilla extract
90 g (3 oz) butter
6 slices of bread

Mix together eggs, milk, salt and vanilla. Microwave a browning dish on 100% for 4 minutes. Add one-third of the butter and microwave for 30 seconds.

Dip two bread slices into egg mixture and microwave in browning dish for 30-40 seconds. Turn slices and microwave for a further 15-25 seconds. Repeat process with remaining bread slices, adding more butter as needed. Serve topped with golden syrup or jam and cream. Serves 6.

Piperade

This French all-in-one dish is ideal for brunch or a hearty breakfast.

100%, 70% .... 16 minutes

6 bacon rashers, rinds removed
2 onions, thinly sliced
1 small green pepper, cut in
** julienne**
1 small red pepper, cut in julienne
3 small ripe tomatoes, skinned,
** seeded and chopped**
5 ml (1 tsp) dried marjoram
generous pinch of dried thyme
6 eggs
5 ml (1 tsp) salt
generous pinch of black pepper

Place bacon in a shallow dish, cover with waxed paper and microwave on 100% for 4 minutes, or to desired crispness. Drain bacon and crumble. Reserve bacon fat. Add onion and peppers to bacon fat and microwave for 3-4 minutes, or until tender. Add tomatoes and herbs and microwave for 3-4 minutes more, stirring twice.

Beat eggs with salt and black pepper and pour into dish with vegetables. Microwave on 70% for 3-4 minutes, stirring gently every minute. (The eggs should still be very moist when removed from the oven.) Sprinkle bacon on each portion and serve with toast. Serves 4.

Hint
Eggs continue to cook after being removed from the microwave, so allow for standing time to complete the cooking process. Always check egg recipes at the minimum suggested time. It is easy to microwave eggs for a few seconds more, but once an egg is overcooked, it becomes tough and leathery.

Scrambled Eggs

100% .... 6 minutes

30 g (1 oz) butter
6 eggs
salt and black pepper
10 ml (2 tsp) milk or single cream per egg

Place butter in a large measuring jug or glass bowl and microwave on 100% for 1 minute. Lightly beat eggs with seasoning and add to butter. Microwave for 3½-4½ minutes, stirring after every minute. (The eggs should still be very moist when removed from the oven.) Stir in milk or, for a more luxurious finish, cream and leave to stand for 1-2 minutes before serving. (The eggs will continue to cook during standing time.)
Serves 3.

Serving suggestions:

SMOKED SALMON
Allowing approximately 2 slices of smoked salmon per person, arrange salmon on a round serving platter and cover with vented plastic wrap. Microwave on 50% for 2 minutes for 8-10 slices. Top with a good grinding of black pepper. Serve with the scrambled eggs, garnished with wedges of lemon and sprigs of parsley.

LUMPFISH ROE AND SOURED CREAM
Top each serving of scrambled eggs with a dollop of soured cream and a generous spoonful of red or black lumpfish roe.

Hint
To cook an egg quickly: Break an egg into a cup (greasing is not necessary), prick the yolk twice with a skewer and microwave on 100% for about 30 seconds.

Brunch-style Frittata

100%, 70% .... 16 minutes

2 eggs
1 egg white
2.5 ml (½ tsp) salt
black pepper
60 ml (4 tbsp) Ricotta cheese
30 ml (2 tbsp) oil
90 g (3 oz) mushrooms, sliced
5 ml (1 tsp) chopped fresh oregano or 2.5 ml (½ tsp) dried oregano
4 spring onions, including green portion, chopped
250 g (9 oz) courgettes, thinly sliced
1 red pepper, cut in julienne
7.5 ml (1½ tsp) lemon juice
30 ml (2 tbsp) Parmesan cheese, grated
60 g (2 oz) Mozzarella cheese, coarsely grated
paprika

Lightly beat together eggs, egg white, seasoning, Ricotta and half the oil. Set aside. Pour remaining oil into a 23-cm (9-in) pie plate and microwave on 100% for 45 seconds. Add mushrooms, oregano, spring onions, salt and black pepper and toss to coat with oil. Microwave for 1 minute, then stir in courgettes, red pepper and lemon juice. Microwave for 4-5 minutes, stirring every minute. Then stir in the Parmesan cheese.

Press vegetables into an even layer and pour egg mixture over. Sprinkle with Mozzarella and paprika. Microwave on 70% for 7-9 minutes until eggs have set and cheese has melted. Serve immediately.
Serves 4.

Hint
Never try to microwave an egg in its shell as the tight membrane surrounding the yolk collects microwave energy, resulting in a build-up of steam and ultimately causing the egg to burst. However, if a boiled egg is found to be undercooked, simply replace its top and microwave on 100% for a few seconds.

Mushroom and Tomato Ramekins

100%, 70% .... 14 minutes

6 large spinach leaves, stalks
  removed
30 g (1 oz) butter
1 small onion, finely chopped
200 g (7 oz) button mushrooms,
  sliced
1-2 tomatoes, skinned and chopped
1 garlic clove, crushed
5 ml (1 tsp) chopped fresh dill or
  2.5 ml (½ tsp) dried dill
salt and black pepper
60 g (2 oz) Gruyère cheese, grated
3 eggs
100 ml (3½ fl oz) single cream
100 g (3½ oz) low-fat soft cheese

Grease or spray six ramekins.
Wash spinach leaves well, place
in a large bowl with only the
water that clings to the leaves and
cover with vented plastic wrap.
Microwave on 100% for
2 minutes. Rinse leaves in cold
water and drain well. Line

prepared ramekins with the
leaves, placing the right side of
each leaf downwards.

Place butter in a shallow
casserole and microwave for
45 seconds. Stir in onion,
microwave for 1 minute, then add
mushrooms, tomatoes, garlic, dill
and seasoning. Stir to coat with
butter and microwave for
3 minutes. Spoon into ramekins,
leaving behind any liquid that
may be at the base of the
casserole. Divide Gruyère cheese
between ramekins.

Lightly beat together eggs,
cream and low-fat cheese. Season
to taste. Spoon into ramekins and
fold any overhanging spinach
leaves over egg mixture. Arrange
ramekins in a circle in the
microwave oven and lightly cover
with greased waxed paper.
Microwave on 70% for
5-7 minutes. The sides should be
set and the centres soft and
creamy.
Serves 6.

Old-fashioned English Breakfast

100% .... 15 minutes

6-8 streaky bacon rashers, rinds
  removed
4 large flat mushrooms
2 tomatoes, thickly sliced
30 g (1 oz) butter
4 eggs
salt and black pepper

Arrange bacon rashers on a bacon
rack, cover with waxed paper and
microwave on 100% for about
5 minutes, depending on size of
rashers. Keep warm. Arrange
mushrooms and slices of tomato
in a circle on a plate, cover lightly
with waxed paper and microwave
for 3-4 minutes. Keep warm.

Heat a browning dish for
3 minutes, add butter and heat
for about 1 minute until sizzling.
Tilt dish to coat evenly with
butter. Break eggs into dish and
very gently pierce each egg yolk
twice with a thin skewer. Season

to taste, cover and microwave for
1½-2 minutes, depending on
whether you prefer your eggs
lightly cooked or well done.
(Remember they will continue to
cook for at least 1 minute after
being removed from the
microwave.) Serve complete
breakfast immediately.
Serves 4.

Breakfast Kippers

Typical breakfast fare, kippers are
easily cooked in the microwave. No
fuss, no smells.

To microwave: Place 250 g (9 oz)
kippers in a shallow dish,
overlapping tails to ensure even
cooking. Dot with butter and
cover with vented plastic wrap.
Microwave on 100% for
2-3 minutes, depending on the
size and thickness of the kippers.
(If you are using 'boil-in-the-bag'
kippers, remember to pierce the
bag before defrosting and
microwaving.)

Peachy Sauce for Porridge

100% .... 5 minutes

425 g (15 oz) canned peach slices
30 ml (2 tbsp) soft brown sugar
10 ml (2 tsp) cornflour
pinch of ground cinnamon
pinch of ground allspice
pinch of salt
125 ml (4 fl oz) orange juice
6 glacé cherries, chopped

Drain peaches, reserving syrup, then chop coarsely and set aside. Combine sugar, cornflour, cinnamon, allspice and salt in a 1-litre (1³/₄-pint) bowl. Stir in orange juice and reserved syrup. Microwave, uncovered, on 100% for 2 minutes. Microwave for 3 minutes longer, stirring after each minute. Add chopped peaches and cherries. Spoon over hot porridge.
Serves 4.

Porridge

All types of breakfast porridge are easily and quickly cooked in the microwave either in one large container or in individual serving dishes.

100% .... 6 minutes

200 g (7 oz) porridge oats
750 ml (1¹/₄ pints) hot water or a
   combination of milk and
   water*
5 ml (1 tsp) salt

Mix dry porridge oats with hot water and salt in a container large enough to prevent mixture from boiling over. Microwave, uncovered, on 100% for 5-6 minutes, stirring mixture halfway through cooking time. Add raisins, sultanas or nuts for variety, or try fresh fruit, honey, butter, jam or marmalade.
Serves 4.

* Do not exceed 50% milk or the mixture will boil too fast.

Home-made Yogurt

100%, 10-15% .... 75 minutes

500 ml (16 fl oz) milk
15 ml (1 tbsp) natural yogurt
30 ml (2 tbsp) dried full-cream milk powder

Pour milk into a large bowl, cover with vented plastic wrap and microwave for 6 minutes on 100%. Uncover and cool over a basin of cold water until warm to the touch – about 45 °C (113 °F). Add yogurt and milk powder and whisk to combine. Cover once more. Microwave on 10-15% for 70 minutes. Cool and refrigerate. Makes about 500 ml (16 fl oz).

Creamy Yogurt

10-15% .... 90 minutes

90 g (3 oz) skimmed milk powder
675 ml (21¹/₂ fl oz) warm water
170 ml (5¹/₂ fl oz) evaporated milk
10 ml (2 tsp) soft brown sugar
45 ml (3 tbsp) natural yogurt

Combine skimmed milk powder and warm water in a large bowl. Add remaining ingredients, mix well and cover with vented plastic wrap. Microwave on 10-15% for 1¹/₂ hours. Cool, then refrigerate. Makes about 875 ml (1¹/₂ pints).

Country Ham Casserole

For a really good breakfast or brunch serve this casserole with hot toast and grilled tomatoes.

100% .... 16 minutes

30 g (1 oz) butter
300 g (11 oz) mushrooms, thickly sliced
300 g (11 oz) cooked ham, diced
4 hard-boiled eggs, sliced
400 g (14 oz) canned cream of celery or cream of asparagus soup
125 ml (4 fl oz) milk
125 g (4 oz) Cheddar cheese, grated
10 ml (2 tsp) Worcestershire sauce
few drops of Tabasco
45 g (1½ oz) butter
75 g (2½ oz) dry brown breadcrumbs

Place 30 g (1 oz) butter in a bowl and microwave on 100% for 1 minute. Add mushrooms, toss to coat and microwave for 2 minutes more. Drain thoroughly.

Arrange alternate layers of ham, egg and mushrooms in a casserole, starting and ending with ham. Combine soup, milk, cheese, Worcestershire sauce and Tabasco. Microwave for 2-3 minutes, stirring every minute until cheese has melted. Pour over casserole.

Microwave 45 g (1½ oz) butter in a bowl for 1 minute, add breadcrumbs and toss to coat. Sprinkle over casserole and microwave for 7-9 minutes, or until hot and bubbling. Brown under a hot grill if desired. Serves 6.

Hint

To dry fresh breadcrumbs: Spread 60 g (2 oz) freshly made bread-crumbs over a plate and microwave on 50% for 3-4 minutes, stirring every minute. Allow to cool before storing. (Because these bread-crumbs do not brown, they are not suitable as a coating for microwaved foods.)

Fish Fondue Casserole

A great combination for a brunch or hearty breakfast. Vary the flavours by changing the ingredients.

100% .... 15 minutes

2 spring onions, sliced
60 g (2 oz) butter
30 ml (2 tbsp) plain flour
salt and black pepper
2.5 ml (½ tsp) dry mustard
375 ml (12 fl oz) milk
200 g (7 oz) canned crab meat or 200 g (7 oz) smoked trout
10 ml (2 tsp) lemon juice
5 ml (1 tsp) fresh dill or 2.5 ml (½ tsp) dried dill
150 g (5 oz) cooked fish, such as hake, flaked
5 slices of white bread
60 g (2 oz) soft breadcrumbs

Place onions in a casserole with 30 g (1 oz) of the butter and microwave on 100% for 1 minute. Stir in flour, salt, black pepper and mustard and gradually blend in milk. Microwave for 3-4 minutes, stirring every minute until sauce thickens and begins to bubble. Add crab or trout and lemon juice, dill and fish. Mix well.

Remove crusts from bread and cut into 1-cm (½-in) cubes. Gently fold into fish mixture. Turn into a 1-litre (1¾-pint) casserole. Microwave remaining butter in a bowl for 1 minute, add breadcrumbs and toss to coat. Sprinkle over casserole and microwave for 7-9 minutes, or until bubbling. Brown under a hot grill if desired. Serves 4.

Tasty Broccoli Dip

100%, 50% .... 12 minutes

150 g (5 oz) frozen broccoli
45 ml (3 tbsp) water
white wine
1 packet of mushroom soup powder
5 ml (1 tsp) Worcestershire sauce
1 garlic clove, crushed
black pepper
250 ml (8 fl oz) soured cream
chopped parsley and slices of
    lemon to garnish

Place broccoli and water in a small bowl, cover and microwave on 100% for 4 minutes. Drain liquid into a measuring jug and add water and enough wine to make up 150 ml (5 fl oz).
   Combine liquid, soup powder, Worcestershire sauce and garlic in a bowl. Microwave for 4-5 minutes, stirring every 30 seconds. Set aside to cool slightly.
   Purée broccoli and soup in a blender or food processor until smooth. Add black pepper and soured cream. Blend to combine. Return to bowl and microwave on 50% for 3 minutes. Spoon into a warmed container. Garnish with parsley and slices of lemon. Makes about 500 ml (16 fl oz).

Aubergine Caviar

100% .... 9 minutes

1 large aubergine, unpeeled and
    diced
salt
45 ml (3 tbsp) water
60 ml (4 tbsp) chopped fresh parsley
1 garlic clove, crushed
$\frac{1}{2}$ onion, chopped
125 ml (4 fl oz) mayonnaise
black pepper
2.5 ml ($\frac{1}{2}$ tsp) dried basil
15 ml (1 tbsp) lemon juice
1 hard-boiled egg, sieved, and
    sprigs of parsley to garnish

Sprinkle aubergine with a little salt and leave to stand for 15 minutes. Rinse and pat dry. Place aubergine and water in a bowl, cover with vented plastic wrap and microwave on 100% for 7-9 minutes until tender. Drain and cool.
   Place all ingredients in a food processor or blender and process until smooth. Adjust seasoning. Spoon into a dish and garnish with egg and parsley. Serve with crudités or biscuits.
Makes about 350 g (12 oz).

Mushroom Bites

100% .... 7 minutes

12 button mushrooms, wiped
15 g (½ oz) butter
15 ml (1 tbsp) dry sherry
1 small garlic clove, crushed
½ small onion, finely chopped
2 sausages, skins removed
3 slices of salami, chopped
30 ml (2 tbsp) dry breadcrumbs
30 ml (2 tbsp) grated Parmesan
   cheese
6 stuffed olives, chopped
parsley sprigs and paprika to
   garnish

Remove stalks from mushrooms. Chop stalks finely and reserve. In a shallow casserole microwave butter on 100% for 45 seconds. Stir in sherry, garlic and onion, toss to ensure that onion is well coated with butter and microwave for 1 minute. Work in sausagemeat and chopped mushroom stalks. Microwave for 2 minutes, stirring twice during cooking time. Add remaining ingredients and combine well.

Fill each mushroom cap with a spoonful of filling and sprinkle with paprika. Arrange mushrooms in a circle on a plate, cover loosely with waxed paper and microwave for 1½-2½ minutes until only just cooked. Garnish with sprigs of parsley.
Makes 12.

Hint
Dips make attractive and easy-to-prepare snacks and are especially tasty when served with an interesting selection of vegetable crudités, such as:
- **carrot sticks**
- **cucumber sticks**
- **tomato wedges**
- **radishes**
- **celery sticks**
- **pineapple sticks**
- **cauliflower or broccoli florets**
- **mushroom caps**
- **courgette sticks**
- **mangetout peas**

Cheesy Bacon Sticks

100% .... 12 minutes

10 streaky bacon rashers, rinds
   removed
45 g (1½ oz) Parmesan cheese,
   grated
20 grissini (Italian breadsticks)

Cut bacon rashers in half lengthways. Sprinkle bacon with Parmesan cheese, press cheese on to bacon and wind one strip in a spiral around each breadstick. Place waxed paper on each of three paper plates. Divide breadsticks between plates, cover with waxed paper and microwave each plate on 100% for 3-4 minutes, or until bacon is cooked.
Makes 20.

Bacon-wrapped Snacks

100% .... 6 minutes

250 g streaky bacon rashers

FILLINGS
400 g (14 oz) canned mussels or
   oysters
pineapple chunks
stuffed olives
stoned prunes
glacé cherries
frankfurter chunks

Remove rinds from bacon and cut each rasher into three. Select filling of your choice. Wrap a piece of bacon around filling and secure with a cocktail stick. Arrange 12 of these snacks on a bacon rack, cover with waxed paper and microwave on 100% for 3 minutes. Turn each snack over, microwave for 2-3 minutes more until bacon is crisp. Serve hot.
Makes about 36 snacks.

Fish Pâté

100% .... 12 minutes

250 g (9 oz) hake
125 g (4 oz) smoked haddock
1 small onion, sliced
bay leaf
peppercorns
100 ml (3½ fl oz) milk
100 ml (3½ fl oz) water
45 ml (3 tbsp) white wine
200 g (7 oz) butter
45 ml (3 tbsp) lemon juice
5 ml (1 tsp) dried dill
45 ml (3 tbsp) single cream
salt and black pepper

GARNISH
lettuce leaves
slices of lemon
sprigs of fresh parsley or dill

Place hake, haddock, onion, bay leaf, a few peppercorns, milk, water and white wine in a shallow casserole. Cover and microwave on 100% for 6 minutes. Drain fish, reserving onion and cooking liquid. Remove skin and bones from fish. Flake flesh and set aside.

Place butter, lemon juice and dill in a bowl. Microwave for 4 minutes, then add fish, cover with vented plastic wrap and microwave for 2 minutes. Stir in cream.

In a food processor or blender, purée fish mixture with the onion and 45 ml (3 tbsp) of the cooking liquid. Season to taste. Pour into a container or prepared mould and refrigerate for at least 6 hours.

If using a mould, turn out on to a bed of lettuce. Garnish with lemon slices and fresh parsley or dill. If not using a mould, place scoops of pâté on crisp lettuce leaves, then garnish with lemon and parsley or dill. Serve with hot toast or Melba toast.
Serves 6.

Note
This fish pâté can be made well in advance and may be frozen for up to three weeks.

Chilli Meatballs

100% .... 21 minutes

1 egg
125 ml (4 fl oz) milk
45 g (1½ oz) dry breadcrumbs
15 ml (1 tbsp) chopped fresh parsley
500 g (18 oz) lean minced beef
salt and black pepper
6 green chillies
12-15 pimento-stuffed green olives, halved
100 g (3½ oz) Cheddar cheese, grated

SAUCE
1 small onion, chopped
1 garlic clove, finely chopped
400 g (14 oz) canned whole tomatoes, chopped
2.5 ml (½ tsp) dried oregano
generous pinch of ground cumin

Beat egg and milk together in a bowl, add breadcrumbs and parsley. Add beef, season with salt and black pepper and mix well to combine. Divide beef into 24-30 portions.

Cut chillies into thin strips, discarding seeds. Wrap a piece of chilli around each half olive, then mould a portion of the meat mixture around each. Place in a circular pattern in a flat microwave dish and microwave on 100% for 8-9 minutes.

To make sauce: Combine all ingredients and left-over chopped chilli strips in a bowl. Microwave, covered, for 8 minutes.

Pour sauce over meatballs and microwave for 2 minutes to heat through. Sprinkle with cheese and microwave for 2 minutes more, or brown under a hot grill. Makes 24-30 meatballs.

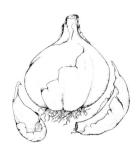

Russian Cheese Spread

A splash of vodka and some lumpfish 'caviar' make this a special dish.

50% .... 2 minutes

15 ml (1 tbsp) powdered gelatine
60 ml (4 tbsp) water
15 ml (1 tbsp) lemon juice
15 ml (1 tbsp) vodka
250 g (9 oz) cream cheese
60 ml (4 tbsp) mayonnaise
60 ml (4 tbsp) soured cream
5 ml (1 tsp) paprika
5 ml (1 tsp) salt
generous pinch of black pepper
15 ml (1 tbsp) finely chopped fresh parsley
15 ml (1 tbsp) finely snipped fresh chives
2.5 ml (½ tsp) dried dill
90 g (3 oz) red lumpfish roe
parsley to garnish

Sprinkle gelatine over water and leave to stand for a few minutes. Microwave on 50% for 45 seconds. Stir and, if necessary, microwave for a few seconds more to dissolve gelatine completely. Add lemon juice and vodka and set aside.

Microwave cream cheese on 50% for 45-60 seconds to soften. Place in a food processor with the mayonnaise, soured cream, paprika, salt, black pepper, parsley, chives and dill. Process until smooth, then add gelatine mixture. Fold in lumpfish roe by hand and turn into a greased 500-ml (16-fl oz) mould. Chill until set, then unmould on to a serving plate and garnish with parsley. Serve with savoury biscuits.
Serves 8.

Cheesy Potatoes

100% .... 13 minutes

12 small new potatoes
60 ml (4 tbsp) water
45 ml (3 tbsp) chopped fresh parsley
5 ml (1 tsp) chopped fresh mint
45 g (1½ oz) Feta cheese
75 g (2½ oz) Ricotta cheese
2-3 slices of ham, chopped
pinch of cayenne
salt and black pepper

Place potatoes in a shallow casserole, add water and cover. Microwave on 100% for 8-10 minutes until just tender. Cool slightly, then cut off tops and carefully scoop out some of the cooked potato, taking care not to break outside skin.

Combine remaining ingredients with potato pulp. Spoon back into potato shells. Arrange in a circle on a flat plate, cover and microwave for 2-3 minutes until heated right through.
Serves 4-6.

Chinese Pork and Ginger Balls

100% .... 5 minutes

500 g (18 oz) lean pork, minced
30 ml (2 tbsp) toasted almonds (page 36), finely chopped
200 g (7 oz) canned water chestnuts, drained and minced
15 ml (1 tbsp) finely grated fresh ginger or 5 ml (1 tsp) squeezed ginger juice (page 61)
15 ml (1 tbsp) soy sauce
1 egg

Combine all ingredients, mixing well. Shape mixture into 2.5-cm (1-in) balls and arrange in a circular pattern on a flat microwave dish. (Do not fill centre of dish.) Cover with waxed paper and microwave on 100% for 4-5 minutes, or until no trace of pink remains on the inside. Serve warm with a mustard or barbecue sauce (page 204).
Makes about 30 balls.

Chicken Liver Pâté de Luxe

100% .... 9 minutes

100 g (3½ oz) butter
250 g (9 oz) chicken livers, cleaned
1 garlic clove, crushed
10 ml (2 tsp) lemon juice
2.5 ml (½ tsp) salt
black pepper
1 slice of white bread, soaked in
  water
75 ml (2½ fl oz) single cream
15 ml (1 tbsp) brandy
15 ml (1 tbsp) port
pinch of ground allspice

GARNISH
1 hard-boiled egg
parsley sprig
Melba toast

Place butter in a casserole and
microwave on 100% for
3 minutes. Carefully pierce
membranes covering livers with a
skewer, add to butter and stir to
coat. Microwave, covered, for
5 minutes, stirring halfway
through cooking time. Add garlic,
lemon juice and seasoning and
microwave for 1 minute more.
  Squeeze excess water out of
bread and add to livers. Process or
liquidize until smooth. Add
cream, brandy, port and allspice.
Pulse to combine. Spoon into a
serving bowl or into a mould and
chill for several hours.
  To serve: Garnish with sieved
egg yolk and chopped egg white
and a sprig of parsley. Serve with
Melba toast.
Serves 6.

Hint
When microwaving chicken livers,
be sure to choose a casserole dish
with a heavy lid. However carefully
you pierce the membrane, chicken
livers tend to spatter.

Mushroom Pâté

100% .... 10 minutes

LAYER ONE
125 g (4 oz) butter
1 small onion, finely chopped
300 g (11 oz) flat mushrooms,
  coarsely chopped
2.5 ml (½ tsp) fresh thyme
75 ml (2½ fl oz) dry sherry
salt and black pepper
125 g (4 oz) cream cheese

LAYER TWO
125 g (4 oz) butter
300 g (11 oz) button mushrooms,
  finely chopped
1 garlic clove, finely chopped
30 ml (2 tbsp) orange juice
generous pinch of grated orange
  rind
salt and white pepper
125 g (4 oz) cream cheese

GARNISH
lemon slices
sprigs of thyme
raw mushroom slices

To make layer one: In a shallow
casserole microwave half the
butter on 100% for 2 minutes.
Add onion and toss to coat.
Microwave for 1 minute. Stir in
mushrooms, thyme, sherry and
seasoning and microwave for
3 minutes. Purée mushroom
mixture in a blender or food
processor, then beat in remaining
butter and cream cheese. Spoon
into a pâté mould or lined loaf
dish and leave till firm.
  To make layer two: Place half
the butter in a bowl and
microwave on 100% for
2 minutes. Stir in mushrooms,
garlic, orange juice and rind and
season to taste. Microwave for
3 minutes. Stir, then allow to cool
slightly before beating in
remaining butter and cheese.
Carefully spoon mixture over first
layer and chill well.
  When set, turn out and garnish
with lemon, thyme and a few
slices of raw mushroom. Serve in
slices with plenty of hot toast.
Serves 6.

Baked Mozzarella

The wonderful aroma combined with the crusty bread and melted cheese make this dish a winner with all age groups. Serve it either as a starter or as a quick supper dish.

100%, 50% .... 10 minutes
Conventional grill ..... 5 minutes

¹/₂ loaf of very crusty bread
100 ml (3¹/₂ fl oz) oil
1 garlic clove, crushed
200 g (7 oz) Mozzarella cheese, thinly sliced
125 ml (4 fl oz) single cream
black pepper
4 anchovy fillets, mashed
15 ml (1 tbsp) chopped capers

Slice bread, cutting slices in half if they are large. Combine oil and garlic and lightly brush both sides of each slice of bread. In a shallow serving dish, arrange slices of bread and cheese alternately, overlapping about three-quarters of each previous slice.

Pour cream into a jug and microwave on 100% for 1 minute. Add black pepper and anchovy fillets, then pour over bread. Sprinkle with capers, cover and microwave on 50% for 4 minutes. Remove cover and place under a preheated grill for about 5 minutes until the cheese is bubbling and the edges are beginning to brown. Serve immediately.
Serves 6 as a starter.

Hint

To slice Mozzarella cheese: Place the cheese in the freezer until it is very cold (about 30 minutes). Fit the slicing disc to the work bowl of a food processor and slice the cheese. This is the most economical method of slicing Mozzarella. Store in the freezer.

Mangetout Peas with Melon

100% .... 2 minutes

350 g (12 oz) mangetout peas, strings removed
45 ml (3 tbsp) water
1 small musk or charentais melon

SAUCE
1 egg
30 ml (2 tbsp) lemon juice
30 ml (2 tbsp) red wine vinegar
15 ml (1 tbsp) sherry
1 garlic clove, finely chopped
2.5 ml (¹/₂ tsp) dried tarragon
2.5 ml (¹/₂ tsp) anchovy paste
salt and black pepper
375 ml (12 fl oz) oil
2 round lettuces
flaked almonds, toasted, to garnish (page 36)

Place peas in 45 ml (3 tbsp) water in a microwave dish. Cover and microwave on 100% for 2 minutes. Refresh in cold water, then drain and pat dry. Peel, seed and cut melon into thin slices.
To make sauce: Combine egg, lemon juice, vinegar, sherry, garlic, tarragon, anchovy paste, salt and black pepper in a food processor. With machine running, slowly add oil until well blended.
To serve: Arrange lettuce leaves on individual plates. Add peas and melon. Spoon sauce over and garnish with toasted almonds.
Serves 6-8.

Artichokes Hollandaise

100%, 70% .... 25 minutes

4 medium-sized globe artichokes
100 ml (3¹/₂ fl oz) water
45 ml (3 tbsp) white wine
2.5 ml (¹/₂ tsp) salt
1 slice of lemon
1 garlic clove, peeled
black peppercorns
5 ml (1 tsp) oil
200 ml (7 fl oz) Hollandaise sauce
  (page 54)

Wash artichokes and trim off
stalks, lower leaves and tips.
Place in a roasting bag or covered
casserole. Combine all remaining
ingredients, except Hollandaise
sauce, and pour over artichokes.
Microwave on 100% for
18-20 minutes. Rearrange
artichokes halfway through
cooking time.
   To test if artichokes are cooked,
remove one of lower leaves. The
leaf should peel off easily. Drain
upside-down and cool. Carefully
lift out middle portion and set
aside. Using the handle of a
teaspoon, scrape away the hairy
choke. Replace leaves and trim
base level so that artichoke can be
served upright.
   To serve: Arrange in a dish,
cover and reheat in microwave on
70% for 4-5 minutes. Serve on
individual plates with plenty of
Hollandaise sauce.
Serves 4.

Note
Artichokes may also be served cold
with a French dressing.

Spaghetti with Pesto

100% .... 4 minutes

45 g (1¹/₂ oz) toasted pine nuts
  (page 36)
100 g (3¹/₂ oz) Parmesan cheese,
  freshly grated
30 g (1 oz) fresh basil leaves
2 garlic cloves
60-80 ml (4-6 tbsp) Italian olive oil
black pepper
200 g (7 oz) spaghetti, cooked
  (page 220)

Using a blender or food
processor, blend pine nuts,
Parmesan cheese, basil and garlic
until mixture is very fine. Slowly
pour oil on to moving blades until
mixture is of a thick consistency.
Season with black pepper. Store
in refrigerator in a tightly-sealed
glass jar until required.
   Serve generous amounts of
pesto on top of hot spaghetti.
Serves 4.

Variation
The following sauce makes an
unusual alternative to pesto:

RICOTTA AND NUT SAUCE
Soak 45 g (1¹/₂ oz) walnuts in boiling
water for 5 minutes, then peel off as
much outer skin as possible. Place
walnuts, 30 g (1 oz) toasted pine
nuts (page 36), 1 garlic clove and
30 g (1 oz) parsley sprigs in the work
bowl of a food processor and
process until finely chopped. Add
salt, black pepper, a generous
pinch of cayenne, 100 g (3¹/₂ oz)
Ricotta cheese and 45 ml (3 tbsp)
hot water. Process to combine.
Add 45 ml (3 tbsp) Italian olive oil
and process for a few seconds
only. Microwave, covered, on
50% for 3-4 minutes until warm.
Serves 4.

Country Terrine

100%, 30% .... 52 minutes

**2 chicken breasts, skinned and
  boned**
15 ml (1 tbsp) brandy
**250 g (9 oz) streaky bacon rashers,
  rinds removed**
250 g (9 oz) chicken livers
225 g (8 oz) boneless lean veal
500 g (18 oz) pork fillet
1 onion, chopped
1 garlic clove, finely chopped
15 g (¹/₂ oz) butter
30 ml (2 tbsp) dry sherry
salt and black pepper
30 ml (2 tbsp) chopped fresh parsley
5 ml (1 tsp) dried tarragon
pinch of ground cloves
pinch of grated nutmeg
125 ml (4 fl oz) single cream
1 small carrot, grated
45 g (1¹/₂ oz) pecan nuts

Cut chicken breasts in half
lengthways and sprinkle with
brandy. Set aside. Use bacon to
line a microwave loaf dish or
terrine and set aside. Mince
chicken livers, veal and pork fillet
and place in a large bowl. In
another bowl combine onion,
garlic and butter and microwave
on 100% for 2 minutes, stirring
after 30 seconds. Add to meat
mixture. Add sherry, salt,
pepper, herbs and spices and mix
well. Stir in cream.

Place one-third of meat mixture
in prepared loaf dish. Arrange
half the strips of chicken breast
down the centre of meat mixture.
Top with half the grated carrot
and arrange pecans on top. Add
half the remaining mixture and
top with remaining chicken,
carrot and nuts. Finally, add
remaining meat mixture and
smooth the top.

Cover tightly with vented
plastic wrap and place dish in
another, larger microwave
container as the mixture has a
tendency to boil over. Microwave
on 30% for 50 minutes. Remove
from microwave and cool for
30 minutes. Then press a heavy
weight (a brick covered in foil
works well) on top of the terrine
and leave to cool. Chill overnight.

To serve: Turn out and cut into
slices. Serve with a mixed
vegetable pickle, pickled onions
and French bread.
Serves 6-8.

Tomato Fondue

100% .... 14 minutes

1 small garlic clove, crushed
45 g (1¹/₂ oz) butter
2 large, very ripe tomatoes,
  skinned, seeded and chopped
5 ml (1 tsp) dried basil
generous pinch of oregano
generous pinch of paprika
salt and black pepper
30 ml (2 tbsp) gin
100 ml (3¹/₂ fl oz) dry white wine
200 g (7 oz) Cheddar cheese, grated
200 g (7 oz) Emmenthal cheese,
  grated

TO SERVE
French bread, cubed
mushroom caps, blanched
cauliflower and broccoli florets,
  blanched

Rub the inside of a deep casserole
with garlic, add butter and
microwave on 100% for 1 minute.
Add tomatoes, herbs, paprika
and season lightly. Microwave for
4 minutes. Add gin and wine.

Microwave for a further
5 minutes, then add cheeses and
stir well. Microwave on 50% for
3-4 minutes, stirring every
minute. Check seasoning and
adjust if necessary. Serve as soon
as possible, using crusty bread
and blanched vegetables to dip
into fondue.
Serves 4-6.

Hint
To skin tomatoes: Arrange 3 or
4 ripe tomatoes in a circle on
absorbent kitchen paper in the
microwave. Microwave on 100%
for 10-15 seconds. Leave to stand
for 5 minutes, then skin.

Savoury Aubergines

100% .... 15 minutes

30 g (1 oz) butter
1 onion, finely chopped
2 lean bacon rashers, rinds
  removed, chopped
2 medium-sized aubergines
125 g (4 oz) tomatoes, chopped
10 ml (2 tsp) tomato paste
salt and black pepper
pinch of garlic powder or garlic salt
30 g (1 oz) black olives, stoned and
  sliced
75 g (2¹/₂ oz) Emmenthal cheese,
  grated
parsley to garnish

Place butter in a casserole and
microwave on 100% for
30 seconds. Add onion and bacon
and microwave for 3 minutes,
stirring once. Cut aubergines in
half lengthways and scoop out
flesh, leaving a thin layer inside
skin. Chop flesh and add to onion
with tomatoes, tomato paste, salt,
black pepper and garlic powder.
Microwave for about 3 minutes,

stirring every minute, then add
olives and microwave for
1 minute more. Stir in half the
cheese and spoon mixture into
aubergine shells.
   Arrange aubergines in a shallow
casserole and microwave for
6 minutes. Sprinkle with
remaining cheese and microwave
for 2 minutes more, or place
under a hot grill to brown. Serve
garnished with parsley.
Serves 4.

Hint
Aubergines, also known as
eggplants and brinjals, are
members of the tomato family. The
spongy, white flesh of these glossy,
purple fruits is often slightly bitter
in flavour. To reduce the bitterness,
cut the fruit into 1-cm (¹/₂-in)-thick
slices, sprinkle with salt and leave
for 30 minutes. Rinse well and pat
dry. This procedure is often
referred to as dégorging.

Shellfish Bowl

100% .... 30 minutes

30 g (1 oz) butter
2 garlic cloves, crushed
1 leek, thinly sliced
1 very ripe tomato, skinned and
  chopped
250 ml (8 fl oz) dry vermouth or
  white wine
10 saffron threads
generous pinch of cayenne
2.5 ml (½ tsp) fresh dill
2.5 ml (½ tsp) fresh thyme
salt and black pepper
8 mussels in shells, cleaned
30 ml (2 tbsp) water
250 g (9 oz) monkfish
500 ml (16 fl oz) fish stock (page 57)
8 large prawns, peeled and
  deveined (leave tails on)
8 small squid, cleaned and cut into
  rings
30 ml (2 tbsp) chopped fresh parsley

Place butter in a large bowl and
microwave on 100% for about
45 seconds. Add garlic and leek.
Stir to coat with butter.

Microwave for 1 minute, stirring
after 30 seconds. Then add
tomato, vermouth or wine,
saffron, cayenne, dill, thyme, salt
and black pepper. Cover with
vented plastic wrap and
microwave for 5 minutes.
Uncover and microwave for
12 minutes until well reduced.
  Place mussels in a bowl with
30 ml (2 tbsp) water, cover with
vented plastic wrap and
microwave for 2-3 minutes until
shells open. (Discard any mussels
that do not open.) Remove and
discard one side of each shell. Set
mussels aside.
  Place monkfish in the stock,
cover and microwave for
4 minutes. Stir, add prawns and
squid, then cover and microwave
for a further 4 minutes. Finally,
stir in mussels, cover and
microwave for 2-3 minutes until
piping hot. Spoon into soup
plates and sprinkle generously
with parsley.
Serves 4.

Eggs with Asparagus

100%, 70% .... 13 minutes

8 fresh green asparagus spears
45 ml (3 tbsp) water
8 eggs
90 ml (3 fl oz) single cream
salt and black pepper
few drops of Tabasco
generous pinch of grated nutmeg
30 g (1 oz) butter
toast wedges to serve

Wash asparagus and trim ends.
Place in a dish with the water and
microwave, covered, on 100% for
5-7 minutes, or until just tender.
Drain and cut into 2.5-cm (1-in)
pieces. Place stalk pieces in a
serving dish or four ramekins and
set tips aside.
  Combine eggs with cream, salt,
black pepper, Tabasco and grated
nutmeg. Microwave butter in a
bowl for 30 seconds, then stir in
egg mixture. Microwave on 70%
for 5-6 minutes, or until just set,
stirring gently every minute.
Transfer egg mixture to serving

dish or ramekins and top with
asparagus tips. Serve at once
with toast.
Serves 4.

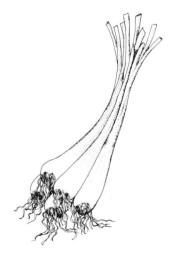

Fish Timbales

100%, 70% .... 30 minutes

10 ml (2 tsp) oil
1 small garlic clove, crushed
1 small onion, sliced
1 leek, sliced
1 tomato, skinned and chopped
250 g (9 oz) firm white fish
10 ml (2 tsp) lemon juice
1 small strip of lemon rind
2.5 ml (½ tsp) snipped fennel
   leaves
1 bay leaf
generous pinch of turmeric
125 ml (4 fl oz) white wine
125 ml (4 fl oz) water
15 ml (1 tbsp) brandy
salt and black pepper
30 g (1 oz) fresh breadcrumbs
1 egg
2 egg yolks
75 ml (2½ fl oz) single cream

SAUCE
1 red pepper, seeded and chopped
1 chilli, seeded and chopped
45 ml (3 tbsp) water
3 canned pimentos
2 garlic cloves, crushed
few drops of Tabasco
30 ml (2 tbsp) oil
15-30 ml (1-2 tbsp) dried
   breadcrumbs

Pour oil into a large casserole, add garlic, onion and leek, toss to coat with oil and microwave on 100% for 2 minutes. Add remaining ingredients, except breadcrumbs, eggs and cream, and mix well. Cover and microwave for 12-15 minutes, stirring twice during cooking time. Purée in a food processor or blender and allow to cool slightly. Mix in breadcrumbs, lightly beaten eggs and cream. Check seasoning.

Pour mixture into six ramekins. Set in a circle in the microwave. Cover lightly with greased waxed paper and microwave on 70% for 5-8 minutes until the middle has just set. Cool, then refrigerate.

To make sauce: In a bowl, place red pepper, chilli and water, cover and microwave on 100% for 5 minutes. Drain. Using a blender, purée red pepper, chilli, pimentos, garlic and Tabasco. Add oil slowly, then add sufficient crumbs to thicken slightly. Season to taste.

To serve: Set each timbale in a pool of sauce. Garnish with a mussel or prawn and a sprig of fennel.
Serves 6.

Pickled Mussels

100%, 50% .... 13 minutes

900 g (2 lb) mussels in shells,
  cleaned
500 ml (16 fl oz) water
1 large onion, sliced
1 lemon, sliced
185 ml (6 fl oz) white wine vinegar
2 bay leaves
10 ml (2 tsp) pickling spice
60 ml (4 tbsp) chopped fresh parsley
salt and black pepper
60 ml (4 tbsp) oil
lettuce leaves to serve

Place mussels and water in a large
microwave container, cover with
vented plastic wrap. Microwave
on 100% for 3 minutes until shells
open. Discard any mussels that
do not open. Remove mussels,
reserving stock. When mussels
are cool enough to handle,
remove from shells and place in a
glass bowl. Top with onion and
lemon slices and set aside.
  In another glass bowl, combine
vinegar, reserved stock, bay

leaves and pickling spice and
microwave for 5 minutes. Reduce
power to 50% and microwave for
5 minutes more. Strain through
muslin and cool to room
temperature, then pour liquid
over mussels, add parsley and
season with salt and black
pepper. Stir in oil and cover.
Marinate in the refrigerator, for
24 hours. Serve slightly chilled
on lettuce leaves.
Serves 4.

Fish Plaits

100%, 70%, 50% ..... 35 minutes

SAUCE
4 large ripe tomatoes
400 ml (13 fl oz) fish stock (page 57)
200 ml (6¹/₂ fl oz) dry white wine
200 ml (6¹/₂ fl oz) single cream
2 egg yolks
few drops of Tabasco
45 ml (3 tbsp) chopped fresh basil

PLAITS
6 rainbow trout fillets
3 sole fillets
15 g (¹/₂ oz) butter
salt and black pepper
400 ml (13 fl oz) dry white wine
bay leaf
chopped celery
basil sprigs to garnish

First make the sauce: Skin, seed
and core tomatoes. Dice flesh
carefully and set aside. Place
skins and seeds in a large bowl.
Add fish stock and wine.
Microwave on 100% for
13-15 minutes until reduced by

half. Strain. Whisk in cream and
yolks. Microwave on 50% for
4 minutes, whisking every
minute. Add tomato flesh,
Tabasco and basil and microwave
for a further 2-3 minutes on 70%.
(The tomatoes should be hot, but
not cooked.) Set aside.
  To prepare fish: Slice each fillet
in half lengthways to make
18 strips in all. Use two pink and
one white strip for each serving.
Plait, tucking ends underneath.
Butter a microwave baking sheet
and arrange fish on the sheet.
Season very lightly and add wine,
bay leaf and a little celery. Cover
with vented plastic wrap and
microwave on 70% for
6-8 minutes, depending on size of
fillets.
  To serve: Reheat sauce on 50%
for 4-5 minutes, then spoon a little
on to each fish plate and top with
a plait. Garnish with basil sprigs.
Serve immediately.
Serves 6.

Mixed Seafood Casserole

100% .... 14 minutes

15 g (½ oz) butter
45 ml (3 tbsp) fresh breadcrumbs
45 ml (3 tbsp) Parmesan cheese, grated
15 ml (1 tbsp) chopped fresh parsley
5 ml (1 tsp) chopped fresh dill or 2.5 ml (½ tsp) dried dill
45 g (1½ oz) butter
45 ml (3 tbsp) plain flour
2.5 ml (½ tsp) dried thyme
salt and black pepper
250 ml (8 fl oz) fish stock (from poaching hake)
125 ml (4 fl oz) single cream
10 ml (2 tsp) lemon juice
400 g (14 oz) hake, skinned, poached and flaked into bite-sized pieces
100 g (3½ oz) peeled shrimps
400 g (14 oz) canned artichoke hearts, drained and coarsely chopped, or 200 g (7 oz) fennel, coarsely chopped and blanched
100 g (3½ oz) mushrooms, sliced

Microwave 15 g (½ oz) butter in a jug on 100% for 30 seconds. Stir in breadcrumbs, Parmesan cheese, parsley and dill. Set aside.

Microwave 45 g (1½ oz) butter in a large jug for 1 minute. Stir in flour, thyme, salt and black pepper. Gradually add fish stock and cream. Microwave for 3-4 minutes, or until thickened, stirring every minute. Stir in lemon juice.

Place hake, shrimps, artichoke hearts and mushrooms in a small casserole and add sauce. Microwave for 6-8 minutes until heated through. Just before serving, sprinkle with crumb mixture.

Serves 4 as a main course, 6 as a starter.

Hint

To open mussels and oysters quickly, place 6 or 8 in a circular pattern on a microwave turntable or on a plate and microwave on 100% for 30 seconds to 1 minute. Any shells which have not opened in this time should be discarded.

Chilled Ratatouille

100% .... 22 minutes

45 ml (3 tbsp) oil
1 onion, chopped
1 green pepper, chopped
1 garlic clove, crushed
1 medium-sized aubergine, diced
2 courgettes, sliced
1 small carrot, grated
4 large tomatoes, skinned and chopped
60 ml (4 tbsp) tomato purée
1 bay leaf
2.5 ml (½ tsp) dried oregano
salt and black pepper
30 ml (2 tbsp) chopped fresh parsley
45 g (1½ oz) strong Cheddar cheese, grated
slices of French bread to serve

Microwave oil in a large bowl on 100% for 1 minute. Add onion, green pepper and garlic. Toss to coat with oil, cover and microwave for 3 minutes. Stir in aubergine, courgettes, carrot, tomatoes, tomato purée, bay leaf, oregano and seasoning. Cover and microwave for 18 minutes, stirring from time to time. Cool, then chill thoroughly.

Before serving, stir in parsley and grated cheese. Serve with plenty of crusty French bread. Serves 4-6.

Note

Originating in Provence, this versatile and colourful vegetable dish may be eaten hot or cold, as a vegetable accompaniment to meat, a starter, or as a salad.

Cheese is not a strictly traditional ingredient but it makes for a tasty variation, as does the inclusion of mint, or other fresh garden herbs.

Smoked Trout Custards

30% .... 20 minutes

175 g (6 oz) smoked trout
2 eggs
250 ml (8 fl oz) single cream
black pepper
5-10 ml (1-2 tsp) lemon juice
5 ml (1 tsp) chopped fresh dill or
 2.5 ml (¹/₂ tsp) dried dill
60 g (2 oz) Emmenthal cheese,
 grated
red lumpfish roe (optional)
fresh dill or parsley and lemon
 slices to garnish

Place trout, eggs, cream, black pepper, lemon juice and dill in a food processor or blender and blend until smooth. Pour into four microwaveproof ramekins and microwave on 30% for 15-20 minutes, or until just set. (If the mixture starts to bubble around the edges, turn off microwave for a few minutes, then continue cooking at 30%.)

Sprinkle with cheese and melt under the grill. Garnish with a little lumpfish roe, fresh dill or parsley and a lemon slice. Serve with toast wedges or Melba toast. Serves 6.

Stuffed Baby Squid

100%, 70% .... 31 minutes

750 g (1¾ lb) small squid
3 streaky bacon rashers, rinds
 removed, chopped
10 ml (2 tsp) oil
1 small onion, chopped
1 thick slice of wholemeal bread,
 made into crumbs
3 brown mushrooms, chopped
2 hard-boiled eggs, chopped
30 ml (2 tbsp) chopped fresh parsley
1 garlic clove, crushed
15 ml (1 tbsp) brandy
salt and black pepper

SAUCE
30 ml (2 tbsp) oil
1 small onion, chopped
1 bay leaf
400 g (14 oz) canned tomatoes,
 drained and chopped
30 ml (2 tbsp) tomato purée
salt and black pepper
2.5 ml (¹/₂ tsp) chopped fresh
 marjoram
5 ml (1 tsp) sugar

Clean squid, set tubes aside and chop tentacles. Microwave bacon and oil in a bowl on 100% for 1 minute. Add onion and microwave for 1 minute more. Stir in chopped tentacles and remaining ingredients, and season to taste. Fill each tube with a little of the mixture, taking care not to overfill as the mixture swells during cooking. Set aside.
 To make sauce: Microwave oil in a shallow casserole on 100% for 1 minute. Add onion, stir to coat with oil and microwave for 1 minute. Add remaining ingredients and microwave for 15 minutes until well thickened.
 Arrange stuffed squid in the dish, spooning a little of the tomato mixture over the top of each. Cover and microwave on 70% for 10-12 minutes, taking care not to over-cook as the squid will become tough.
Serves 6.

Orange and Tomato Soup

100% .... 24 minutes

30 g (1 oz) butter
1 celery stick, chopped
1 onion, chopped
1 carrot, chopped
2 bacon rashers, rinds removed, chopped
45 ml (3 tbsp) plain flour
15 ml (1 tbsp) tomato purée
500 g (18 oz) ripe tomatoes, skinned and chopped
1 litre (1¾ pints) chicken stock
salt and black pepper
5 ml (1 tsp) sugar
5 ml (1 tsp) dried basil
10 ml (2 tsp) grated orange rind
100 ml (3½ fl oz) orange juice
30 ml (2 tbsp) medium sherry
double cream and grated orange rind to garnish

In a large casserole, microwave butter on 100% for 30 seconds. Add vegetables and bacon and microwave for 4-5 minutes,
stirring every minute. Stir in flour and tomato purée, then add tomatoes, stock, salt, black pepper, sugar and basil. Cover and microwave for 15 minutes.

Pour soup into a food processor or blender and process till smooth. Return to casserole, stir in orange rind and juice and microwave for 2-3 minutes to heat through. Add sherry and spoon into individual bowls. Garnish with a little cream and grated orange rind.
Serves 6.

Cream of Onion Soup

100% .... 26 minutes

60 g (2 oz) butter
3 large onions, finely chopped
2 celery sticks, finely chopped
1 litre (1¾ pints) chicken stock
1 bay leaf
pinch of grated nutmeg
salt and black pepper
30 g (1 oz) plain flour
125 ml (4 fl oz) milk
125 ml (4 fl oz) single cream
fried croûtons and chopped fresh parsley to garnish

In a large casserole, microwave butter on 100% for 45 seconds. Add onion and celery and microwave for 3 minutes, stirring once. Add stock, bay leaf, nutmeg and season well. Microwave, covered, for 15-18 minutes, or until vegetables are very tender. Remove bay leaf.

Purée soup in a food processor or blender, then return to casserole. Carefully blend flour with milk and gradually beat into
soup. Microwave for about 4 minutes, stirring every minute, then stir in cream. Garnish with fried croûtons and sprinkle with parsley.
Serves 4-6.

Hint

To make basic croûtons: Place 60 g (2 oz) butter in a large, shallow baking dish and microwave on 100% for 1 minute. Stir in bread cubes cut from 4 slices of bread, ensuring that all sides are coated with butter, and microwave for 4-6 minutes. Leave to stand for 5 minutes to crisp completely before using. Store in an air-tight container.
• To make garlic croûtons: Microwave 1 sliced garlic clove in the melted butter for 45 seconds. Remove garlic before adding bread cubes.
• To make herby croûtons: Add 2.5-5 ml (½-1 tsp) dried herbs with the bread cubes.
• To make cheese croûtons: Add 45 ml (3 tbsp) grated Parmesan cheese immediately after microwaving but before standing time.

Hearty Mussel Soup

100% .... 36 minutes

30 ml (2 tbsp) oil
1-2 garlic cloves, crushed
1 onion, chopped
1 carrot, diced
2 celery sticks, chopped
1 litre (1³/₄ pints) chicken stock
30 ml (2 tbsp) tomato paste
400 g (14 oz) canned tomatoes,
  chopped
250 g (9 oz) white fish
2.5 ml (¹/₂ tsp) sugar
salt and black pepper
2.5 ml (¹/₂ tsp) dried basil
800 g (1 lb 14 oz) fresh mussels with
  shells, cooked (page 55)
90 g (3 oz) frozen peas

Pour oil into a large bowl and
microwave on 100% for 1 minute.
Add garlic, onion, carrot and
celery and stir to coat. Cover and
microwave on 100% for
5 minutes. Stir in chicken stock,
tomato paste and chopped
tomatoes and microwave,
covered, for 10 minutes.

Add fish, sugar, seasoning and
basil. Microwave, covered, for
10 minutes. Discard fish, then
add mussels and peas. Cover and
microwave for a further
10 minutes.
Serves 8.

Basic Chicken Stock

Place 1 kg (2¹/₄ lbs) chicken bones,
trimmings and giblets in a large
bowl. Pour over 2 litres
(3¹/₂ pints) of boiling water and
leave to stand for 5 minutes.
Drain and pour over 2 litres
(3¹/₂ pints) of cold water.
  Add 6 peppercorns, 1 bay leaf,
a little thyme, 4 parsley sprigs,
1 sliced onion, 1 thickly sliced
celery stalk and 1 thickly sliced
carrot. Microwave on 100% for
10-12 mintues, then reduce power
to 50% and microwave for about 1
hour. Strain stock and cool.
Remove fat and keep stock
refrigerated until required.
Makes about 1.5 litres (2³/₄ pints).

Chilled Cucumber Soup

100%, 70% .... 20 minutes

1 large cucumber, peeled and diced
1 litre (1³/₄ pints) chicken stock
¹/₂ onion, chopped
30 g (1 oz) butter
45 ml (3 tbsp) plain flour
salt and black pepper
15 ml (1 tbsp) lemon juice
2 egg yolks
100 ml (3¹/₂ fl oz) single cream
fresh mint leaves and cucumber
  slices to garnish

Place cucumber in a casserole
with the stock and onion. Cover
and microwave on 100% for
10-12 minutes, or until cucumber
is tender. Cool, then purée
mixture in a blender or food
processor.
  Microwave butter in a bowl for
30 seconds. Stir in flour and
gradually mix in cucumber purée.
Microwave for 4 minutes, stirring
every minute until mixture
thickens. Season with salt,
pepper and lemon juice.

Blend egg yolks with cream,
then beat in a little of the soup.
Pour back into soup and stir to
combine. Microwave on 70% for
about 3 minutes, stirring every
minute. (Do not let mixture boil.)
Cool soup, then chill thoroughly.
Serve garnished with mint and
cucumber slices.
Serves 6.

Cream of Pumpkin Soup

100% .... 28 minutes

60 g (2 oz) butter
1 onion, sliced
1.5 kg (2¼ lb) pumpkin, peeled,
    seeded and chopped
2.5 ml (½ tsp) mild curry powder
500 ml (16 fl oz) chicken stock
500 ml (16 fl oz) milk
salt and black pepper
generous pinch of grated nutmeg
75 ml (2½ fl oz) single cream
snipped fresh chives

Place butter in a large casserole
and microwave on 100% for
30 seconds. Add onion and
microwave for 2 minutes. Then
add pumpkin, curry powder and
stock and microwave, covered,
for 18-20 minutes, stirring every
4 minutes.

   Purée pumpkin with stock in a
food processor or blender and
return to dish. Add milk and
microwave for 4-5 minutes,
stirring every minute. Season well
with salt, black pepper and
nutmeg. Stir in cream just before
serving and sprinkle with chives.
Serves 6.

Smoked Haddock Soup

70% .... 14 minutes

500 g (18 oz) smoked haddock,
    skinned
1 onion, sliced
400 ml (13 fl oz) water
100 ml (3½ fl oz) dry white wine
500 ml (16 fl oz) milk
salt and black pepper
150 g (5 oz) mashed potato, hot
60 g (2 oz) butter
60 ml (4 tbsp) single cream
30 ml (2 tbsp) lemon juice
10 ml (2 tsp) chopped fresh dill or
    5 ml (1 tsp) dried dill

Place fish in a casserole with onion,
water and wine. Cover and microwave on 70% for 8-10 minutes.
Leave to stand for 10 minutes.
Remove and flake fish.

   Strain cooking liquid into a dish
and add milk, flaked fish, salt and
black pepper. Microwave for
3-4 minutes, or until boiling, then
beat in enough of the mashed
potato to give a good consistency.
Stir in butter, cream and lemon
juice. Serve in individual bowls,
sprinkled with dill.
Serves 4-6.

Carrot and Coriander Soup

100% .... 42 minutes

60 g (2 oz) butter
1 small onion, chopped
1 kg (2¼ lb) carrots, peeled and thinly sliced
60 ml (4 tbsp) Madeira or medium dry sherry
15 ml (1 tbsp) whole coriander
15 ml (1 tbsp) sugar
salt and black pepper
1 litre (1¾ pints) chicken stock

GARNISH
60 ml (4 tbsp) soured cream
30 ml (2 tbsp) grated carrot
15 ml (1 tbsp) chopped fresh coriander or snipped chives

Place butter in a large casserole and microwave on 100% for 45 seconds. Add onion and carrots, stir to coat with butter and microwave for 4 minutes. Then add Madeira, coriander, sugar and seasoning. Cover and microwave for about 25 minutes until carrots are soft, stirring from time to time.

Pour in stock and microwave for a further 5 minutes. Process soup in batches in a food processor or blender, then rub through a sieve. Reheat in microwave oven for 5-7 minutes.

To serve: Spoon into warmed soup bowls, top each serving with soured cream, grated carrot and chopped coriander or snipped chives.
Serves 6.

Spring Onion Soup

100% .... 18 minutes

30 g (1 oz) butter
2 bunches of spring onions, including green portion, chopped
15 ml (1 tbsp) plain flour
750 ml (1¼ pints) chicken stock, boiling
salt and black pepper
10 ml (2 tsp) chopped fresh dill or 2.5 ml (½ tsp) dried dill
200 ml (6½ fl oz) single cream or soured cream
15 ml (1 tbsp) brandy

GARNISH
45 ml (3 tbsp) soured cream
snipped spring onion tops
dill sprigs

Place butter in a 2-litre (3½-pint) casserole and microwave on 100% for 45 seconds. Add spring onions and toss to coat with butter. Microwave for 4 minutes, stirring at least once during cooking time.

Add flour, stir well, then gradually add stock. Season to taste with salt and black pepper and add dill. Stir to combine. Cover and microwave for 10 minutes, then stir in cream and brandy. Microwave for 2-3 minutes until piping hot.

Ladle into warmed soup bowls, add a spoonful of soured cream to each serving and garnish with a sprinkling of spring onions and a sprig of dill.
Serves 6.

Hint

There is nothing quite like the flavour of garden-fresh herbs but all things have their season, and when your herbs are at their peak it is a good time to dry some for the leaner months. That way you can enjoy the year-round satisfaction of using home-grown.

To dry herbs in the microwave: Place 90 g (3 oz) fresh herbs in layers between sheets of absorbent kitchen paper. Microwave on 100% for 4-6 minutes. (The time will vary according to the water content of the herbs.) Cool to room temperature, then crush and store in an air-tight container.

Lightly Curried Vichyssoise

100% .... 26 minutes

60 g (2 oz) butter
6 large leeks, sliced
4 medium-sized potatoes, peeled
  and sliced
2.5-5 ml (^{1}/$_2$-1 tsp) curry paste
700 ml (22 fl oz) chicken stock
salt and black pepper
pinch of grated nutmeg
250 ml (8 fl oz) single cream
30 ml (2 tbsp) snipped chives

Place butter in a large casserole
and microwave on 100% for
1-1^1/$_2$ minutes. Add leeks, stir to
coat with butter, then cover and
microwave for 4 minutes, stirring
every minute. Add potatoes and
curry paste, stir to coat with
butter, cover and microwave for
3 minutes.

Pour in half the stock, season
very lightly and add nutmeg.
Cover and microwave for
15 minutes, stirring at least once

during cooking time. Add
remaining stock and microwave
for 2 minutes more.

Purée soup in a blender or food
processor, then add cream,
reserving a little for garnishing.
Adjust seasoning. Cool, then chill
well. Serve with a little of the
remaining cream lightly stirred
into each portion and top with a
sprinkling of chives.
Serves 6.

Chilled Avocado Soup

100% .... 12 minutes

45 g (1^1/$_2$ oz) butter
45 ml (3 tbsp) chopped onion
60 ml (4 tbsp) plain flour
750 ml (1^1/$_4$ pints) chicken stock
2 medium-sized ripe avocados
15 ml (1 tbsp) lemon juice
salt and black pepper
125 ml (4 fl oz) milk
125 ml (4 fl oz) single cream
few drops of Tabasco
avocado slices and soured cream
  to garnish

Place butter in a large casserole
and microwave on 100% for
30 seconds. Add onion and
microwave for 2 minutes. Stir in
flour and gradually mix in stock.
Microwave for 5 minutes, stirring
twice.

Peel and quarter avocados, then
chop roughly. Add to soup
together with lemon juice, salt
and black pepper. Microwave for
4 minutes, stirring after
2 minutes. Purée mixture in a

food processor or blender, then
return to dish. Stir in milk and
cream, add a few drops of
Tabasco and chill well. Serve
garnished with soured cream and
thin slices of avocado.
Serves 4-6.

Hint
Garnish bowls of soup with:
• chopped or snipped fresh herbs
• a spoonful of cream, feathered by
drawing a cocktail stick through it
once or twice
• the flowers of herbs or any other
edible flower
• a few cooked pasta shapes
• grated or thinly-sliced vegetables
of the type that are included in the
soup
• tiny plain or cheese choux puffs
• herb-flavoured crêpe cut into thin
shreds
• egg threads (stir lightly beaten
egg into piping hot soup at the last
moment and microwave on 70% for
1-2 minutes)

Corn and Bacon Chowder

100% .... 20 minutes

30 g (1 oz) butter
4 bacon rashers, rinds removed,
  finely chopped
1 onion, finely chopped
2 celery sticks, sliced
2 potatoes, peeled and diced
15 ml (1 tbsp) plain flour
600 ml (19 fl oz) beef stock
300 ml (10 fl oz) milk
400 g (14 oz) canned sweetcorn
  kernels
1 bay leaf
salt and black pepper
15 ml (1 tbsp) snipped chives
Melba toast or crusty rolls to serve

Place butter in a large bowl or casserole and microwave on 100% for 45 seconds. Add bacon and microwave for 2-3 minutes. Remove bacon from bowl and set aside.

To the bowl add onion, celery and potatoes. Stir to coat with fat, then cover and microwave for 7-8 minutes. Stir in flour, then gradually add stock and milk, followed by the sweetcorn and bay leaf. Microwave for about 8 minutes, stirring at least twice during cooking time. Remove bay leaf, season to taste and add bacon. Spoon into soup bowls, sprinkle with chives and serve with Melba toast or crusty rolls. Serves 6.

Hints

• To separate bacon rashers easily: Microwave bacon on 100% for a few seconds.
• To defrost a 250 g (9 oz) packet of bacon: Place the packet on a plate and microwave on 30% for 3-4 minutes. Turn the packet over after half the cooking time and leave to stand for 5 minutes before using. Do not microwave foil packets.

Creole Fish Soup

100%, 70% .... 20 minutes

30 ml (2 tbsp) oil
1 onion, sliced
2 celery sticks, sliced
1 large green pepper, cored, seeded
  and sliced
3 garlic cloves, finely chopped
750 ml (1¼ pints) seasoned tomato
  sauce, (page 204)
375 ml (12 fl oz) chicken stock
5 ml (1 tsp) salt
5 ml (1 tsp) sugar
few drops of Worcestershire sauce
few drops of Tabasco
350 g (12 oz) fish fillets, skinned
275 g (10 oz) hot cooked rice
  (page 220)
chopped fresh parsley to garnish

Microwave oil on 100% for 1 minute. Add vegetables, toss to coat and microwave for 3 minutes, stirring once. Add tomato sauce, stock, salt, sugar, Worcestershire sauce and Tabasco. Microwave, covered, for 6 minutes.

Cut fish into bite-sized pieces and add to soup. Microwave on 70% for 8-10 minutes, stirring gently from time to time. Spoon into bowls and top each with a mound of rice. Sprinkle with parsley.
Serves 4-6.

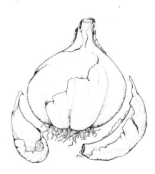

Mexican Chicken Soup

100% .... 47 minutes

750 g (1¾ lb) chicken pieces
1 litre (1¾ pints) water
1 onion, sliced
3 celery sticks, roughly chopped
5 ml (1 tsp) salt
black pepper
1-2 chillies, chopped
1 bay leaf
300 g (11 oz) tomatoes, skinned and
   chopped
2-3 carrots, thinly sliced
1 medium-sized onion, chopped
250 ml (8 fl oz) chicken stock
1 large courgette, sliced
200 g (7 oz) peas
1 avocado, sliced, to garnish

Place chicken, water, onion,
celery, seasoning, chillies and bay
leaf into a 3-litre (5-pint)
casserole. Cover and microwave
on 100% for 25 minutes. Remove
chicken from broth and set aside.
Strain broth, discard vegetables
and return broth to casserole.
Add tomatoes, carrots, onion and
chicken stock. Cover and
microwave for 15 minutes.
   When chicken is cool enough to
handle, remove flesh from bones
and discard skin. Cube flesh and
add to cooked liquid with
courgette and peas. Cover and
microwave for 5-7 minutes more
until all vegetables are tender.
Before serving, garnish with
slices of avocado.
Serves 6.

Beef Chilli and Potato Soup

**Served with crusty rolls, this hearty
soup makes a satisfying meal.**

100% .... 19 minutes

250 g (9 oz) minced beef
1 small onion, chopped
1 celery stick, sliced
400 g (14 oz) canned whole
   tomatoes, coarsely chopped
2 medium-sized potatoes, peeled
   and diced
600 ml (19 fl oz) beef stock
5 ml (1 tsp) chilli powder
salt and black pepper
2.5 ml (½ tsp) Worcestershire
   sauce
400 g (14 oz) canned red kidney
   beans, drained
125 ml (4 fl oz) soured cream

Crumble meat into a large
casserole and microwave on 100%
for 3 minutes, stirring once to
break up meat. Drain off all fat.
Add onion and celery and
microwave for 2 minutes. Add
tomatoes, potatoes, stock, chilli
powder, salt, black pepper and
Worcestershire sauce. Cover and
microwave for about 12 minutes,
or until potatoes are very tender.
Stir in beans and microwave for a
further 2 minutes. Serve in
individual bowls, topped with
soured cream.
Serves 6.

Hints
• Soups can be left simmering in
the microwave over a lengthy
period with minimal attention. On
a low power level, soup will neither
boil over nor dry out.
• To heat one portion of chilled
soup, allow 2-3 minutes on 100%.
• To reheat a portion of frozen
soup, first defrost on 30% for about
5 minutes, then heat as for chilled
soup. (Times will vary quite
considerably depending on the fat
content of the soup, as well as the
size of the portion.)

Apple Soup with Brandy

100% .... 19 minutes

60 g (2 oz) butter
2 large leeks, thinly sliced
½ onion, sliced
2 apples, peeled, cored and grated
3 large potatoes, peeled and diced
750 ml (1¼ pints) chicken stock
generous pinch of ground nutmeg
250 ml (8 fl oz) milk
375 ml (12 fl oz) whipping cream
salt and white pepper
30 ml (2 tbsp) brandy
chopped spring onion to garnish (optional)

Microwave butter on 100% for 1 minute. Add leeks, onion and apples, tossing to coat, then microwave for 3 minutes, stirring twice. Add potatoes, stock and nutmeg. Microwave, covered, for 12-15 minutes, or until potatoes are very tender.

Cool slightly, then purée mixture in batches in a blender or food processor. Stir in milk and 300 ml (10 fl oz) of the cream and season to taste with salt and pepper. Cover and chill for at least 3 hours.

Before serving, stir in brandy. Spoon into individual bowls and top with remaining cream, which has been whipped. Sprinkle with chopped spring onion if desired. (This soup makes a great summer starter.)
Serves 6.

Peanut Soup

100%, 50% .... 20 minutes

30 g (1 oz) butter
6 spring onions, sliced
1 celery stick, thinly sliced
2.5 ml (½ tsp) curry powder
45 ml (3 tbsp) plain flour
500 ml (16 fl oz) chicken stock
375 ml (12 fl oz) milk
125 g (4 oz) smooth peanut butter
20 ml (4 tsp) lemon juice
few drops of Tabasco
salt
30 ml (2 tbsp) snipped chives and a few peanuts to garnish

In a large casserole, microwave butter on 100% for 1 minute. Add onions and celery and microwave for 3 minutes. Add curry powder, mix well and microwave for 30 seconds more. Stir in flour and gradually stir in chicken stock and milk. Microwave for about 5 minutes, stirring every minute until mixture has thickened.

Strain liquid and purée vegetables. Return purée to soup together with peanut butter and beat until well blended. Add lemon juice, Tabasco and salt to taste. Microwave on 50% for about 10 minutes, stirring occasionally. Spoon into individual bowls and garnish with snipped chives and a few peanuts.
Serves 6.

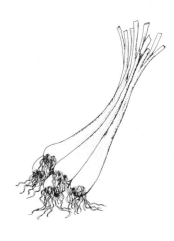

Melon Salad

100% .... 1 minute

1 sweet melon
lettuce leaves
1 bunch of spring onions, chopped
30 ml (2 tbsp) Dijon mustard
2.5 ml (¹/₂ tsp) sugar
60 ml (4 tbsp) white wine vinegar
90 ml (3 fl oz) oil
2.5 ml (¹/₂ tsp) finely chopped fresh mint leaves
mint sprigs to garnish

Peel melons, halve and remove seeds. Cut into slices. Arrange a few slices attractively on each salad plate with a lettuce leaf. Place onions, mustard, sugar and vinegar in a jug and microwave on 100% for 1 minute. Whisk in oil and chopped mint. Continue whisking until thickened, then drizzle over melon. Garnish with sprigs of mint and serve warm. Serves 4-6.

Almond and Dill Potato Salad

100% .... 25 minutes

1.5 kg (3 lb) potatoes, peeled and diced
125 ml (4 fl oz) water
salt and black pepper
10 ml (2 tsp) chopped fresh dill or 2.5 ml (¹/₂ tsp) dried dill
45 g (1¹/₂ oz) flaked almonds, toasted

DRESSING
30 g (1 oz) butter
1 onion, finely chopped
1 garlic clove, minced
10 ml (2 tsp) chopped fresh dill or 2.5 ml (¹/₂ tsp) dried dill
30 ml (2 tbsp) honey
60 ml (4 tbsp) soured cream
250 ml (8 fl oz) mayonnaise
2.5 ml (¹/₂ tsp) French mustard
2.5 ml (¹/₂ tsp) sugar

Place potatoes in a casserole. Add water, cover and microwave on 100% for 18-22 minutes, stirring gently three times. (Potatoes should be just tender.) Drain and sprinkle with salt, black pepper and dill.
   To make dressing: Microwave butter in a bowl for 30 seconds. Add onion and garlic and microwave for 2 minutes. Leave to cool. Combine dill, honey, soured cream, mayonnaise, mustard and sugar with onion mixture. Spoon over potatoes, tossing to mix. Sprinkle with toasted almonds just before serving.
Serves 8.

Hint
To toast pine nuts and almonds: Place pine nuts, or flaked or blanched almonds in a browning dish and microwave on 100% for 4-5 minutes, stirring every minute.

Tangy Pasta Salad

100% .... 5 minutes

200 g (7 oz) spiral noodles, cooked (page 220)
30 ml (2 tbsp) Italian olive oil
450 g (1 lb) canned tomatoes, chopped
salt and black pepper
generous pinch of cayenne
pinch of sugar
10 ml (2 tsp) chopped fresh basil or 2.5 ml (¹/₂ tsp) dried basil
1 garlic clove, finely chopped
5 ml (1 tsp) whole coriander seeds, crushed
2-3 courgettes, sliced
30 ml (2 tbsp) capers, chopped

Toss drained, hot pasta in oil and allow to cool. In a large bowl combine all ingredients except capers. Microwave on 100% for 5 minutes. Stir and allow to cool. Combine sauce and pasta and turn into a glass serving bowl. Sprinkle with capers.
Serves 6.

Brown Rice Salad

100% .... 25 minutes

200 g (7 oz) brown rice
600 ml (19 fl oz) boiling water
1 chicken stock cube
5 ml (1 tsp) oil
pinch of turmeric
1/2 small onion, chopped
1 small green pepper, seeded and chopped
2 celery sticks, chopped
1 mango, peeled and diced
100 ml (3 1/2 fl oz) mayonnaise
pinch of cayenne
2.5 ml (1/2 tsp) dried thyme
2-3 slices of mango and thyme sprigs to garnish

Place rice in a large glass jug, add boiling water, stock cube, oil and turmeric. Microwave on 100% for 25 minutes, stirring twice during cooking time. Allow to stand, covered, for 20 minutes, then cool.

Toss all remaining ingredients in a large bowl and finally add rice. Season to taste. Garnish with a few slices of mango and thyme sprigs.
Serves 6.

Hint
Flavoured vinegars made from herbs, strawberries or other fruits soaked in wine vinegar add subtle flavour to salad dressings and sauces.

STRAWBERRY VINEGAR
Place 1 litre (1 3/4 pints) white wine vinegar in a jug and microwave on 50% for 2 minutes until warm. Place 90 g (3 oz) sliced strawberries in a large bowl and sprinkle with 30 g (1 oz) caster sugar. Pour warm vinegar over, cover and leave to stand for 24 hours. Gently pour mixture into a jar, seal and leave for 2 weeks. Then, when vinegar has a rosy colour, strain into a clean jar and seal. Makes 1 litre (1 3/4 pints).

Warm Lettuce Salad

100% .... 5 minutes

6 bacon rashers, rinds removed
6 spring onions, chopped
60 ml (4 tbsp) white vinegar
60 ml (4 tbsp) water
15 ml (1 tbsp) sugar
2.5 ml (1/2 tsp) salt
black pepper
1 lettuce
3 fresh mint leaves, finely chopped
300 g (11 oz) fresh young spinach
1 small bunch of radishes, sliced
2 hard-boiled eggs, chopped

Arrange bacon on a plate or bacon rack, cover with waxed paper and microwave on 100% for about 5 minutes until cooked. Drain bacon fat into a bowl. When bacon is sufficiently cool, crumble and set aside.

Add spring onions to bacon fat and microwave for 2 minutes. Add vinegar, water, sugar, salt and black pepper and microwave for about 2 minutes, or until boiling. Stir well.

Tear lettuce into small pieces and place in a large microwave-proof bowl. Add mint. Tear spinach leaves and add to bowl, tossing well. Pour hot dressing over and toss. Microwave for 1 minute, toss again and add crumbled bacon, radishes and eggs. Serve while still warm. Serves 6.

Ring Potato Salad

100% .... 15 minutes

500 g (18 oz) potatoes, peeled and
　diced
45 ml (3 tbsp) water
30 ml (2 tbsp) oil
15 ml (1 tbsp) vinegar
2.5 ml (½ tsp) dry mustard
pinch of cayenne
salt and black pepper
75 ml (2½ fl oz) mayonnaise
2 hard-boiled eggs, chopped
1 small green pepper, chopped
250 g (9 oz) cottage cheese
1 small onion, chopped
30 ml (2 tbsp) chopped fresh parsley

GARNISH
endive
red and green pepper strips
olives
tomato wedges

Soak diced potato in cold water
for 5 minutes. Drain, place in a
large bowl with 45 ml (3 tbsp)
water and cover with vented
plastic wrap. Microwave on 100%

for 12-15 minutes until tender.
Drain.
　Combine oil, vinegar, mustard,
cayenne and seasoning. Sprinkle
over hot potatoes and allow to
cool. Combine remaining
ingredients and carefully mix
with cooled potatoes. Pack into a
greased 18-cm (7-in) ring mould
and refrigerate for 1 hour.
　To serve: Loosen edges with a
spatula, shake well and turn out
on to a bed of endive. Garnish by
arranging green and red pepper
strips over the top and filling the
middle with endive and olives.
Arrange tomato wedges around
the outside.
Serves 4 to 6.

Hint
A sprinkling of cumin or caraway
seeds does much to enhance a quick
potato salad. Finely chopped
gherkin, a few sliced and lightly
sautéed mushrooms, chopped
celery and freshly cooked French
beans are good additions, too.

Marinated Fish Salad

70% .... 8 minutes

500 g (18 oz) firm white fish or
　cleaned squid
60 ml (4 tbsp) lemon or lime juice
20 ml (4 tsp) oil
10 ml (2 tsp) grated ginger root,
　squeezed (page 61)
300 g (11 oz) medium-sized prawns,
　with shells

SALAD
2 small onions, sliced
1 green pepper, diced
½ Chinese cabbage, shredded
2-3 tomatoes, chopped
100 g (3½ oz) green beans,
　trimmed and cut in half
150 g (5 oz) beansprouts
3 medium-sized carrots, grated

DRESSING
45 ml (3 tbsp) oil
45 ml (3 tbsp) lemon or lime juice
15 ml (1 tbsp) light soy sauce
15 ml (1 tbsp) chilli sauce
5 ml (1 tsp) soft brown sugar

Remove skin and bones from fish.
Place fish in a shallow dish.
Combine lemon juice, oil and
ginger and sprinkle over fish.
Add prawns, cover with vented
plastic wrap and marinate for at
least 3 hours.
　Microwave on 70% for
5-8 minutes, depending on fish
chosen. Cool fish, remove from
marinade and slice. Remove
shells from prawns, leaving tails
intact, and slice prawns in half
lengthways. Place fish in a large
bowl.
　Rinse onions and place in a bowl
with iced water for 10 minutes.
Drain thoroughly. Add all
vegetables to fish and toss well.
Make dressing by combining all
ingredients. Add to fish and toss
carefully just before serving.
Serves 6.

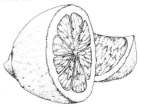

Oriental Avocado Salad

100% .... 3 minutes

4 bacon rashers, rinds removed,
 chopped
4 small avocados
15 ml (1 tbsp) spring onion,
 chopped
45 g (1½ oz) beansprouts

DRESSING
100 ml (3½ fl oz) oil
45 ml (3 tbsp) wine vinegar
10 ml (2 tsp) lemon juice
7.5 ml (1½ tsp) soy sauce
15 ml (1 tbsp) honey
5 ml (1 tsp) spring onion, chopped
salt and black pepper

Place bacon in a microwave dish,
cover loosely with waxed paper
and microwave on 100% for
2-3 minutes, or until crisp. Drain
and pat dry. Peel and slice
avocados and arrange on eight
individual serving plates.
Sprinkle with bacon, chopped
spring onion and beansprouts.
 To make dressing: Combine all
ingredients for dressing and
shake well. Spoon over salad.
Serves 8.

Spinach Soy Salad

100% .... 5 minutes

500 g (18 oz) young spinach leaves,
 trimmed and washed
15 ml (1 tbsp) sesame seeds, toasted
 (page 44)
5 ml (1 tsp) orange rind,
 finely grated
30 ml (2 tbsp) pecan nuts,
 coarsely chopped

DRESSING
45 ml (3 tbsp) soy sauce
30 ml (2 tbsp) oil
45 ml (3 tbsp) orange juice
2.5 ml (½ tsp) Worcestershire
 sauce
5 ml (1 tsp) sugar

Place spinach in a large casserole
with only the water clinging to the
leaves after washing. Cover and
microwave on 100% for
5 minutes. Drain and coarsely
chop.
 Combine all ingredients for
dressing in a jar and shake well.
Pour dressing over spinach and
chill. Before serving, sprinkle
with sesame seeds, orange rind
and pecan nuts.
Serves 4.

From left: Basic Salad Dressing, Watercress Dressing and Angostura Salad Dressing

Basic Salad Dressing

100% .... 5 minutes

125 ml (4 fl oz) water
¹/₂ packet of lemon jelly
500 ml (16 fl oz) mayonnaise
185 ml (6 fl oz) evaporated milk
60 ml (4 tbsp) vinegar
30 ml (2 tbsp) lemon juice
10 ml (2 tsp) French mustard
5 ml (1 tsp) salt
2.5 ml (¹/₂ tsp) black pepper

Microwave water in a glass
measuring jug for 2 minutes on
100%. Add jelly cubes and stir
to dissolve. Microwave for
3 minutes more. Add to
mayonnaise along with remaining
ingredients. Mix well, then chill
thoroughly. Makes about
750 ml (1¹/₄ pints).

Variations

THOUSAND ISLAND SALAD
DRESSING
To 250 ml (8 fl oz) of basic salad
dressing add 60 ml (4 tbsp) chilli
sauce, 30 ml (2 tbsp) chopped
green pepper, 5 ml (1 tsp) paprika
and mix well. Makes about
300 ml (10 fl oz).

BLUE CHEESE SALAD DRESSING
To 250 ml (8 fl oz) of basic salad
dressing add 60 g (2 oz) crumbled
blue cheese, 30 ml (2 tbsp) milk,
few drops of Tabasco and a
generous pinch of black pepper.
Makes about 300 ml (10 fl oz).

CREAMY GARLIC SALAD DRESSING
To 250 ml (8 fl oz) of basic salad
dressing add 60 ml (4 tbsp) grated
Cheddar cheese, 45 ml (3 tbsp)
milk and a pinch of garlic powder.
Mix until smooth. Makes about
300 ml (10 fl oz).

Watercress Dressing

**Very good on fish or chicken
salads.**

70% .... 1¹/₂ minutes

1 bunch of watercress, trimmed
1 large parsley sprig
¹/₂ small onion
60 ml (4 tbsp) wine vinegar
1 egg yolk
60 ml (4 tbsp) oil
salt and black pepper

Wash watercress and shake off
water. Place in a microwaveproof
dish, cover and microwave on
70% for 1¹/₂ minutes. Drain and
place in a food processor or
blender with parsley, onion,
vinegar, egg yolk, oil and
seasoning. Blend until mixture
is emulsified. Keep chilled.
Makes about 125 ml (4 fl oz).

Angostura Salad Dressing

70% .... 1 minute

generous pinch of celery seeds or
2.5 ml (¹/₂ tsp) finely chopped
celery leaves
5 ml (1 tsp) dry mustard
2.5 ml (¹/₂ tsp) Angostura bitters
60 ml (4 tbsp) lemon juice
250 ml (8 fl oz) oil (or use half olive
oil and half vegetable oil)
2 garlic cloves, lightly crushed

Whisk all ingredients except
garlic together in a bowl. Add
garlic and microwave on 70% for
1 minute. Allow to stand until
dressing has completely cooled,
then remove garlic. Store in the
refrigerator and shake before
using.
Makes about 250 ml (8 fl oz).

Chicken and Pasta Salad

100% .... 7 minutes

3 chicken breasts, boned and halved
125 ml (4 fl oz) chicken stock
500 g (18 oz) tagliatelle, cooked (page 220)
400 g (14 oz) canned chick-peas, drained
400 g (14 oz) canned artichoke hearts, drained and coarsely chopped
300 g (11 oz) frozen peas, thawed
300 g (11 oz) button mushrooms, sliced
90 g (3 oz) stuffed olives, sliced
1 green pepper, cored, seeded and cut into strips
1 celery stick, thinly sliced
60 g (2 oz) toasted almonds to garnish (page 36)

DRESSING
150 ml (5 fl oz) oil
45 ml (3 tbsp) red wine vinegar
45 ml (3 tbsp) chopped fresh parsley
15 ml (1 tbsp) French mustard
2.5 ml ('/₂ tsp) curry powder
salt and black pepper
1 small garlic clove, peeled and chopped

Place chicken pieces, skin-side up, in a round dish. Pour chicken stock over, cover and microwave on 100% for 5-7 minutes, or until just cooked. Leave to cool in stock, then drain and remove skin. Cut into chunks and place in a large bowl. Add tagliatelle, chick-peas, artichokes, peas, mushrooms, olives, green pepper and celery to chicken. Toss and chill well.
 To make dressing: Combine all ingredients in a blender and blend well.
 Pour dressing over salad, tossing well, and chill until ready to serve. Sprinkle with toasted almonds to garnish.
Serves 10.

Green Salad with Dill Dressing

100% .... 12 minutes

45 ml (3 tbsp) water
2.5 ml ('/₂ tsp) salt
500 g (18 oz) green beans, sliced
1 round lettuce
6 spring onions, sliced
60 g (2 oz) Cheddar cheese, grated
4 radishes, sliced
125 g (4 oz) croûtons (page 28)

DRESSING
150 ml (5 fl oz) oil
60 ml (4 tbsp) red wine vinegar
15 ml (1 tbsp) sugar
5 ml (1 tsp) salt
10-15 ml (2 tsp-1 tbsp) chopped fresh dill or 2.5-5 ml ('/₂-1 tsp) dried dill
generous pinch of curry powder
black pepper

First make the dressing: Combine all ingredients in a large jug and microwave on 100% for 2 minutes, stirring once. Chill.

Combine water and salt in a large casserole. Add green beans and microwave, covered, on 100% for 8-10 minutes. Drain and refresh in cold water. Tear lettuce into small pieces and combine with beans and spring onions. Toss gently and chill thoroughly.
 To serve, add desired amount of dressing to salad and toss.
Top with cheese, radishes and croûtons.
Serves 6.

Warm Liver Salad

Duck livers are the ultimate choice for this dish. However, as they are not easily obtained, chicken livers make a good substitute.

100% .... 6 minutes

250 g (9 oz) carefully cleaned duck
   or chicken livers
5 ml (1 tsp) orange rind, finely
   grated
juice of 1 orange
30 ml (2 tbsp) brandy or cognac
salt and black pepper
1 small fennel bulb, sliced
selection of salad leaves, such as
   endive, round lettuce, iceberg
   and red curly leaf
mung beansprouts
cress
1 bunch of spring onions, including
   some of the green portion,
   chopped
mushrooms, sliced
cherry tomatoes
30 g (1 oz) butter
paprika

DRESSING
60 ml (4 tbsp) oil
30 ml (2 tbsp) strawberry vinegar
   (page 37)
pinch of sugar
salt and black pepper
pinch of cayenne
generous pinch of dry mustard

Lay livers in a flat glass dish. Sprinkle with orange rind, orange juice, brandy, salt and black pepper. Cover and marinate for at least 2 hours. Meanwhile prepare salad.

Place fennel in a bowl, add 45 ml (3 tbsp) water and cover with vented plastic wrap. Microwave on 100% for 1 minute. Drain and refresh under cold water. Combine all vegetables in a large bowl, cover and refrigerate until required. Combine all ingredients for dressing and set aside.

Drain livers and pat dry. Microwave butter in a shallow casserole on 100% for 1½ minutes. Add livers and turn to coat with butter. Cover and microwave for 2-3 minutes. (Livers should not be cooked through as they will become tough and bitter.) Set aside to cool slightly before arranging on the side of the salad.

To serve: Toss salad with dressing and place a large spoonful on each plate. Add livers and sprinkle with paprika. Serve immediately.
Serves 6.

Fennel and Walnut Salad

100% .... 4 minutes

3 small fennel bulbs, cleaned and
  sliced
125 ml (4 fl oz) dry white wine
salt and black pepper
1 small bunch of radishes
100 g (3½ oz) walnuts
2 round lettuces, washed and patted
  dry

DRESSING
1 egg yolk
30 ml (2 tbsp) fresh lemon juice
15 ml (1 tbsp) French mustard
salt and black pepper
90 ml (3 fl oz) oil
90 ml (3 fl oz) soured cream

Place fennel in a bowl with wine
and seasoning. Microwave,
covered, on 100% for 3-4 minutes,
or until just tender. Drain and
chill. Grate radishes and coarsely
chop walnuts, saving a few whole
ones for garnishing.

To make dressing: Combine egg
yolk, lemon juice, mustard, salt
and black pepper in a food
processor or blender and process
for a few seconds to mix. With
machine running, gradually pour
in oil and blend well. Stir in
soured cream and chill well.

To serve: Arrange lettuce leaves
on six individual plates. Top with
a little dressing. Add fennel,
radishes and nuts. Add a little
more dressing and garnish with
whole walnuts.
Serves 6.

Fennel and Anchovy Salad

Slice 1 large fennel bulb and
1 leek. Place in a dish with 30 ml
(2 tbsp) dry white wine, cover
and microwave on 100% for
4 minutes. Leave to stand, then
drain and chill. Grate 2 carrots
and slice 8 anchovy fillets into
2.5-cm (½-in) lengths. Add to
fennel and combine with a few
black olives and 125 ml (4 fl oz)
French dressing. Adjust
seasoning and leave to marinate
for 30 minutes. Serve on a bed of
butterhead lettuce. Serves 4.

French Bean Salad

100% .... 8 minutes

500 g (18 oz) young green beans,
  trimmed
45 ml (3 tbsp) water
salt and black pepper
125 ml (4 fl oz) French dressing
1 garlic clove, crushed
4 tomatoes, sliced
2 hard-boiled eggs, chopped

Place beans and water in a
microwave dish and microwave,
covered, on 100% for about
8 minutes. Refresh under cold
running water, then drain well.
Add salt, black pepper, dressing
and garlic and toss lightly. Chill
well.

To serve: Arrange one sliced
tomato on each of four individual
plates. Top with beans and
sprinkle with chopped hard-
boiled egg.
Serves 4.

Moulded Green Vegetable Salad

100% .... 3 minutes

250 ml (8 fl oz) water
90 g (3 oz) lime jelly cubes
3 celery sticks, chopped
1 small green pepper, chopped
15 ml (1 tbsp) snipped chives
125 g (4 oz) cucumber, diced
250 g (9 oz) low-fat soft cheese
250 ml (8 fl oz) mayonnaise

Microwave water on 100% for
2-2½ minutes until boiling. Pour
over lime jelly in a bowl and stir to
dissolve. Return dissolved jelly to
microwave for 30 seconds.
Remove and cool until partially
set.

Using an electric mixer, beat
jelly, then add vegetables, cottage
cheese and mayonnaise, mixing
well. Spoon into a serving bowl or
ring mould and chill until set
(about 3 hours).
Serves 6-8.

Spinach, Bacon and Sesame Salad

100% .... 3 minutes

2-3 streaky bacon rashers, rinds
  removed
300 g (11 oz) spinach, washed,
  trimmed and broken into small
  pieces
100 g (3½ oz) button mushrooms,
  sliced
1 small onion, thinly sliced

DRESSING
15 ml (1 tbsp) toasted sesame seeds
  (page 44)
15 ml (1 tbsp) tahini (sesame seed
  paste)*
45 ml (3 tbsp) oil
30 ml (2 tbsp) chicken stock
15 ml (1 tbsp) soy sauce
2.5 ml (½ tsp) squeezed ginger
  juice (page 61)
5 ml (1 tsp) lemon juice
black pepper

Place bacon rashers on a rack and
cover loosely with waxed paper.

Microwave on 100% for about
3 minutes until beginning to
become crisp. Set aside and
crumble when cool.
    Next make dressing by
combining all ingredients in a
blender and blending until
smooth. Carefully combine
vegetables in a salad bowl, pour
in dressing, toss lightly and top
with crumbled bacon.
Serves 4-6.

* Tahini is available from speciality
shops.

Hint
To toast sesame seeds: Microwave a
browning dish on 100% for
3 minutes. Sprinkle 45 ml (3 tbsp)
seeds on to the dish and cover with
waxed paper. Leave to stand for 2-3
minutes, stirring every 20 seconds.

Broccoli and Mushroom Salad

100% .... 6 minutes

1 large leek, sliced
15 ml (1 tbsp) lemon juice
generous pinch of fresh thyme
15 ml (1 tbsp) oil
salt and black pepper
½ green pepper, finely chopped
300 g (11 oz) button mushrooms
300 g (11 oz) broccoli, broken into
  evenly-sized florets
45 ml (3 tbsp) water

DRESSING
45 ml (3 tbsp) oil
5 ml (1 tsp) coarse-grained mustard
30 ml (2 tbsp) red wine vinegar
2.5 ml (½ tsp) honey
15 ml (1 tbsp) chopped fresh parsley
2.5 ml (½ tsp) chopped fresh
  oregano
salt and black pepper

Place leek, lemon juice, thyme, oil
and seasoning in a large bowl and
microwave on 100% for 1 minute.

Add green pepper and
mushrooms, toss to coat with
mixture and cover with vented
plastic wrap. Microwave for
2 minutes. Cool and chill well in
marinade.
    Place broccoli in a bowl with
45 ml (3 tbsp) water, cover with
vented plastic wrap and
microwave for 3 minutes. Drain
and refresh with plenty of cold
water. Add to mushroom
mixture.
    Combine all ingredients for
dressing and pour over
vegetables. Chill for at least
2 hours before serving.
Serves 6.

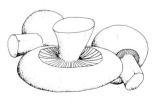

Spicy Three-bean Salad

This dish goes well with barbecued meat.

100% .... 21 minutes

15 ml (1 tbsp) oil
2 bacon rashers, rinds removed, diced
2 medium-sized onions, chopped
1 green pepper, cored, seeded and chopped
2 garlic cloves, crushed
10 ml (2 tsp) chopped fresh ginger
5 ml (1 tsp) curry paste
800 g (1 lb 14 oz) canned whole tomatoes, chopped
salt and black pepper
2.5 ml (1/2 tsp) sugar
1 bay leaf
400 g (14 oz) canned baked beans
400 g (14 oz) canned butter beans, drained
400 g (14 oz) canned kidney beans, drained
parsley to garnish

Use a large, deep casserole for this. Microwave oil on 100% for 1 minute. Add bacon, onions, green pepper, garlic, ginger and curry paste. Stir well and microwave for 5 minutes. Add tomatoes with their juice, seasoning, sugar and bay leaf. Microwave, uncovered, for 15 minutes, stirring from time to time. Remove bay leaf and add all the beans. Garnish with sprigs of parsley. Serve hot or cold. Serves 12.

Sweet-and-sour Beans

Microwave 5 diced bacon rashers on 100% for 4 minutes. Set aside. Combine bacon fat with 100 g (3½ oz) sugar, 15 ml (1 tbsp) cornflour, 150 ml (5 fl oz) vinegar, 5 ml (1 tsp) prepared English mustard, salt and black pepper. Microwave for 3 minutes, stirring twice. Add 1 sliced onion and 400 g (14 oz) each of drained, canned green beans, red kidney beans and butter beans. Mix well, cover and microwave for 6 minutes, stirring once. Leave to stand for 10 minutes, sprinkle with bacon and serve. Serves 6.

Marinated Cauliflower Salad

100%, 50% .... 7 minutes

1 large cauliflower, washed and trimmed
250 ml (8 fl oz) water
125 ml (4 fl oz) oil
60 ml (4 tbsp) vinegar
90 ml (3 fl oz) lemon juice
5 ml (1 tsp) dried fennel seeds
2.5 ml (1/2 tsp) dried chervil
2.5 ml (1/2 tsp) dried thyme
1 small bay leaf
2.5 ml (1/2 tsp) ground coriander
6 peppercorns
5 ml (1 tsp) salt
1 celery stick, sliced
2 garlic cloves, crushed
12 black olives

Break cauliflower into small florets and place in a large casserole. Combine all ingredients, except olives, pour over cauliflower, cover and microwave on 100% for 3 minutes. Reduce power to 50% and microwave for 4 minutes more. Remove from microwave, add olives and allow to cool. Chill for at least 24 hours. Serve by spooning drained cauliflower mixture on to lettuce leaves.
Serves 4-6.

Cauliflower with Creamy Stilton Dressing

Break 1 medium-sized cauliflower into small florets and place in a large casserole with 45 ml (3 tbsp) water. Cover with vented plastic wrap and microwave on 100% for 3 minutes. Set aside to cool, then chill. Combine 45 g (1½ oz) crumbled Stilton cheese and 45 ml (1 tbsp) white wine in a jug and microwave on 50% for 1½ minutes. Mix until smooth. Microwave for a few seconds more if necessary. Cool slightly, then add 45 ml (3 tbsp) soured cream and 45 ml (3 tbsp) mayonnaise and season to taste. Serve spooned over cauliflower and garnished with 10 ml (2 tsp) snipped chives. Serves 6.

Stuffed Hake Florentine

100%, 70% .... 25 minutes

750 g (1¾ lb) fresh spinach,
  trimmed
1 small onion, chopped
30 g (1 oz) butter
2 egg yolks
pinch of grated nutmeg
salt and black pepper
4 large fillets of hake,
  skinned and trimmed
100 ml (3½ fl oz) dry white wine
juice of 1 lemon
lemon wedges and parsley
  to garnish

SAUCE
30 g (1 oz) butter
60 ml (4 tbsp) plain flour
300 ml (10 fl oz) milk
5 ml (1 tsp) French mustard
100 g (3½ oz) Cheddar cheese,
  grated
pinch of cayenne
45 ml (3 tbsp) single cream

Place spinach in a large microwave dish with just the water from washing clinging to the leaves. Microwave, covered, on 100% for 2 minutes. Drain and cool, then chop finely.

Microwave chopped onion in 30 g (1 oz) butter for 3 minutes, stirring at least once. Add spinach and microwave for 2 minutes more. Carefully stir in egg yolks, nutmeg, salt and pepper to taste. Divide spinach mixture between hake fillets and roll up from tail to head. Place in a casserole with wine and lemon juice. Cover and microwave on 70% for 8-10 minutes, or until fish flakes easily.

To make sauce: Microwave butter in a 1-litre jug on 100% for 45 seconds, stir in flour and gradually stir in milk. Microwave for 1 minute, then stir in mustard. Microwave for 3-4 minutes more, stirring every minute until the sauce is thick and bubbling. Stir in most of the cheese, cayenne and cream.

Drain fish and transfer to a serving dish. Pour sauce over, sprinkle with remaining cheese and microwave on 70% for 1-2 minutes more, or place under a hot grill to brown. Garnish with lemon wedges and parsley. Serves 4.

Cod with Feta Topping

70% .... 11 minutes

4 cod steaks
10 ml (2 tsp) lemon juice
salt and black pepper
pinch of paprika
15 g (½ oz) butter
1 large tomato, skinned and
  chopped
100 g (3 ½ oz) Feta cheese,
  crumbled
30 ml (2 tbsp) chopped fresh parsley
15 ml (1 tbsp) snipped spring
  onion tops
15 ml (1 tbsp) chopped capers
2.5 ml (½ tsp) chopped fresh
  marjoram

Remove skin from fish, sprinkle
with lemon juice, salt, pepper and
paprika. Arrange steaks in a
shallow casserole and top each
steak with a little butter. Cover
and microwave on 70% for
4-6 minutes, depending on
thickness of fish. (The fish should
be about two-thirds cooked at this
point.)

Combine remaining ingredients
and season lightly. Divide mixture
between cod steaks, heaping
it slightly on top of each. Cover
and microwave for 5 minutes
more. Serve immediately.
Serves 4.

Hint
**Serve the following savoury butter
with plain poached fish: Combine
60 g (2 oz) butter, 15 ml (1 tbsp)
Dijon mustard and 30 ml (2 tbsp)
chopped fresh basil. Chill well,
then form into pats or scoop into
balls with a melon baller.**

Spicy Prawns

**Prawns cooked this way are
succulent and full of flavour.
Remember to supply finger bowls
and plenty of paper napkins.**

100% .... 22 minutes

1 kg (2¼ lb) uncooked prawns in
  shells
250 g (9 oz) butter
200 ml (6 ½ fl oz) bottled tomato
  sauce
15 ml (1 tbsp) Worcestershire sauce
30 ml (2 tbsp) lemon juice
pinch of salt
chilli powder to taste
oil
lemon roses and parsley
  or cress to garnish
buttered rice to serve (page 220)

Devein prawns and remove heads
if desired. Rinse and pat dry, then
set aside. Place butter, tomato
sauce, Worcestershire sauce,
lemon juice, salt and chilli
powder in a 3-litre (5-pint)
casserole and microwave on 100%

for 6 minutes. Add half the
prawns and microwave for about
8 minutes. Stir twice during
cooking time. Prawns are cooked
when they turn deep pink and
become opaque.)

Drain prawns well and set aside.
Repeat with remaining prawns.
Then heat a little oil in a frying
pan and fry prawns conventionally
for 2-3 minutes, turning once
during cooking time. Garnish
with lemon roses and parsley and
serve immediately with buttered
rice and the sauce the prawns
were first cooked in.
Serves 6-8.

Home-made Chilli Sauce
In a blender, combine 100 g
(3½ oz) small, red, dried
Portuguese chillies, 500 ml
(16 fl oz) oil, 2-3 crushed garlic
cloves, 5 ml (1 tsp) salt, 5 ml
(1 tsp) black pepper, juice of
1 lemon and 30 ml (2 tbsp)
whisky. Blend for 45 seconds,
then pour into a bottle and use as
required. (This sauce is extremely
hot.) Makes about 600 ml
(17½ fl oz).

Seafood Crêpes

100%, 70% .... 22 minutes

300 g (11 oz) hake, skinned
150 ml (5 fl oz) water
150 ml (5 fl oz) white wine
juice of 1 lemon
75-100 g (2½ -3½ oz) smoked
  trout fillet
3 hard-boiled eggs, coarsely
  chopped
90 g (3 oz) butter
½ onion, chopped
200 g (7 oz) mushrooms, sliced
45 g (1½ oz) plain flour
250 ml (8 fl oz) single cream
45 ml (3 tbsp) milk
15 ml (1 tbsp) chopped fresh
  parsley
salt and black pepper
8 crêpes (page 132)
60 ml (4 tbsp) grated Parmesan
  cheese
parsley to garnish

Place hake in a casserole. Add
water, wine and lemon juice
and microwave on 70% for
9-11 minutes. Leave to stand for
10 minutes, then drain fish,
reserving liquid. Coarsely flake
hake and trout and combine with
eggs.

In a bowl, microwave butter on
100% for 45 seconds. Add onion
and microwave for 2 minutes.
Add mushrooms and microwave
for l minute more. Stir in flour,
then add reserved cooking liquid.
Microwave for 2 minutes, stirring
once. Add half the cream and all
the milk and microwave for a
further 3 minutes, stirring every
minute. Add parsley, season to
taste with salt and black pepper,
then add to fish and mix well.

Divide mixture between crêpes
and roll up. Place in a lightly
greased casserole. Drizzle
remaining cream over and
sprinkle with Parmesan cheese.
Microwave on 70% for 2 minutes
to heat through, or place under a
hot grill to brown. Garnish with
parsley.
Serves 4 as a main course, 8 as a
starter.

Crab and Artichoke Casserole

100% .... 9 minutes

400 g (14 oz) canned artichoke
  hearts
30 g (1 oz) butter
225 g (8 oz) cooked crab meat
  or crab sticks, chopped
275 g (10 oz) button mushrooms,
  sliced, or 275 g (10 oz) canned
  sliced mushrooms, drained
5-7.5 ml (1-1½ tsp) Worcestershire
  sauce
60 ml (4 tbsp) dry sherry
1 egg yolk
salt and black pepper
45 ml (3 tbsp) grated Parmesan
  cheese
45 ml (3 tbsp) grated Cheddar
  cheese

WHITE SAUCE
30 g (1 oz) butter
30 ml (2 tbsp) plain flour
salt and black pepper
250 ml (8 fl oz) milk

First make the sauce: Microwave
butter in a 1-litre (1¾ -pint) glass
jug on 100% for about 30 seconds.
Stir in flour, salt and black
pepper. Microwave for
45 seconds. Stir, then slowly
whisk in milk, blending well.
Microwave for about 2 minutes,
stirring twice. Remove from oven
and stir well.

Drain artichoke hearts and
arrange in the bottom of a greased
23-cm (9-in) baking dish. In a
glass bowl, microwave butter on
100% for 30 seconds. Add crab
meat and mushrooms and toss
lightly. Spread crab mixture over
artichoke hearts.

Mix together white sauce,
Worcestershire sauce, sherry and
egg yolk, and season to taste with
salt and black pepper. Spoon over
crab mixture. Sprinkle with
Parmesan and Cheddar cheeses
and microwave for 7-9 minutes to
heat through.
Serves 4-6.

Turban of Smoked Salmon and Sole

100%, 50% .... 26 minutes

3 lemon soles, filleted
salt and black pepper
250 g (9 oz) smoked salmon
30 g (1 oz) butter

MOUSSELINE
500 g (18 oz) fresh haddock
left-over smoked salmon pieces
2 egg whites
a few drops of Tabasco
10-15 ml (2-3 tsp) lemon juice
30 ml (2 tbsp) chopped fresh parsley
500 ml (16 fl oz) whipping cream,
** well chilled**
2.5 ml (½ tsp) dried thyme
pistachio nuts (optional)
1 recipe Hollandaise sauce
** (page 54)**

First make the mousseline: Place
fish into work bowl of a food
processor fitted with metal
blades. Season and process until
smooth. Add egg whites,
Tabasco, lemon juice and parsley
and process for a few seconds.
With the blades running, slowly
add cream. Process until well
blended. (Care must be taken not
to over-mix at this point.) Add
thyme and pistachio nuts. Pulse
to combine.

  Grease a 23-cm (9-in) microwave
ring mould. Lightly season sole
fillets and arrange crossways in
mould, alternating with smoked
salmon and overlapping fish
slightly. Allow ends of fish to
hang over sides of mould. Pack
mousseline into mould. Fold fish
ends over mousseline.

  Cut a circle of baking parchment
slightly larger than mould and cut
a few crosses in the centre of the
paper to allow for expansion.
Place paper on top of fish. (The
dish may be prepared to this stage
a few hours in advance.)

  Microwave on 50% for
20-25 minutes. Leave to stand for
a few minutes, then drain off any
excess liquid. Turn out on to a
heated serving platter.
Microwave butter on 100% for
30 seconds, then brush over
mould. Serve with Hollandaise
sauce.
Serves 6.

Paella

100%, 70% .... 21 minutes

30 ml (2 tbsp) oil (olive and
   sunflower mixed are excellent)
1 onion, chopped
1 garlic clove, crushed
1 green pepper, chopped
200 g (7 oz) long-grain rice
few threads of saffron or 2.5 ml
   (½ tsp) ground turmeric
500 ml (16 fl oz) chicken stock,
   boiling
45 ml (3 tbsp) tomato paste
black pepper
150 g (5 oz) firm white fish
175 g (6 oz) frozen peas, thawed
200 g (7 oz) prawns, peeled and
   deveined
150 g (5 oz) cooked chicken, cut into
   bite-sized pieces
100 g (3 ½ oz) ham, diced
800 g (1 lb 14 oz) cooked fresh
   mussels, with 1 shell from
   each removed
1 canned pimento, cut into strips
75 ml (2 ½ fl oz) dry white wine

GARNISH
black olives
1 lemon, cut into wedges
chopped fresh parsley

Microwave oil in a large casserole
on 100% for 1 minute. Add onion,
garlic and green pepper. Toss to
coat with oil. Microwave for
4 minutes, stirring once. Stir in
rice and saffron, then pour in
boiling stock. Stir in tomato paste,
season with pepper, cover and
microwave for 8 minutes.

Add white fish (whole), peas,
prawns, chicken and ham. Cover
and microwave for 4 minutes. Stir
carefully, then allow to stand for
10 minutes, covered. Remove fish
from dish, flake into bite-sized
pieces and return to rice mix. Stir
in mussels, pimento and wine,
then cover and microwave on
70% for 4 minutes. Garnish with
olives, lemon and parsley before
serving.
Serves 4.

Caribbean Fish Stew

Hot pickled fish and potatoes in a
well-seasoned tomato sauce.

100%, 70% .... 25 minutes

1 kg (2¼ lb) hake fillets,
   skinned
4 potatoes, diced
1 large onion, sliced
1 small red pepper, sliced
1 small green pepper, sliced
15 ml (1 tbsp) sugar
10 ml (2 tsp) salt
2.5 ml (½ tsp) black pepper
15 ml (1 tbsp) Worcestershire sauce
7.5 ml (1 ½ tsp) pickling spices
1.25 kg (2¾ lb) canned tomatoes,
   coarsely chopped
30 g (1 oz) butter
1 lemon

Cut fish into bite-sized pieces and
set aside. In a large casserole,
combine potatoes, onion,
peppers, sugar, salt, black
pepper, Worcestershire sauce,
pickling spices tied in a bag, and
tomatoes. Microwave, covered,
on 100% for 15-17 minutes, or
until potatoes are tender.

Add fish and microwave on 70%
for 6-8 minutes, or until fish flakes
easily. Remove spice bag. Stir in
juice of half the lemon and all the
butter. Garnish with lemon slices
from remaining half of lemon.
Serves 8.

Hint
Poaching is the most usual method
of cooking fish in the microwave.
Arrange fish pieces with the
thinnest part towards the centre of
the dish. Cover loosely with waxed
paper and microwave on 100%,
allowing 4-6 minutes per 500 g
(18 oz) for thick fish steaks and
3-4 minutes per 500 g (18 oz) for
thinner portions.

The poaching liquid can be varied
by using white wine, chicken stock
or even tomato juice. For extra
flavour, add onion, herbs,
peppercorns or lemon slices.

Rolls of Trout with Mustard Sauce

100% .... 22 minutes

2 carrots, cut in julienne
2-3 celery sticks, cut in julienne
1 leek, cut in julienne
1 small cucumber, cut in julienne
spring onion tops
45 ml (3 tbsp) water
4 trout, filleted and skinned
salt and black pepper
15 g (½ oz) butter
2 spring onions, chopped
200 ml (6½ fl oz) white wine

MUSTARD SAUCE
poaching liquid from fish
30 ml (2 tbsp) single cream
5-10 ml (1-2 tsp) lemon juice
15 ml (1 tbsp) moutarde de Meaux
   (coarse-grained French mustard)
2.5 ml (½ tsp) mustard seed
15 g (½ oz) butter, softened

GARNISH
8 lemon slices
parsley or mustard and cress

Take a few julienne strips from each vegetable and carefully tie into a bundle with a spring onion top, making eight bundles. Arrange bundles in a circle in a shallow dish. Add water, cover with vented plastic wrap and microwave on 100% for 3-4 minutes. (Vegetables should still be crisp.)

Lightly season trout fillets and lay on a board, skinned-side uppermost. Place a bundle of vegetables on each fillet, roll up and secure with a cocktail stick. Microwave butter in a shallow casserole for 1 minute. Add spring onions and microwave for 1 minute more. Add wine and microwave for a further 2 minutes. Arrange trout rolls in liquid, cover with vented plastic wrap and microwave for 5-7 minutes. Remove fish rolls and keep warm.

To make sauce: Strain fish cooking liquid and discard solids. Microwave liquid for 4-5 minutes to reduce it by about half. Add cream, lemon juice, mustard and mustard seed. Microwave for 2 minutes, stirring every 30 seconds. Then add butter and adjust seasoning if necessary. Remove cocktail sticks from fish, arrange on a serving plate and spoon a little sauce over each of the fillets. Garnish with lemon and parsley or a little mustard and cress.
Serves 4.

Hints
• When microwaving whole fish, fold the thin tail section underneath to achieve even cooking, or shield the tail with foil.
• Make two or three slashes in the sides of a large whole fish to prevent the skin from bursting and to promote even cooking.

Savoury Fish Fillets

100% .... 8 minutes

500 g (18 oz) firm white fish
   fillets or steaks
125 ml (4 fl oz) French
   or Italian dressing
90 g (3 oz) savoury biscuit
   crumbs or seasoned cornflake
   crumbs
paprika
salt

Place fillets in a glass dish and pour dressing over. Marinate for about 30 minutes, then lift out of dressing and coat with crumbs. Place in a greased baking dish and sprinkle with paprika and salt. Cover with waxed paper and microwave on 100% for 6-8 minutes, or until fish flakes easily.
Serves 4.

Spicy Fish Curry

100%, 70% .... 26 minutes

750 g (1¾ lb) firm white fish
45 ml (3 tbsp) oil
generous pinch of black pepper
2.5 ml (½ tsp) salt
2.5 ml (½ tsp) ground turmeric
generous pinch of cayenne
7.5 ml (1½ tsp) coriander seeds, crushed
2.5 ml (½ tsp) ground aniseed
2.5 ml (½ tsp) ground fenugreek
2 garlic cloves, crushed
1 fresh chilli, chopped
10 ml (2 tsp) fresh lemon juice
12 curry leaves
2.5-5 ml (½ -1 tsp) garam masala
1 large onion, sliced
5 ml (1 tsp) tamarind pulp
60 ml (4 tbsp) warm water
400 g (14 oz) canned tomatoes, chopped
15 ml (1 tbsp) plain flour
5 ml (1 tsp) sugar
15 ml (1 tbsp) chopped fresh coriander to garnish

First, cut fish into serving portions, then, using half the oil, make a paste with all the spices, garlic, chilli and lemon juice. Spread over fish and marinate for 2-3 hours.

Pour remaining oil into a large shallow casserole. Microwave on 100% for 45 seconds. Add curry leaves, garam masala and onion, stir to coat with oil and microwave for 3 minutes.

Soak tamarind pulp in the warm water for 10 minutes. Strain and set aside. Tip tomatoes and their juice into a blender, together with the flour and sugar. Blend until smooth. Add to onion mixture, together with tamarind liquid. Cover and microwave for 10 minutes.

Arrange fish in sauce, spooning a little sauce over each portion. Cover and microwave on 70% for 10-12 minutes, depending on thickness of portions. Sprinkle with chopped coriander. Serve with rice, chutney and sambals. Serves 4.

Fish Stroganoff

100%, 70% .... 14 minutes

750 g (1¾ lb) firm white fish fillets
salt and black pepper
45 g (1 ½ oz) butter
2.5 ml (½ tsp) paprika
generous pinch of dried thyme
200 g (7 oz) button mushrooms, sliced
100 ml (3 ½ fl oz) fish stock (page 57)
15 ml (1 tbsp) brandy
15 ml (1 tbsp) dry sherry
15 g (½ oz) butter
15 ml (1 tbsp) plain flour
150 ml (5 fl oz) soured cream
10 ml (2 tsp) lemon juice
15 ml (1 tbsp) chopped fresh parsley
10 ml (2 tsp) poppy seeds

Slice fish into strips 6 cm (2 ½ in) long and about 8 mm (½ in) wide. Season lightly. In a large, shallow casserole microwave butter on 100% for 1 minute. Add fish, toss to coat with butter and microwave for 3 minutes. Add paprika, thyme, mushrooms, stock, brandy and sherry. Stir to combine. Cover and microwave for 4-6 minutes, or until almost cooked.

Work together 15 g (½ oz) butter and flour and add to hot liquid, blending in a little at a time. Then stir in soured cream and lemon juice. Microwave, covered, on 70% for 4 minutes, stirring twice. Sprinkle with parsley and poppy seeds and serve immediately. Serves 4.

Fish Fillets in Sherry Cream Sauce with Basil

In a shallow casserole, combine 125 ml (4 fl oz) single cream with 15 g (½ oz) butter, 15 ml (1 tbsp) finely chopped fresh basil, 15 ml (1 tbsp) grated Parmesan cheese and 30 ml (2 tbsp) dry sherry. Microwave on 100% for 2 minutes, then place about 750 g (1¾ lbs) fish fillets in a single layer in the sauce. Spoon a little sauce over, cover and microwave for about 5 minutes. Serve at once. Serves 3-4.

Tuna Steaks with Rouille

Rouille is a robust sauce usually served with a bouillabaisse, but here it is an ideal complement to the full flavour of fresh tuna.

70% .... 8 minutes

4 small fresh tuna steaks or fillets
45 ml (3 tbsp) oil
salt and black pepper
4 onion slices
4 lemon slices
60 ml (4 tbsp) white wine
15 ml (1 tbsp) capers to garnish

ROUILLE
1 thick slice of white bread
75 ml (2½ fl oz) water
2 garlic cloves
1 fresh chilli, finely chopped
1 large canned pimento
30 ml (2 tbsp) oil
salt and black pepper

Arrange tuna steaks in a shallow casserole. Brush tuna with oil and sprinkle with salt and pepper. Place a slice of onion and a slice of lemon on top of each steak, then pour wine around. Cover with vented plastic wrap and micro-wave on 70% for 6-8 minutes. (The tuna may take longer to cook if the steaks are thick.)

To make sauce: Remove crusts then soak bread in water for a few minutes. Squeeze excess water out of bread, then place in a blender with all the other ingredients and blend until smooth. Thin down slightly with a little cooking liquid from the fish.

To serve: Arrange fish on a warmed platter, top with a spoonful of sauce and garnish with a few capers. Serve remaining sauce separately. Serves 4.

Fish Cutlets with Pepper Sauce

100% .... 14 minutes

4 fish cutlets, such as cod or turbot
15 ml (1 tbsp) lemon juice
15 ml (1 tbsp) brandy
salt and black pepper
15 g (½ oz) butter
200 ml (6 ½ fl oz) single cream
1 small canned pimento,
  roughly chopped
pinch of cayenne
15 g (½ oz) butter
10 ml (2 tsp) plain flour
paprika

Arrange fish cutlets in a shallow casserole. Sprinkle with lemon juice and brandy, season lightly and dot with 15 g (½ oz) butter. Cover and microwave on 100% for 7-9 minutes, depending on thickness of fish. Drain off liquid and reserve. Keep fish warm.

Microwave cream and pimento in a large jug for 3 minutes, then add cayenne and reserved liquid. Work together 15 g (½ oz) butter and flour and add to contents of jug. Pour into a blender and blend until smooth. Return to microwave for 2 minutes until piping hot and thickened. Place fish on serving platter, spoon sauce over and sprinkle lightly with paprika. Serve immediately.
Serves 4.

Squid Steaks With Minty Hollandaise Sauce

100% .... 11 minutes

4 squid steaks
salt and black pepper
15 ml (1 tbsp) plain flour
15 g (½ oz) butter
15 ml (1 tbsp) chopped fresh mint

HOLLANDAISE SAUCE
125 g (4 oz) butter
2 egg yolks
15 ml (1 tbsp) lemon juice
2.5 ml (½ tsp) dry mustard
salt and white pepper

First make the sauce: Microwave butter in a glass jug on 100% for 3 minutes until hot and bubbling. Place remaining ingredients in a blender or food processor. When butter is ready, turn blender or processor to highest speed and slowly add butter, mixing until sauce is creamy and thickened.

Lightly season squid steaks and sprinkle very lightly with flour. Microwave a browning dish on 100% for 6 minutes. Add butter and if not very hot microwave for ½-1 minute more. Arrange steaks in butter and microwave for 2 minutes on each side. Place on an ovenproof serving dish. Stir mint into sauce and spoon over steaks. Place under grill for a few minutes, watching carefully as the sauce burns very easily. Serve immediately. Serves 4.

Hint
Fish should always be fully defrosted before microwaving and pieces should be separated during defrosting time.

Lemon Soles with Orange Sauce

100%, 70%, 50% ..... 10 minutes

4 lemon soles, skinned, with
    side bones removed
100 ml (3½ fl oz) orange juice
grated rind of 1 orange
salt and white pepper
fresh thyme sprigs
45 g (1½ oz) butter
1 egg yolk
5 ml (1 tsp) cornflour
15 ml (1 tbsp) water
45 ml (3 tbsp) single cream
paprika and grated orange rind
    to garnish

Arrange soles in a large, shallow dish, overlapping tails to prevent overcooking. Sprinkle with orange juice, orange rind, seasoning and thyme, then dot with butter. Cover with vented plastic wrap and microwave on 70% for 5-7 minutes. (Do not overcook as sole is a rather thin fish.) Remove fish and keep

warm. Reserve liquid from fish.
    Combine egg yolk, cornflour, water and cream in a bowl, mixing thoroughly. Microwave fish liquid on 100% for 1 minute, then add to cornflour mixture, stirring well. Microwave on 50% for 2 minutes, whisking every 30 seconds. Place fish in a serving dish and pour sauce over. Sprinkle with paprika and orange rind before serving.
Serves 4.

Hints
• To keep fish from drying out during microwaving, brush with melted butter.
• When microwaving 'boil-in-the-bag' fish, remember to pierce the bag before cooking.

Chilled Italian Mussels

100% .... 16 minutes

1 kg (2¼ lb) fresh mussels in
  shells
150 ml (5 fl oz) dry white wine
few black peppercorns
1 thick onion slice
60 ml (4 tbsp) oil
2 streaky bacon rashers,
  rinds removed, diced
1 onion, chopped
1-2 garlic cloves, crushed
1 small carrot, grated
400 g (14 oz) canned tomatoes,
  chopped
125 ml (4 fl oz) dry white wine
salt and black pepper
5 ml (1 tsp) fresh thyme
1 bay leaf
5 ml (1 tsp) sugar
60 ml (4 tbsp) chopped fresh parsley
60 ml (4 tbsp) chopped almonds
60 ml (4 tbsp) currants

GARNISH
parsley
lemon wedges
15 ml (1 tbsp) snipped chives

Remove 'beards' from mussels
and scrub well. Stand mussels in
plenty of cold water for
20 minutes. Drain mussels and
place in a large casserole. Add dry
white wine, a few black
peppercorns and a thick slice of
onion. Cover and microwave for
7-9 minutes, stirring halfway
through cooking time. Discard
any mussels that do not open
during cooking time.

  Drain mussels. Remove and
discard half the shells and arrange
mussels in a shallow serving dish.
Set aside.

  Microwave oil in a casserole on
100% for 30 seconds. Add bacon
and microwave for 2 minutes. Stir
in onion, garlic and carrot and
microwave for 3 minutes. Then
add tomatoes and their juice,
wine, seasoning, thyme, bay leaf
and sugar. Microwave,
uncovered, for 10 minutes,
stirring from time to time. Stir in
parsley, almonds and currants,
and while still hot spoon a little of
the mixture into each mussel.

  Cool, then cover and refrigerate
for at least 2 hours. Garnish with
parsley, lemon wedges and
sprinkle with snipped chives.
Serves 4.

Salmon Steaks de Luxe

100%, 10-15% .... 17 minutes

4 salmon steaks, about 2.5 cm (1 in)
   thick
100 ml (3½ fl oz) water
100 ml (3 ½ fl oz) white wine
15 ml (1 tbsp) lemon juice
1 bay leaf
1 onion slice
a few peppercorns
1 small carrot, sliced
generous pinch of salt
1 blade of mace
60 g (2 oz) butter
60 ml (4 tbsp) whipping cream
chopped parsley and lemon slices
   to garnish

Wipe salmon steaks, pat dry and
set aside. Place water, wine,
lemon juice, bay leaf, onion,
peppercorns, carrot, salt and
mace in a large, shallow casserole.
Cover and microwave on 100%
for 3 minutes. Add salmon and
dot with butter. Replace cover
and microwave for 6 minutes, or
until fish starts to turn opaque.

Transfer fish to a serving dish,
cover and keep warm. Strain
liquid and return to casserole.
Microwave, uncovered, for
5 minutes. Whisk in cream, then
microwave on 10-15% for
3 minutes. Pour over fish and
serve immediately, garnished
with chopped parsley and slices
of lemon.
Serves 4.

Hints
• To steam fish: Cover the fish dish
tightly with plastic wrap to hold in
as much moisture as possible
during cooking and pierce wrap
with the sharp point of a knife to
prevent 'ballooning'.
• To 'grill' fish: The browning dish
provides an excellent means of
grilling fish in the microwave,
especially for thicker steaks or
cutlets. Always turn fish over when
juices appear on top and cover with
waxed paper.

Tuna and Mushroom Lasagne

100%, 50% .... 22 minutes

75 g (2½ oz) butter
1 onion, chopped
3 celery sticks, chopped
1 small green pepper, chopped
200 g (7 oz) mushrooms, sliced
45 g (1½ oz) plain flour
345 ml (11 fl oz) milk
15 ml (1 tbsp) lemon juice
generous pinch of salt
a few drops of Tabasco
60 ml (4 tbsp) single cream
400 g (14 oz) canned tuna,
   drained and flaked
30 ml (2 tbsp) chopped
   fresh parsley
100 g (3½ oz) Cheddar cheese,
   grated
5 ml (1 tsp) paprika
250 g (9 oz) ribbon noodles,
   cooked (page 220)

Place butter in a large casserole
and microwave on 100% for
2 minutes. Add onion, celery and

green pepper, toss in butter and
microwave for 3 minutes. Add
mushrooms and stir to combine
ingredients. Microwave for
1 minute. Stir in flour. Then add
milk and stir well. Microwave for
4 minutes, stirring every
30 seconds. Add lemon juice,
salt, Tabasco, cream, tuna,
parsley and half the cheese. Stir
well. Combine remaining cheese
with paprika and set aside.
   Arrange noodles in a shallow
casserole, pour tuna sauce over
and sprinkle remaining cheese on
top. Cover and microwave on
50% for about 12 minutes until
cheese has melted and the edges
begin to bubble.
Serves 6-8.

Baked Lobster Tails

100%, 70% .... 27 minutes

4 lobster tails
45 ml (3 tbsp) water
30 ml (2 tbsp) white wine
2.5 ml (½ tsp) salt
100 ml (3½ fl oz) water
100 ml (3½ fl oz) white wine
1 onion slice
1 parsley sprig
1 bay leaf
10 ml (2 tsp) lemon juice
5 ml (1 tsp) dry mustard
200 g (7 oz) monkfish, filleted
45 g (1½ oz) butter
200 g (7 oz) mushrooms, sliced
45 ml (3 tbsp) plain flour
100 ml (3½ fl oz) milk
45 ml (3 tbsp) single cream
30 ml (2 tbsp) brandy
30 ml (2 tbsp) chopped fresh parsley
30 ml (2 tbsp) chopped fresh dill
30 g (1 oz) fresh white breadcrumbs
30 ml (2 tbsp) grated Parmesan cheese
30 g (1 oz) butter, melted
sprigs of dill and slices of lemon to garnish

Arrange tails in a circle in a shallow dish, the thin ends facing inwards. Add 50 ml water, 30 ml wine and salt, cover with vented plastic wrap and microwave on 70% for 12-14 minutes, depending on size of tails. (The cooked flesh should be white and tender.)

Leave tails to stand for 2 minutes then, using a pair of scissors, cut down both sides of the underside and peel away. Starting at the thick end, peel flesh out of shells. Reserve shells and cut flesh into 1-cm (½ -in) slices. Set aside.

Place 100 ml water, 100 ml wine, onion, parsley, bay leaf, lemon juice and mustard into a casserole and microwave on 100% for 2 minutes. Add monkfish fillets and cover. Microwave for 3-4 minutes until fish is just tender. Remove, slice and set aside.

Microwave wine mixture for 3 minutes, then strain. Then microwave 45 g (1½ oz) butter for 45 seconds in a bowl. Add mushrooms and stir to coat with butter. Microwave for 1 minute. Stir in flour, milk and strained liquid and microwave for 2 minutes, stirring every 30 seconds. Stir in cream, brandy, parsley and dill. Adjust seasoning. Add fish to sauce and carefully spoon mixture into crayfish shells.

Combine breadcrumbs, Parmesan cheese and 30 g (1 oz) butter and sprinkle a little over each tail. Place under a hot grill for about 2 minutes until golden brown. Garnish with dill and lemon slices. Serve immediately. Serves 4.

Note
Crayfish microwave particularly well, but care must be taken not to overcook them or they will lose their succulence and flavour. When cooking whole crayfish, do not attempt to microwave more than two at a time. Cook as for crayfish tails, adhering to the same cooking time for two whole crayfish as for four tails.

Fish Stock

100%, 50% .... 26 minutes

45 g (1½ oz) butter
1 small onion, chopped
1 carrot, chopped
1 celery stick, chopped
6 peppercorns
3 whole cloves
125 ml (4 fl oz) dry white wine
30 ml (2 tbsp) white vinegar
750 ml (1¼ pints) cold water
twist of lemon rind
750 g (1¾ lb) fish bones, heads and trimmings
½ bay leaf
3 parsley sprigs
thyme leaves

Microwave butter in a large bowl for 45 seconds on 100%. Add onion, carrot and celery. Microwave for 3 minutes. Add remaining ingredients and microwave for 8-10 minutes, then microwave on 50% for 10-12 minutes. Strain stock, cool and use for fish soups or sauces. Makes about 750 ml (1¼ pints).

Chicken and Apple Scallop

A quick dish using left-over cooked chicken or turkey.

70% .... 15 minutes

15 ml (1 tbsp) French mustard
generous pinch of ground ginger
300 g (11 oz) cooked chicken, cut into cubes
2 large apples, peeled and sliced
2.5 ml (½ tsp) dried tarragon
15 ml (1 tbsp) lemon juice
2.5 ml (½ tsp) salt
400 g (14 oz) canned cream of mushroom soup
75 ml (2½ fl oz) single cream
15-30 ml (1-2 tbsp) sherry
30 g (1 oz) butter
60 g (2 oz) dry brown breadcrumbs

Combine mustard and ginger in a large bowl, then stir in chicken, mixing well to coat. Spread evenly over base of a greased, 1-litre (1¾ pint) baking dish. Place apple slices in another baking dish and sprinkle with tarragon, lemon juice and salt. Microwave on 70% for 2-3 minutes, stirring gently after 1 minute. Arrange apple slices over chicken.

Combine soup, cream and sherry, spoon over apples and microwave on 70% for 8-10 minutes, or until heated through. Place butter in a bowl and microwave for 30 seconds. Add breadcrumbs and stir gently to coat. Sprinkle over casserole. Microwave for 2 minutes more or brown under a hot grill.
Serves 4-6.

Chicken Teriyaki

This dish is typically Japanese - good to look at and light to eat.

100%, 70% .... 28 minutes

6 chicken thighs
15 ml (1 tbsp) oil
spring onions to garnish

MARINADE
45 ml (3 tbsp) soy sauce (light Japanese is best)
30 ml (2 tbsp) mirin* or dry sherry
15 ml (1 tbsp) sugar
5 ml (1 tsp) ginger juice (page 61)

First make the marinade by combining all ingredients in a jug and microwaving them on 70% for 1 minute. Stir to dissolve sugar. Next, using a fork, prick chicken skin to allow marinade to penetrate and place thighs in a non-metallic dish. Pour marinade over and leave to stand for 30 minutes.

Microwave a browning dish on 100% for 6 minutes. Add oil and microwave for 30 seconds. Remove chicken thighs from marinade and pat dry. Place in browning dish, skin-side down, cover and microwave for 6 minutes, turning halfway through cooking time. Reduce power to 70% and microwave for a further 6-8 minutes.

Remove chicken from dish, add marinade and microwave for 3-4 minutes until well boiled. Return chicken to dish, skin-side down, and microwave for 2-3 minutes until skin has a good sheen on it.

To serve: Slice chicken diagonally into 15-cm (6-in) pieces. Garnish with spring onions which have been trimmed and chilled in iced water. Serve with rice.
Serves 3-4.

* Mirin is a type of semi-sweet saki, available at speciality shops which stock Japanese ingredients.

Tomato and Basil Chicken with Fettuccine

A delicious chicken, tomato and herb sauce to serve with pasta.

100%, 50% .... 22 minutes

30 g (1 oz) butter
500 g (18 oz) chicken breasts,
   boned, skinned and cubed
1 garlic clove, finely chopped
125 g (4 oz) chopped fresh basil
   (do not use dried)
2 x 400 g (14 oz) cans or jars of
   seasoned tomato sauce or
   2 x recipe (page 204)
200 ml (6½ fl oz) water
15 ml (1 tbsp) sugar
60 ml (4 tbsp) dry white wine
salt and black pepper
500 g (18 oz) fettuccine, cooked
   (page 220)
grated Parmesan cheese to serve

Place butter in a medium-sized casserole and microwave on 100% for 1 minute. Add chicken, garlic, half the basil and stir. Microwave

for 2-3 minutes, stirring after each minute. Set aside.

Combine tomato sauce, water, sugar and wine in a casserole. Microwave for 3 minutes, or until heated through. Add remaining basil and microwave on 50% for 15 minutes, stirring occasionally. (The mixture should thicken slightly.) Add chicken, season with salt and black pepper and serve over hot fettuccine. Serve Parmesan cheese separately. Serves 4-6.

Clay-baked Chicken

This chicken, baked in a clay cooking dish, has a deliciously spicy, barbecued flavour.

100% .... 33 minutes

1 chicken, about 1.5 kg (3 lb)
salt and black pepper
2 onions, cut into rings
1 garlic clove, finely chopped
125 ml (4 fl oz) seasoned tomato
   sauce (page 204)
30 ml (2 tbsp) soft brown sugar
15 ml (1 tbsp) cider vinegar
15 ml (1 tbsp) lemon juice
5 ml (1 tsp) chilli powder,
   or to taste
5 ml (1 tsp) Worcestershire sauce

Soak the top and bottom of a clay cooking dish in water for 15 minutes, then drain. Rinse chicken and pat dry. Season cavity with salt and black pepper and place a few onion rings inside. Place chicken in cooking dish and surround with remaining onion rings.

Combine all remaining ingredients and spoon over chicken. Cover with lid and microwave on 100% for 28-33 minutes, basting two or three times while cooking. Leave to stand for a few minutes before carving. Serve each portion with onions and some of the sauce. Serves 4-6.

Lemon Chicken

Divide a 1.5 kg (3 lb) chicken in quarters and coat with 45 ml (3 tbsp) flour seasoned with 5 ml (1 tsp) garlic salt, 5 ml (1 tsp) paprika, pinch of black pepper and 2.5 ml (½ tsp) dried thyme. Place chicken, skin-side down, in a pre-soaked clay cooking dish, cover and microwave on 100% for 15 minutes. Turn quarters over. Combine 45 ml (3 tbsp) honey, 20 ml (4 tsp) lemon juice, 15 ml (1 tbsp) dry sherry, 10 ml (2 tsp) soy sauce and a pinch of ground ginger and pour over chicken. Cover and microwave for 10-15 minutes, or until cooked, basting twice. Serves 4.

Poultry Timbales with Tarragon Béarnaise

This is a great way to use left-over chicken or turkey.

100%, 70% .... 20 minutes

45 g (1½ oz) butter
30 ml (2 tbsp) plain flour
250 ml (8 fl oz) hot milk
salt and black pepper
400 g (14 oz) cooked chicken or turkey
2 egg yolks
2 eggs
90 ml (3 fl oz) single cream
5 ml (1 tsp) chopped fresh tarragon or 2.5 ml (½ tsp) dried tarragon
30 ml (2 tbsp) brandy
fresh tarragon or parsley to garnish

TARRAGON BÉARNAISE
60 ml (4 tbsp) tarragon vinegar
60 ml (4 tbsp) dry vermouth
15 ml (1 tbsp) chopped spring onion
15 ml (1 tbsp) chopped fresh tarragon or 5 ml (1 tsp) dried tarragon
salt and black pepper
3 egg yolks
30 g (1 oz) butter, chilled
125 g (4 oz) butter, melted
15 ml (1 tbsp) chopped fresh tarragon or 5 ml (1 tsp) dried tarragon

Microwave butter in a large jug on 100% for 1 minute. Stir in flour and hot milk. Microwave for 3-4 minutes, stirring every minute until sauce is thick and bubbling. Season with salt and black pepper, then leave to cool.

Cut cooked poultry into small pieces and place in a food processor fitted with metal blades. Add egg yolks and eggs. Blend until smooth, then add cooled sauce, cream, tarragon and brandy. Mix well and spoon into six or eight well-greased ramekins.

Place ramekins in a circular pattern on oven turntable. Cover with greased waxed paper and microwave on 70% for 5-8 minutes, or until the outside is set and the middle is just firm. Leave to stand, covered, for about 5 minutes before turning out on to serving plates.

To make sauce: In a bowl, combine vinegar, vermouth, spring onion, 15 ml (1 tbsp) fresh tarragon or 5 ml (1 tsp) dried tarragon, salt and black pepper to taste and microwave on 100% for 3-5 minutes, or until liquid is reduced to about 30 ml (2 tbsp). Strain liquid and cool. Place egg yolks and reduced liquid in a blender or food processor and blend with the chilled butter. Microwave the 125 g (4 oz) melted butter for 1-2 minutes until just boiling, then slowly add in a steady stream to ingredients in blender or food processor, keeping the motor running. Adjust seasoning and beat in remaining tarragon.

To serve: Spoon equal quantities of Béarnaise sauce on to each serving plate, set a timbale in the centre of the sauce and garnish with fresh tarragon or parsley. Serves 6-8.

Note

The timbale mixture can be made up and the liquid for the sauce can be reduced well in advance. Microwave the timbales just before serving and make the Béarnaise sauce during standing time.

Chicken and Vegetable Stir-fry

100% .... 13 minutes

175 g (6 oz) mangetout peas
**600 g (1 lb 5 oz) chicken breasts,
   boned and skinned**
10 ml (2 tsp) cornflour
75 ml (2½ fl oz) chicken stock
30 ml (2 tbsp) oil
salt and black pepper
2 spring onions, sliced
**15 ml (1 tbsp) freshly grated
   ginger root**
1 garlic clove, finely chopped
6 button mushrooms, sliced
20 ml (4 tsp) soy sauce
15-30 ml (1-2 tbsp) medium sherry

Top and tail and remove strings from peas, cut chicken into bite-sized pieces and dissolve cornflour in chicken stock.

Microwave a browning dish on 100% for 5 minutes. Add oil and heat for 1 minute longer. Sprinkle chicken with salt and pepper, add to browning dish and microwave for 2 minutes, stirring after 1 minute. Add peas and onions. Microwave for a further minute. Add ginger, garlic and mushrooms, mixing gently, and microwave for 1 minute more.

With a slotted spoon, remove chicken and vegetables and keep warm. Add cornflour mixture, soy sauce and sherry to dish and microwave for about 3 minutes, or until sauce thickens, stirring every minute. Return chicken and vegetables and toss to coat with sauce. If necessary, microwave for l minute more to heat through. Serve immediately with rice. Serves 4.

Hint
Ginger is often tough and woody and difficult to chop, so try the following Japanese tip: Peel a piece of ginger and grate it on a medium-sized grater. Pick the pulp up in your fingers and squeeze out as much juice as possible. You need never use ginger any other way.

Stuffed, Honeyed Chicken Thighs

100% .... 22 minutes

6 chicken thighs
30 g (1 oz) butter
15 ml (1 tbsp) clear honey
2 red apples, cored and sliced
15 ml (1 tbsp) redcurrant jelly
fresh sage sprigs to garnish

STUFFING
15 g (½ oz) butter
½ small onion, chopped
**1 slice of white bread, made into
   crumbs**
125 g (4 oz) smooth low-fat cheese
4-6 fresh sage leaves
salt and black pepper
**1 red apple, quartered, cored and
   coarsely grated**

Loosen skin on each chicken thigh to form a pocket for stuffing. Set aside.

To prepare stuffing: Microwave butter in a small bowl on 100% for 45 seconds. Add onion and toss to coat. Microwave for 1 minute. Add remaining ingredients, seasoning well. Divide stuffing between chicken thighs, pushing it between the skin and flesh. Secure with two cocktail sticks.

Arrange chicken thighs in a well-greased, shallow casserole. In a small bowl combine half the butter and all the honey. Microwave for 45 seconds, then brush over chicken. Cover lightly with waxed paper and microwave for 12-15 minutes, or until chicken is just cooked. Drain chicken and keep warm.

Add remaining butter to dish and microwave for 1 minute. Add apple slices and microwave for 1-2 minutes until apple is just tender. Arrange chicken on a serving platter with apple slices around. Add redcurrant jelly to juices in dish and microwave for 45 seconds. Spoon sauce over chicken and garnish with sage leaves.
Serves 4.

Fruit 'n Spice Chicken with Toasted Almonds

100%, 70% .... 36 minutes

pinch of saffron
125 ml (4 fl oz) boiling water
30 ml (2 tbsp) oil
1 chicken, about 1.5 kg (3 lb),
  cut into portions
salt and black pepper
1 onion, chopped
1 x 2.5-cm (1-in) cinnamon stick
125 g (4 oz) prunes
60 ml (4 tbsp) sultanas
60 ml (4 tbsp) honey
5 ml (1 tsp) ground cinnamon
10 ml (2 tsp) lemon juice
10 ml (2 tsp) toasted sesame seeds
  (page 44)
30 ml (2 tbsp) toasted almonds
  (page 36)

Soak saffron in boiling water for
20 minutes. Microwave a
browning dish on 100% for
6 minutes. Add oil and
microwave for 1 minute more.
Sprinkle chicken with salt and
black pepper, arrange in
browning dish and microwave for
3 minutes. Turn and rearrange
chicken. Microwave for a further
2 minutes.

Remove chicken, add onion
and microwave for 3 minutes.
Return chicken and add saffron
liquid and cinnamon stick. Cover
and microwave on 70% for
8-10 minutes, or until chicken is
nearly cooked. Remove chicken,
add prunes and sultanas.
Microwave for 2 minutes,
uncovered. Add honey, cinnamon
and lemon juice. Microwave on
100% for 5-7 minutes, or until
mixture is thick and syrupy.

Return chicken once more to dish
and microwave on 70% for about
2 minutes to heat through.
Sprinkle with sesame seeds and
almonds before serving. Serve
with rice.
Serves 4-6.

Asparagus and Mushroom Chicken Casserole

100%, 70%, 50% ..... 46 minutes

1 chicken, about 1.5 kg (3 lb)
250 ml (8 fl oz) dry white wine
salt and a few black peppercorns
2 small bay leaves
large sprig of thyme
large sprig of parsley
1 small onion, chopped
200 g (7 oz) mushrooms, sliced
15 g (½ oz) butter
200 g (7 oz) canned asparagus pieces
100 ml (3½ fl oz) milk
60 g (2 oz) butter
60 g (2 oz) plain flour
75 ml (2½ fl oz) single cream
2.5 ml (½ tsp) Dijon mustard
salt and black pepper

Place rinsed chicken, breast-side
down, in a deep casserole and
add wine, seasoning, herbs and
onion. Cover and microwave on
70% for 28-32 minutes, turning
chicken after 20 minutes. Drain
chicken and leave to stand for at
least 10 minutes before carving
into portions.

Place mushrooms in a small dish
with 15 g (½ oz) butter and
microwave on 100% for
2 minutes, stirring after 1 minute.
Set aside. Strain liquid in which
chicken was cooked into a
measuring jug. Add liquid from
asparagus and enough milk to
make up 550 ml (18 fl oz).

In another large jug microwave
60 g (2 oz) butter for 1½ minutes.
Stir in flour, whisk in all the liquid
and microwave for 4-5 minutes,
stirring every minute until sauce
has boiled and thickened. Add
cream, mustard, asparagus and
mushrooms and season to taste.
Place chicken portions in a
serving dish and pour sauce over.
Adjust seasoning to taste.
Microwave on 50% for
4-5 minutes to reheat.
Serves 6.

Chicken with Chilli

A chicken dish with a Mexican touch.

100%, 70% .... 26 minutes

8 chicken drumsticks
salt and black pepper
15 ml (1 tbsp) oil
1 onion, chopped
3 garlic cloves, chopped
1 small green pepper, sliced
15 ml (1 tbsp) chilli powder, or to taste
400 g (14 oz) canned whole tomatoes, coarsely chopped
400 g (14 oz) canned red kidney beans, drained and rinsed
125 g (4 oz) frozen sweetcorn
60 ml (4 tbsp) chopped fresh coriander leaves
extra coriander leaves to decorate

SIDE DISHES
soured cream
black olives
grated Cheddar cheese
chopped fresh tomato

Cut joints off each drumstick and scrape around bones to free tendons. Sprinkle chicken with salt and black pepper.

Heat a browning dish on 100% for 5 minutes. Add oil and heat for 1 minute more. Add chicken and microwave for 3 minutes. Turn and microwave for 2 minutes more. Add onion, garlic and green pepper. Microwave for a further 2 minutes. Stir well, then add chilli powder and tomatoes in their juice. Cover and microwave on 70% for 8-10 minutes more, or until chicken is just cooked. Stir in beans and sweetcorn and microwave for 2-3 minutes to heat through.

Just before serving, stir in coriander leaves and scatter a few whole leaves on top to decorate. Serve side dishes in separate bowls and let everyone help themselves.
Serves 4.

Note

This dish can be made in advance. Just cool, then cover and refrigerate. To reheat, microwave on 70% for 6-9 minutes, or until heated through. Stir in coriander leaves just before serving.

Chicken and Dill Chowder

100%, 70% .... 17 minutes

1 onion, chopped
1 garlic clove, finely chopped
30 g (1 oz) butter
60 ml (4 tbsp) plain flour
salt and black pepper
750 ml (1¼ pints) chicken stock
3-4 courgettes, grated
1 carrot, grated
45 ml (3 tbsp) dry white wine
300 g (11 oz) cooked chicken (or turkey), cubed
250 ml (8 fl oz) single cream
30 ml (2 tbsp) chopped fresh parsley
15 ml (1 tbsp) chopped fresh dill or 5 ml (1 tsp) dried dill

In a large casserole, microwave onion and garlic in butter on 100% for 2-3 minutes, stirring after 1 minute. Stir in flour, salt and black pepper to taste, and mix well. Gradually add stock. Microwave for 4-5 minutes, stirring every minute.

Add courgettes, carrot and wine. Microwave, covered, for 4-5 minutes, stirring every 2 minutes. Stir in chicken, cream and herbs. Microwave on 70% for 3-4 minutes, or until heated through, stirring after 2 minutes. Serves 6.

Hint

To add an extra dash of piquancy to soups, keep on hand the following magic combination:

CHILLI SHERRY
Pour 250 ml (8 fl oz) dry sherry into a jug and microwave on 100% for 1 minute to warm. Pierce 6 small, dried Portuguese chillies in a few places with the tip of a knife. Add them to the sherry and store in a small decanter for at least one week before using. Serve with any soup, adding 5-10 ml (1-2 tsp) per serving at the table. Makes about 250 ml (8 fl oz).

Roast Chicken with Sausage Stuffing

100% .... 39 minutes

1 chicken, about 1.5 kg (3 lb)
90 g (3 oz) butter
5 ml (1 tsp) chicken spice

STUFFING
3 slices of bread, toasted
1 small bunch of seedless green grapes
175 g (6 oz) pork sausagemeat
30 ml (2 tbsp) chopped onion
2.5 ml (½ tsp) dried thyme
generous pinch of of dried sage
60 ml (4 tbsp) single cream
30 ml (2 tbsp) brandy
salt and black pepper

First make the stuffing: Cut toast into small cubes and put into a bowl. Halve grapes and add to bread. Crumble sausagemeat into a shallow dish and microwave with the onion on 100% for 3 minutes, stirring every minute. Drain and add to bread, together with thyme, sage, cream and brandy. Season to taste.

Loosen skin of chicken breast and spread butter under skin. Stuff bird and truss. Sprinkle with chicken spice. Shield drumsticks and wing tips with small pieces of foil to prevent overcooking. Place bird in a roasting bag or a covered casserole, then microwave on 100% for 10-12 minutes per 500 g (18 oz) – about 30-36 minutes for a 1.5 kg (3 lb) chicken. Remove foil shields after half the cooking time. Leave to stand for 10 minutes before carving. Serves 4-6.

Note

For an unstuffed chicken, base the cooking time on 10 minutes per 500 g (18 oz), and for stuffed poultry, use 12 minutes per 500 g (18 oz). If you wish to microwave on 70%, increase the time by about one-third.

Hint

To promote even cooking of roast chicken, truss the legs and wings close to the body.

Poussins with Peaches and Curry Butter

100% .... 24 minutes

2 poussins, 500-600 g (18 oz-1 lb
  5 oz) each
30 g (1 oz) butter
2 large, firm peaches
watercress to garnish (optional)

CURRY BUTTER
90 g (3 oz) butter
1 lemon
1 orange
1 spring onion, chopped
1 small garlic clove, chopped
2.5-5 ml (½ -1 tsp) curry powder
salt and black pepper

First make the curry butter: Place butter in a dish and microwave on 100% for 20 seconds to soften. Grate 5 ml (1 tsp) lemon rind and squeeze 20 ml (4 tsp) lemon juice from half of the lemon. Keep separate. Slice other half of lemon thinly and set aside. Grate 15 ml (1 tbsp) orange rind and squeeze 30 ml (2 tbsp) orange juice from half of the orange. Slice other half thinly and set aside.

Place spring onion, garlic, lemon and orange rind, butter, curry powder, salt and black pepper in a food processor and process until smooth. Gradually add lemon and orange juice. Set aside.

Place poussins on a work surface and carefully loosen skin from breast meat, starting at the neck end. Spread 30 ml (2 tbsp) of the curry butter under the skin of each chicken, then pat skin back into place. Reserve remaining curry butter.

Place a few slices of lemon and orange in each poussin and truss. Spread half of the plain butter over each poussin. Shield wing tips and ends of legs with foil and place poussins in a casserole. Cover and microwave on 100% for about 8 minutes. Remove foil and baste poussins with cooking juices. Microwave, covered, for 8-10 minutes more, basting every 3 minutes. Leave to stand for 10 minutes before serving.

Meanwhile, prepare peaches. Halve peaches, remove stones, but do not peel. Place peaches, cut-side up, in a shallow baking dish and spread with reserved curry butter. Add a little water to the bottom of the dish and microwave for 2-3 minutes to heat through.

To serve: Split poussins, placing one half poussin and one half peach on each plate. Garnish with watercress if desired.
Serves 4.

Hint
Because the surface temperature of food does not change enough in microwave cooking to bring about natural browning, it is necessary to use a browning agent on the surface of meats.

Chicken can be brushed with melted butter and sprinkled with herbs, paprika, brown onion soup powder or crumbled chicken stock cube before microwaving. Soy sauce, Worcestershire sauce and barbecue sauce are also useful coatings.

Baked Spicy Chicken

100% .... 22 minutes

8 chicken portions

MARINADE
125 ml (4 fl oz) seasoned tomato
  sauce (page 204)
5 ml (1 tsp) salt
2.5 ml (½ tsp) cayenne pepper
2.5 ml (½ tsp) ground cumin
2.5 ml (½ tsp) garam masala
30 ml (2 tbsp) lemon juice
5 ml (1 tsp) grated lemon rind
5 ml (1 tsp) chilli powder
15 ml (1 tbsp) chopped fresh
  coriander
2 small garlic cloves, crushed

Place chicken portions in a large casserole. Combine ingredients for marinade, pour over chicken and marinate for at least 4 hours. Cover and microwave on 100% for 18-22 minutes. Rearrange and turn chicken halfway through cooking time. Leave to stand for 10 minutes before serving.
Serves 4-6.

Chicken with Orange and Mint Sauce

For your next barbecue let the microwave speed up the cooking. Gently cook the chickens, then finish off over hot coals with this delicious basting sauce.

100% .... 18 minutes
Barbecue time ..about 15 minutes

2 chickens, about 1.5 kg (3 lb) each, cut into serving pieces
125 ml (4 fl oz) orange juice
125 ml (4 fl oz) chicken stock
10 fresh mint leaves

SAUCE
175 g (6 oz) orange marmalade
45 g (1½ oz) butter
30 ml (2 tbsp) clear honey
15 ml (1 tbsp) chopped fresh mint or
  5 ml (1 tsp) dried mint

Make the sauce first by combining marmalade, butter, honey and mint in a bowl and microwaving

on 100% for 2-3 minutes, stirring after 1 minute. Set aside.

Place chicken pieces in a single layer in a large, shallow casserole. Combine orange juice, chicken stock and mint leaves and pour over chicken. Microwave, covered, on 100% for 10 minutes. Turn and rearrange chicken pieces and microwave for 5 minutes more.

Remove chicken pieces from liquid, pat dry and place on the barbecue. Cook for about 15 minutes, or until cooked to taste, turning once and brushing with the sauce.
Serves 8-10.

Caucasian Chicken

100%, 70% .... 35 minutes

8 chicken thighs
30 ml (2 tbsp) plain flour
salt and black pepper
30 g (1 oz) butter
30 ml (2 tbsp) oil
1 onion, sliced
1 apple, grated
2.5 ml (½ tsp) dried marjoram
2.5 ml (½ tsp) dried rosemary
15 ml (1 tbsp) Worcestershire sauce
125 g (4 oz) prunes, soaked
  overnight, reserving liquid
400 g (14 oz) canned tomato soup
30 ml (2 tbsp) sweet sherry
green olives

Wipe chicken thighs and pat dry. Combine flour and seasoning and rub into chicken. Microwave a browning dish on 100% for 6 minutes. Add butter and oil and microwave for 30 seconds. Add chicken thighs and microwave for 2 minutes on each side. Drain chicken and set aside.

Add onion and apple to dish. Toss to coat with oil, then microwave for 4 minutes, stirring at least once during cooking time. Return chicken to dish, together with herbs, Worcestershire sauce, prune liquid and half the soup. Cover and microwave on 70% for 15 minutes. (Halfway through cooking time turn chicken thighs over and around.) Stir in remaining soup, prunes and sherry. Cover and microwave for 5-7 minutes more. Add a few olives and serve with either rice or pasta.
Serves 4.

Hints
• Microwaving renders a good amount of fat from chicken. The fat should be drained off before adding sauces or other ingredients.
• Microwave chicken pieces with the skin-side up and place the thicker parts towards the outer edge of the dish.

Chicken Tonnato

100% .... 12 minutes

**6 chicken breasts, boned and
  skinned**

STOCK
100 ml (3½ fl oz) dry white wine
1 onion slice
1 small carrot, grated
**1 small celery stick, roughly
  chopped**
black peppercorns
salt

SAUCE
1 egg yolk
150 ml (5 fl oz) oil
1 small garlic clove
**100 g (3½ oz) canned tuna,
  drained**
20 ml (4 tsp) capers
4 anchovy fillets
15-25 ml (3-5 tsp) lemon juice
**100 ml (3½ fl oz) reserved cooking
  liquid**
salt and white pepper
75 ml (2½ fl oz) single cream

GARNISH
black olives
15 ml (1 tbsp) chopped fresh parsley
capers
lemon wedges
paprika

Combine all ingredients for stock
in a large shallow casserole.
Cover and microwave on 100%
for 2 minutes. Next, arrange
chicken breasts in a circle in the
dish, the thickest part facing
outwards. Cover and microwave
for 8-10 minutes, turning once
during cooking time. Drain
chicken, set aside to cool and
reserve liquid.

  To make sauce: Using a blender
or food processor, blend together
egg yolk, oil, garlic, tuna, capers
and anchovies. Add lemon juice
and cooled cooking liquid. Blend
again. Season lightly, add cream
and blend to combine.

  To serve: Place a little of the
sauce on a serving platter. Slice
chicken breasts in half
horizontally and arrange on top
of sauce. Mask slices with sauce,
cover and allow to stand for
2-3 hours (refrigerated, if you
have the space) before serving.
Garnish with black olives,
parsley, capers and lemon
wedges that have been dipped in
paprika.
Serves 6.

Chicken and Mushroom Crêpes

100%, 50% .... 20 minutes

60 g (2 oz) butter
225 g (8 oz) mushrooms, cleaned
  and sliced
½ small onion, finely chopped
60 ml (4 tbsp) plain flour
500 ml (16 fl oz) milk
2 chicken stock cubes, crumbled
freshly ground black pepper
2.5 ml (½ tsp) dried tarragon
125 ml (4 fl oz) soured cream
45 ml (3 tbsp) dry sherry
225 g (8 oz) cooked chicken, diced
30 ml (2 tbsp) finely chopped
  parsley
12 crêpes (page 132)

Microwave butter in a deep
casserole on 100% for 45 seconds.
Add mushrooms and onion,
stir to coat with butter and
microwave, covered, for
2-2 ½ minutes.
  Blend in flour and microwave
for 30 seconds. Stir and

microwave for 45 seconds more.
Stirring well, gradually mix in
milk, followed by crumbled stock
cubes, pepper and tarragon, then
cover and microwave for
3 minutes, stirring after each
minute. Finally, mix in soured
cream and sherry. Set aside
250 ml (8 fl oz) of the sauce and
add chicken and half the parsley
to remaining sauce. Mix well.
  Spoon a little chicken mixture
on to each crêpe. Roll up crêpes
and place in two casseroles.
Spoon reserved sauce over
crêpes, cover and microwave each
dish on 50% for 5-6 minutes until
heated through. Sprinkle with
remaining parsley before serving.
Serves 6.

Hint
**To defrost frozen crêpes: Place a
stack of 10 crêpes on a plate, cover
with plastic wrap and microwave
on 30% for 4 minutes.**

Chicken and Cheese Salad

70 % .... 8 minutes

4 chicken breasts, skinned and
  boned
125 ml (4 fl oz) chicken stock
125 ml (4 fl oz) dry white wine
5 ml (1 tsp) fresh tarragon or 2.5 ml
  (½ tsp) dried tarragon
2 round lettuces, torn into pieces
2 tomatoes, sliced
45 g (1½ oz) black olives
45 ml (3 tbsp) chopped spring
  onions
1 avocado, peeled and cubed
lemon juice
100 g (3½ oz) Cheddar cheese,
  grated

RASPBERRY AND APPLE
VINAIGRETTE
1 spring onion, chopped
¼ small apple, peeled and sliced
60 ml (4 tbsp) apple juice
30 ml (2 tbsp) raspberry vinegar
  (see strawberry vinegar on
  page 37)

75 ml (2½ fl oz) oil
salt and black pepper

Place chicken breasts in a
casserole. Add chicken stock,
wine and tarragon. Cover and
microwave on 70% for 4 minutes.
Turn chicken over and microwave
for about 4 minutes more, or until
chicken is just done. Let stand to
cool.
  To make vinaigrette: Place
spring onion, apple, apple juice
and vinegar in a small bowl and
microwave on 100% for
3-4 minutes, or until liquid is
reduced by half. Cool mixture and
then slowly beat in oil. Season to
taste.
  Cut chicken into chunks. Place
lettuce in a large bowl. Add other
ingredients and just before
serving, toss with raspberry and
apple vinaigrette.
Serves 4-6.

Stir-fried Chicken and Cashews

100% .... 20 minutes

3 chicken breasts, boned, skinned and sliced into 1-cm (½ -in) wide strips
salt and black pepper
20 ml (4 tsp) sesame seed oil
30 ml (2 tbsp) oil
5 ml (1 tsp) ginger root, finely chopped or squeezed (page 61)
1-2 garlic cloves, finely chopped
1 onion, chopped
200 g (7 oz) broccoli, trimmed into florets
2 carrots, thinly sliced
6 water chestnuts, sliced
60 ml (4 tbsp) salted cashew nuts
30 ml (2 tbsp) cornflour
15 ml (1 tbsp) soy sauce
15 ml (1 tbsp) dry sherry
250 ml (8 fl oz) chicken stock
6 spring onions, sliced diagonally

Season chicken lightly. Microwave a browning dish on 100% for 6 minutes. Add half the oils and microwave for 1 minute more. Add chicken, ginger and garlic, toss to coat evenly, then microwave for 4 minutes, stirring twice during cooking time. Transfer chicken to another plate.
  Add remaining oil to browning dish and microwave for 1 minute. Then add onion, broccoli florets and carrots, toss to coat with oil and microwave for 2 minutes. Stir in chicken, water chestnuts and cashews. Microwave for 2 minutes. Combine cornflour, soy sauce and sherry, add to stock, then pour into dish. Stir well. Microwave for 4 minutes, stirring every minute. Sprinkle with spring onions and serve at once.
Serves 4.

Honey-soy Chicken

100% .... 25 minutes

1 chicken, about 1.5 kg (3 lb), cut into serving portions
60 ml (4 tbsp) clear honey
generous pinch of ground ginger
1 garlic clove, crushed
10 ml (2 tsp) lemon juice
30 ml (2 tbsp) soy sauce
1 large carrot, thinly sliced
45 ml (3 tbsp) water
250 g (9 oz) mangetout peas
250 g (9 oz) mushrooms, sliced
15 ml (1 tbsp) oil
15 ml (1 tbsp) sesame seeds

Place chicken portions in a casserole. Combine honey, ginger, garlic, lemon juice and 15 ml (1 tbsp) of the soy sauce. Brush half the mixture over chicken, cover with waxed paper and microwave on 100% for 14-16 minutes, or until chicken is just cooked. (Brush several times with remaining honey mixture.) Set aside and keep warm.
  Place carrot in a casserole with the water, cover and microwave for 3-4 minutes. Add peas and microwave for a further 3 minutes. Drain, then stir in mushrooms, oil and sesame seeds. Add remaining soy sauce and microwave for 1-1 ½ minutes to heat through. Serve vegetables with the chicken on a bed of hot rice, if desired.
Serves 4.

Hint
Crumbed chicken portions make a wonderfully quick meal in the microwave, but as they do not cook to a golden brown the coating must be made up of interesting and tasty ingredients.
  Try a combination of 125 g (4 oz) dried breadcrumbs or toasted sesame seeds (page 44), 60 ml (4 tbsp) grated Parmesan cheese, 10 ml (2 tsp) finely snipped chives, 2.5 ml (½ tsp) chicken seasoning, black pepper and 25 ml chopped fresh parsley. Coats 10 drumsticks dipped first in beaten egg.

Stuffed Roast Turkey

100%, 70% .... 96 minutes
Conventional oven:
180 °C (350 °F, gas 4) 45-60
minutes

1 turkey, about 4.5 kg (10 lb)
60 g (2 oz) butter
salt and black pepper
generous pinch of paprika
10 ml (2 tsp) Worcestershire sauce
10 ml (2 tsp) lemon juice
10 ml (2 tsp) soft brown sugar

STUFFING
100 ml (3½ fl oz) oil
2 onions, chopped
liver from turkey, finely chopped
175 g (6 oz) fresh white
**   breadcrumbs**
250 g (9 oz) pork sausagemeat
salt and black pepper
45 ml (3 tbsp) chopped fresh parsley
100 ml (3½ fl oz) unsweetened
**   chestnut purée**
1 apple, peeled and diced
2 eggs
2 celery sticks, chopped

First make the stuffing:
Microwave oil in a large bowl on
100% for 2 minutes. Add onion
and liver, stir to coat with oil.
Microwave for 4 minutes, stirring
twice. Add remaining ingredients
and mix well. Fill both body and
neck cavities with stuffing. Secure
neck skin with cocktail sticks.

Spread turkey skin with butter
and season with salt, black
pepper and paprika. Truss with
string. Shield wing tips,
drumstick ends and top of breast
with foil. Place in a large roasting
bag, make two or three small
incisions in bag to allow excess
steam to escape and tie open end
loosely with string.

Weigh turkey and calculate
microwaving time, allowing
10 minutes per 500 g (18 oz) on
70%. Place turkey in microwave,
breast-side down. Microwave for
about one-third of calculated
time, then turn turkey over. Baste
with butter, microwave for one-
third longer, turn and baste
again. Microwave for remaining
time.

Remove turkey from bag and
remove foil shields. Place turkey
in a roasting pan. Combine
Worcestershire sauce, lemon
juice, soft brown sugar and 30 ml
(2 tbsp) of the pan juices. Pour
over turkey and roast at 180 °C
(350 °F, gas 4) for 45 minutes to
1 hour, basting at least twice.
Leave turkey to stand for 10
minutes before carving. (To test if
turkey is cooked, press drumstick
between fingers - it should be soft
and move up and down easily.)
Serves 10.

Variation
APRICOT AND ORANGE STUFFING
100 g (3½ oz) dried apricots
250 ml (8 fl oz) orange juice
turkey liver and heart, if available
250 g (9 oz) butter
4 celery sticks, chopped
1 large onion, chopped
500 g (18 oz) pork sausagemeat
500 g (18 oz) bread, cut into cubes
5 ml (1 tsp) dried sage
5 ml (1 tsp) dried tarragon
2.5 ml (½ tsp) dried thyme
15 ml (1 tbsp) chopped fresh parsley
100 g (3½ oz) flaked almonds

125 ml (4 fl oz) orange-flavoured
**   liqueur**
chicken stock to moisten
salt and black pepper

Place apricots and orange juice in
a jug and microwave on 100% for
3 minutes. Next, microwave
turkey liver and heart in a little
stock for 3 minutes on 70%. Leave
to stand until cool.

Microwave 125 g (4 oz) of the
butter in a bowl for 2 minutes,
add celery and onion and
microwave for 4 minutes, stirring
twice, then turn into a large bowl.
Microwave sausagemeat for
4-5 minutes, stirring twice. Add
to celery mixture with the bread,
herbs, almonds and apricots in
orange juice. Dice liver and heart
and add to stuffing. Mix well.

Microwave remaining butter for
1 minute and pour over stuffing
mixture. Add orange-flavoured
liqueur and enough chicken stock
to moisten. Stir well and season to
taste. Stuff body and neck cavity
of turkey.
Makes enough stuffing for
2 × 4.5 kg (10 lb) turkeys.

Guinea Fowl with Caramelized Cherry Sauce

100%, 70% .... 70 minutes

1 young guinea fowl, about 1 kg
  (2 lb 4 oz)
150 g (5 oz) pork fillet
fresh basil leaves
15 ml (1 tbsp) snipped chives
2 apples, peeled, cored and sliced
salt and black pepper
few bacon rashers, rinds removed
30 g (1 oz) butter

SAUCE
90 g (3 oz) soft brown sugar
125 ml (4 fl oz) red wine vinegar
375 ml (12 fl oz) orange juice
30 ml (2 tbsp) cherry brandy
30 ml (2 tbsp) sweet red Cinzano

Rinse out cavity of bird and pat dry with absorbent kitchen paper. Mince or process pork fillet with basil, chives, apples and seasoning. Combine well and use to fill cavity. Cover breast of bird with bacon and secure rashers with wooden cocktail sticks.

Microwave a browning dish on 100% for 6 minutes. Add butter and microwave for 30 seconds. Place guinea fowl in dish, breast-side down, and microwave for 8-10 minutes, giving bird a quarter turn every 2 minutes. Set aside.

To make sauce: Place soft brown sugar and vinegar in a microwaveproof bowl or casserole. Microwave for 4-6 minutes until beginning to caramelize. Add orange juice and stir well. (At this point there will be thick, tacky strands of caramel in the bowl.) Continue microwaving for a further 5-7 minutes until these strands disappear. Stir from time to time. Add cherry brandy and Cinzano.

Place bird in sauce, breast-side down, cover and microwave on 70% for 30-40 minutes. Turn bird over halfway through cooking time. Remove from oven and carve after 5 minutes' standing time. Arrange joints in sauce and reheat if necessary.
Serves 4.

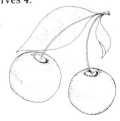

Duck with Gooseberries

100%, 70% .... 57 minutes

1 duck, about 1.5 kg (3 lb)
salt and black pepper
2 leeks, roughly chopped
parsley sprigs
large thyme sprig
15 g (½ oz) butter
2.5 ml (½ tsp) ground ginger
45 ml (3 tbsp) clear honey
45 ml (3 tbsp) jellied marmalade
45 ml (3 tbsp) Grand Marnier
30 g (1 oz) butter
175 g (6 oz) gooseberries

SAUCE
10 ml (2 tsp) cornflour
10 ml (2 tsp) gravy powder
250 ml (8 fl oz) giblet stock
  (page 73)
100 ml (3½ fl oz) cooking liquid,
  strained
15 ml (1 tbsp) Grand Marnier

Rinse duck well and pat dry.
Season lightly inside and out.

Place leeks, parsley and thyme in
the cavity. Tie duck into shape
with string and shield wings with
small strips of foil. Secure neck
skin with a cocktail stick, then
place duck, breast-side down, on
a roasting rack or in a roasting
bag. (Calculate cooking time by
allowing 14-15 minutes per
500 g (18 oz).)
  Microwave on 100% for
10 minutes. Drain off excess fat.
Combine 15 g (½ oz) butter with
the ginger and spread over breast
and thighs. Return duck to rack,
breast-side down. Microwave on
70% for approximately half
remaining cooking time. Drain off
excess fat, turn duck over and
microwave for 5 minutes more.
  Combine honey, marmalade
and Grand Marnier, spoon over
duck and complete cooking time,
basting with glaze once or twice.
Remove string and cocktail stick
and keep duck warm.
  Microwave 15 g (½ oz) butter on
100% for 45 seconds. Add
gooseberries, stir to coat with
butter and microwave for
1 minute just to heat through.

Keep warm. Combine all sauce
ingredients in a jug and microwave for 5 minutes, stirring from
time to time.
  To serve: Carve duck, place a
portion on each dinner plate and
serve with a little sauce and a
spoonful of gooseberries.
Serves 3-4.

Caramelized Duck

100%, 70% .... 58 minutes

1 duck, about 1.5 kg (3 lb)
salt and black pepper
1 onion, peeled
1 apple, quartered
15 g (½ oz) butter
2.5 ml (½ tsp) ground ginger
45 ml (3 tbsp) clear honey
45 ml (3 tbsp) soft brown sugar
45 ml (3 tbsp) orange-flavoured
  liqueur
2 oranges
30 g (1 oz) butter
100 ml (3½ fl oz) water
cress to garnish (optional)

SAUCE
10 ml (2 tsp) cornflour
10 ml (2 tsp) gravy powder
150 ml (5 fl oz) giblet stock
100 ml (3½ fl oz) orange juice
100 ml (3½ fl oz) strained cooking
  juices
15 ml (1 tbsp) orange-flavoured
  liqueur

Rinse duck and pat dry with
absorbent kitchen paper. Scrape
skin thoroughly with a knife to
remove any feathers. Season
inside and outside. Place onion
and apple in cavity. Tie duck into
shape with string, and shield
wing tips with small strips of foil.
Secure neck skin with a cocktail
stick, then place duck, breast-side
down, on a roasting rack or in a
roasting bag. (To calculate
cooking time, allow 14-15 minutes
per 500 g (18 oz).)
  Microwave on 100% for
10 minutes. Drain off excess fat.
Combine 15 g (½ oz) butter with
the ginger, and spread over breast
and thighs. Return duck to rack,
breast-side down. Microwave for
about half remaining cooking
time on 70%. Drain off excess fat
and turn duck over. Microwave
for 5 minutes more.
  Combine honey, brown sugar
and liqueur. Spread this mixture
over duck and microwave for
remaining time, basting with
glaze once or twice. When
cooked, strain cooking juices,
skim off fat and set juices aside.

Remove string and cocktail stick
from duck, leave to stand for
10-15 minutes and keep warm.
  Remove zest from oranges, peel
and slice thickly. Microwave 30 g
(1 oz) butter on 100% in a shallow
casserole for 1 minute and add
orange slices. Turn slices over
immediately, then microwave for
2-3 minutes. Keep warm. Place
zest and 100 ml (3 ½ fl oz) water in
a bowl. Microwave on 100% for
4 minutes, then drain.
  To make sauce: Combine
cornflour, gravy powder, giblet
stock and orange juice in a bowl.
Add reserved cooking juices,
orange zest and liqueur, and stir
to blend. Microwave on 100% for
5 minutes, stirring every minute.
  To serve: Arrange orange slices
along duck breast, spoon a little
sauce over and carve at table.
Serve remaining sauce separately.
Garnish with cress if desired.
Serves 3-4.

Giblet Stock

100%, 50% .... 12 minutes

1 set of giblets (duck or chicken),
  cleaned
1 thick onion slice
1 small carrot, roughly chopped
1 parsley sprig
salt and black pepper
1 bay leaf
200 ml (6½ fl oz) water

Place all ingredients in a bowl.
Cover and microwave on 100%
for 5 minutes. Reduce power to
50% and microwave for a further
7 minutes. Strain and use as
required.
Makes about 200 ml (6½ fl oz).

Cajun Meat Loaf

A spicy meat loaf served with soured cream.

100% .... 27 minutes

7.5 ml (1½ tsp) salt
7.5 ml (1½ tsp) black pepper
5 ml (1 tsp) cayenne
2.5 ml (½ tsp) ground cumin
2.5 ml (½ tsp) grated nutmeg
1 bay leaf
30 g (1 oz) butter
1 small onion, chopped
½ green pepper, chopped
2 garlic cloves, finely chopped
10-15 ml (2-3 tsp) Tabasco, or to
   taste
15 ml (1 tbsp) Worcestershire sauce
15 ml (1 tbsp) chopped fresh parsley
2.5 ml (½ tsp) dried thyme
125 ml (4 fl oz) milk
125 ml (4 fl oz) seasoned tomato
   sauce (page 204)
675 g (1½ lb) minced beef
1 egg, beaten
45 ml (3 tbsp) seasoned tomato
   sauce
60 ml (4 tbsp) grated Cheddar
   cheese
soured cream to serve

Combine salt, pepper, cayenne, cumin, nutmeg and bay leaf and set aside. Microwave butter in a large dish on 100% for 1 minute. Add onion and microwave for 3 minutes, stirring once. Add green pepper and garlic and microwave for 3 minutes more, stirring once. Then add combined seasonings, Tabasco and Worcestershire sauce, parsley and thyme. Microwave for a further minute. Stir in milk and 125 ml (4 fl oz) tomato sauce and microwave for 1 minute. Let mixture cool slightly.

Remove bay leaf and add onion mixture to beef. Pour in egg, mix well and turn into a deep square or rectangular casserole and smooth top. Spread with 45 ml (3 tbsp) tomato sauce, cover loosely with waxed paper and microwave on 100% for about 18 minutes, or until cooked through. Sprinkle with cheese during last minute of microwaving. Leave to stand for 10 minutes, then cut into squares and serve with soured cream. Serves 6-8.

Easy Beef Stew

Cook this stew in a clay cooking dish for perfect results.

100%, 50%, 30% ..... 75 minutes

1 kg (2¼ lb) stewing steak,
    cubed
30 ml (2 tbsp) plain flour
7.5 ml (1½ tsp) salt
black pepper
2.5 ml (½ tsp) paprika
3 small carrots, peeled and sliced
2 small onions, sliced
1-2 garlic cloves, finely chopped
125 ml (4 fl oz) water
2 tomatoes, skinned, seeded and
    chopped
60 ml (4 tbsp) chilli sauce, or to taste
2.5 ml (½ tsp) dried thyme
1 beef stock cube
100 g (3½ oz) fresh green beans,
    quartered
200 g (7 oz) mushrooms, halved

Soak the top and bottom of a
3-litre (5-pint) clay cooking dish in
water for 15 minutes, then drain.
Coat beef cubes with a mixture of
flour, salt, black pepper and
paprika and place in dish. Cover
and microwave on 100% for
15 minutes. Stir beef cubes and
add carrots, onions and garlic.
   Combine water, tomatoes, chilli
sauce, thyme and crumbled beef
stock cube. Stir into meat and
vegetables. Cover and microwave
on 50% for 20 minutes. Add
green beans and mushrooms
and microwave on 30% for
30-40 minutes, or until meat and
vegetables are tender.
Serves 6.

Hint
**To ensure the even cooking of meat
in stews, meat must be completely
defrosted before microwaving.
(Refer to meat chart on page 218.)
   Cooking times for stews will
depend on the type and amount of
meat used and on the quantity of
vegetables added to the dish. Cut
the meat and vegetables into
smaller pieces than you would for
conventional cooking and make
them more or less uniform in size.**

Beef Bolognese

A tasty sauce to serve with pasta.

100% .... 20 minutes

500 g (18 oz) lean minced beef
1 onion, chopped
2 garlic cloves, finely minced
2 celery sticks, chopped
2 carrots, peeled and grated
125 g (4 oz) chicken livers, chopped
2.5 ml (½ tsp) dried oregano
pinch of cayenne
3 tomatoes, skinned, seeded and
    chopped
250 ml (8 fl oz) red wine
salt and black pepper

Crumble mince into a large
casserole. Microwave on 100% for
4 minutes, breaking up meat with
a fork every minute. Remove
meat with a slotted spoon, then
add onion, garlic, celery, carrots
and chicken livers. Microwave for
4 minutes, covered, stirring every
minute.
   Return meat to casserole and
add remaining ingredients. Cover
and microwave for 10-12 minutes,
stirring twice. Adjust seasoning
to taste. Cool and refrigerate until
needed. Reheat by microwaving
on 100% for 3-4 minutes, stirring
frequently. Serve with spaghetti.
Serves 4.

Variation
CREAMY MACARONI BOLOGNESE
For an alternative dish, reduce the
quantity of wine used in cooking
to 150 ml (5 fl oz) and add 150 ml
(5 fl oz) soured cream once the
sauce is completely cooked. Then
add 250 g (9 oz) cooked macaroni
(raw weight) and turn into a
casserole. Cover with 60 g (2 oz)
grated Cheddar cheese and
microwave on 70% for 4-5
minutes until meat sauce and
cheese bubble. Serves 4.

Note
**Use this sauce to make delicious
savoury pancakes or Greek
pastitsio. Serve any left-over sauce
on toast as a quick snack.**

Beef and Spinach Pie

100% .... 25 minutes

1 onion, finely chopped
60 g (2 oz) butter
1 garlic clove, finely chopped
600 g (1 lb 5 oz) minced beef
300 g (11 oz) fresh spinach, trimmed
  and washed
125 g (4 oz) noodles, cooked
  (page 220)
60 ml (4 tbsp) chopped fresh parsley
2.5 ml (½ tsp) dried marjoram
125 ml (4 fl oz) beef stock
60 ml (4 tbsp) single cream
generous pinch of grated nutmeg
salt and black pepper
100 g (3½ oz) Cheddar cheese,
  grated

Place onion and butter in a large
casserole and microwave for
3 minutes on 100%. Add garlic,
microwave for 1 minute more,
then crumble in beef and microwave for 3-4 minutes, or until
meat is no longer pink. (Stir twice
during cooking time, breaking up
meat with a fork.) Place spinach in
another dish, with water still
clinging to leaves, and microwave
for 3 minutes, covered with
vented plastic wrap. Drain well
and chop.
  Add spinach and noodles to
meat mixture, together with
herbs, stock, cream, nutmeg,
seasoning and half the cheese.
Mix well and turn into a greased
baking dish. Microwave, covered,
for 8 minutes, then uncover, stir
gently and microwave for 4-6
minutes longer until bubbling.
Sprinkle with remaining cheese
during last minute of cooking.
Leave to stand for at least
5 minutes before serving.
Serves 4-6.

Variation
QUICK CRUMB TOPPING
Melt 60 g (2 oz) butter on 100%
for 1 minute, stir in 60 g (2 oz)
dried breadcrumbs, 60 ml (4 tbsp)
grated Parmesan cheese and
2.5 ml (½ tsp) paprika. Sprinkle
mixture over pie and microwave
for 1 minute before serving. (This
topping is appropriate for most
casseroles, too.)

Beef Kebabs

50%, 100% .... 12 minutes

750 g (1¾ lb) rump or fillet steak,
  cut into large cubes
200 g (7 oz) button mushrooms
8-10 pickling onions
1-2 green peppers, cut into squares
8-10 cherry tomatoes
4 canned pineapple rings, cut
  into pieces

MARINADE
10 ml (2 tsp) ginger juice (page 61)
1 garlic clove, chopped
15 ml (1 tbsp) finely chopped onion
100 ml (3½ fl oz) soy sauce
30 ml (2 tbsp) mirin* or 15 ml
  (1 tbsp) dry sherry and 15 ml
  (1 tbsp) medium sherry
10 ml (2 tsp) soft brown sugar
15 ml (1 tbsp) oil

Place steak in a non-metallic dish.
Combine all ingredients for
marinade in a bowl, microwave
on 50% for 2 minutes, stir well
and pour over steak. Leave to
stand for at least 1 hour.

  Place mushrooms in a bowl,
pour boiling water over them and
leave to stand for 1 minute, then
drain. Pour off marinade from
meat and push pieces on to
skewers together with the
vegetables and pineapple.
  Place 5-6 kebabs at a time on a
plate, brush with marinade and
cover loosely with waxed paper.
Microwave on 100% for about
5 minutes, turning kebabs
halfway through cooking time
and brushing them with a little
marinade. Repeat with remaining
kebabs. Serve on a bed of rice.
Serves 4.

*** Mirin is a type of semi-sweet saki,
available at speciality shops which
stock Japanese ingredients.**

Fillet Steak with Brandy Vinaigrette

100% .... 10 minutes

15 ml (1 tbsp) oil
4 slices of beef fillet, about 1.5 cm
  (¾ in) thick

VINAIGRETTE
15 ml (1 tbsp) chopped fresh thyme
  or 5 ml (1 tsp) dried thyme
3 spring onions, chopped
30 g (1 oz) butter
15 ml (1 tbsp) white wine vinegar
30 ml (2 tbsp) brandy
30 ml (2 tbsp) oil
salt and black pepper

First make vinaigrette: Place thyme, spring onions and butter in a bowl and microwave on 100% for 1 minute. Beat in vinegar, brandy, oil and seasoning and microwave for 1 minute more. Beat well and keep warm.

Either cook the beef under the grill or, if using the microwave, heat a browning dish on 100% for

6 minutes. Add enough oil to coat bottom of dish, then add meat and brown for 1 minute. Turn meat over and microwave for 1 minute more, or until cooked to taste. Serve with warm vinaigrette sauce.
Serves 4.

Tangy Tomato Marinade

In a bowl, combine 250 ml (8 fl oz) seasoned tomato sauce (page 204), 15 ml (1 tbsp) French mustard, 60 ml (4 tbsp) red wine vinegar, 15 ml (1 tbsp) brown sugar, 1 minced garlic clove, 5 ml (1 tsp) dried oregano, 2.5 ml (½ tsp) Worcestershire sauce and pepper to taste. Microwave, covered with waxed paper, on 100% for 1½ minutes. Stir well. Reduce power to 50% and microwave for 5 minutes more. Cool, then pour over steaks or cubed beef for kebabs. Makes about 280 ml (9 fl oz).

Stuffed Cabbage Casserole

100% .... 26 minutes

12 large cabbage leaves
60 ml (4 tbsp) water
350 g (12 oz) minced beef
350 g (12 oz) minced pork
200 g (7 oz) cooked rice (page 220)
salt and black pepper
15 ml (1 tbsp) lemon juice
5 ml (1 tsp) dried mixed herbs
15 ml (1 tbsp) chopped fresh parsley
30 ml (2 tbsp) finely chopped onion
1 garlic clove, finely chopped
400 g (14 oz) canned condensed
  tomato soup
185 ml (6 fl oz) seasoned tomato
  sauce (page 204)
60 ml (4 tbsp) water
30 ml (2 tbsp) dry sherry
5 ml (1 tsp) sugar
4 bacon rashers, rinds removed,
  chopped

Place cabbage leaves in a 3-litre (5-pint) casserole. Add water and microwave, covered, on 100% for

5-6 minutes until leaves are pliable. Drain and remove heavy core from each. Mix together beef, pork, rice, salt, black pepper, lemon juice, mixed herbs, parsley, onion and garlic, blending well.

Divide mixture into twelve portions and place one on each cabbage leaf. Roll up each leaf, beginning at the wide end and folding sides in. Secure rolls with cocktail sticks and place seam-side down in a lightly-greased casserole.

Mix together soup, tomato sauce, water, sherry and sugar and pour over rolls. Sprinkle bacon on top, then cover and microwave for 17-20 minutes, turning dish during cooking if necessary. Leave to stand for 5-8 minutes before serving.
Serves 6.

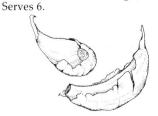

Beef and Broccoli Stir-fry

100% .... 12 minutes

60 g (2 oz) rice-shaped noodles
500 g (18 oz) broccoli
7.5 ml (1½ tsp) cornflour
5 ml (1 tsp) oil
15 ml (1 tbsp) soy sauce
30 ml (2 tbsp) thinly sliced red pepper
few drops of Tabasco
15 ml (1 tbsp) white wine vinegar
220 ml (7 fl oz) chicken stock
10 ml (2 tsp) lemon juice
15 ml (1 tbsp) oil
600 g (1 lb 5 oz) sirloin steak, cut into thin strips
4 spring onions, chopped
15 ml (1 tbsp) grated fresh ginger root
30 ml (2 tbsp) beansprouts

Soak rice-shaped noodles in boiling water for about 5 minutes, then drain well. Trim broccoli, slice stems thinly and blanch in boiling water. Break broccoli heads into small florets. Set aside. Combine cornflour, 5 ml (1 tsp) oil, soy sauce, red pepper, Tabasco, vinegar, chicken stock and lemon juice. Set aside.

Heat a browning dish for 6 minutes on 100%. Add 15 ml (1 tbsp) oil, tilting dish to coat. Add meat and brown quickly, microwaving for 1 minute. Remove meat from dish. Add spring onions and ginger and microwave for 1 minute. Add soy sauce mixture and microwave for 1-2 minutes, or until slightly thickened, stirring once or twice. Stir in softened noodles, steak and broccoli. Microwave for 2 minutes, stirring once. Adjust seasoning, adding more soy sauce if desired. Add beansprouts and serve.
Serves 4.

Note
Rice-shaped noodles are available from speciality food shops.

Beef and Mushroom Cobbler

100%, 30% .... 72 minutes
Conventional oven:
200 °C (400 °F, gas 6) .. 15 minutes

30 ml (2 tbsp) oil
2 bacon rashers, rinds removed,
  chopped
1 onion, chopped
2 celery sticks, sliced
1 garlic clove, crushed
1 kg (2¼ lb) stewing steak,
  cut into 2.5-cm (1-in) cubes
salt and black pepper
2.5 ml (½ tsp) paprika
2.5 ml (½ tsp) dried mixed herbs
250 ml (8 fl oz) beef stock
250 ml (8 fl oz) red wine
45 ml (3 tbsp) tomato purée
15 g (½ oz) butter
20 ml (4 tsp) plain flour
200 g (7 oz) mushrooms, quartered
175 g (6 oz) frozen peas

TOPPING
250 g (9 oz) plain flour
5 ml (1 tsp) salt
15 ml (1 tbsp) baking powder
60 ml (4 tbsp) oil
1 egg
5 ml (1 tsp) vinegar
milk and water

Place oil and bacon in a large
casserole and microwave on
100% for 2 minutes. Add onion
and celery, stir to coat with oil and
microwave for 2 minutes. Add
garlic, beef, seasoning, paprika,
herbs, stock, wine and tomato
purée. Stir well, cover and
microwave for 8 minutes. Stir
again, then reduce power to 30%
and microwave for at least 1 hour
until meat is tender. Stir from
time to time.
  Work butter and flour together
and stir into meat mixture. Add
mushrooms and peas and stir
again. Turn into a large shallow
casserole suitable for serving.
  To make topping: Sift dry
ingredients into a bowl. Combine
oil, egg and vinegar in a jug, then
add milk and water to measure a

total of 250 ml (8 fl oz). Pour on to
dry ingredients and mix to a firm
dough. Dust a board lightly with
flour, press out dough to a
thickness of 10 mm (½ in) and cut
into rounds with a 4-cm (1½ -in)
pastry cutter. Arrange scones on
top of meat mixture, overlapping
each scone slightly. Brush with
beaten egg and bake conventionally at 200 °C (400 °F, gas 6) for
15 minutes.
Serves 6-8.

Hints
• Simmering stews or casseroles
gently on a low power setting (for
example, 50%) and adding an acid
ingredient, such as vinegar,
pineapple juice, tomato juice or
wine, will help to tenderize meat as
well as give added flavour.
• To convert favourite stew or
casserole recipes for microwave
use, reduce the quantity of liquid
called for by about one third as
there is little evaporation during
microwave cooking.

Savoury Swiss Steak

50% .... 70 minutes

750 g (1¾ lb) rump steak, sliced
  8 mm (¾ in) thick
60 g (2 oz) plain flour
salt and black pepper
2 large onions, thinly sliced
400 g (14 oz) canned tomatoes, juice
  included, roughly chopped
125 ml (4 fl oz) beer
15 ml (1 tbsp) sugar
10 ml (2 tsp) prepared mild mustard
30 ml (2 tbsp) brown onion soup
  powder

Cut steak into six serving pieces.
Combine flour, salt and pepper
and use to coat steak. Layer meat
with onions in a casserole.
Combine remaining ingredients,
mix well and pour over meat.
Cover and microwave on 50% for
60-70 minutes, or until meat is
tender. (Rearrange meat after
40 minutes.) Serve each portion
with sauce.
Serves 6.

Roast Beef with Mushroom Gravy

70%, 100% .... 23-32 minutes
Conventional oven:
220 °C (425 °F, gas 7).. 25 minutes

1.5 kg (3 lb) topside of beef
salt and black pepper
2-2.5 ml (½ tsp) dry mustard
15 ml (1 tbsp) oil

GRAVY
200 g (7 oz) brown mushrooms,
  sliced
125 ml (4 fl oz) boiling beef stock
60 ml (4 tbsp) red wine
5 ml (1 tsp) gravy powder
5 ml (1 tsp) creamed horseradish

Pat meat dry, season lightly with
salt, black pepper and mustard
and brush with oil. Place meat on
a roasting rack with fat-side
underneath and cover loosely
with waxed paper. Turning meat
halfway through cooking time,
microwave on 70% for 17 minutes
(rare), for 22 minutes (medium),

or 26 minutes (well done).
Remove meat from microwave
oven and place in a conventional
oven at 220 °C (425 °F, gas 7) for
25 minutes.
To make gravy: Pour juices from
meat into a shallow casserole, add
mushrooms and stir to coat.
Microwave on 100% for
2 minutes, then add stock and
microwave for 1 minute more.
Mix red wine, gravy powder and
horseradish together, add to
mushrooms and stir to combine.
Microwave for 2-3 minutes until
boiling and slightly thickened.
Slice meat thinly and serve with
the gravy.
Serves 6.

Hint
**To assist the browning of joints of
meat cooked in the microwave,
brush with Worcestershire sauce or
soy sauce, or add soy sauce to a
marinade. Sprinkling the meat
surface with brown onion soup
powder, herbs or a little crumbled
beef stock cube, or brushing it with
tomato purée will also give a good
finish.**

Sloppy Joes

**Make this mixture in advance and
keep ready for quick filled rolls and
sandwiches.**

100% .... 6 minutes

500 g (18 oz) minced beef
½ small onion, chopped
250 ml (8 fl oz) bottled tomato sauce
30 ml (2 tbsp) prepared mild
  mustard
salt and black pepper
15 ml (1 tbsp) soft brown sugar
10 ml (2 tsp) vinegar
2.5 ml (½ tsp) curry powder
  (optional)
60 g (2 oz) Cheddar cheese, grated

Crumble minced beef into a
1.25-litre (2¼-pint) casserole. Add
onion and microwave on 100% for
4 minutes. Break up meat with a
fork, then microwave until meat
is cooked (1-2 minutes). Drain off
excess liquid and add remaining
ingredients. Mix well, cover and
refrigerate until needed.
To serve: spoon about 75 g

(2½ oz) of the mixture inside each
roll or sandwich and microwave
on 100% for about 1 minute per
roll.
Makes enough for 8 rolls or
sandwiches.

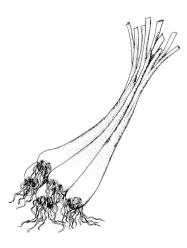

Fillet Steak with Pineapple Béarnaise

100% .... 18 minutes

5 ml (1 tsp) oil
salt and black pepper
4-6 thick slices of fillet steak
ground ginger
4-6 canned pineapple rings
15 ml (1 tbsp) water

SAUCE
45 ml (3 tbsp) dry white wine
60 ml (4 tbsp) unsweetened
  pineapple juice
15 ml (1 tbsp) tarragon vinegar
2 spring onions, roughly chopped
2 egg yolks
salt and white pepper
100 g (3½ oz) butter
60 ml (4 tbsp) mayonnaise

Microwave a browning dish on 100% for 6 minutes, add oil and sprinkle dish very lightly with salt. Arrange steaks in dish, pushing them down flat. Sprinkle with pepper and ginger and microwave for 4-6 minutes, turning only once. (Cooking times will vary according to thickness of steaks and degree of rareness required.) Remove steaks and keep warm.

Microwave pineapple rings for 1 minute in browning dish, then add 15 ml (1 tbsp) water to dish and reserve this residue for the sauce.

To make sauce: Place wine, pineapple juice, vinegar and spring onions in a jug and microwave for 2 minutes, or until reduced to approximately half the original quantity. Add to residue in browning dish.

Place egg yolks and seasoning in work bowl of a food processor, blend for a few seconds, then add liquid. Blend again for 45 seconds. Meanwhile, microwave butter for 2-3 minutes until very hot. Pour in through feed tube in a slow but constant stream and continue processing until mixture thickens. Add mayonnaise and process to combine.

To serve: Arrange steaks on a serving platter, place a pineapple ring on top of each steak and spoon sauce over. Serve at once with new potatoes and a selection of fresh vegetables.
Serves 4-6.

Mexican Beef Pittas

100% .... 12 minutes

500 g (18 oz) minced beef
1 small onion, chopped
1 garlic clove, finely chopped
½ green pepper, chopped
60 ml (4 tbsp) raisins
5 ml (1 tsp) salt
30-45 ml (2-3 tbsp) chilli sauce
45 ml (3 tbsp) chutney
2.5 ml (½ tsp) ground cinnamon
90 g (3 oz) tomatoes, chopped
45 g (1½ oz) stuffed olives, sliced
45 g (1½ oz) toasted almonds
    (page 36)
6-8 pitta breads, halved

GARNISH
½ small round lettuce, shredded
250 ml (8 fl oz) soured cream

Crumble beef into a casserole with onion and garlic. Cover with waxed paper and microwave on 100% for 3 minutes. Break up meat and stir. Cover and microwave for 2-3 minutes longer, or until very little pink remains in meat. Drain.
    Add green pepper, raisins, salt, chilli sauce, chutney and cinnamon. Microwave, covered, for 3-4 minutes, or until hot. Stir in tomatoes, olives and half the almonds. Microwave, covered, for 1-2 minutes until heated through. Spoon mixture into pitta bread halves and garnish with shredded lettuce, soured cream and remaining almonds.
Serves 6-8.

Note
Pitta bread is unleavened flat bread from the Middle East. It is called 'pocket bread' as it is hollow inside. Make your own or purchase pitta bread from delicatessens and large supermarkets.
    To thaw frozen pitta bread: Separate pittas and defrost 3 at a time. Place them on absorbent kitchen paper and microwave on 30% for 30-40 seconds. Leave to stand for 1-2 minutes.

Beef Olives

100% .... 13 minutes

400 g (14 oz) frying steak or topside,
    cut in one large, thin slice
¼ onion, finely chopped
30 ml (2 tbsp) finely chopped celery
60 g (2 oz) mushrooms, finely
    chopped
2.5 ml (½ tsp) prepared
    horseradish
2.5 ml (½ tsp) mixed herbs
45 ml (3 tbsp) beef stock
60 g (2 oz) fresh breadcrumbs
salt and black pepper
250 ml (8 fl oz) beef stock
125 ml (4 fl oz) red wine
fresh herbs to garnish (optional)

SAUCE
15 g (½ oz) butter
½ onion, chopped
60 g (2 oz) mushrooms, sliced
15 g (½ oz) plain flour
cooking liquid
salt and black pepper

Cut meat into four neat pieces and pound out thinly. Combine vegetables, horseradish, herbs, 45 ml (3 tbsp) stock and breadcrumbs. Season with salt and black pepper to taste. Divide mixture between meat slices, roll up, tie neatly and place in a casserole. Pour 250 ml (8 fl oz) stock and red wine over rolls and microwave, covered, on 100% for 5 minutes. (Turn rolls over and rearrange once during cooking time.) Remove rolls from cooking liquid and keep warm.
    To make sauce: Microwave butter for 30 seconds. Add onion and microwave for 2 minutes, then add mushrooms and microwave for 1 minute more. Stir in flour and gradually add cooking liquid. Microwave for 3-4 minutes, stirring every minute, until thickened and bubbling. Season to taste with salt and black pepper.
    To serve: Place one roll on a warmed serving plate and spoon sauce over. Garnish with fresh herbs if desired.
Serves 4.

Cottage Pie

100% .... 29 minutes

750 g (1¾ lb) potatoes, peeled and
   cubed
60 ml (4 tbsp) water
1 onion, chopped
500 g (18 oz) minced beef
100 g (3½ oz) frozen carrots, sliced
   or diced
60 g (2 oz) mushrooms, sliced
30 ml (2 tbsp) tomato purée
2.5 ml (½ tsp) sugar
2 tomatoes, skinned and chopped
15 ml (1 tbsp) chopped fresh parsley
2.5 ml (½ tsp) dried thyme
salt and black pepper
10 ml (2 tsp) gravy powder
15 ml (1 tbsp) HP sauce
125 ml (4 fl oz) water
30 g (1 oz) butter
about 60 ml (4 tbsp) milk
5 ml (1 tsp) prepared mild mustard
100 g (3½ oz) Cheddar cheese,
   grated
parsley to garnish

Place potatoes in a large bowl
with the water and microwave,
covered, on 100% for
10-12 minutes. Leave to stand,
covered, while preparing meat.
   Place onion in a large casserole,
crumble in beef and microwave,
covered, for 3 minutes. Break up
meat with a fork, then stir in
carrots and mushrooms and
microwave for 2 minutes more.
Stir again. Add tomato purée,
sugar, chopped tomatoes and
herbs and season well.
Microwave for 4 minutes, stirring
twice. Combine gravy powder,
HP sauce and water, stir into
casserole and microwave for
2 minutes.
   Drain potatoes and mash with
butter and enough milk to give a
good consistency. Stir in mustard
and half the cheese. Smooth
surface of meat mixture and pipe
or spoon potato over. Microwave
for 4-5 minutes until heated
through. Sprinkle with remaining
cheese and microwave for
1 minute more or brown under
the grill. Serve garnished with a
little parsley.
Serves 4-6.

Beef Mexican

100% .... 18 minutes

60 g (2 oz) butter
1 onion, sliced
1 carrot, peeled and sliced
1 green pepper, seeded and sliced
1 potato, peeled and diced
2 garlic cloves, finely chopped
5 ml (1 tsp) chopped fresh oregano
   or 2.5 ml (½ tsp) dried oregano
5 ml (1 tsp) fresh thyme or 2.5 ml
   (½ tsp) dried thyme
15 ml (1 tbsp) chopped fresh parsley
2.5-5 ml (½ -1 tsp) chilli powder
2.5 ml (½ tsp) Worcestershire
   sauce
500 g (18 oz) topside of beef, sliced
   into thin strips
salt and black pepper
30 ml (2 tbsp) plain flour
400 g (14 oz) canned tomatoes,
   chopped
125 ml (4 fl oz) beef stock
10 ml (2 tsp) lemon juice
5 ml (1 tsp) grated lemon rind

In a large casserole, microwave
butter on 100% for 1 minute.
Add onion, carrot, green pepper,
potato and garlic. Microwave for
7 minutes, stirring twice. Add
herbs, chilli powder,
Worcestershire sauce, beef, salt
and pepper. Cover and
microwave for 5 minutes, stirring
once. Stir in flour, then add
tomatoes with their liquid, beef
stock, lemon juice and rind.
Cover and microwave for
5 minutes more, stirring twice.
Allow to stand for a few minutes.
Serve with hot rice if desired.
Serves 4.

Hamburgers

This chart is for cooking lean minced beef hamburgers in a browning dish. Each hamburger should weigh about 125 g (4 oz). Use 100% power and turn hamburgers after half the cooking time. Season burgers after turning.

No. of patties	Preheat browning dish	Cooking time
1	4 minutes	2-3 minutes
2	6 minutes	3-4 minutes
3	6 minutes	4-5 minutes
4	8 minutes	5-6 minutes

To cook hamburgers in a glass dish, increase cooking time by about 20 seconds per burger. To add good colour to hamburgers not cooked in a browning dish, brush with barbecue, soy or Worcestershire sauce, or sprinkle each side with a little brown onion soup powder.

Cheese and Wine Burgers

100% .... 14 minutes

500 g (18 oz) minced beef
45 ml (3 tbsp) bottled tomato sauce
60 ml (4 tbsp) dry red wine
90 g (3 oz) Cheddar cheese, grated
salt and black pepper
30 ml (2 tbsp) chopped onion
4 cheese slices or onion rings
4 hamburger buns

Combine beef, tomato sauce, wine, cheese, salt, black pepper and chopped onion. Mix well and shape into four burgers. Preheat browning dish on 100% for 7-8 minutes. Place burgers in dish, cover and microwave on 100% for 2½ minutes. Turn burgers, cover and microwave for 2½ minutes more. Top each burger with a slice of cheese or onion rings and microwave for 1 minute. Serve on toasted hamburger buns.
Serves 4.

Baked Green Peppers

100% .... 16 minutes

4 green peppers
15 ml (1 tbsp) oil
2 bacon rashers, rinds removed, chopped
1 onion, chopped
250 g (9 oz) minced beef
salt and black pepper
60 g (2 oz) mushrooms, chopped
1 egg
125 g (4 oz) cooked rice (page 220)
15 ml (1 tbsp) chopped fresh parsley
pinch of dried thyme
60 ml (4 tbsp) grated Cheddar cheese

Cut a slice off the top of each green pepper. Remove core and seeds. Place peppers in a casserole, cover and microwave on 100% for 4 minutes, turning them over halfway through cooking time.

In a shallow dish, microwave oil for 1 minute. Add bacon and onion and microwave for 3 minutes. Add minced beef and microwave for a further 3 minutes. Season well. Add mushrooms, egg, rice, parsley, thyme and three-quarters of the cheese.

Stuff green peppers with this mixture and top with remaining cheese. Stand peppers in a shallow serving dish and cover. Microwave for 5 minutes. Serve immediately.
Serves 4.

Variation

VEGETARIAN STUFFING
Microwave 45 ml (3 tbsp) oil on 100% for 45 seconds. Add 1 chopped onion, stir to coat and microwave for 2 minutes. Stir in 200 g (7 oz) sliced mushrooms, cover and microwave for 2 minutes more. Add 2.5 ml (½ tsp) dried thyme, salt and pepper, a pinch of cayenne, 175-250 g (6-9 oz) cooked rice (page 220) and 75 g (2½ oz) grated Cheddar cheese and stir to combine. Divide between peppers and microwave as above.

Beef and Vegetable Casserole with Cheese Topping

100% .... 15 minutes

1 recipe cheese sauce (page 131)
1 onion, chopped
l carrot, diced
l large potato, peeled and thinly sliced
1 courgette, thinly sliced
45 ml (3 tbsp) water
100 g (3½ oz) mushrooms, sliced
15 ml (1 tbsp) tomato purée
400 g (14 oz) minced beef
15 ml (1 tbsp) chopped fresh parsley
2.5 ml (½ tsp) dried oregano
pinch of dried thyme
salt and black pepper
45 ml (3 tbsp) grated Cheddar cheese

Make the cheese sauce first, then set aside. Combine onion, carrot, potato and courgette in a casserole. Add water and microwave, covered, on 100% for 4 minutes, stirring once. Drain, then add mushrooms, tomato purée, crumbled minced beef, herbs and seasoning. Cover and microwave for 6-8 minutes more, stirring at least once to break up beef.

Turn into an ovenproof serving dish and top with cheese sauce. Microwave for 2-3 minutes to heat through, then sprinkle with grated cheese and brown under a grill if desired.
Serves 4.

Note
Casseroles can be topped with crushed potato crisps, crumbled cooked bacon or buttered bread-crumbs to give an attractive finish.

To make buttered breadcrumbs: Microwave 30-45 g (1-1½ oz) butter in a dish on 100% for 45-60 seconds. Add 60 g (2 oz) small cubes of bread or freshly made breadcrumbs and toss to coat thoroughly. Microwave for 1 minute more before using as required.

Mince and Noodle Bake

100%, 70% .... 27 minutes

45 ml (3 tbsp) oil
1 onion, chopped
200 g (7 oz) bacon rashers, rinds removed, chopped
500 g (18 oz) minced beef
salt and black pepper
5 ml (1 tsp) mixed herbs
400 g (14 oz) canned creamed sweetcorn
400 g (14 oz) canned tomato soup
200 g (7 oz) shell noodles or macaroni cooked (page 220)
100 g (3½ oz) mature Cheddar cheese, grated

Microwave oil in a large casserole on 100% for 45 seconds. Add onion and bacon and stir to coat. Microwave for 5 minutes, covered with vented plastic wrap, stirring twice during cooking time. Add minced beef, seasoning and herbs. Stir with a fork, then microwave for 5-7 minutes, breaking up meat with a fork every 2 minutes.

Mix in sufficient sweetcorn and tomato soup to give a soft mixture, then microwave for 5 minutes. Then reduce power to 70% and microwave for 5 minutes more. Stir in noodles and about half the cheese. Transfer to a casserole and sprinkle with remaining cheese. Either brown under a grill or microwave on 70% for 3-4 minutes until cheese begins to bubble.
Serves 6.

Hint
An easy way to microwave and drain minced beef is to put the meat in a microwaveproof colander. Place the colander in a casserole, cover loosely and microwave as any recipe directs for minced beef.

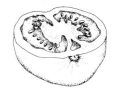

Veal with Cream Sauce

100%, 50% .... 53 minutes

750 g (1¾ lb) stewing veal, cubed
about 750 ml (1½ pints) water
1 onion, roughly chopped
1 bouquet garni
6 baby carrots, halved
200 g (7 oz) button mushrooms,
quartered
parsley to garnish

SAUCE
45 g (1½ oz) butter
45 ml (3 tbsp) plain flour
150 ml (5 fl oz) milk
60 ml (4 tbsp) single cream
10-15 ml (2-3 tsp) lemon juice
1 egg yolk
salt and white pepper

Place meat in a casserole with sufficient water to cover (about 750 ml [1½ pints]). Place onion in a colander and pour boiling water over to remove strong flavour. Tie herbs and spices for bouquet garni in a piece of muslin and add to meat along with onion.

Cover and microwave on 100% for 7 minutes. Add carrots, then lower power to 50% and microwave for 30 minutes, or until meat is tender, stirring from time to time. Remove meat and vegetables with a slotted spoon and set aside in a large casserole together with mushrooms. Discard bouquet garni. Reserve stock.

To make sauce: Microwave butter in a large jug on 100% for 1 minute. Stir in flour, then milk and about 300 ml (10 fl oz) of the reserved stock. Microwave for 4-5 minutes until boiling and thickened, stirring every minute. Add cream, lemon juice and egg yolk and season to taste. Combine sauce with meat and vegetables. Cover dish and microwave for 10 minutes on 50% to heat through and cook mushrooms. Garnish with parsley.
Serves 4.

Note
This dish looks particularly attractive garnished with pastry crescents:
Roll out scraps of puff pastry thinly and use a small scone cutter to cut half-moon shapes. Lay on a greased baking sheet and brush with a little beaten egg. Bake at 190 °C (375 °F, gas 5) for about 8 minutes until golden brown.

Hints
• Because veal is a delicate, lean meat, whenever possible cover it during cooking time or use a roasting bag. Microwaving on 70% also helps to prevent the meat from drying out.
• When selecting joints for roasting, look for evenly shaped pieces of meat.

Saltimbocca

100% .... 16 minutes

8 veal escalopes
8 thin slices of ham
fresh sage leaves, chopped
2.5 ml (½ tsp) dried oregano
salt and black pepper
90 g (3 oz) butter
90 ml (3 fl oz) medium cream sherry
60 ml (4 tbsp) chicken stock

Pound veal very thin, then halve each slice. Cut slices of ham in half and lay a piece of ham on each half-slice of veal. Top with sage and oregano. Lightly season, then roll up meat and fasten with cocktail sticks.
Microwave a browning dish for 7 minutes. Add butter and tip dish to melt. Add veal rolls and microwave for 3-4 minutes, turning several times until meat is browned. Add sherry and stock and stir. Microwave, covered, for 3-5 minutes, or until meat is tender.
Serves 8.

Veal Roulade with Tomato Sauce

100%, 50% .... 22 minutes

4 veal schnitzels, beaten until very thin
salt and black pepper
15 ml (1 tbsp) lemon juice
2 carrots, cut into sticks
45 ml (3 tbsp) water
10 green beans
8-10 fresh asparagus spears
45 g (1½ oz) butter

SAUCE
400 g (14 oz) canned tomatoes, drained and chopped
60 ml (4 tbsp) cream sherry
60 ml (4 tbsp) water
1 garlic clove, finely chopped
1 bay leaf
60 ml (4 tbsp) soured cream

Lay schnitzels on a board, season, sprinkle with lemon juice and set aside. Place carrots in a bowl with 45 ml (3 tbsp) water, cover and microwave on 100% for 2 minutes. Add beans and asparagus, cover again and microwave for 2-3 minutes more. (The vegetables should still be undercooked.)

Place a carrot stick, a couple of beans and 1 or 2 asparagus spears along short end of each schnitzel. Roll up and secure with a wooden cocktail stick. Arrange rolls in a shallow dish, dot liberally with butter, cover and microwave for 5 minutes. Turn and microwave on 50% for 5 minutes more. Remove roulades and keep warm.

To make sauce: In a large jug combine meat juices with all sauce ingredients, except cream. Microwave on 100% for 5-7 minutes. Remove bay leaf and pour liquid into a blender. Blend until smooth, then strain and add cream. Thin with a little water if necessary. Remove cocktail sticks from meat and slice thickly. Pour a spoonful of sauce on to each plate, arrange slices of meat on top of sauce and serve with rice or boiled potatoes.
Serves 4.

Veal Normandy

100%, 70% .... 26 minutes

15 ml (1 tbsp) oil
15 g (½ oz) butter
4 medium-sized veal escalopes
15 ml (1 tbsp) plain flour
5 ml (1 tsp) paprika
salt and black pepper
1-2 onions, sliced
100 ml (3½ fl oz) chicken stock
5 ml (1 tsp) dried oregano
2 large Granny Smith apples, cored, quartered and cut into wedges
100 ml (3½ fl oz) single cream
60 ml (4 tbsp) brandy

Heat a browning dish on 100% for 6 minutes. Add oil and butter and microwave for 30 seconds. Sprinkle escalopes very lightly with flour, paprika and seasoning and arrange in browning dish with thinner ends in the centre. Microwave for 3 minutes on each side. Remove from dish.

Add onions, scraping base of dish to loosen brown bits, and microwave for 2 minutes. Then add chicken stock and oregano and microwave for 4 minutes to reduce slightly. Stir in apples, cream and brandy, then add escalopes, spooning a little of the sauce over them. Cover and microwave on 70% for 7-10 minutes, stirring from time to time. Serve immediately.
Serves 4.

Browning Dish Hints

• To increase the browning of foods, use a spatula to flatten or press food against the base of the dish for better contact.
• Make sure that all frozen foods have completely thawed before placing in a browning dish as ice crystals in food prevent browning.
• Browning dishes may also be used for general microwave cooking as the surface does not function as a browner when covered with food.
• To remove burned-on food from a browning dish, soak the dish in hot soapy water, then wash out. Never use abrasive pads on the surface.

Peach-stuffed Lamb

100% .... 16 minutes

1 kg (2¼ lb) boned breast of lamb

STUFFING
30 ml (2 tbsp) oil
250 g (9 oz) dried peaches, chopped
100 g (3½ oz) pecan nuts, chopped
30 ml (2 tbsp) ground almonds
90 g (3 oz) wholemeal breadcrumbs
100 g (3½ oz) sultanas
salt and black pepper
generous pinch of ground cumin
2.5 ml (½ tsp) dried rosemary
2 small eggs, beaten
45 ml (3 tbsp) peach chutney
milk

Trim meat and wipe dry, then make stuffing. Pour oil into a bowl and microwave on 100% for 45 seconds. Add peaches, nuts, breadcrumbs and sultanas. Stir in all seasoning, rosemary, eggs, chutney and enough milk to make a moist stuffing.

Lay boned lamb flat (two pieces) on a board and spread stuffing over meat. Roll each piece tightly and tie with string. Place in a shallow microwave dish and microwave for 5 minutes. Baste with meat juices, then microwave for 8-10 minutes longer, or until meat is almost cooked. Wrap in foil, shiny-side inwards, and allow to stand for 10 minutes before cutting into slices to serve. Serves 4-6.

Variation

ORANGE AND HERB STUFFING
Combine 1 chopped onion, 60 g (2 oz) soft butter, 1 chopped garlic clove, 125 g (4 oz) fresh breadcrumbs, 2.5 ml (½ tsp) dried rosemary, salt and black pepper to taste, 2.5 ml (½ tsp) grated lemon rind, 5 ml (1 tsp) grated orange rind, 30 ml (2 tbsp) orange juice or orange-flavoured liqueur, 30 g (1 oz) sultanas and 1 beaten egg. Mix well. (This stuffing is ideal for any boned joint of lamb.)

Peach-stuffed Lamb, (top) and
Lamb and Courgette Kebabs

Roast Leg of Lamb

Lamb and Courgette Kebabs

100%, 70% .... 9 minutes

750 g (1³/₄ lb) boneless lamb, cubed
3 courgettes, cut in 1.5-cm (³/₄-in) pieces

MARINADE
250 ml (8 fl oz) oil
60 ml (4 tbsp) fresh lemon juice
30 ml (2 tbsp) orange juice
5 ml (1 tsp) grated orange rind
3 spring onions, chopped
10 ml (2 tsp) coarse-grained French mustard
5 ml (1 tsp) dried rosemary
2.5 ml (¹/₂ tsp) dried tarragon
5 ml (1 tsp) salt

Combine all ingredients for marinade in a bowl and microwave on 100% for 1 minute. Place lamb cubes and courgettes in a large flat container and pour marinade over. Stir to coat. Cover and refrigerate for at least 6 hours, stirring occasionally. Drain and reserve liquid.

Thread lamb and courgette pieces alternately on wooden skewers. Brush with marinade and place half the kebabs on a microwave plate. Microwave on 70% for 6-8 minutes, turning once and brushing with marinade several times. Remove and keep warm. Repeat with remaining kebabs. Serve with savoury rice and vegetables.
Serves 4-6.

Roast Leg of Lamb

100% .... 33 minutes

1 leg of lamb, about 1.5 kg (3 lb)
2 garlic cloves, sliced
1 large rosemary sprig
45 ml (3 tbsp) seasoned tomato sauce (page 204)
30 ml (2 tbsp) Dijon mustard

Wipe lamb dry with absorbent kitchen paper and make incisions in surface of meat with a sharp knife. Insert slivers of garlic and pieces of rosemary into meat. Combine tomato sauce and mustard and brush over meat.

Place meat in a covered casserole or roasting bag and microwave on 100% for 8-11 minutes per 500 g (18 oz) (24-33 minutes for 1.5 kg [3 lb]). Shield bone end of lamb with a strip of foil halfway through cooking time. Cover lamb in a tent of foil and leave to stand for about 15 minutes before carving.
Serves 6-8.

Cumberland Gravy

100% .... 4 minutes

cooking juices from lamb
water or stock
30 ml (2 tbsp) redcurrant jelly
generous pinch of dry mustard
pinch of ground ginger
5 ml (1 tsp) lemon juice
10 ml (2 tsp) plain flour
45 ml (3 tbsp) red wine

Combine cooking juices from lamb with enough water or stock to make up 300 ml (10 fl oz). Add redcurrant jelly, mustard, ginger and lemon juice and mix well. Microwave on 100% for 1 minute. Combine flour with red wine and stir into gravy. Microwave for 2-3 minutes, stirring every minute, until bubbling and slightly thickened.
Makes about 345 ml (11 fl oz).

Galantine of Lamb

100% .... 47 minutes

1 x 2 kg (4¹/₂ lb) leg of lamb, boned
375 ml (12 fl oz) dry white wine
10 ml (2 tsp) chopped fresh mint
10 ml (2 tsp) crushed fresh rosemary
peppercorns, bruised
125 ml (4 fl oz) white wine
30 ml (2 tbsp) whisky
black pepper
3 garlic cloves, bruised
5 ml (1 tsp) salt

STUFFING
500 g (18 oz) chicken breasts,
  skinned and boned
125 g (4 oz) cooked ham, diced
4 bacon rashers, rinds removed,
  chopped
45 g (1¹/₂ oz) pecan nuts
10 ml (2 tsp) grated lemon rind
1 garlic clove, finely chopped
5 ml (1 tsp) chopped fresh mint
5 ml (1 tsp) chopped fresh rosemary

Pat lamb dry and place in a large
glass container. Pour wine over
and sprinkle with mint, rosemary
and a few bruised peppercorns.
Marinate overnight in
refrigerator, turning several
times. Drain well and reserve
marinade.
    To make stuffing: Cut one
chicken breast into thin strips and
set aside. Chop remaining breasts
and place in a food processor
together with the ham, bacon,
nuts, lemon rind, garlic, mint and
rosemary. Process until well
blended.
    Pour 125 ml (4 fl oz) wine into a
bowl and microwave on 100% for
about 3 minutes, uncovered, or
until reduced by half. Stir into
chicken mixture together with
whisky. Season with black pepper
to taste, then layer stuffing in
pocket of lamb made by removal
of bone, alternating with strips of
chicken breast. Sew up neatly.
    Roll lamb in a double thickness
of muslin, shape neatly and tie
ends securely. Place lamb in a
large microwaveproof (preferably
clay*) dish and pour reserved
marinade over meat. Add just
enough water to cover meat, then
add bruised garlic and salt. Cover
and microwave on 100% for
8-11 minutes per 500 g (18 oz),
depending on how well done you
like lamb.
    To serve hot: Remove lamb from
liquid, cover with a tent of foil and
leave to stand for 20 minutes
before carving.
    To serve cold: Remove lamb
from liquid, cool, then chill well.
Remove muslin and slice thinly.
Place on a platter and garnish as
desired.
Serves 10-12.

* If the galantine is cooked in a clay
dish, allow an extra 10 minutes'
cooking time.

Wine-braised Lamb Chops

70% .... 12 minutes

6 lamb chops
1 onion, sliced
1 garlic clove, finely chopped
1 green pepper, thinly sliced
125 g (4 oz) button mushrooms,
  sliced
salt and black pepper
2 tomatoes, skinned and sliced
75 ml (2¹/₂ fl oz) red wine
15 ml (1 tbsp) soy sauce
15 ml (1 tbsp) seasoned tomato
  sauce (page 204)

Soak a clay cooking dish in water
for 15 minutes. Arrange chops in
base, with the thickest part
outwards. Cover with vegetables
and season lightly. Top with
tomatoes. Combine remaining
ingredients and pour over chops.
Cover and microwave on 70% for
10-12 minutes. Stand for
5 minutes before serving.
Serves 3-4.

Malay-style Curried Mince

100%, 70%, 50% ..... 46 minutes

30 ml (2 tbsp) oil
1 onion, chopped
7.5-10 ml (1½-2 tsp) curry powder
1 slice of white bread
200 ml (6½ fl oz) milk
500 g (18 oz) minced lamb
15 ml (1 tbsp) apricot jam
15 ml (1 tbsp) lemon juice
60 ml (4 tbsp) spicy chutney
45 g (1½ oz) seedless raisins
6 dried apricots, chopped
salt and black pepper
2 eggs
2.5 ml (½ tsp) curry powder
blanched almonds
2 lemon or bay leaves

Pour oil into a large casserole and microwave on 100% for 1 minute. Add onion and curry powder, mixing well, then microwave for 5 minutes, stirring once. Soak bread in half the milk for a few minutes, mash it and add to onion mixture. Stir in meat, jam, lemon juice, chutney, raisins, apricots and seasoning. Mix well and microwave on 70% for 8-10 minutes, stirring once or twice.

Turn mixture into a shallow casserole and smooth top. Combine remaining milk, eggs and curry powder. Pour over meat mixture. Spike top with almonds and lay lemon or bay leaves in the middle. Microwave on 50% for 25-30 minutes until egg mixture has set. Serve with saffron rice, onion and tomato salad, chutney and desiccated coconut, if desired.
Serves 4.

Lamb Patties with Melon and Mint

100%, 70% .... 17 minutes

30 ml (2 tbsp) toasted flaked almonds (page 36)
1 egg, beaten
salt and black pepper
30 ml (2 tbsp) dry breadcrumbs
1 garlic clove, finely chopped
1 onion, finely chopped
30 ml (2 tbsp) finely chopped fresh mint
500 g (18 oz) lean lamb, minced
30 ml (2 tbsp) soy sauce
30 ml (2 tbsp) oil
1 small musk melon
45 ml (3 tbsp) orange juice
orange wedges and fresh mint sprigs to garnish
mint sauce to serve

Combine almonds, egg, salt, black pepper, breadcrumbs, garlic, onion, chopped mint and lamb. Mix well and shape into four patties. Brush both sides with soy sauce.

Microwave a browning dish on 100% for 7 minutes, then add oil and microwave for 1 minute more. Place lamb patties in dish and microwave for 3 minutes. Turn patties over and microwave for 2-3 minutes more. Remove from oven and keep warm.

Cut melon into wedges and remove rind. Place wedges on a flat microwave dish and brush with orange juice. Microwave on 70% for 2-3 minutes to heat through. Arrange patties and melon on a warmed plate and garnish with orange wedges and fresh mint. Serve with mint sauce.
Serves 4.

Mint Sauce

Combine 250 g (9 oz) smooth apricot jam, 100 g (3½ oz) sugar, 250 ml (8 fl oz) white vinegar and microwave on 100% for 4-5 minutes. Stir well to dissolve sugar, then stir in 60 g (2 oz) chopped fresh mint. Cool and bottle. Store in the refrigerator for up to 6 months. Makes about 600 ml (19 fl oz).

Moussaka

100%, 70% .... 67 minutes

2 medium-sized aubergines, sliced
salt
60 ml (4 tbsp) oil
3 medium-sized potatoes
30 g (1 oz) Cheddar cheese, grated

CHEESE SAUCE
300 ml (10 fl oz) milk
1 thick onion slice
1 small carrot, coarsely chopped
1 parsley sprig
2 cloves
1 blade of mace
black peppercorns
1 bay leaf
45 g (1½ oz) butter
45 g (1½ oz) plain flour
salt
30 g (2 oz) Cheddar cheese, grated
2 eggs, lightly beaten

MEAT SAUCE
1 medium-sized onion, chopped
2 garlic cloves, finely chopped
500 g (18 oz) lamb, minced
30 ml (2 tbsp) tomato paste

400 g (14 oz) canned whole
  tomatoes, chopped
2.5 ml (½ tsp) dried oregano
2.5 ml (½ tsp) mixed herbs
2.5 ml (½ tsp) ground cinnamon
salt and black pepper

Sprinkle aubergine slices with salt
and set aside for 30 minutes.

Next, make the cheese sauce:
Place milk, onion, carrot, parsley,
cloves, mace, a few peppercorns
and bay leaf in a jug. Microwave
on 100% for 3 minutes, then leave
to stand for 15 minutes. Strain
and discard vegetables and
seasonings.

Microwave butter on 100% for
1 minute. Stir in flour and
gradually add milk. Microwave
for 4-5 minutes, stirring every
minute. Add salt to taste, then
add in cheese. Stir half the sauce
into the eggs, then return to
remaining sauce and set aside.

Rinse, drain and dry aubergine
slices. Brush both sides with oil
and arrange at the bottom of a
large shallow dish. Microwave,
covered, for 6 minutes. Drain on
absorbent kitchen paper. Wash

and prick potatoes, place on a
sheet of absorbent kitchen paper
and microwave on 100% for 8-10
minutes. Leave to cool slightly,
then peel and slice thickly. (The
potatoes should be only partially
cooked.)

To make meat sauce: pour a little
oil into a large casserole and
microwave for 1 minute. Add
onion and garlic and toss well.
Microwave for 5 minutes.
Crumble meat into dish and
microwave for a further
5 minutes, stirring at least once.
Add remaining ingredients and
microwave for 10 minutes,
stirring occasionally.

Fill a large greased casserole
with layers of meat mixture,
aubergine and potato. Pour sauce
over top layer of potatoes and
microwave on 70% for 15-20
minutes until mixture is very hot
and tomatoes bubble around
edges. Sprinkle with remaining
30 g (2 oz) cheese and microwave
for 1 minute more or brown under
a hot grill. Leave to stand for
15 minutes before serving.
Serves 6.

Tzatziki

This typically Greek dish is
excellent with moussaka or served
as a starter with other rich lamb
dishes. Serve with plenty of French
bread or pieces of pitta.

½ cucumber, grated (including
  skin)
1 garlic clove, crushed
15 ml (1 tbsp) tarragon vinegar
200 ml (6½ fl oz) plain yogurt
  (preferably made with whole
  milk)
200 ml (6½ fl oz) soured cream
salt and black pepper
15 ml (1 tbsp) chopped fresh mint

Place cucumber in a colander for
15 minutes, allowing excess
moisture to drain off. Combine
all ingredients with cucumber
and leave to stand for at least
15 minutes before serving.
Serves 4.

Greek Meatballs with Fresh Tomato Sauce

100%, 70% .... 31 minutes

500 g (18 oz) minced lamb
2 eggs
1 garlic clove, finely chopped
1 onion, finely chopped
45 ml (3 tbsp) chopped fresh
  coriander leaves
2.5 ml (½ tsp) ground cinnamon
5 ml (1 tsp) salt
black pepper
100 g (3½ oz) fresh breadcrumbs
oil

FRESH TOMATO SAUCE
30 ml (2 tbsp) oil
2 onions, chopped
2 garlic cloves, finely chopped
4 large tomatoes, skinned and
  chopped
salt and black pepper
90 ml (3 fl oz) red wine
1 bay leaf
thyme and rosemary sprigs

First make the sauce: Pour oil into
a large casserole and microwave
on 100% for 1 minute. Add onions
and garlic and microwave for
3 minutes. Add tomatoes,
seasoning, wine and herbs and
microwave on 70% for
15 minutes. Set aside.
  To make meatballs: Combine all
ingredients, except oil, and mix
well. Shape into small balls. In a
shallow casserole microwave oil
on 100% for 1 minute, then add
half the meatballs, turning to
coat. Microwave for 3-4 minutes,
or until just done. Remove cooked
meatballs and keep warm. Repeat
with remaining meatballs.
  Add meatballs to tomato sauce
and microwave on 70% for
2-3 minutes to heat through.
Then serve with hot, cooked rice
or spaghetti (page 220).
Serves 4.

Lamb Casserole

100%, 50% .... 120 minutes

200 g (7 oz) lentils
200 g (7 oz) chick-peas
30 ml (2 tbsp) oil
1.5 kg (3 lb) knuckle end of lamb
30 g (1 oz) plain flour
2 medium-sized onions, chopped
1 garlic clove, crushed
500 ml (16 fl oz) chicken stock
2.5 ml (¹/₂ tsp) ground turmeric
2.5 ml (¹/₂ tsp) dried thyme
cardamom seeds from 1 or 2 pods
5 ml (1 tsp) salt
black pepper
2 tomatoes, skinned and chopped
15 ml (1 tbsp) lemon juice
5 ml (1 tsp) chopped fresh mint

Wash lentils and chick-peas, place in a large bowl, cover with water and allow to soak for 12 hours. Drain before using.

Heat a browning dish on 100% for 6 minutes, add oil, then lamb which has been tossed in flour. Microwave, uncovered, for 5-7 minutes, stirring every minute until slightly brown all over. Add onions and garlic, stir to combine and microwave for 2 minutes more.

Turn meat into a large casserole and add all remaining ingredients, except mint. Cover and microwave for 15 minutes, stirring twice during cooking time. Reduce power to 50% and microwave for about 1¹/₂ hours until both meat and dried pulses are soft, stirring from time to time. If necessary add a little extra water during cooking time. Sprinkle meat with mint just before serving.
Serves 6.

Marinated Lamb Ribs

The combination of whisky, soy sauce, molasses and mustard gives a delicious flavour to the ribs. Finish them off on the barbecue.

100%, 50% .... 31 minutes
Plus barbecue time

1.5 kg (3 lb) breast of lamb, cut into serving portions

MARINADE
75 ml (2¹/₂ fl oz) whisky
60 ml (4 tbsp) soy sauce
30 ml (2 tbsp) molasses
1 onion, chopped
45 ml (3 tbsp) coarse-grained French mustard
5 ml (1 tsp) Worcestershire sauce
90 ml (3 fl oz) orange juice

Combine all ingredients for marinade in a bowl, mix well and microwave on 100% for 1 minute. Place ribs in a large container and pour marinade over. Cover and refrigerate for at least 6 hours, turning frequently.

Place ribs in a large microwave dish. Add marinade, cover and microwave on 50% for 30 minutes, stirring and basting every 10 minutes. Let ribs cool in marinade and refrigerate until needed. Grill over hot coals, brushing with marinade, until crisp and cooked through.
Serves 4.

Orange Marinade
Combine 125 ml (4 fl oz) orange marmalade, 150 ml (5 fl oz) orange juice, 75 ml (2¹/₂ fl oz) Worcestershire sauce, 45 ml (3 tbsp) lemon juice and 2.5 ml (¹/₂ tsp) each of dry mustard and ground ginger. Season well with salt and black pepper and add 1 finely chopped garlic clove.

Microwave on 100% for 1¹/₂ minutes, then pour over ribs. Refrigerate, covered, for at least 4 hours before cooking. Makes enough for 2 kg (4¹/₂ lbs) ribs.

Lamb with Lemon and Wine Sauce

100% .... 7 minutes

45 g (1½ oz) butter
45 ml (3 tbsp) plain flour
1 chicken stock cube, crumbled
15 ml (1 tbsp) chopped fresh dill or 5 ml (1 tsp) dried dill
150 ml (5 fl oz) water
75 ml (2½ fl oz) white wine
45 ml (3 tbsp) lemon juice
salt and black pepper
500 g (18 oz) cooked lamb, cubed
paprika
grated lemon rind

Microwave butter on 100% for 45 seconds. Stir in flour, stock cube and dill. Gradually stir in water, wine and lemon juice. Microwave for 2-3 minutes, or until sauce has thickened, stirring every minute. Season to taste with salt and black pepper. Add meat and stir well. Cover and microwave for 2-3 minutes, or until meat is heated through, stirring frequently. Sprinkle with paprika and lemon rind before serving. Serve with hot rice if desired.
Serves 4.

Variation
ROAST LAMB IN GRAVY
In a casserole, microwave 15 ml (1 tbsp) oil on 100% for 45 seconds. Add 1 sliced onion, stir to coat and microwave for 2 minutes. Arrange slices of cooked roast lamb in the dish and top with 6 quartered button mushrooms.

Combine 200 ml (6½ fl oz) left-over gravy with 10 ml (2 tsp) tomato purée and 30 ml (2 tbsp) red wine or sweet sherry. Pour over meat and mushrooms. Cover and microwave for 2 minutes. Stir to rearrange meat, re-cover dish and microwave on 70% for 7 minutes. (A mixture of left-over vegetables, such as carrots and courgettes also may be added.)
Serves 2.

Traditional Lamb Curry

100%, 70%, 30% ..... 76 minutes

750 g (1¾ lb) neck of lamb
15 ml (1 tbsp) plain flour
salt and black pepper
2 cardamom pods
15 ml (1 tbsp) whole coriander
10 ml (2 tsp) cumin seeds
15 ml (1 tbsp) ground turmeric
2.5-5 ml (½-1 tsp) chilli powder
30 ml (2 tbsp) oil
2 garlic cloves, crushed
2 onions, thinly sliced
125 ml (4 fl oz) chicken stock and 125 ml (4 fl oz) beef stock
30 ml (2 tbsp) tomato paste
2 bay leaves
15 ml (1 tbsp) lemon juice

Place meat in a large bowl. Combine flour and all spices in a liquidizer or spice mill and grind until powdered. Rub into meat.

Microwave a browning dish on 100% for 6 minutes. Add oil, onions and garlic and fry for 4-5 minutes until beginning to turn brown, stirring frequently. Remove onions from dish, add meat to browning dish and microwave for 5 minutes, stirring frequently.

Return onions to dish together with stock, tomato paste, bay leaves and lemon juice. Cover and microwave for 5 minutes. Reduce power to 70% and microwave for 15 minutes. Remove lid and microwave on 30% for 40 minutes, stirring once or twice Serve with rice and side dishes of your choice.
Serves 4.

Cucumber Sambal
Grate 1 cucumber and squeeze out all water. Grate 1 very small carrot and mix into cucumber. Combine 10 ml (2 tsp) cumin seeds, 1 chopped green chilli and 5 ml (1 tsp) each of dry mustard, salt and lemon pepper. Stir into 250 ml (8 fl oz) plain yogurt. Combine with cucumber and carrot and garnish with chopped fresh coriander. Serve chilled.
Serves 4.

Casserole of Lamb with Wholemeal Topping

100%, 70% .... 52 minutes

1 kg (2¼ lb) lean lamb
15 g (½ oz) plain flour
salt and black pepper
2.5 ml (½ tsp) dried mixed herbs
30 ml (2 tbsp) oil
1 garlic clove, crushed
2 medium-sized onions, sliced
400 ml (13 fl oz) stock (half chicken,
   half beef)
2 celery sticks, chopped
2-3 carrots, thinly sliced
200 g (7 oz) frozen peas
250 g (9 oz) brown mushrooms

DUMPLINGS
45 g (1½ oz) self-raising flour
45 g (1½ oz) wholemeal flour
2.5 ml (½ tsp) baking powder
2.5 ml (½ tsp) salt
45 g (1½ oz) margarine
15 ml (1 tbsp) chopped fresh parsley
75-100 ml (2½-3½ fl oz) water

Cut meat into 2.5-cm (1-in) cubes,
place in a large bowl and add
flour, seasoning and herbs. Pour
oil into a shallow casserole and
microwave on 100% for 1 minute.
Add meat and cover. Microwave
for 12-14 minutes, stirring from
time to time.

Add garlic and onions and stir
to combine. Microwave for
4 minutes. Stir in stock, celery
and carrots. Cover and microwave for 5 minutes. Reduce
power to 70% and microwave for
20 minutes more. Stir in peas and
mushrooms.

Meanwhile, make dumplings:
Sift self-raising flour into a mixing
bowl, then add wholemeal flour,
baking powder and salt. Rub in
butter. Add parsley and sufficient
water to form a soft dough. Spoon
dough (about 12 portions) over
casserole. Cover and microwave
on 100% for 7-8 minutes. Leave to
stand for 5 minutes before
serving.
Serves 6.

Noisettes of Lamb with Plums

For a really special effect, garnish each serving with a whole plum.

100% .... 16 minutes

30 g (1 oz) butter
8 noisettes of lamb
salt and black pepper
watercress or parsley to garnish

SAUCE
**400 g (14 oz) canned plums,
  drained, syrup reserved**
400 ml (13 fl oz) red wine
1 small piece of cinnamon stick

First make the sauce: Place plums, about half the reserved syrup, wine and cinnamon stick in a large jug. Microwave on 100% for 5 minutes. Remove cinnamon stick and make sure that all stones have been removed from fruit, then pour sauce into a blender or food processor. Blend until smooth. Thin sauce with a little

extra syrup if necessary. Set aside and keep warm.

Microwave a browning dish on 100% for 6 minutes. Add butter and microwave for 30 seconds. Lightly season noisettes, arrange in dish and microwave for 5 minutes, turning over halfway through cooking time. (Do not overcook lamb as it becomes tough.)

To serve: Pour a little sauce on to four plates and swirl to coat evenly. Top sauce with two noisettes and garnish with watercress or parsley.
Serves 4.

Lamb Chops with Redcurrant Glaze

100%, 50% .... 20 minutes

8 lamb loin chops
salt and black pepper

GLAZE
60 ml (4 tbsp) redcurrant jelly
**250 ml (8 fl oz) canned beef
  consommé**
1 small piece of cinnamon stick
**30 ml (2 tbsp) spring onion, finely
  sliced, including part of green
  portion**
2.5-5 ml (½-1 tsp) cornflour
15 ml (1 tbsp) water

First make the glaze: Place jelly, consommé, cinnamon stick and spring onion into a jug. Microwave on 100% for 5 minutes, stirring from time to time until jelly has melted. Remove cinnamon stick. Combine cornflour and water and add sufficient to melted jelly to thicken slightly. Microwave for

1-2 minutes until well boiled. Set aside and keep warm.

Arrange chops, thickest ends outwards, in a shallow dish. Cover loosely with greaseproof paper. Microwave chops for 8-10 minutes, turning over after 5 minutes. Do not overcook. Drain off any excess fat and season chops to taste. Spoon glaze over chops, reduce power to 50% and microwave for 2-3 minutes. Spoon glaze over chops once more before serving. Serves 4.

Hint
Lamb chops are uneven in shape and need special care when microwaving. When cooking several chops at a time, make sure that the narrow bone end is towards the middle of the microwave dish. This will help to prevent overcooking.

Lamb and Nut Curry

100%, 50% .... 75 minutes

60 ml (4 tbsp) oil or ghee
1 onion, chopped
salt and black pepper
750 g (1¾ lb) lamb, boned and
  cubed
100 ml (3½ fl oz) plain yogurt
15 ml (1 tbsp) lemon juice
30 g (1 oz) plain cashew nuts,
  chopped
30 ml (2 tbsp) chopped fresh
  coriander

SPICE MIXTURE
30 g (2 oz) plain cashew nuts
small piece of fresh ginger, peeled
5 ml (1 tsp) whole coriander
150 ml (5 fl oz) water
1 small piece of cinnamon stick
3 cloves
seeds from 4 cardamom pods
3 garlic cloves
2.5-5 ml (½-1 tsp) chilli powder
15 ml (1 tbsp) poppy seeds
2.5 ml (½ tsp) ground turmeric

First, place all ingredients for
spice mixture in a blender and
blend until smooth. Next, place
oil or ghee in a large casserole and
microwave on 100% for 1 minute.
Add onion, toss to coat with oil
and microwave for 2 minutes.
Season meat lightly, then add to
oil with spice mixture. Stir well.
   Cover dish and microwave for
7 minutes, stirring at least once
during cooking time. Stir in
yogurt, cover and microwave for
5 minutes, then reduce power to
50% and microwave for 50-60
minutes, stirring from time to
time. Before serving, transfer
meat to a clean dish, stir in lemon
juice and sprinkle with chopped
cashew nuts and fresh coriander.
Serve with a pilau.
Serves 4.

Hint
**Poppadums cook well in the
microwave. Lightly brush 4 small
poppadums with oil on one side
only. Place in a single layer around
the edge of a plate and microwave
on 100% for about 2 minutes,
turning after 1 minute.**

Pilau

100% .... 14 minutes

200 g (7 oz) long-grain rice
30 ml (2 tbsp) ghee or 30 g (1 oz)
  butter
3 cardamom pods
2 cloves
1 small piece of cinnamon stick
2.5 ml (½ tsp) cumin seeds
1 bay leaf
500 ml (16 fl oz) weak chicken
  stock, boiling
30 ml (2 tbsp) almonds, flaked
30 ml (2 tbsp) currants or raisins
30 ml (2 tbsp) oil
1 onion, sliced
onion rings to garnish

Soak rice in cold water for about
30 minutes. Drain well.
Microwave ghee or butter in a
medium-sized casserole on 100%
for 1 minute. Using a pestle and
mortar or spice mill, grind spices
and add to hot ghee or butter
together with bay leaf. Microwave
for 1 minute.
   Add rice, stir to coat and
microwave for 2 minutes. Add
stock, cover and microwave for
10 minutes. Stir, cover again and
allow to stand for 10-15 minutes.
Add almonds and currants and
fluff with a fork. Turn into a
serving dish and garnish with
fried onion rings.
Serves 4.

Note
While it is possible to make onion
rings in the microwave oven, it will
take longer than it would conventionally.
   To make onion rings: Heat a little
oil in a frying pan on top of the
stove. Toss onion rings in flour and
fry until a golden colour. Drain on
absorbent kitchen paper until
required.

Savoury Lamb Stew

Long, slow cooking builds in flavour and it really is carefree when cooked in a clay dish in the microwave.

100%, 30% .... 83 minutes

1.5 kg (3 lb) stewing lamb, cubed
30 ml (2 tbsp) plain flour
salt
generous pinch of cayenne
2.5 ml (½ tsp) ground coriander
generous pinch of paprika
1 large onion, thinly sliced
1 garlic clove, finely chopped
2 celery sticks, sliced
1 carrot, thinly sliced
½ green pepper, diced
800 g (1 lb 14 oz) canned whole
    tomatoes, chopped
2.5 ml (½ tsp) dried marjoram
2.5 ml (½ tsp) dried rosemary
30 ml (2 tbsp) tomato paste
100 g (3½ oz) frozen green beans
100 g (3½ oz) frozen peas

Soak top and bottom of a 3-litre (5-pint) clay cooking dish in water for 15 minutes, then drain. Toss lamb in flour mixed with salt, cayenne, coriander and paprika and place in clay cooking dish. Cover and microwave on 100% for 12 minutes. Stir, then microwave for 5 minutes more.

Add onion, garlic, celery, carrot and green pepper to dish. Combine tomatoes with their liquid, herbs and tomato paste and pour over vegetables. Cover and microwave on 30% for about 1 hour, or until meat is tender, stirring occasionally. Add beans and peas. Stir gently and microwave for 5-6 minutes more. Serves 6-8.

Braised Shoulder of Lamb

100%, 50% .... 60 minutes

blanched spinach leaves
1.5 kg (3 lb) boned shoulder of lamb
salt and black pepper
30 g (1 oz) butter
250 ml (8 fl oz) clear apple juice

STUFFING
350 g (12 oz) cooked rice (page 220)
75 g (2½ oz) seedless raisins
1 egg
5 ml (1 tsp) curry paste
200 g (7 oz) ham, minced
30 ml (2 tbsp) tomato purée
pinch of cayenne

Arrange a few spinach leaves on meat and season lightly. Combine ingredients for stuffing and spread over spinach leaves. Roll and sew up firmly. Melt butter in a pan on top of cooker and brown meat well all over, then transfer lamb to a deep casserole.

Pour over half the apple juice, cover and microwave on 100% for 10 minutes. Reduce power level to 50% and microwave for 45-50 minutes, adding remaining apple juice and turning meat about halfway through cooking time. Allow meat to stand for 5 minutes before carving. Serve on a bed of rice with vegetables in season. Serves 4-6.

Hint
Gravy-making is easy in the microwave. Just measure pan dripping or juices from roast meat or poultry into a jug. Add flour and microwave on 100% for 1-2 minutes, then gradually add well-flavoured stock, wine or water, or a combination of liquids. Microwave for 2-3 minutes, stirring from time to time, until thick and smooth.

For 300 ml (10 fl oz) gravy you will need about 30 ml (2 tbsp) pan dripping, 25 ml (5 tsp) plain flour, 300 ml (10 fl oz) liquid and salt and black pepper to taste.

Glazed Baked Ham

TO MICROWAVE RAW HAM

50% ...... 14-16 minutes per 500 g
(18 oz)

Shield top cut edge with a thin
strip of foil. Place ham in a
roasting dish and cover tightly
with vented plastic wrap, or place
in a roasting bag and tie ends.
(Make at least two holes in the bag
to allow steam to escape.)

  Microwave on 50% for the
minimum time, then check
internal temperature by inserting
a meat thermometer and allowing
2 minutes for temperature to
register. If internal temperature
has not reached 71 °C (160 °F),
remove thermometer and return
ham to microwave oven for a few
more minutes. Leave ham to
stand for 5-10 minutes after
cooking.

TO MICROWAVE COOKED HAM
(INCLUDING CANNED HAMS)

50% ...... 10-13 minutes per 500 g
(18 oz)

Place ham in a roasting dish. (Pre-
cooked hams should be placed
with the fat-side up and shielded
on the thin edge with a strip of
foil.) Cover tightly with vented
plastic wrap and microwave on
50% for the minimum time. Test
internal temperature by inserting
a meat thermometer and allowing
2 minutes for temperature to
register. If the internal
temperature has not reached 46 °C
(115 °F), remove thermometer and
return ham to microwave oven for
a few more minutes. Leave ham to
stand for 5-10 minutes after
cooking.

Glazes

PINEAPPLE MUSTARD GLAZE
**400 g (14 oz) canned pineapple
  slices**
100 g (3½ oz) soft brown sugar
**30 ml (2 tbsp) pineapple syrup
  from can**
**30 ml (2 tbsp) prepared English
  mustard**

Arrange pineapple slices over
ham and secure with cocktail
sticks. Combine soft brown sugar,
pineapple syrup and mustard and
pour over finished ham.
Microwave on 100% for
3-4 minutes.

HONEY-SOY GLAZE
60 ml (4 tbsp) clear honey
60 ml (4 tbsp) soy sauce
5 ml (1 tsp) dry mustard

Combine all ingredients and
brush over microwaved ham.
Leave to stand for a few minutes
to set.

Note
**It is often a good idea to leave
glazing ham to the last 3-5 minutes
of cooking time, as adding a sugary
glaze any sooner may result in an
overcooked outer layer of meat.**

Pork Stroganoff

100%, 70% .... 21 minutes

500 g (18 oz) pork fillet
125 ml (4 fl oz) apple juice
15 ml (1 tbsp) cider vinegar
1 garlic clove, crushed
1 bay leaf
2.5 ml (½ tsp) fresh thyme
30 ml (2 tbsp) plain flour
generous pinch of paprika
salt and black pepper
generous pinch of dry mustard
30 ml (2 tbsp) oil
15 g (½ oz) butter
1 large onion, sliced
200 g (7 oz) button mushrooms,
  sliced
15 ml (1 tbsp) tomato paste
150 ml (5 fl oz) soured cream
paprika

Trim meat and cut diagonally into
thin strips. Combine apple juice,
vinegar, garlic, bay leaf and
thyme. Pour over meat, cover and
let stand for at least 2 hours. Drain
meat, pat dry and reserve
marinade.

Combine flour with paprika,
salt, black pepper and mustard
and dust meat with this mixture.
Microwave a browning dish on
100% for 6 minutes. Add oil and
butter and microwave for
45 seconds. Add meat and onions
and microwave for 4 minutes,
stirring every minute. Then stir in
reserved marinade, mushrooms,
tomato paste and soured cream.

Cover and microwave on 70%
for 10 minutes, stirring twice
during cooking time. Correct
seasoning if necessary and
sprinkle with paprika. Serve with
a green salad and boiled potatoes
sprinkled with chopped parsley.
Serves 4.

Hints
• **To remove the last of the cream
from a carton, microwave the carton
on 100% for 10-15 seconds.**
• **To heat serving plates, pour 30 ml
(2 tbsp) water on to each of 4 plates,
stack them and microwave on 100%
for about 2 minutes. Give them a
quick wipe to dry before using.
Dampened absorbent kitchen
paper may be used instead of water.**

Honeyed Gammon

100%, 70% .... 36 minutes

15 g (½ oz) butter
4 canned pineapple rings
4 gammon steaks
45 g (1½ oz) butter
45 ml (3 tbsp) clear honey
45 ml (3 tbsp) soft brown sugar
45 ml (3 tbsp) toasted breadcrumbs
100 ml (3½ fl oz) pineapple juice
5-10 ml (1-2 tsp) cornflour
30 ml (2 tbsp) water
4 glacé cherries

Heat a browning dish on 100%
for 6 minutes, add butter and
pineapple rings and microwave
for 1 minute on each side.
Remove and keep warm.

Pat gammon steaks dry.
Place 45 g (1½ oz) butter and half
the honey in a jug. Microwave on
100% for 1-2 minutes until
melted. Brush both sides of steaks
generously with this mixture.
Combine soft brown sugar and
breadcrumbs and pat on to steaks,
coating evenly.

Arrange steaks in a shallow
casserole with the thicker side
outwards. Cover loosely and
microwave on 70% for
10-12 minutes. Remove from dish
and keep warm.

Add remaining honey and
pineapple juice to dish and
microwave on 100% for
2 minutes. Mix cornflour with
cold water and add to hot liquid.
Stir to combine. Microwave for
1-2 minutes until boiling and
thickened.

To serve: Arrange steaks on a
serving platter. Garnish with
pineapple rings and cherries.
Serve sauce separately.
Serves 4.

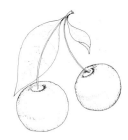

Pork and Pasta, left, and Pork Chops with Sweet-and-sour Sauce

Pork Chops with Sweet-and-sour Sauce

100%, 30% .... 34 minutes

4 thick pork chops, trimmed
1 onion, sliced
1 carrot, thinly sliced
1 celery stick, thinly sliced
200 g (7 oz) canned pineapple
  chunks, drained
15 ml (1 tbsp) lemon juice
1 garlic clove, finely chopped
75 g (2½ oz) soft brown sugar
75 ml (2½ fl oz) red wine vinegar
60 ml (4 tbsp) seasoned tomato
  sauce (page 204)
60 ml (4 tbsp) chutney
15 ml (1 tbsp) soy sauce
1 green pepper, diced
salt and black pepper
10 ml (2 tsp) cornflour
30 ml (2 tbsp) pineapple juice
  from can

Soak top and bottom of a clay
cooking dish in water for
15 minutes, then drain. Place
pork chops in dish and top with
onion rings, carrot and celery
slices, pineapple, lemon juice and
garlic. Sprinkle with soft brown
sugar. Mix together the vinegar,
tomato sauce, chutney and soy
sauce and pour over chops and
vegetables. Top with green
pepper, cover and microwave on
30% for 20 minutes. Turn chops
and microwave, covered, for
10-12 minutes more, or until pork
is completely cooked.

  Remove chops to a serving dish.
Remove vegetables and pineapple
from cooking liquid and spoon
over chops. Keep warm. Season
liquid with salt and black pepper.
Mix cornflour with pineapple
juice and stir into liquid.
Microwave, uncovered, on 100%
for 2 minutes, stirring after
1 minute. Pour sauce over chops
and serve.
Serves 4.

Pork and Pasta

**Serve this delicious sauce over
spaghetti or any of the other pasta
shapes.**

100%, 30% .... 30 minutes

30 ml (2 tbsp) oil
l onion, chopped
400 g (14 oz) lean pork, minced
125 g (4 oz) chicken livers, minced
400 g (14 oz) canned whole
  tomatoes, chopped
15 ml (1 tbsp) chilli sauce
2.5 ml (½ tsp) dried sage
2.5 ml (½ tsp) dried basil
45 ml (3 tbsp) brandy
salt and black pepper
1 beef stock cube, crumbled
100 g (3½ oz) mushrooms, sliced
175 g (6 oz) pasta, cooked (page 220)
fresh herbs to garnish

Pour oil into a large casserole and
microwave for l minute on 100%.
Add onion and microwave for
2 minutes. Stir in pork and
chicken livers and microwave for
4 minutes, stirring once to break
up meat. Add tomatoes with their
juice, chilli sauce, herbs, brandy,
salt, black pepper and crumbled
stock cube. Cover and microwave
for 3 minutes.

  Add mushrooms, stir, then
reduce power to 30% and
microwave for 20 minutes more,
stirring occasionally. Serve over
hot pasta and garnish with fresh
herbs.
Serves 4.

Mandarin Roast Pork

Injecting the pork with orange-flavoured liqueur gives a delicious flavour. Garnish with mandarin orange segments.

100%, 50% .... 51 minutes

1 boned loin of pork, about 1.5 kg (3 lb)
4 garlic cloves, sliced
8 fresh sage leaves
125 ml (4 fl oz) orange-flavoured liqueur
10-15 ml (2-3 tsp) oil
salt and black pepper
125 ml (4 fl oz) chicken stock
30 ml (2 tbsp) orange-flavoured liqueur
90 ml (3 fl oz) single cream
mandarin orange segments to garnish

Tie meat into a good shape and place, fat-side up, on a microwave roasting rack. Make a number of slits in meat and insert slices of garlic and sage leaves. Inject 125 ml (4 fl oz) liqueur evenly into meat.* Score skin, rub with oil and sprinkle with salt, then cover with a tent of waxed paper and microwave on 50% for 13-15 minutes per 500 g (18 oz). (About 39-45 minutes.)

If crackling is not crisp, place under a hot grill for a few minutes, taking care that crackling does not burn. Leave meat to stand, covered, for 10-15 minutes before serving.

While meat is standing, add stock to roasting dish and microwave for 2 minutes on 100%. Turn liquid into a bowl, add 90 ml (3 fl oz) liqueur and cream and season well. Microwave, loosely covered, for 3-4 minutes, stirring every minute until bubbling and thickened. Carve pork and serve, garnished with mandarin orange segments, with the sauce.
Serves 6-8.

* Inexpensive, disposable plastic syringes are available from chemists and make the injection of the liqueur very easy.

Sweet-and-sour Kasseler Chops

100% .... 22 minutes

1 kg (2¼ lb) kasseler chops or loin pork
15 ml (1 tbsp) oil
1 onion, sliced
1 green pepper, sliced
2 celery sticks, sliced
400 g (14 oz) canned pineapple chunks, drained
black pepper
15 ml (1 tbsp) cornflour
30 ml (2 tbsp) water

MARINADE
60 ml (4 tbsp) white vinegar
30 ml (2 tbsp) clear honey
15 ml (1 tbsp) soy sauce
1 garlic clove, crushed
30 ml (2 tbsp) soft brown sugar
150 ml (5 fl oz) pineapple juice from can

Place chops in a flat dish. Combine all ingredients for marinade. Pour over chops and leave to stand for at least 1 hour. Drain chops, place in a shallow casserole and cover. Microwave on 100% for 10 minutes. Keep warm.

In another shallow dish microwave oil for 1 minute. Add onion, green pepper and celery. Microwave for 4 minutes, stirring once during cooking time. Add pineapple chunks and marinade. Season with black pepper, then cover and microwave for 4 minutes. Mix cornflour with water, then a little of the hot liquid. Stir mixture into sauce, cover and microwave for a further 3 minutes. Pour over meat and serve immediately.
Serves 4.

Hint
To soften honey: Remove the lid of the honey jar and microwave the honey on 100% for 1-2 minutes. Microwave a small quantity of honey for a few seconds only.

When requiring a quantity of honey for a recipe, a more accurate measure is obtained if the honey has been heated first.

Pork in Wine Sauce

100% .... 13 minutes

2 pork fillets, about 250 g (9 oz) each
30 ml (2 tbsp) plain flour
2.5 ml (½ tsp) dried rosemary
2.5 ml (½ tsp) dried sage
generous pinch of black pepper
60 g (2 oz) butter
1 onion, chopped
90 ml (3 fl oz) dry white wine
grated rind and juice of 1 orange
185 ml (6 fl oz) single cream
orange slices to garnish

Cut fillets into 1-cm (½ -in) slices.
Combine flour, herbs and pepper
and coat meat with mixture.
Microwave butter in a large
casserole on 100% for 1 minute.
Add onion and microwave for
3 minutes, stirring every minute.
Add pork and microwave for
3 minutes, stirring every minute.
Add wine, orange rind and juice.
Microwave for 2 minutes. Stir in
cream and microwave for
4 minutes more, stirring every
minute. Serve garnished with
orange slices.
Serves 4.

Devilled Pork Chops

100%, 70% .... 21 minutes

30 ml (2 tbsp) oil
salt and black pepper
4 pork chops, trimmed
1 onion, sliced
400 g (14 oz) canned tomato soup
10 ml (2 tsp) Worcestershire sauce
5 ml (1 tsp) prepared English
  mustard
30 ml (2 tbsp) spicy fruit chutney

Microwave a browning dish on
100% for 6 minutes. Add oil and
microwave for 30 seconds. Season
chops lightly, arrange in
browning dish with the thickest
portion towards the outside and
microwave for 2-3 minutes on
each side.
  Remove chops and add onion.
Microwave for 1 minute, then stir
in remaining ingredients and
microwave for 3 minutes. Return
chops to dish, spoon a little sauce
over each, cover and microwave
on 70% for 5-7 minutes.
Serves 4.

Devilled Pork Chops

Roast Loin of Pork

100%, 70% .... 38 minutes

1 kg (2¼ lb) loin of pork, boned and rolled, with skin well scored
10 ml (2 tsp) oil
salt and black pepper
2.5 ml (½ tsp) dry mustard
2.5 ml (½ tsp) dried sage

STUFFING
90 g (3 oz) butter
1 small onion, chopped
1 small garlic clove, crushed
90 g (3 oz) fresh white breadcrumbs
4 apple rings, soaked and chopped
2.5 ml (½ tsp) dried sage
10 ml (2 tsp) chopped fresh parsley
grated rind of 1 lemon
salt and black pepper
stock to moisten

Rub meat with oil and then with seasonings. Place pork on a roasting rack and microwave on 70% for 26-30 minutes. Wrap meat in a tent of foil and let it stand for 10 minutes, then brown under grill until crackling is crisp.

Meanwhile, make the stuffing. Microwave butter on 100% in a bowl for 1 minute. Add onion and microwave for a further minute. Add remaining ingredients and season to taste. Pack into a small microwaveproof serving dish and cover. Microwave for 4-6 minutes until cooked through. Serve with slices of pork, accompanied by apple sauce.
Serves 4-6.

Apple Sauce

Peel, core and slice 500 g (18 oz) cooking apples and place in a bowl with 45 ml (3 tbsp) water and 2 whole cloves. Cover with vented plastic wrap and microwave on 100% for 8 minutes. Remove from the microwave, discard cloves and mash apples. Stir in a pinch of salt and sugar to taste. Makes about 300 ml (9 fl oz).

Pork and Brown Rice Casserole

100%, 70% .... 49 minutes

30 ml (2 tbsp) oil
6 pork chops
5 ml (1 tsp) salt
pinch of black pepper
30 g (1 oz) butter
1 small onion, chopped
1 celery stick, chopped
200 g (7 oz) brown rice
560 ml (18 fl oz) water, boiling
5 ml (1 tsp) salt
2 medium-sized pears, unpeeled and chopped
60 ml (4 tbsp) seedless raisins
pinch of ground coriander
pinch of crushed cardamom seeds

Heat a browning dish on 100% for 6 minutes. Add oil and heat for 1 minute more. Season chops, arrange in dish and microwave for 1 minute on each side. Remove chops and set aside.

Microwave butter for 45 seconds. Add onion and celery and microwave for 2 minutes. Add rice, boiling water and 5 ml (1 tsp) salt and microwave, covered, for 25 minutes. Leave to stand for 20 minutes.

Mix pears, raisins, coriander and cardamom into rice and transfer to a casserole. Top with chops, browned-side upwards. Microwave, covered, on 70% for 10-12 minutes, or until chops are cooked.
Serves 6.

Hints for Reheating Food

• When reheating most food, cover with waxed paper to hold in the heat but at the same time allow the steam to escape.
• Stir stews and casseroles when reheating.
• When reheating a plate of food, all the food should be at the same temperature, with the food which takes the longest to heat on the outside.
• Food is usually heated through when the centre of the underside of the container is warm.

Steak and Kidney Pudding

100%, 70%, 30% ..... 69 minutes

500 g (18 oz) stewing steak, cubed
125 ml (4 fl oz) beer
45 ml (3 tbsp) oil
1 onion, chopped
2.5 ml (½ tsp) chopped fresh
  rosemary
2.5 ml (½ tsp) fresh thyme
200 g (7 oz) ox kidney, skinned,
  cored and chopped
30 ml (2 tbsp) plain flour
salt and black pepper
5 ml (1 tsp) Worcestershire sauce
4 brown mushrooms, sliced
15 ml (1 tbsp) chopped fresh parsley

SUETCRUST PASTRY
250 g (9 oz) self-raising flour
2.5 ml (½ tsp) salt
125 g (4 oz) suet, shredded
about 185 ml (6 fl oz) cold water

Place stewing steak in a bowl and marinate in beer overnight. Drain meat and reserve liquid. Place oil, onion, and herbs in a large casserole and microwave on 100% for 2 minutes. Stir in meat, kidney, flour, salt, black pepper, Worcestershire sauce and beer marinade. Microwave, covered, for 10 minutes, stirring once during cooking time. Reduce power to 30% and microwave for 45 minutes, stirring in mushrooms and parsley about 5 minutes before end of cooking time. Set aside to cool.

To make suetcrust pastry: Sift flour and salt into a large mixing bowl, add suet and mix to a firm dough with water. Roll out about two-thirds of the pastry and line a well-greased 1-litre (1¾-pint) pudding bowl. Roll out remaining pastry to form a lid.

Spoon in cooled filling. Moisten edges of pastry and top with pastry lid, making sure that the edges are well sealed. Cover loosely with plastic wrap. Then microwave on 70% for 10-12 minutes. Leave to stand for 5 minutes before turning out and serving.
Serves 4.

Liver with Mustard Sauce

100% .... 17 minutes

500 g (18 oz) calf's liver, sliced
30 ml (2 tbsp) plain flour
salt and black pepper
60 g (2 oz) butter
60 ml (4 tbsp) dry white wine
60 ml (4 tbsp) beef stock
5 spring onions, chopped
1 tomato, skinned, seeded
  and chopped
2.5 ml (½ tsp) dried thyme
15 ml (1 tbsp) lemon juice
75 ml (2½ fl oz) single cream
20 ml (4 tsp) Dijon mustard

Dredge liver slices with seasoned flour. Heat a browning dish on 100% for 6 minutes. Add butter and microwave for 30 seconds more. Add liver and microwave for 1½ minutes on each side. Remove from dish and keep warm.

Add wine and stock to dish along with chopped spring onions, tomato, thyme and lemon juice. Microwave for 2 minutes. Stir in cream and microwave for 4-5 minutes until boiling and thickened. Stir in mustard and spoon sauce over liver.
Serves 4.

Hint
To defrost liver: Place 250 g (9 oz) liver in a shallow dish. Cover with waxed paper and microwave on 30% for 4 minutes. Leave to stand for 10 minutes before using.

Devilled Kidneys on Toast

100% .... 12 minutes

8 lamb's or calf's kidneys
15 ml (1 tbsp) plain flour
salt and black pepper
45 g (1½ oz) butter
3 bacon rashers, rinds removed, chopped
30 ml (2 tbsp) tomato purée
5 ml (1 tsp) prepared English mustard
5 ml (1 tsp) Worcestershire sauce
generous pinch of cayenne
30 ml (2 tbsp) spicy chutney
5 ml (1 tsp) gravy powder
75 ml (2½ fl oz) water
4 large brown mushrooms, thickly sliced
4 slices of hot buttered toast to serve
15 ml (1 tbsp) chopped fresh parsley

Remove and discard skins and cores from kidneys, then slice each kidney into four. Toss in seasoned flour. Microwave butter in a shallow casserole on 100% for 1 minute. Add bacon and microwave for 2 minutes. Then add kidneys, toss to coat with butter, cover and microwave for 1 minute.

Add all remaining ingredients, stir well, cover and microwave for 7-8 minutes, stirring at least once during cooking time. Serve on toast, sprinkled with parsley. Serves 4.

Variation

SAUTÉED BREAKFAST KIDNEYS
Heat a browning dish on 100% for 5 minutes, add 15 g (½ oz) butter and microwave for 30 seconds. Arrange 6 halved lamb's kidneys, prepared as above and seasoned with salt and black pepper, cut-side downwards in the dish. Microwave for 30 seconds. (Cover with waxed paper to prevent spattering.) Turn kidneys over and microwave for 1 minute more. Serve immediately. Serves 4-6.

Sweetbreads in Wine Sauce

100%, 70% .... 23 minutes

350 g (12 oz) sweetbreads, well cleaned
300 ml (10 fl oz) water
15 ml (1 tbsp) lemon juice
2.5 ml (½ tsp) salt
30 g (1 oz) butter
1 large carrot, grated
1 small onion, sliced
125 ml (4 fl oz) chicken stock
125 ml (4 fl oz) dry white wine
20 ml (4 tsp) redcurrant jelly
7.5 ml (1½ tsp) fresh thyme or 2.5 ml (½ tsp) dried thyme
5 ml (1 tsp) lemon juice
8 mushrooms, sliced
7.5 ml (1½ tsp) cornflour
30 ml (2 tbsp) brandy
60 ml (4 tbsp) single cream
salt and black pepper

Place sweetbreads in a casserole with water, 15 ml (1 tbsp) lemon juice and salt. Cover and microwave on 100% for 7-9 minutes, or until firm and no pink remains. Leave to stand for 10 minutes, then drain. Remove membranes and any tubes from sweetbreads. Break or cut into small clusters.

Place butter in a casserole and microwave on 100% for 45 seconds. Add carrot and onion and microwave, covered, for 3 minutes. Add stock, wine, jelly, thyme and 5 ml (1 tsp) lemon juice. Microwave for 3 minutes more. Add mushrooms and microwave for 1 minute.

Combine cornflour and brandy and stir into vegetable mixture. Microwave for 2-3 minutes, stirring every minute. Add cream and sweetbreads and microwave, covered, for 2-3 minutes on 70%. Season to taste with salt and black pepper and serve with hot toast if desired. Serves 4 as a starter, 2 as a main course.

Note

Sweetbreads are generally the thymus glands taken from a calf. They have a similar appearance and texture to brains.

Venison Casserole

100%, 70%, 50% …. 104 minutes

1.5 kg (3 lb) venison, cubed
30 ml (2 tbsp) plain flour
30 ml (2 tbsp) oil
1 onion, chopped
1 garlic clove, chopped
1 carrot, chopped
2 tomatoes, skinned and chopped
200 ml (6½ fl oz) beef stock
100 ml (3½ fl oz) good red wine
5 ml (1 tsp) ground coriander
salt and black pepper
bouquet garni comprising:
  2 bay leaves, 1 large fresh
  thyme sprig, 1 small piece of
  cinnamon stick and
  6 juniper berries
100 ml (3½ fl oz) soured cream
  (optional)

Place venison in a large bowl with
the flour and toss to coat evenly.
In a large casserole, microwave oil
on 100% for 45 seconds. Add
onion, garlic and carrot and
microwave for 3 minutes, stirring

once during cooking time. Add
meat, stir to combine and
microwave for 5 minutes. Stir in
tomatoes, stock, wine, coriander,
salt, black pepper and bouquet
garni. Cover and microwave for
5 minutes.

Reduce power to 70% and
microwave for 30 minutes,
stirring from time to time. Then
microwave on 50% for about
1 hour until meat is tender.
Remove bouquet garni and stir in
soured cream before serving.
Serves 6.

Note
Venison requires long, slow
cooking to become tender, so little
time is saved when it is cooked in
the microwave. However,
microwave cooking keeps the
kitchen and house cool and free of
the normal strong venison smell.

The gamey flavour of venison
combines well with sweet jellies,
such as redcurrant, apple and
cranberry, as well as chestnut
purée. Serve one of these separately
with the meat.

Southern-style Rabbit

100%, 70%, 30% ….. 46 minutes

45 ml (3 tbsp) oil
2 onions, chopped
2 red peppers, diced
30-45 ml (2-3 tbsp) mild chilli
  powder, or to taste
2.5 ml (½ tsp) ground cumin
5 ml (1 tsp) dried oregano
2.5-5 ml (½ -1 tsp) cayenne
5 ml (1 tsp) ground coriander
5 ml (1 tsp) salt
black pepper
1 rabbit, about 1 kg (2¼ lb), cut
  into serving pieces
375 ml (12 fl oz) beer
125 ml (4 fl oz) chicken stock
15 ml (1 tbsp) vinegar
30 ml (2 tbsp) clear honey

Microwave oil in a large
microwave dish on 100% for
2 minutes. Add onions, stir and
microwave, covered, for
5 minutes. Add peppers and
microwave for 4 minutes more.
Add chilli powder, cumin,

oregano, cayenne, coriander, salt
and black pepper. Microwave,
uncovered, for 4 minutes.

Then add rabbit, arranging so
that the thickest part of each piece
is towards the outside of the dish.
Pour beer and chicken stock over
rabbit, cover and microwave on
30% for 8 minutes. Turn pieces
and continue microwaving,
covered, for 8 minutes more.
Increase power to 70% and
microwave for 12-15 minutes,
or until meat is tender.

Transfer rabbit to a warmed dish
and keep warm. Pour cooking
liquid and vegetables into a food
processor or blender, add vinegar
and honey and process to a purée.
Correct seasoning and serve over
rabbit.
Serves 4.

Note
A versatile meat, mild in flavour,
rabbit is at its best in sauces
containing wine, herbs and spices.

Microwaved Sausages

Sausages microwaved in a browning dish look good and taste good. Leave to stand for 2-3 minutes before serving.

FOR 500 g (18 oz) SAUSAGES
Microwave a browning dish on 100% for 6 minutes. Brush sausages lightly with soy or Worcestershire sauce, prick with a fork or skewer and arrange on a dish. Cover with waxed paper and microwave for 2 minutes. Turn sausages over and microwave for a further 2 minutes.

FOR 2 SAUSAGES
Microwave a browning dish for 6 minutes on 100%. Microwave sausages for 35-45 seconds each side.

Sausage and Bean Bake

100%, 70% .... 22 minutes

3 bacon rashers, rinds removed, chopped
20 ml (4 tsp) oil
500 g (18 oz) pork or beef sausages
1 garlic clove, finely chopped
1 small onion, chopped
1 small cauliflower, broken into florets
15 ml (1 tbsp) tomato purée
2.5 ml (½ tsp) dried sage
250 ml (8 fl oz) apple juice
salt to taste
generous pinch of cayenne
400 g (14 oz) canned red kidney beans, drained
400 g (14 oz) canned green beans, drained

Place bacon in a dish and microwave on 100% for 1-1½ minutes. Remove from oven and set aside. Heat a browning dish for 6 minutes, add oil and microwave for 30 seconds more. Add sausages and microwave for 2 minutes. Turn and microwave for 1 minute more.
 Add bacon, garlic, onion, cauliflower, tomato purée, sage, apple juice, salt and cayenne. Cover and microwave on 70% for about 8 minutes, or until cauliflower is tender. Add drained beans and microwave on 100% for 2-3 minutes, or until heated through.
Serves 4.

Baked Potato with Bacon Cheese Topping

Baked Potato with Toppings

Quantity	Timing	100%
1 potato	4-6 minutes	
2 potatoes	6-8 minutes	
3 potatoes	8-12 minutes	
4 potatoes	12-16 minutes	
5 potatoes	16-20 minutes	
6 potatoes	20-25 minutes	

Wash potatoes and pat dry. Pierce with a skewer. Place potatoes on absorbent kitchen paper at least 2.5'cm (1 in) apart. If microwaving several potatoes, arrange them in a circle. Microwave on 100% and turn them over half-way through cooking time. Potatoes may still feel firm when done, but will soften while standing. If you wrap them in foil, shiny-side in, after they have been microwaved, they will keep warm for up to 30 minutes.

Potato toppings

BACON CHEESE TOPPING
Combine 15 ml (1 tbsp) finely chopped onion, 60 ml (4 tbsp) grated Cheddar cheese and 3 cooked, chopped bacon rashers with 250 ml (8 fl oz) soured cream and season well with black pepper. Makes enough for 4 potatoes.

VEGETABLE CHEESE TOPPING
To 200 g (7 oz) cheese spread, add 1 finely chopped courgette, 6 chopped button mushrooms and 45 ml (3 tbsp) finely chopped onion. Stir in a little milk and a few drops of Tabasco. Slit the potato skin crossways to expose some of the flesh and place 2 generous spoonfuls of the mixture on top. Serve at once. Makes enough for 4 potatoes.

Pickled Vegetables

100% .... 5 minutes

1 small head of cauliflower, broken into florets
1 small bunch of broccoli, broken into florets
175 g (6 oz) green beans, sliced
2 courgettes, cut in julienne
1 large turnip, peeled and cut in julienne
1 red pepper, cut in julienne
125 ml (4 fl oz) water
60 ml (4 tbsp) sea salt
15 ml (1 tbsp) peppercorns
5 slices of peeled ginger root
4 small dried chilli peppers (or to taste), crumbled
250 ml (8 fl oz) water
250 ml (8 fl oz) white vinegar
1 litre (1³/₄ pints) cold water

Combine vegetables in a large casserole, add 125 ml (4 fl oz) water and microwave, covered, on 100% for 2 minutes. Drain and refresh under cold running water.
Combine salt, peppercorns, ginger root, chilli peppers and 250 ml (8 fl oz) water in a large bowl. Microwave for 3 minutes, then stir to dissolve salt. Add vinegar and cold water and pour liquid over vegetables. Leave to stand for 30 minutes, then transfer to glass jars. Refrigerate, covered, for 3 days before using. (Vegetables prepared this way will keep for up to 2 weeks in the refrigerator.)

Hint
When microwaving frozen vegetables, there is no need to thaw them, nor to add water. Just place them in a suitable container or a roasting bag (but never use wire ties).
Before microwaving, cover the container and pierce the plastic wrap or cooking bag. (Frozen vegetables may be cooked in the bags they are purchased in if the bags are first pierced.) Microwave for about two-thirds of the time required for fresh vegetables. (Refer to vegetable chart on page 220.)

Spiced Pumpkin, left, and Sugared Onion Slices

Sugared Onion Slices

100% .... 4 minutes

6 thick slices from large onions
45 g (1½ oz) butter, melted
salt
15 ml (1 tbsp) soft brown sugar
30 ml (2 tbsp) chopped walnuts

Preheat a browning dish for about 6 minutes. Brush onion slices with half the melted butter. Place in browning dish and microwave on 100% for about 2 minutes. Turn slices, season with salt and sprinkle with brown sugar. Add chopped walnuts and drizzle with remaining butter. Cover and microwave for about 2 minutes until just tender.
Serves 6.

Spiced Pumpkin

100% .... 17 minutes

1 kg (2¼ lb) pumpkin
45 ml (3 tbsp) water
pinch of salt
60 g (2 oz) butter
10 ml (2 tsp) soft brown sugar
generous pinch of ground allspice
5 ml (1 tsp) grated orange rind
45 ml (3 tbsp) orange juice

With a melon-baller, make pumpkin balls, using as much of the pumpkin as possible. Combine water and salt in a bowl, add pumpkin, cover and microwave on 100% for 12-14 minutes, or until pumpkin is tender. Drain and keep warm.

Microwave butter in a bowl for 30 seconds. Stir in sugar, allspice and orange rind. Microwave for 1 minute. Add orange juice and microwave for 1-1½ minutes, or until mixture boils. Pour over pumpkin balls and toss gently to mix.
Serves 4-6.

Cottage Potatoes

100%, 70% .... 32 minutes

5 large potatoes, diced
90 ml (3 fl oz) water
2 slices of white bread, coarsely crumbed
125 g (4 oz) butter
1 green pepper, diced
1 red pepper, diced
60 ml (4 tbsp) chopped onion
salt and black pepper
15 ml (1 tbsp) chopped fresh parsley
5 ml (1 tsp) chopped fresh thyme or 2.5 ml (½ tsp) dried thyme
200 g (7 oz) Cheddar cheese, grated
milk
60 g (2 oz) potato crisps, crushed

Place potatoes in a large casserole, add water, cover and microwave on 100% for 16 minutes. Drain. Mix potatoes with bread and set aside.

Microwave 30 g (1 oz) of the butter for 30 seconds. Add green and red peppers and onion. Microwave for 3 minutes, stirring once. Add to potatoes along with salt, black pepper, parsley and thyme. Stir in three-quarters of the cheese and place mixture in a greased casserole.

Microwave remaining butter for 1 minute and pour over mixture. Add enough milk to half-fill dish. Sprinkle with potato crisp crumbs and microwave on 70% for 8-10 minutes. Sprinkle with remaining cheese and microwave for 1 minute more to melt.
Serves 6.

Hints

• Cut vegetables into even-sized pieces or slices.
• Allow 2-4 minutes' standing time as vegetables will continue cooking after they have been removed from the microwave. (Vegetables should still be firm at the end of the cooking time.)
• If using a cooking liquid, add salt to the liquid. If not, add a little salt to the vegetable after it has been microwaved. Remember, less salt is needed than in conventional cooking.
• Refer to the vegetable chart on page 220 for cooking details.

Stuffed Squash

100% .... 14 minutes

12 small squash
60 ml (4 tbsp) water
30 ml (2 tbsp) olive oil
1 small garlic clove, finely chopped
2 spring onions, chopped
3 small plum tomatoes, skinned, seeded and chopped
2.5 ml (¹/₂ tsp) lemon juice
2.5 ml (¹/₂ tsp) sugar
7.5-10 ml (1¹/₂-2 tsp) chopped fresh lemon thyme or 2.5 ml (¹/₂ tsp) dried thyme
black pepper
30 ml (2 tbsp) chopped fresh parsley

Place six squash with 30 ml (2 tbsp) water in a casserole. Cover and microwave on 100% for 3 minutes. Rinse in cold water. Repeat with remaining six squash. Using a melon-baller, remove core and pulp from centre of each squash. Reserve pulp.

Pour oil into a bowl and microwave for 45 seconds. Add garlic and spring onions and microwave for 1 minute. Add squash pulp, tomatoes, lemon juice, sugar, lemon thyme, black pepper and half the parsley. Microwave for 2 minutes. Turn mixture into a blender or food processor and blend until smooth. Fill squash with the mixture and arrange six on a microwave baking sheet. Microwave for 2 minutes, or until heated through. Repeat with remaining squash and serve sprinkled with remaining parsley as an accompaniment to lamb or beef.
Serves 6.

Hint
To make pumpkin easier to cut and peel, microwave a piece on 100% for 1¹/₂-2 minutes, depending on the size. Some hard varieties of squash may also be treated this way.

Couscous Timbales

100% .... 9 minutes

15 g (¹/₂ oz) butter
6 spring onions, including green portion, chopped
pinch of crushed caraway seeds
generous pinch of ground turmeric
pinch of ground cinnamon
400 g (14 oz) canned tomatoes
45 g (1¹/₂ oz) currants
250 ml (8 fl oz) water
salt and black pepper
225 g (8 oz) couscous
45 ml (3 tbsp) chopped fresh parsley

Place butter in a bowl and microwave on 100% for 30 seconds. Add spring onions, stir to coat and microwave for 1 minute. Stir in crushed caraway seeds, turmeric and cinnamon. Drain, chop and re-drain tomatoes and add to onion together with currants, water and seasoning. Microwave for 5 minutes. Stir in couscous, cover and microwave for 2 minutes. Leave to stand for 10 minutes, then add parsley and fluff with a fork.

Pack into six well-greased timbale moulds or ramekins, cover and leave to stand in a warmer drawer for 5 minutes. Turn out on to a platter.

These may be made some time in advance and refrigerated. If packed into ramekins, reheat in the microwave on 50% for 6-7 minutes before turning out. Makes 6.

Note
Still relatively unknown, this granular cereal is made from semolina and originates in North Africa. It may be used as an accompaniment to a main dish, as part of a spicy casserole, or even in combination with fruit as a dessert.

Green Beans with Lightly Curried Hollandaise Sauce

100% .... 11 minutes

500 g (18 oz) young green beans
45 ml (3 tbsp) water
salt
1 recipe Hollandaise sauce
  (page 54)
2.5 ml (¹/₂ tsp) curry paste
45 ml (3 tbsp) single cream

Top and tail beans, removing strings if necessary. Leave very young beans whole, cut larger beans in half. Place in a bowl with water and salt and cover with vented plastic wrap. Microwave on 100% for 9-11 minutes, stirring once during cooking time. Drain beans and place in a serving dish. Mix Hollandaise sauce with curry paste and cream. Spoon over beans and serve immediately.
Serves 6.

Peas with Ham

100% .... 16 minutes

8 pearl onions
45 ml (3 tbsp) water
15 g (¹/₂ oz) butter
5 ml (1 tsp) caster sugar
2 slices of ham, chopped
350 g (12 oz) frozen peas
15 g (¹/₂ oz) butter
salt and black pepper
generous pinch of dried chervil

Place onions and water in a bowl, cover with vented plastic wrap and microwave on 100% for 3-4 minutes. Drain and dry.
  Microwave a browning dish for 6 minutes. Add butter and sugar, arrange onions in dish and microwave for 4-5 minutes. Stir in remaining ingredients, microwave for 1 minute, then spoon into a serving dish.
Serves 4-6.

Broccoli with Pecan Butter

100% .... 13 minutes

90 g (3 oz) butter
45 g (1¹/₂ oz) pecan nuts, chopped
500 g (18 oz) broccoli, trimmed and
  broken into florets
45 ml (3 tbsp) water
salt and black pepper

Place butter in a bowl and microwave on 100% for 30 seconds. Add pecan nuts and microwave for 1 minute more. Set aside. Place broccoli in a casserole with water and microwave, covered, for 9 minutes. Drain. Add pecan butter to broccoli, season to taste and microwave for 2 minutes more to heat through.
Serves 4-6.

Cabbage and Cheese Casserole

100% .... 15 minutes

750 g (1³/₄ lb) cabbage, shredded
30 ml (2 tbsp) water
400 g (14 oz) canned cream of celery
  soup
black pepper
15 ml (1 tbsp) lemon juice
100 g (3¹/₂ oz) Cheddar cheese,
  grated
45 g (1¹/₂ oz) potato crisps,
  crushed

Place cabbage in a large casserole, sprinkle with water and cover. Microwave on 100% for 6 minutes, then drain. Combine soup, pepper and lemon juice. Layer cabbage with cheese and soup in a buttered casserole, ending with a layer of soup. Sprinkle with potato crisp crumbs and microwave for 6-9 minutes, or until heated through and bubbling.
Serves 6-8.

Brussels Sprouts and Bacon

100% .... 18 minutes

450 g (1 lb) Brussels sprouts, trimmed
45 ml (3 tbsp) water
6 streaky bacon rashers, rinds removed
1 small onion, chopped
salt and black pepper

Place sprouts and water in a casserole, cover and microwave on 100% for 10 minutes. Drain and set aside. In a shallow dish microwave bacon, covered with waxed paper, for 3 minutes, or until crisp. Remove from oven and chop, reserving bacon fat.
   Pour bacon fat into a casserole, add onion and microwave for 3 minutes, stirring twice, or until onion is tender. Add Brussels sprouts, toss well, season to taste and microwave for 2 minutes to heat through. Serve sprinkled with bacon.
Serves 4-6.

Braised Celery with Pecans

100% .... 17 minutes

450 g (1 lb) celery, trimmed
45 ml (3 tbsp) water
60 g (2 oz) butter
1 onion, chopped
45 g (1½ oz) pecan nuts
15 ml (1 tbsp) lemon juice
15 ml (1 tbsp) grated lemon rind
salt and black pepper

Slice celery diagonally into 1-cm (½-in) pieces. Place in a casserole with water, cover and microwave on 100% for 8-9 minutes. Drain and set aside. Microwave half the butter for 1 minute, add onion and microwave for 2 minutes. Set aside.
   In a separate dish, microwave remaining butter for 1 minute, add pecans and microwave for 2 minutes, stirring after 1 minute. Combine celery, onion and butter, pecans and butter, then add the lemon juice and rind, salt and black pepper. Microwave for 1-2 minutes more to heat through.
Serves 4.

Cherry Tomato Sauté

These hot cherry tomatoes make an ideal garnish for any main dish.

100%, 70% .... 4 minutes

15 g (¹/₂ oz) butter
1 punnet of cherry tomatoes
2.5 ml (¹/₂ tsp) sugar
salt and black pepper
2.5 ml (¹/₂ tsp) dry mustard
10 ml (2 tsp) brandy
10 ml (2 tsp) chopped fresh basil or
  2.5 ml (¹/₂ tsp) dried basil

Microwave butter in a shallow casserole on 100% for 30 seconds. Prick tomatoes all over with a small skewer, add to butter and stir to coat. Microwave for 2-3 minutes on 70%, stirring every 30 seconds. Add remaining ingredients. Microwave for 30 seconds more.
Serves 6 as a garnish.

Cauliflower Bake

100%, 70% .... 20 minutes

1 medium-sized cauliflower, cut
  into florets
45 g (1¹/₂ oz) butter
1 small onion, chopped
2 large tomatoes, skinned and
  chopped
15 ml (1 tbsp) plain flour
150 ml (5 fl oz) chicken stock
5 ml (1 tsp) prepared mild mustard
generous pinch of ground coriander
generous pinch of ground turmeric
black pepper
75 g (2¹/₂ oz) Cheddar cheese,
  grated

Soak cauliflower florets in cold, well-salted water for 10 minutes. Drain off water, turn cauliflower into a bowl, cover with vented plastic wrap and microwave on 100% for 5 minutes. Drain and set aside.
  Microwave butter in a bowl for 45 seconds, stir in onion and microwave for 1 minute. Stir in tomatoes and flour and

microwave for a further minute. Stir in stock and remaining ingredients, except cheese. Microwave for 5 minutes, stirring every minute. Stir in half the cheese.
  Turn cauliflower into a shallow casserole, spoon sauce over and microwave for 4 minutes. Sprinkle with remaining cheese, reduce to 70% and microwave for 2-3 minutes until cheese begins to bubble. Serve immediately.
Serves 6-8.

Leeks in Cream

100% .... 17 minutes

60 g (2 oz) butter
8 leeks, sliced
grated nutmeg to taste
salt and black pepper
250 ml (8 fl oz) single cream
15 ml (1 tbsp) lemon juice
30 ml (2 tbsp) grated Parmesan
  cheese

Place butter in a shallow casserole and microwave on 100% for 1 minute. Add leeks and microwave for 3 minutes, stirring gently once. Add nutmeg, salt, black pepper and cream and microwave for 2 minutes.
  Strain leeks and place in a clean microwave dish. Add lemon juice to cream mixture and microwave for 5 minutes, or until somewhat reduced. Pour over leeks and microwave for 5 minutes more. Sprinkle with Parmesan cheese. Microwave for 1 minute to melt cheese. Serve immediately.
Serves 4-6.

Broccoli Timbales

100%, 50% .... 13 minutes

400 g (14 oz) broccoli
45 ml (3 tbsp) water
4 eggs
250 ml (8 fl oz) single cream
60 g (2 oz) Cheddar cheese, grated
salt and black pepper
1 small garlic clove, crushed
5 ml (1 tsp) chopped fresh tarragon
 or generous pinch of dried
 tarragon
10 ml (2 tsp) lemon juice
tarragon or parsley sprigs to garnish

Place washed broccoli in work bowl of a food processor and chop finely. Place in a bowl, add water and cover with vented plastic wrap. Microwave on 100% for 5 minutes, then drain well. Lightly beat eggs in a bowl, add remaining ingredients and stir to combine. Stir in broccoli. Divide mixture between eight well-greased ramekins.
 Arrange ramekins in a circle in the microwave. Cover loosely with waxed paper and microwave on 50% for 6-8 minutes. Leave to stand for a few minutes before serving. (The mixture should be completely set, like a custard.)
 Run a spatula around the edge of each ramekin and turn out on to a heated platter. Garnish with sprigs of fresh tarragon or parsley.
Serves 8.

Hints
• To prepare broccoli for cooking: Trim spears, leaving up to 5 cm (2 in) of stalk. To ensure even cooking, arrange in a dish with the stems pointing outwards.
• Toss hot, cooked broccoli with melted butter, toasted almonds (page 36) and toasted sesame seeds (page 44).
• Spoon Hollandaise sauce (page 54) over hot, cooked broccoli and sprinkle with paprika and finely grated lemon rind.
• Sprinkle chopped fresh basil and grated Cheddar cheese over hot, cooked broccoli.

Parsnips in Orange Sauce

100% .... 16 minutes

3 medium-sized parsnips, peeled
 and cubed
30 ml (2 tbsp) water
125 ml (4 fl oz) orange juice
30 ml (2 tbsp) soft brown sugar
30 ml (2 tbsp) golden syrup
2.5 ml (½ tsp) salt
pinch of paprika
30 g (1 oz) butter
grated rind of 1 orange

Place parsnips and water in a casserole and microwave, covered, on 100% for 8 minutes, stirring once. Drain and keep warm in dish.
 Combine orange juice, sugar, syrup, salt, paprika, butter and orange rind in a bowl and microwave for 1 minute, then mix well. Pour over parsnips and microwave for 5-7 minutes, stirring at least twice.
Serves 6.

Mushrooms Magnifique

70% .... 12 minutes

12 large flat mushrooms
salt
30 g (1 oz) butter, softened
60 g (2 oz) pecan nuts, chopped
30 ml (2 tbsp) chopped fresh parsley
½ garlic clove, finely chopped
2.5 ml (½ tsp) fresh thyme or
 generous pinch of dried thyme
salt and black pepper
125 ml (4 fl oz) single cream

Remove stalks from mushrooms and chop finely. Lightly salt mushroom caps. Mix together butter, chopped stalks, pecans, parsley and garlic. Add thyme, salt and black pepper to taste. Stuff mushrooms with mixture and arrange in two shallow baking dishes. Drizzle cream over mushrooms and microwave each dish on 70% for about 6 minutes, or until well heated and bubbling.
Serves 4-6.

Fennel au Gratin

100% .... 14 minutes

3 large fennel bulbs, washed
thoroughly and thinly sliced
45 ml (3 tbsp) water
salt and black pepper
60 g (2 oz) butter
60 ml (4 tbsp) plain flour
2000 ml (6¹/₂ fl oz) chicken stock
60 ml (4 tbsp) dry white wine
250 ml (8 fl oz) single cream
5 ml (1 tsp) paprika
60 g (2 oz) Gouda cheese, finely
grated

Place fennel and water in a
casserole. Cover and microwave
on 100% for 6 minutes, stirring at
least once. Drain well and season
to taste with salt and black
pepper.

In a separate casserole,
microwave butter for 1 minute.
Stir in flour, then gradually mix in
chicken stock and wine. Lastly,
add cream and paprika.
Microwave for 3 minutes, or until
sauce is thick and bubbling,
stirring every minute. Add fennel
to sauce and stir well.

Transfer to a baking dish and
microwave for 2-3 minutes to heat
through. Sprinkle with cheese.
Microwave for 1 minute more, or
brown under a hot grill.
Serves 4-6.

Hint

REDUCED CREAM FOR SAUCES
**Place 250 ml (8 fl oz) single cream in
a 1.5-litre (2³/₄-pint) casserole.
Microwave on 100% for 2 minutes.
Stir and microwave for a further 2
minutes. Stir and reduce power to
50% and microwave for 6-8 minute,
stirring every 2 minutes.**

**Various flavourings can be added
to reduced cream such as wine,
lemon juice, salt and pepper, grated
cheese, savoury butter or mustard.
This makes a rich, smooth sauce to
serve with vegetables, meat or fish.**

Spicy Beetroot with Orange

100% .... 37 minutes

1 kg (2¼ lb) young beetroot
250 ml (8 fl oz) water
grated rind and juice of 1 lemon
15 ml (1 tbsp) grated orange rind
45 ml (3 tbsp) sugar
2.5 ml (¹/₂ tsp) salt
2.5 ml (¹/₂ tsp) ground cloves
generous pinch of grated nutmeg
45 ml (3 tbsp) frozen orange juice
concentrate
20 ml (4 tsp) cornflour
30 ml (2 tbsp) water
15 g (¹/₂ oz) butter

Trim beetroot and prick skins
carefully. Place in a large
microwaveproof dish and add
water. Cover and microwave on
100% for 28-32 minutes, or until
tender. Cool, then drain,
reserving liquid. Peel and slice
beetroot.

Pour cooking liquid into a large
jug. Add grated rind and juice of
lemon, orange rind, sugar, salt,
cloves, nutmeg and frozen orange
juice concentrate. Dissolve
cornflour in water and add to jug.
Microwave for 3-4 minutes,
stirring every minute, until
mixture is clear and thickened.
Add beetroot and butter and
microwave for 1 minute more
to heat through. Serve hot.
Serves 6-8.

Vegetable Biriani

100%, 70%, 50% ..... 74 minutes

200 g (7 oz) brown lentils
750 ml (1¼ pints) water
60 g (2 oz) butter
5 ml (1 tsp) cumin seeds
5 ml (1 tsp) mustard seeds
generous pinch of cayenne
2.5 ml (½ tsp) salt
1 garlic clove, crushed
generous pinch of ground turmeric
generous pinch of ground ginger
2.5 ml (½ tsp) ground cinnamon
2.5 ml (½ tsp) ground coriander
1 red chilli, seeded and chopped
1 large aubergine, peeled and diced
1 large onion, sliced
1 bunch of spring onions, sliced
200 g (7 oz) green beans, sliced
100 ml (3½ fl oz) water
1 large potato, peeled and diced
30 ml (2 tbsp) water
2 tomatoes, skinned and diced
275 g (10 oz) cooked white rice
  (page 220)
275 g (10 oz) cooked yellow rice
60 g (2 oz) cashew nuts, coarsely
  chopped
60 g (2 oz) peanuts, coarsely
  chopped
60 g (2 oz) seedless raisins
chutney or lime pickle to serve

Place lentils and water in a casserole, cover and microwave on 70% for about 30 minutes. Leave to stand for 10 minutes, then drain and set aside.

Microwave butter in a bowl on 100% for 1 minute, then add cumin and mustard seeds, cayenne, salt, garlic, turmeric, ginger, cinnamon, coriander and chilli. Microwave for 2 minutes, stirring every 30 seconds, then set aside.

Place aubergine, onion, spring onions and green beans in a casserole. Add 100 ml (3½ fl oz) water, cover and microwave on 100% for 8 minutes, stirring gently every 2 minutes. Drain vegetables, reserving liquid. Place potato in a casserole with 30 ml (2 tbsp) water and microwave for 3 minutes. Drain. Then combine all vegetables, including tomatoes, with spice mixture, mixing thoroughly.

Place cooked white rice in a large casserole, then add lentils. Top with vegetable mixture, then yellow rice. Sprinkle nuts and raisins on top and spoon reserved vegetable liquid over. Cover and microwave on 50% for 30 minutes. Serve with chutney or lime pickle if desired. Serves 6-8.

Melanzane

100%, 70% .... 25 minutes

3-4 medium-sized aubergines, cut into 1-cm (½ -in) slices
salt
plain flour
oil for frying
30 ml (2 tbsp) oil
1 medium-sized onion, chopped
400 g (14 oz) canned tomatoes, puréed
45 ml (3 tbsp) tomato purée
10 ml (2 tsp) chopped fresh basil
5 ml (1 tsp) sugar
black pepper
250 g (9 oz) Mozzarella cheese, thinly sliced
45 g (1½ oz) Parmesan cheese, grated

Sprinkle aubergine slices with salt, then leave to stand for about 20 minutes. Rinse well, pat dry and sprinkle lightly with flour. Using a large frying pan, fry slices in oil until lightly browned. Drain on absorbent kitchen paper.

To make sauce: Pour 30 ml (2 tbsp) oil into a large bowl and microwave on 100% for 45 seconds. Add onion, puréed canned tomatoes, tomato purée, basil, sugar and pepper and microwave, uncovered, for 7-9 minutes, stirring from time to time. (The mixture should have thickened slightly.)

Pour a thin layer of tomato sauce into a shallow casserole, arrange aubergine slices over this, then cover with a layer of Mozzarella, followed by a sprinkling of Parmesan cheese. Repeat these layers, then cover with vented plastic wrap and microwave on 70% for 10-15 minutes until piping hot. For a crusty brown top, place under the grill for a few seconds before serving.
Serves 4-6.

Warm Lentil Hot Pot

70% .... 25 minutes

200 g (7 oz) brown lentils, soaked in cold water for 6 hours
1 small onion, chopped
1 large carrot, grated
500 ml (16 fl oz) vegetable stock, boiling
2.5 ml (½ tsp) salt
1 bouquet garni comprising: peppercorns, blade of mace, sprigs of fresh herbs, 1 bay leaf, whole allspice, piece of lemon rind
30 ml (2 tbsp) lemon juice
45 ml (3 tbsp) oil
1 bunch of spring onions, including green portion, chopped
45 ml (3 tbsp) pecan nuts, coarsely chopped
60 g (2 oz) Feta cheese, cubed
chopped fresh parsley to garnish

Drain soaked lentils and place in a large casserole. Add onion, carrot, stock, salt and bouquet garni. Microwave on 70% for 20-25 minutes, stirring

occasionally. (The lentils should be tender, not soft.) Remove bouquet garni. Add lemon juice, oil, spring onions and pecan nuts and stir carefully to combine. Serve warm as a main dish or chilled as a salad, sprinkled with Feta cheese and parsley.
Serves 4.

Note
There are many varieties of lentils, the most popular being red, brown and black. Whole brown or black lentils need to be soaked in plenty of cold water for at least 6 hours before being cooked. Red lentils, which resemble small, reddish-yellow split peas, do not need to be soaked before cooking.

Lentil Salad
To 250 g (9 oz) (raw weight) of cooked lentils, add 100 ml (3½ fl oz) French dressing, 5 ml (1 tsp) turmeric, 5 ml (1 tsp) curry paste, 1 chopped onion, 1 crushed garlic clove and 45 ml (3 tbsp) lemon juice. Leave to stand overnight before serving.
Serves 4-6.

Spiced Chick-peas

100%, 30% .... 78 minutes

200 g (7 oz) chick-peas, soaked in cold water overnight
1 litre (1¾ pints) water, boiling
5 ml (1 tsp) salt
60 ml (4 tbsp) oil
5 ml (1 tsp) chopped fresh ginger
2.5 ml (½ tsp) coriander seeds, crushed
5 ml (1 tsp) curry paste
generous pinch of ground cumin
1 small aubergine, cubed
1 small onion, chopped
1 garlic clove, crushed
400 g (14 oz) canned tomatoes, chopped
15 ml (1 tbsp) chopped fresh coriander

Drain soaked chick-peas and place in a large casserole. Add boiling water and salt. Cover and microwave on 100% for 20 minutes, stirring at least twice. Reduce power to 30% and microwave for 35-40 minutes, or until tender, stirring occasionally.

Pour oil into a large casserole and microwave on 100% for 1 minute. Add ginger, coriander, curry paste and cumin. Stir and microwave for 30 seconds, then add aubergine, onion and garlic. Microwave for 2 minutes. Add cooked chick-peas, stir to combine, then microwave for 4 minutes. Now stir in tomatoes with their juice. Cover and microwave for 10 minutes. Stir well and sprinkle with chopped coriander before serving.
Serves 4-6.

Cabbage and Aubergine with Cheese Sauce

100% .... 27 minutes

½ medium cabbage, shredded
30 ml (2 tbsp) water
60 g (2 oz) butter
1 small onion, chopped
1 small aubergine, peeled and diced
30 ml (2 tbsp) plain flour
250 ml (8 fl oz) beer
200 g (7 oz) mature Cheddar cheese, grated
30 ml (2 tbsp) Worcestershire sauce
2.5 ml (½ tsp) salt
2.5 ml (½ tsp) dry mustard
few drops of Tabasco
black pepper
carraway seeds
30 g (1 oz) fresh wholemeal breadcrumbs
2.5 ml (½ tsp) paprika

Place cabbage and water in a large casserole and microwave, uncovered, on 100% for 6 minutes. Drain and set aside. In another casserole microwave 30 g

(1 oz) of the butter for 30 seconds and add onion. Microwave for 2 minutes. Add aubergine, stir, then microwave for 5 minutes more, stirring every 2 minutes. Remove aubergine from onion and add to cabbage.

Add remaining butter to onions left in casserole and microwave for 30 seconds. Stir in flour, then gradually stir in beer. Microwave for 3-4 minutes, stirring every minute until bubbling. Add cheese a little at a time, stirring to melt, then add Worcestershire sauce, salt, dry mustard, Tabasco, black pepper and caraway seeds. Microwave for 1 minute more, then pour over cabbage mixture, mixing well.

Turn into a greased casserole, top with breadcrumbs and sprinkle with paprika. Microwave for 5-6 minutes, until bubbling and hot.
Serves 4.

Vegetable Lasagne

100%, 70%, 50% ..... 40 minutes

15 ml (1 tbsp) oil
1 onion, chopped
1 green pepper, sliced
2 celery sticks, chopped
1-2 garlic cloves, crushed
2 tomatoes, skinned and chopped
30 ml (2 tbsp) tomato purée
salt and black pepper
2.5 ml (½ tsp) dried marjoram or oregano
1 bay leaf
150 g (5 oz) mushrooms, sliced
250 g (9 oz) courgettes, sliced lengthways
100 ml (3½ fl oz) plain yogurt or single cream
200 g (7 oz) Ricotta cheese
125 g (4 oz) Mozzarella cheese, grated
60 ml (4 tbsp) grated Parmesan cheese
15 ml (1 tbsp) chopped fresh parsley
2.5 ml (½ tsp) paprika

BÉCHAMEL SAUCE
250 ml (8 fl oz) milk
1 onion slice
2 cloves
1 small bay leaf
1 small carrot
celery slices
parsley sprig
30 g (1 oz) butter
30 ml (2 tbsp) plain flour
salt and black pepper

Microwave oil in a casserole on 100% for 45 seconds. Add onion, green pepper and celery. Stir to coat and microwave for 4 minutes, stirring at least twice during cooking time. Then add garlic, tomatoes, tomato purée, seasoning and herbs. Stir well. Microwave for 8 minutes, stirring twice during cooking time.

Spoon half the mixture into a greased, shallow casserole and cover with half the mushrooms and half the courgettes. Combine yogurt and Ricotta and spread over vegetable mixture. Repeat vegetable layers once more.

To make sauce: Pour milk into a large jug with onion, cloves, bay leaf, carrot, a few celery slices and parsley and microwave on 100% for 2 minutes. Cover and leave to stand for 10 minutes. Microwave butter in a bowl for 30 seconds, then stir in flour, add strained milk and stir well. Microwave for 2 minutes until thick and bubbling, stirring every 30 seconds. Season to taste. Makes about 300 ml (10 fl oz).

Stir in half the Mozzarella cheese and pour sauce over vegetable layers. Combine remaining Mozzarella, Parmesan cheese, parsley and paprika and sprinkle on top of sauce. Microwave on 70% for 10 minutes, then on 50% for a further 10-12 minutes until piping hot and cooked through.
Serves 4-6.

Savoury Onions

100% .... 14 minutes

4 large onions, peeled
15 ml (1 tbsp) water
30 ml (2 tbsp) dry sherry
100 g (3½ oz) mushrooms
90 g (3 oz) wholemeal breadcrumbs
10 ml (2 tsp) chopped fresh sage
10 ml (2 tsp) chopped fresh parsley
45 ml (3 tbsp) finely chopped celery
salt and black pepper
100 g (3½ oz) Cheddar cheese, grated

Place onions in a shallow dish, add water and half the sherry. Cover and microwave on 100% for 10 minutes. Chop mushrooms and mix with breadcrumbs, sage, parsley and celery. Moisten with remaining dry sherry.

Remove centres from onions, finely chop, add to mushroom mixture and season well. Press stuffing into onions, microwave for 3-4 minutes, then sprinkle with cheese and grill to brown.
Serves 4.

Mushrooms Newburg

100%, 50% .... 14 minutes

60 g (2 oz) butter
675 g (1½ lb) mushrooms
45 ml (3 tbsp) chopped onion
45 ml (3 tbsp) sherry

SAUCE
30 g (1 oz) butter
30 ml (2 tbsp) plain flour
500 ml (16 fl oz) single cream*
2 egg yolks
30 ml (2 tbsp) water
salt
pinch of cayenne
pinch of grated nutmeg
hot toast to serve

Place butter in a shallow casserole and microwave on 100% for 1 minute. Add whole mushrooms and onion. Microwave for 5 minutes. Stir, add sherry and microwave on 50% for a further 3 minutes. Remove from oven and keep warm.

To make sauce: Place butter in a large jug and microwave on 100% for 1 minute. Stir in flour, then gradually add cream and microwave for about 3 minutes, or until cream begins to thicken. Beat egg yolks with water, then stir about half the cream sauce into the beaten egg yolks. Pour back into jug, stir well and microwave for 1 minute more. Add salt, cayenne and nutmeg. Stir, then pour sauce over mushrooms. Mix well, adjust seasoning to taste and serve over hot toast.
Serves 4-6.

* If a less rich sauce is preferred, use 250 ml (8 fl oz) single cream and 250 ml (8 fl oz) milk.

Baked Tomatoes with Basil

100%, 70% .... 11 minutes

6 large firm tomatoes
45 ml (3 tbsp) chopped fresh basil or 15 ml (1 tbsp) dried basil
60 ml (4 tbsp) chopped fresh parsley
generous pinch of dried thyme
2.5 ml (½ tsp) chopped fresh mint or generous pinch of dried mint
salt and black pepper
15 ml (1 tbsp) oil
3 spring onions, chopped
2 garlic cloves, finely chopped
90 g (3 oz) fresh wholemeal breadcrumbs
15 ml (1 tbsp) lemon juice
lemon wedges to garnish

Cut a small round from the top of each tomato. Scoop out pulp and strain off any liquid. Invert tomatoes on a plate to drain. Combine drained tomato pulp with basil, parsley, thyme, mint, salt and black pepper.

Pour oil into a small bowl and microwave on 100% for 30 seconds. Add spring onions and garlic and microwave for 2 minutes. Add to herb mixture along with breadcrumbs and lemon juice. Combine well and spoon into tomato shells. Oil a baking dish and arrange tomatoes in it. Cover and microwave on 70% for 5-8 minutes, depending on size of tomatoes. (The tomatoes should be hot but not broken up.) Serve garnished with lemon wedges.
Serves 6.

Spinach Provençale

100%, 70% .... 15 minutes

1 kg (2¼ lb) fresh spinach
30 ml (2 tbsp) oil
1 large onion, chopped
1 garlic clove, finely chopped
2 eggs, beaten
90 ml (3 fl oz) single cream
salt and black pepper
pinch of freshly grated nutmeg
90 g (3 oz) Pecorino sheep's milk
　cheese, grated
30 g (1 oz) butter

Wash spinach and discard stalks
and large white ribs. Chop leaves
coarsely. Microwave oil in a large
casserole on 100% for l minute.
Add onion and garlic and
microwave for 2 minutes. Add
spinach leaves, cover and
microwave for 2 minutes. Stir
well, then microwave for a further
2 minutes.

　Combine eggs, cream, salt,
black pepper, nutmeg and three-
quarters of the grated cheese.
Add to spinach and turn into a

greased baking dish. Dot with
butter. Microwave on 70% for
5-7 minutes, or until set. Sprinkle
remaining cheese over top and
microwave for 30 seconds more to
melt. Leave to stand for about
8 minutes, return to microwave
for 1 minute on 100%. Serve hot.
Serves 4.

Spinach-stuffed Mushrooms

Wipe 10 large mushrooms,
remove stems and arrange on two
microwave dishes. Drain and
chop 250 g (9 oz) cooked spinach
and mix with 30 ml (2 tbsp) thick
white onion soup powder, 60 ml
(4 tbsp) low-fat soft cheese, pinch
of nutmeg, 30 ml (2 tbsp) dried
breadcrumbs (page 13), 30 ml
(2 tbsp) finely grated Cheddar
cheese and seasoning to taste.

　Place a spoonful of the mixture
in each mushroom cap and
sprinkle a little extra grated
Cheddar cheese over each.
Microwave each dish on 100% for
2½-3 minutes. Makes 10 stuffed
mushrooms.

Couscous with Vegetables

100% .... 16 minutes

175 g (6 oz) couscous
250 ml (8 fl oz) water, boiling
generous pinch of salt
15 ml (1 tbsp) oil
3 tomatoes, skinned and chopped
1 small onion, chopped
1 garlic clove, crushed
small piece of pumpkin, cubed
few broccoli or cauliflower florets
1 small carrot, thinly sliced
75 ml (2½ fl oz) vegetable stock
generous pinch of ground turmeric
salt and black pepper
cayenne
100 g (3½ oz) okra or green beans

Place couscous, water and salt in a
casserole and microwave on 100%
for 1 minute, then allow to stand
for 10 minutes.

　Meanwhile, microwave oil in a
large casserole on 100% for
45 seconds. Add all vegetables

except okra. (Combine green
beans with the other vegetables if
you are not using okra.) Mix
together, then add stock,
turmeric, salt and black pepper.
Cover and microwave for
10-12 minutes, stirring from time
to time. Add okra and microwave
for 2-3 minutes.

　Fluff couscous with a fork before
adding vegetable mixture and
adjust seasoning to taste.
Serves 4.

Tagliatelle with Mussels

If you happen to be a sparkling wine drinker use a little in this dish instead of the white wine!

100%, 70% .... 11 minutes

1 orange
75 g (2½ oz) butter
125 ml (4 fl oz) single cream
75 ml (2½ fl oz) white wine
200 g (7 oz) mussels, cooked, without shells
salt and black pepper
30 ml (2 tbsp) chopped fresh parsley
200 g (7 oz) tagliatelle, cooked (page 220) and kept warm

Using a zester, cut fine julienne shreds of rind from the orange, then squeeze out juice. Microwave butter in a bowl on 100% for 2 minutes. Add orange rind and juice and microwave for 1 minute. Add cream, microwave for 3 minutes, then stir in wine, mussels and seasoning.

Reduce power to 70% and microwave for 4-5 minutes, stirring once. Sprinkle with parsley and spoon over portions of cooked tagliatelle. Serve with an interesting salad. Serves 2.

Variation

CLAM SAUCE
Microwave 45 ml (3 tbsp) oil in a casserole on 100% for 45 seconds. Add 1 chopped onion and 2 chopped garlic cloves, stir and microwave for 3 minutes. Drain 2 × 300 g (11 oz) cans of clams. Add clam juice and 125 ml (4 fl oz) dry white wine to onion mixture and microwave on 70% for 5 minutes. Stir in clams, 15 ml (1 tbsp) chopped fresh parsley and black pepper to taste. Microwave for 1-2 minutes to heat through, then add 30 g (1 oz) butter and stir to melt. Serves 4.

Cheesy Tuna Imperial

A tuna and noodle casserole with a difference.

100%, 70% .... 19 minutes

125 g (4 oz) butter
45 g (1½ oz) plain flour
5 ml (1 tsp) salt
generous pinch of black pepper
625 ml (1 pint) milk
250 g (9 oz) low-fat soft cheese
200 g (7 oz) canned tuna, drained and flaked
75 g (2½ oz) pimento-stuffed olives, coarsely chopped
30 ml (2 tbsp) chopped spring onions
250 g (9 oz) noodles or other pasta, cooked (page 220)
175 g (6 oz) Cheddar cheese, grated
90 g (3 oz) soft breadcrumbs

In a large bowl, microwave 75 g (2½ oz) of the butter on 100% for 1 minute. Stir in flour, salt and black pepper and microwave for 45 seconds. Gradually stir in milk. Microwave for 5-6 minutes, or

until sauce thickens and bubbles, stirring every minute. Stir in low-fat soft cheese, mixing well, then add tuna, olives, and spring onions. Mix thoroughly.

Place about 150 ml (5 fl oz) of the sauce in a greased baking dish. Add half the noodles, half the remaining sauce, half the grated cheese, then repeat layers. Microwave remaining butter in a bowl for 1 minute, add bread-crumbs and toss lightly to coat. Sprinkle over casserole. Microwave on 70% for 8-10 minutes, or until mixture begins to bubble. Serve with a salad for a complete supper. Serves 6.

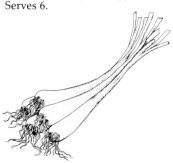

Pasta with Four Cheeses

100%, 50% .... 11 minutes

90 g (3 oz) Gruyère cheese, diced
90 g (3 oz) Gouda cheese, diced
60 g (2 oz) Parmesan cheese, finely grated
10 ml (2 tsp) plain flour
30 g (1 oz) butter
125 ml (4 fl oz) milk
250 g (9 oz) pasta shells, cooked (page 220) and kept warm
90 g (3 oz) Mozzarella cheese, coarsely grated
black pepper

Mix together Gruyère, Gouda and Parmesan cheeses and toss together with the flour. Microwave butter and milk together on 100% for l-2 minutes, or until butter has melted. Add a little of the combined cheeses, stir gently with a wooden spoon and microwave on 50% for 1 minute. Stir well, add a little more cheese and repeat process until cheese has melted and sauce is smooth (about 8 minutes).

Pour cheese sauce over pasta and stir gently. Mix in Mozzarella cheese and serve immediately with freshly ground black pepper. Serves 4 as a starter, 2-3 as a main course.

Salsa Verde

Microwave a browning dish on 100% for 6 minutes. Cut 1 medium-sized green pepper in half lengthways and remove seeds. Place halves, skin-side down, in the dish and microwave for 1-2 minutes, pressing halves flat a few times, until skin begins to blister. Rub off skin.

Break sprigs off stems of 200 g (7 oz) parsley. Place green pepper, parsley, 3 anchovy fillets, 15 ml (1 tbsp) lemon juice, 45 ml (3 tbsp) capers and a generous grinding of black pepper in the container of a blender or food processor. Blend until smooth. Slowly add 250 ml (8 fl oz) oil and blend to combine. Serve with pasta, cold tongue or beef. Serves 6.

Pasta with Summer Vegetables

100% .... 14 minutes

6 bacon rashers, rinds removed
125 g (4 oz) green beans, trimmed and cut into 1-cm (½ -in) pieces
1 small red pepper, diced
4 small squash, sliced
2 courgettes, sliced
45 ml (3 tbsp) water
30 g (1 oz) butter
4 spring onions, chopped
250 g (9 oz) pasta twists, cooked (page 220) and kept warm
15 ml (1 tbsp) lemon juice
salt and black pepper
5 ml (1 tsp) fresh thyme or 2.5 ml (½ tsp) dried thyme

Place bacon on a plate or rack, cover with waxed paper and microwave on 100% for 4-5 minutes, or until crisp. Drain, crumble and set aside.

Combine green beans, red pepper, squash and courgettes with 45 ml (3 tbsp) water.

Microwave, covered, for 4 minutes, then drain well.

In a bowl, microwave butter for 30 seconds, add spring onions and microwave for 1 minute. Add drained vegetables and toss to coat. Combine with pasta, then add lemon juice, salt, black pepper, thyme and reserved bacon. Toss gently to mix and microwave for 2-3 minutes to heat through before serving. Serves 4-6.

Note
Dried pasta needs to be reconstituted in plenty of boiling salted water and therefore it is not faster to cook pasta in the microwave.

Hint
Pasta reheats in the microwave with excellent results. Just place the pasta in a suitable container, cover and microwave on 100% for 2-3 minutes, or longer, depending on the quantity.

Pasta del Sol

100% .... 1 minute

400 g (14 oz) canned pineapple
  chunks
250 g (9 oz) pasta shells, cooked
  (page 220)
2 oranges, peeled to remove all pith
  and coarsely chopped
1 red pepper, cut in julienne
1 celery stick, sliced
250 g (9 oz) cooked ham, cut in
  julienne
175 g (6 oz) frozen peas
lettuce to serve
60 ml (4 tbsp) cashew nuts (salted or
  unsalted)

DRESSING
125 ml (4 fl oz) unsweetened orange
  juice
30 ml (2 tbsp) lemon juice
125 ml (4 fl oz) oil
30 ml (2 tbsp) grated orange rind
15 ml (1 tbsp) sugar
5 ml (1 tsp) dried sweet basil
generous pinch of black pepper
pinch of grated nutmeg

Drain pineapple, reserving juice
for another use, and place in a
large bowl. Add cooked pasta to
pineapple along with all
remaining salad ingredients,
except nuts.

To make dressing: Combine all
ingredients in a jug and
microwave on 100% for 1 minute.
Stir and pour over salad, tossing
gently to mix. Cover and chill for
several hours, or overnight,
stirring gently from time to time.
Serve on lettuce-lined plates and
sprinkle with cashew nuts.
Serves 6-8.

Note
**Left-over cooked chicken also
makes a good salad when used
instead of ham.**

Cream Cheese Gnocchi with Butter and Parmesan

100% .... 13 minutes

250 g (9 oz) cream cheese
2 eggs
60 g (2 oz) butter, softened
60 g (2 oz) Parmesan cheese, grated
100 ml (3½ oz) plain flour
salt and black pepper
pinch of grated nutmeg
1.5 litres (2¾ pints) water, boiling
90 g (3 oz) butter

Beat cream cheese with eggs, 60 g
(2 oz) softened butter, 30 g (1 oz)
of the Parmesan cheese and flour.
Season to taste with salt, black
pepper and nutmeg. Form into
oval gnocchi about 10 ml (2 tsp)
each, then roll in a little extra
flour.

Pour boiling water into a large
bowl and microwave on 100% for
1 minute to bring back to boil.

Add gnocchi a few at a time and
poach for 2-3 minutes. Check
gnocchi every minute and lift
them out as they rise to the top of
the bowl. Drain and keep warm
while repeating process until all
gnocchi are cooked. Then
microwave 90 g (3 oz) butter in a
jug for 1 minute and serve with
the gnocchi. Sprinkle with
remaining Parmesan cheese.
Serves 4 as a starter, 2 as a main
course.

Variation
GNOCCHI WITH CREAMY BLUE
CHEESE SAUCE
Prepare gnocchi as above, then
make the sauce as follows:
Crumble 75 g (2½ oz) of any blue
cheese into a jug, add 250 ml
(8 fl oz) single cream and microwave on 100% for 2-3 minutes
until very hot. Stir to ensure that
cheese mixes in completely, then
add 5 ml (1 tsp) Dijon mustard
and black pepper to taste. Whisk
until smooth. Serve piping hot
over gnocchi. Serves 3-4.

Spaghetti Mould

It is very much easier to fry the aubergines on top of the cooker while making the filling in the microwave.

100%, 70% .... 39 minutes

2 large aubergines
salt
plain flour
oil for frying
30 ml (2 tbsp) oil
350 g (12 oz) topside of beef, minced
1 onion, chopped
1-2 garlic cloves, finely chopped
400 g (14 oz) canned tomatoes, chopped
30 ml (2 tbsp) tomato paste
2.5 ml (½ tsp) dried oregano
salt and black pepper
125 g (4 oz) frozen peas
200 g (7 oz) spaghetti, cooked (page 220)
60 g (2 oz) Cheddar cheese, grated
45 ml (3 tbsp) grated Parmesan cheese
45 g (1½ oz) dry breadcrumbs

Wash, dry and trim aubergines. Cut into slices, 3-mm (⅛-in) thick. Sprinkle with salt and leave to stand for 20 minutes. Rinse well, pat dry and dust lightly with flour. Heat a little oil in a frying pan and brown slices quickly on both sides, cooking a few at a time.

To make filling: Microwave 30 ml (2 tbsp) oil in a large casserole on 100% for 45 seconds. Crumble mince into dish and microwave for 5 minutes, using a fork to break up mince from time to time. Add onion and garlic. Microwave for 2 minutes, then stir in tomatoes with their liquid, tomato paste, oregano and seasoning. Microwave for 7 minutes. Stir in peas and microwave for another 4 minutes. Fold in cooked spaghetti and cheeses.

Grease a straight-sided 20-cm (8-in) square casserole or soufflé dish and sprinkle base and sides generously with breadcrumbs. Place a slice of aubergine in the middle of the dish, arrange

remaining slices in a circle around it, overlapping each other, then arrange overlapping slices around the sides. (To prevent aubergine slices from collapsing, spoon in a little of the filling as you arrange them.)

Spoon in remaining filling and pack down firmly. Arrange any remaining slices of aubergine on top and sprinkle with any left-over breadcrumbs. Cover with vented plastic wrap and microwave on 70% for 15-20 minutes. Leave to stand for 5 minutes before turning out. Cut into wedges and serve with a crisp green salad.
Serves 6.

Gazpacho Rice

100% .... 19 minutes

500 g (18 oz) minced beef
1 onion, sliced
1 garlic clove, finely chopped
200 g (7 oz) rice
625 ml (1 pint) tomato juice
60 ml (4 tbsp) red wine vinegar
salt and black pepper
few drops of Tabasco
1 medium-sized green pepper, chopped
1 tomato, skinned and chopped
100 g (3½ oz) cucumber, chopped

Crumble beef into a large casserole and microwave on 100% for 3 minutes. Break up mince and drain off any fat. Add onion, garlic, rice, tomato juice, vinegar, salt, black pepper and Tabasco. Cover and microwave for 15 minutes, or until liquid is absorbed and rice is tender. Stir in green pepper, tomato and cucumber and microwave for 1 minute to heat through.
Serves 4-6.

Apple and Walnut Wild Rice

100% .... 21 minutes

150 g (5 oz) brown and wild rice,
  mixed
500 ml (16 fl oz) chicken stock,
  boiling
45 ml (3 tbsp) sherry
45 g (1½ oz) butter
salt and black pepper
pinch of MSG
15 ml (1 tbsp) fresh chives
2 apples, peeled and sliced
30 g (1 oz) butter
30 ml (2 tbsp) soft brown sugar
3 celery sticks, sliced
60 g (2 oz) walnuts, chopped
2.5 ml (½ tsp) grated orange rind

Place rice in a casserole dish with
the stock and microwave on 100%
for 25-30 minutes. Add sherry,
45 g (1½ oz) butter, seasoning,
msg and chives. Stir to mix well.
Cover and leave to stand for 20
minutes.
  Microwave apples with

remaining 30 g (1 oz) butter for
3 minutes, stirring once. Sprinkle
with brown sugar and microwave
for 1 minute more. Stir gently to
dissolve sugar. Add to rice along
with celery, walnuts and orange
rind. Microwave for a further
2 minutes to heat through.
Serves 6.

Note
As with pasta, rice must be fully
hydrated during the cooking
process and the microwave cannot
speed up this process. However,
when cooked in the microwave, rice
will not burn if neglected. It also
reheats better in the microwave
than it does conventionally.

Hint
**To reheat rice: Place rice in a dish or
bowl, cover tightly and microwave
on 100% for 1-3 minutes,
depending on the quantity. (No
additional liquid is necessary.) Stir
lightly with a fork to 'fluff up' the
rice.**

Orange Rice and Raisins

100% .... 20 minutes

100 g (3½ oz) butter
200 g (7 oz) rice
400 ml (13 fl oz) water, boiling
100 ml (3½ fl oz) orange juice
5 ml (1 tsp) salt
pinch of ground turmeric
1 orange, peeled and chopped
45 ml (3 tbsp) chopped almonds
100 g (3½ oz) seedless raisins
30 ml (2 tbsp) sugar

Microwave butter in a large
casserole on 100% for 2 minutes.
Add rice, stir to coat and
microwave for 1 minute.
Add boiling water, orange juice,
salt and turmeric. Stir in orange
pieces and almonds and
microwave, covered, for
12-15 minutes. Stir in raisins and
sugar. Leave to stand for
20 minutes, then microwave for
2 minutes to heat through.
Serves 6.

Risotto

100%, 70% .... 16 minutes

60 g (2 oz) butter
1 small onion, chopped
125 g (4 oz) chicken livers, halved
salt and black pepper
2 slices ham, diced
125 g (4 oz) rice
250 ml (8 fl oz) beef stock
75 g (2½ oz) frozen peas
45 ml (3 tbsp) cream
30 ml (2 tbsp) grated Parmesan
chopped parsley to garnish

Microwave butter in a casserole
on 100% for 1 minute. Stir in
onion and microwave for
1 minute. Add livers, stir to coat,
cover and microwave for a further
minute. Add seasoning, ham, rice
and stock. Microwave, covered,
for 10 minutes, stirring twice.
Add peas, cover and leave to
stand for 10 minutes. Stir in
cream and Parmesan cheese.
Reheat on 70% for 2-3 minutes.
Serve sprinkled with parsley.
Serves 4.

Curried Banana Rice

Served cold, this makes an unusual salad to accompany barbecued meat or fish.

100% .... 15 minutes

200 g (7 oz) rice
500 ml (16 fl oz) water, boiling
5 ml (1 tsp) salt
pinch of ground turmeric
20 g (¾ oz) butter
4 bananas
15 ml (1 tbsp) lemon juice
2 celery sticks, sliced
75 g (2½ oz) sultanas
75 g (2½ oz) salted peanuts
30 ml (2 tbsp) chopped red pepper
15 ml (1 tbsp) snipped chives
lettuce to serve

DRESSING
200 ml (6½ fl oz) mayonnaise
45 ml (3 tbsp) single cream
15 ml (1 tbsp) lemon juice
15 ml (1 tbsp) curry powder,
  or to taste
2.5 ml (½ tsp) dry mustard
few drops of Tabasco

Combine rice, water, salt, turmeric and butter in a large casserole. Cover and microwave on 100% for 15 minutes. Leave to stand for 20 minutes, then chill.
  To make salad: Peel and slice bananas, sprinkle with lemon juice and set aside. Combine rice, celery, sultanas, peanuts, red pepper and chives and toss to mix.
  To make dressing: Combine mayonnaise, cream, lemon juice, curry powder, dry mustard and Tabasco. Mix well and add to rice mixture. Toss lightly, fold in bananas and chill until needed. Serve on crisp lettuce.
Serves 6-8.

Aubergine Rolls

100%, 70% .... 28 minutes

2 large aubergines, peeled and
   sliced lengthways
oil for brushing
200 g (7 oz) Feta cheese, crumbled
200 g (7 oz) Ricotta cheese
45 g (1½ oz) Parmesan cheese,
   grated
15 ml (1 tbsp) lemon juice
1 bunch of spring onions, chopped
1 large egg, lightly beaten
20 g (¾ oz) chopped fresh parsley

SAUCE
45 ml (3 tbsp) oil
1 large carrot, finely grated
2-3 leeks, chopped
1 onion, chopped
1-2 garlic cloves, crushed
800 g (1 lb 14 oz) canned tomatoes,
   chopped
1 bay leaf
5 ml (1 tsp) dried thyme
salt and black pepper

Sprinkle aubergines with salt and
leave to stand for 15 minutes.

Next, make the sauce. Microwave
oil in a casserole on 100% for
45 seconds. Add carrot, leeks,
onion and garlic. Stir to coat and
microwave for 5 minutes, stirring
twice. Add tomatoes and
remaining ingredients. Microwave for 10 minutes, stirring
occasionally. Remove bay leaf.

Rinse aubergine and pat dry.
Arrange slices on a baking sheet,
brush both sides with oil and grill
to brown.

Combine Feta, Ricotta and half
the grated Parmesan with lemon
juice, spring onions, egg and half
the parsley. Season lightly. Place
30 ml (2 tbsp) of this mixture
across the short side of each
aubergine slice and roll up.

Spread 60 ml (4 tbsp) of the
sauce on the base of a shallow
casserole. Arrange rolls on sauce
in one layer. Pour remaining
sauce over the top and sprinkle
with remaining Parmesan cheese
and parsley. Microwave on 70%
for 10-12 minutes to heat through.
Serves 4-6.

Puffy Omelette

100%, 50% .... 9 minutes

3 eggs, separated
45 ml (3 tbsp) mayonnaise
30 ml (2 tbsp) water
salt and black pepper
30 g (1 oz) butter

Whisk egg whites until soft peaks
form. In a separate bowl, beat egg
yolks, mayonnaise, water and
seasoning, then gently fold into
whisked whites.

Microwave butter in a 20-cm
(8-in) glass pie dish on 100% for
1 minute. Swirl to coat dish. Pour
in egg mixture and spread evenly
over the dish. Microwave on 50%
for 6-8 minutes, rotating dish if
necessary, until mixture is set but
still glossy on top. Leave to set for
30 seconds to 1 minute, then run a
spatula around sides of dish. Fold
half of the omelette over and
gently slide on to a serving plate.
Serves 1-2.

Oriental Omelette Filling

100% .... 7 minutes

45 ml (3 tbsp) oil
4 mushrooms, sliced
3 spring onions, sliced
100 g (3½ oz) cooked ham, diced
15 ml (1 tbsp) chopped sweet pickle
75 g (2½ oz) cooked rice (page 220)
45 ml (3 tbsp) dry white wine
10 ml (2 tsp) soy sauce
5 ml (1 tsp) cornflour
salt and black pepper

Microwave oil in a casserole on
100% for 45 seconds. Add
mushrooms, onions, ham and
pickle. Microwave for 2 minutes,
stirring once. Add rice and microwave for 1 minute. Combine wine
and soy sauce, stir in cornflour
and add to vegetables. Microwave
for 2-3 minutes, stirring every
minute. Season to taste.
Fills 2-3 omelettes.

Macaroni Cheese and Ham Bake

100% .... 15 minutes

300 ml (10 fl oz) cheese sauce
  (see opposite)
200 g (7 oz) Cheddar cheese, grated
4 eggs, beaten
30 ml (2 tbsp) plain flour
400 g (14 oz) canned cream of
  mushroom soup
200 g (7 oz) cooked ham, chopped
60 g (2 oz) mushrooms, sliced
30 ml (2 tbsp) chopped spring onion
30 ml (2 tbsp) chopped fresh parsley
45 ml (3 tbsp) chopped stuffed
  olives
60 ml (4 tbsp) mayonnaise
375 g (13 oz) macaroni, cooked
  (page 220)

Combine cheese sauce with three-quarters of the grated cheese. Mix in eggs, flour and mushroom soup. Add ham, mushrooms, spring onion, parsley and olives. Stir in mayonnaise, then fold in macaroni.

Turn into a 2-litre (3½-pint) casserole. Microwave, covered, on 100% for 10-13 minutes, or until mixture is almost set. Uncover, sprinkle with remaining cheese and microwave for about 2 minutes more to melt cheese. Leave to stand for 8-10 minutes before serving.
Serves 6-8.

Hints
• Cheese takes only a short time to cook in the microwave because it has a high fat content, therefore timing should be in seconds rather than minutes. Where cheese must be cooked for more than a few moments, layer it between other ingredients and use a lower power level.
• When adding cheese to cooked sauces, it is not usually necessary to cook the sauce further. Just stir the cheese into the sauce until it melts.
• If a recipe calls for a topping of cheese, add it just before the dish is cooked and microwave for 30 seconds to 1 minute.

Cheese Sauce

100% .... 6 minutes

45 g (1½ oz) butter
45 ml (3 tbsp) plain flour
2.5 ml (½ tsp) dry mustard
600 ml (19 fl oz) milk
100 g (3½ oz) Cheddar cheese,
  finely grated
salt and white pepper
15 ml (1 tbsp) chopped fresh parsley
  (optional)

Microwave butter in a large jug on 100% for 45 seconds. Stir in flour and dry mustard. Gradually stir in milk and microwave on 100% for 4-5 minutes, or until bubbling and thickened, stirring well every minute. Add cheese. Stir to melt. Season to taste with salt and white pepper and stir in parsley if desired.
Makes about 600 ml (19 fl oz).

Brie with Almonds and Butter

100%, 70% .... 5 minutes

150 g (5 oz) piece Brie cheese
30 g (1 oz) unsalted butter
30 ml (2 tbsp) flaked almonds

Place cheese on a microwaveproof serving plate. Combine butter and almonds in a bowl and microwave on 100% for 3-4 minutes, or until almonds are toasted. Spoon almond mixture over Brie and microwave on 70% for about 1 minute, or until cheese is heated through. Serve as a spread with savoury biscuits or Melba toast.
Serves 6-8.

Manicotti Crêpes

100%, 70% .... 22 minutes

**300 g (11 oz) spinach, trimmed and
  washed**
1 onion, chopped
1 garlic clove, finely chopped
30 g (1 oz) butter
500 g (18 oz) minced beef
salt and black pepper
**60 ml (4 tbsp) grated Parmesan
  cheese**
12 crêpes (see below)
**225 g (8 oz) Mozzarella cheese,
  thinly sliced**
1 recipe cheese sauce (page 131)

Place spinach in a casserole with
just the water clinging to the
leaves from washing. Microwave,
covered, on 100% for 4 minutes.
Drain well and chop. Set aside.
  In a large casserole, microwave
onion, garlic and butter for
2 minutes. Add beef and
microwave for 4 minutes, stirring
twice to break up meat. Drain,
then stir in spinach, salt, black
pepper and Parmesan cheese.

Fill prepared crêpes with
mixture and roll up loosely. Place
in two buttered baking dishes and
top with slices of Mozzarella
cheese. Spoon cheese sauce over
and microwave on 70% for
4-6 minutes until heated through
and bubbling. Brown under a grill
if desired. Keep warm and repeat
with remaining crêpes.
Serves 6 as a main course, 12 as a
starter.

Basic Crêpe Mixture

Combine 125 g (4 oz) plain flour,
generous pinch of salt, 2 eggs,
150 ml (5 fl oz) milk and 150 ml
(5 fl oz) water in a blender and
blend for 30 seconds. Scrape
down sides of glass jug and
process for a further 30 seconds.
Microwave 30 g (1 oz) butter on
100% for 30 seconds, add to
batter and blend for a few
seconds. Let batter stand for
30 minutes before cooking in a
crêpe pan in the usual way.
Makes about 12 crêpes.

Cheese and Asparagus Quiche

100%, 50% .... 19 minutes

**23-cm (9-in) shortcrust pastry case
  (page 157)**
5 ml (1 tsp) Worcestershire sauce
1 egg yolk

FILLING
**400 g (14 oz) canned asparagus
  pieces, drained**
15 g (½ oz) butter
1 onion, chopped
5 ml (1 tsp) dried mixed herbs
125 g (4 oz) Cheddar cheese, grated
4 eggs
125 ml (4 fl oz) single cream
125 ml (4 fl oz) milk
salt and black pepper

Brush pastry case with a mixture
of Worcestershire sauce and egg
yolk. Microwave on 100% for
2 minutes, then cool.
  Spread asparagus pieces in
pastry case. Microwave butter in a
bowl for 30 seconds. Add onion,

microwave for 2 minutes, then
add herbs. Sprinkle three-
quarters of the cheese over
asparagus and top with onion
mixture. Combine eggs, cream,
milk, salt and black pepper and
mix well. Pour into pastry case.
  Microwave on 50% for
11-13 minutes. Sprinkle with
remaining cheese and microwave
for 1 minute more. Leave to stand
for at least 5 minutes before
serving.
Serves 6-8.

Variations

MOZZARELLA AND ASPARAGUS
QUICHE
Substitute Mozzarella cheese for
the Cheddar, and basil for the
mixed herbs. Proceed as above.
In the last minute of cooking,
arrange sliced tomatoes on top.

SPINACH QUICHE
Instead of asparagus, mix 125 g
(4 oz) cooked, drained, chopped
spinach with the onion. Stir in a
pinch of grated nutmeg and
substitute soured cream for
cream. Proceed as above.

Cheese and Herb Fondue

100%, 50% .... 8 minutes

30 g (1 oz) butter
45 ml (3 tbsp) dry white wine
30 ml (2 tbsp) brandy
500 g (18 oz) blue cheese, crumbled
125 g (4 oz) Brie cheese, cubed
60 g (2 oz) button mushrooms, sliced
15 ml (1 tbsp) chopped fresh herbs, such as parsley or tarragon
generous pinch of freshly grated nutmeg
1 large French loaf

Microwave butter in a casserole on 100% for 1 minute. Add wine and brandy and microwave for 1 minute. Add cheeses, stir and microwave on 50% for 1 minute more. Stir thoroughly and microwave for about 4 minutes, stirring well after each minute. Add mushrooms, herbs and nutmeg and microwave for 1 minute more.

Place over a spirit burner at the table. Cut French bread into cubes and dip into fondue. Serve with salad, olives and gherkins if desired.
Serves 4.

Egg and Potato Soufflé

100% .... 10 minutes
Conventional oven:
190 °C (375 °F, gas 5) .. 40 minutes

2 large potatoes, peeled and diced
45 ml (3 tbsp) water
45 g (1½ oz) butter
salt and black pepper
125 ml (4 fl oz) soured cream
90 g (3 oz) mature Cheddar cheese, grated
4 eggs, separated
10 ml (2 tsp) chopped fresh parsley
30 ml (2 tbsp) chopped spring onion
pinch of cream of tartar

Add potatoes to water in a casserole and microwave, covered, on 100% for 8-10 minutes. Drain and mash with butter, salt, pepper and soured cream. Mix in cheese, egg yolks, parsley and spring onion.

Whisk egg whites with a pinch of cream of tartar to form stiff peaks. Fold into potato mixture and pile into a greased soufflé dish. Bake at 190 °C (375 °F, gas 5) for about 40 minutes.
Serves 4.

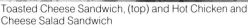
Toasted Cheese Sandwich, (top) and Hot Chicken and
Cheese Salad Sandwich

Hot Chicken and Cheese Salad Sandwiches

100% .... 2 minutes

250 g (9 oz) cooked chicken, diced
1 large dill pickle, finely chopped
30 ml (2 tbsp) finely chopped onion
5 ml (1 tsp) prepared mild mustard
60 ml (4 tbsp) mayonnaise
75 g (2½ oz) Cheddar cheese, grated
salt and black pepper
4 slices of rye bread or wholemeal bread, lightly toasted

Mix all ingredients except bread and season to taste. Refrigerate until needed. To heat, spread a quarter of the mixture on each slice of bread. Place two slices on a serving plate and microwave on 100% for about 1 minute, or until cheese has melted and mixture is hot. Repeat with remaining slices and serve at once. Serves 4.

Toasted Cheese Sandwich

100% .... 7 minutes

2 slices of wholemeal bread, lightly toasted
prepared mustard
2 slices of processed cheese
chopped spring onion or chives
butter

Spread one side of each slice of bread with a little mustard. Top with a slice of cheese and sprinkle one side with chopped spring onion or chives. Sandwich bread slices together. Spread outside of both slices with a little butter.
　Heat a browning dish on 100% for 5 minutes. Place sandwich on browning dish, press down slightly and leave for 25 seconds. Turn sandwich over and leave for another 25 seconds. Microwave for 30-40 seconds to melt cheese. Serve at once.
Serves 1.

Variations
HAM AND CHEESE
Place one slice of cooked ham between the slices of cheese and proceed as above.

CHEESE AND TOMATO
Place three thin slices of tomato between the slices of cheese and proceed as above.

Note
When making two sandwiches, add 10-15 seconds to the cooking time. If making several sandwiches, the browning dish will have to be reheated. Wipe the surface very clean to prevent burning.

Corn Custard

100%, 70% .... 14 minutes

30 g (1 oz) butter
½ onion, chopped
½ green pepper, chopped
½ red pepper, chopped
2 eggs, beaten
500 ml (16 fl oz) single cream
300 g (11 oz) frozen sweetcorn
30 ml (2 tbsp) chopped fresh parsley
100 g (3½ oz) Cheddar cheese, grated
salt and black pepper

Microwave butter in a casserole on 100% for 1 minute. Add onion and peppers and microwave for 3 minutes, stirring once. Combine eggs, cream, peppers and onion, corn, parsley, 75 g (2½ oz) of the cheese and seasoning. Turn into casserole and microwave on 70% for 6-10 minutes, or until just set. Sprinkle with remaining cheese during last minute of cooking. Allow to stand for 10 minutes before serving. Serves 6.

Spiced Feta

The taste of fresh herbs and garlic makes this cheese wonderful to serve with French bread. Use the oil in salad dressings.

100% .... 1 minute

750 g (1¾ lb) Feta cheese,
　preferably in one piece
1 litre (1¾ pints) milk
sprigs of fresh herbs (rosemary,
　basil or oregano)
long thin strips of lemon rind
250 ml (8 fl oz) sunflower seed oil
3 green chillies, seeds removed
3 garlic cloves, peeled
15 ml (1 tbsp) mustard seeds
4 bay leaves
30 ml (2 tbsp) juniper berries
15 ml (1 tbsp) fennel seeds

Cut Feta into 3-cm (1¼-in) slices. Place in a bowl, cover with milk and refrigerate for 24 hours to reduce saltiness. Drain cheese and pat dry. Arrange cheese alternately with sprigs of herbs and lemon rind in a wide-necked decorative jar.

Place remaining ingredients in a jug and microwave on 100% for 1 minute. Leave to stand for 10 minutes before pouring on to the cheese. Cover and refrigerate for 3 days before using. Use within 10 days.
Serves 6.

Baked Feta

In a casserole, microwave 45 g (1½ oz) butter on 100% for 1 minute. Slice 450 g (1 lb) Feta cheese and arrange slices in layers in the dish. Microwave on 70% for 3 minutes, checking every minute until cheese softens and begins to bubble slightly. Add juice of 1 lemon, 2.5 ml (½ tsp) poppy seeds and season with pepper. Serve immediately with French bread or Melba toast as a snack or starter. Serves 3-4.

Baked Eggs in Courgettes with Hollandaise Sauce

100%, 70% .... 7 minutes

1 kg (2¼ lb) courgettes
5 ml (1 tsp) salt
15 g (½ oz) butter
15 ml (1 tbsp) oil
6 spring onions, chopped
salt and black pepper
4 eggs
1 recipe Hollandaise sauce
　(page 54)

Grate courgettes coarsely and toss with 5 ml (1 tsp) salt. Leave to stand for 5 minutes, then drain in a sieve, pressing gently to remove excess water. Drain again on absorbent kitchen paper.

Place butter and oil in a casserole and microwave on 100% for 45 seconds. Add spring onions and microwave for 1 minute. Add courgettes, stir to coat and microwave for 2 minutes, stirring once. Season with salt and black pepper and divide among four individual casseroles.

Make a hollow in the centre of each portion, then carefully break an egg into each. Prick yolks with a skewer. Microwave on 70% for 2-3 minutes, or until eggs are just set. Serve with hot Hollandaise sauce.
Serves 4.

Variation

CREAMED SPINACH NESTS
Combine 300-500 g (11-18 oz) cooked, drained, chopped spinach with 45 g (1½ oz) melted butter, a generous pinch of grated nutmeg, salt, pepper and about 60 ml (4 tbsp) cream. Mix well and use to line four or six individual casseroles. Proceed as above.

Creamy Chocolate Pots

100%, 50% .... 6 minutes

**200 g (7 oz) chocolate chips or plain
  chocolate, broken into pieces**
125 ml (4 fl oz) single cream
60 ml (4 tbsp) milk
1 egg
30 g (1 oz) caster sugar
**30 ml (2 tbsp) orange-flavoured
  liqueur**
pinch of salt
**whipped cream, grated orange rind
  and chocolate rolls to decorate**

Pour chocolate chips into a large
bowl and microwave on 50% for
3-4 minutes, or until just melted,
stirring twice. Stir until smooth.
In a jug, microwave cream and
milk together on 100% for
1½-2 minutes. Beat egg, sugar,
liqueur and salt into chocolate,
then slowly add hot milk mixture.
  Pour into six small, pretty tea or
demitasse cups and chill well.
Serve decorated with whipped
cream, a little grated orange rind
and chocolate rolls.
Serves 6.

Chocolate Rolls

**It is important to use cooking
chocolate for these rolls, as ordinary
dessert chocolate does not harden
sufficiently for this purpose.**

50% .... 5 minutes

75 g (2½ oz) cooking chocolate

Break chocolate into small pieces
and place in a bowl. Microwave
for 4-5 minutes on 50%, stirring
from time to time. Use a metal
spatula or long, straight-edged
knife to spread chocolate very
thinly on a marble slab or
stainless steel surface. Leave
chocolate to just set.
  Holding a straight-bladed knife
or a 20-cm (8-in) cook's knife with
two hands at an angle of
approximately 45°, pull knife
firmly over chocolate towards
you. This action will lift a thin
layer off the surface and the
chocolate will curl into rolls. Store
rolls in an airtight container for up
to one week. (The quantity made
will depend on the size of the
rolls.)

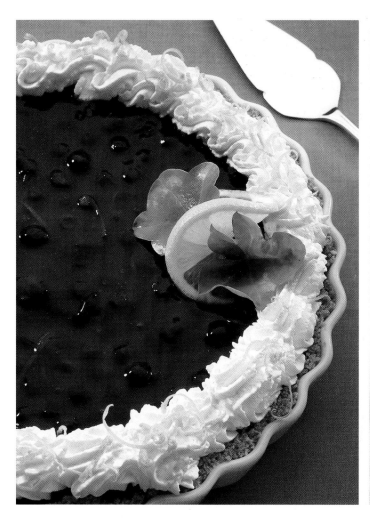

Blueberry Cheesecake

100%, 70%, 50% ..... 15 minutes

125 g (4 oz) Marie biscuit crumbs
45 g (1½ oz) icing sugar
60 g (2 oz) butter

FILLING
2 eggs
75 g (2½ oz) caster sugar
250 g (9 oz) cream cheese
125 ml (4 fl oz) single cream
pinch of salt
15 ml (1 tbsp) lemon juice
5 ml (1 tsp) finely grated lemon rind

TOPPING
350 g (12 oz) fresh blueberries
100 g (3½ oz) caster sugar
30 ml (2 tbsp) cornflour
pinch of salt
185 ml (6 fl oz) water
2.5 ml (½ tsp) grated lemon rind

DECORATION
whipped cream
lemon slices

Combine crumbs and sugar in a bowl. Microwave butter on 100% for 1 minute and stir into crumb mixture. Press mixture into the base of a 23-cm (9-in) round or square baking dish and set aside.

To make filling: Combine all ingredients in a large bowl and beat until smooth. Microwave on 70% for 4-6 minutes, stirring well every minute until mixture begins to thicken. Turn into prepared dish and microwave on 50% for 3-4 minutes, or until mixture is set. Remove from oven and cool. Cover with half the blueberries.

To make topping: Combine sugar, cornflour, salt and water. Add remaining blueberries and lemon rind and microwave on 70% for 3-4 minutes, stirring gently every minute until thick and clear. Spoon over cheesecake and chill.

Serve decorated with whipped cream and lemon slices, if desired.
Serves 8.

Almond Ice Cream

100%, 70% .... 14 minutes

100 g (3½ oz) caster sugar
75 ml (2½ fl oz) water
450 ml (14½ fl oz) milk
345 ml (11 fl oz) single cream
6 egg yolks
30 ml (2 tbsp) caster sugar
3 egg whites
45 g (1½ oz) toasted almonds, chopped (page 36)
45 ml (3 tbsp) Amaretto liqueur

Place 100 g (3½ oz) sugar and water in a large bowl and microwave on 100% for 2 minutes, stirring every 30 seconds. Brush sides of bowl with water to remove sugar crystals. Microwave for 6 minutes, or until syrup turns a deep caramel colour. Very carefully add milk and cream. Stir, then microwave for 3 minutes.

Beat together egg yolks and 30 ml (2 tbsp) caster sugar thoroughly. Pour hot milk and cream mixture on to egg yolk mixture and beat again. Microwave on 70% for 3 minutes. Stir well, cool, then freeze until firm.

Whisk egg whites until stiff. Cut frozen ice cream into chunks and process one-third at a time in a food processor until smooth. Add about one-third of the egg white to each batch and process until combined. Place ice cream mixture in a large bowl, then add nuts and liqueur, stirring well. Pour into freezer trays or one large container. Freeze until firm.
Serves 6-8.

Hint
To soften ice cream: Place a block of ice cream in a container and microwave on 100% for 20 seconds. Check for desired softness and continue microwaving until the ice cream is as soft as needed.

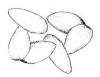

Caramel Slice

50% .... 45 seconds

200 g (7 oz) boudoir biscuits
200 ml (6½ fl oz) milk
30 ml (2 tbsp) coffee-flavoured
** liqueur**
45 g (1½ oz) butter
100 g (3½ oz) icing sugar
30 ml (2 tbsp) cocoa powder
2 egg yolks
30 ml (2 tbsp) brandy
375 ml (12 fl oz) whipping cream
10 ml (2 tsp) instant coffee granules
15 ml (1 tbsp) water
7.5 ml (1½ tsp) powdered gelatine
45 g (1½ oz) pecan nuts, chopped
2 rolls of Toffos, chopped
whipped cream and chocolate rolls
** (page 136) to decorate**

Line the base of a 23 x 12-cm
(9 x 5-in) microwave loaf pan with
greaseproof paper. Dip biscuits
into milk flavoured with coffee
liqueur and lay them in a row at
the bottom of the pan.
  Cream together thoroughly
butter, icing sugar, cocoa powder
and egg yolks. Add brandy to
cream and whip until fairly stiff.
Fold into creamed mixture.
Combine coffee, water and
gelatine, leave to stand for
5 minutes, then microwave on
50% for 45 seconds. Stir into
creamed mixture.
  Combine chopped nuts and
caramels in a bowl. First, spread
about one-third of creamed
mixture on to the biscuits, then
sprinkle liberally with nut
mixture. Repeat all layers twice
more. Cover and refrigerate.
  Before serving, loosen sides of
caramel slice with a spatula and
turn out on to a serving platter.
Decorate top with swirls of cream
and chocolate rolls.
Serves 8.

Pears Alicia

100% .... 19 minutes

250 ml (8 fl oz) water
75 g (2½ oz) caster sugar
125 ml (4 fl oz) dessert wine
45 ml (3 tbsp) Curaçao
2 strips of thinly pared orange rind
15 ml (1 tbsp) apple jelly
small piece of cinnamon stick
6 firm pears, peeled
20 ml (4 tsp) cornflour
30 ml (2 tbsp) brandy
angelica and strips of orange rind
** to decorate**
whipped cream to serve

Pour water into a casserole dish,
add sugar and cover. Microwave
on 100% for 4 minutes. Add wine,
Curaçao, orange rind, apple jelly
and cinnamon stick. Stir to
combine. Add pears, cover and
microwave for 7-10 minutes. (The
time will vary depending on the
type and ripeness of pears used.)
Remove pears and cinnamon
stick.
  Blend together cornflour and
brandy. Add a little hot poaching
syrup to cornflour mixture and
stir to combine, then pour
cornflour mixture into syrup. Stir
well and microwave, covered, for
5 minutes, stirring twice during
cooking time. (The liquid should
be of a pouring consistency, as it
thickens when cold.) Add pears
and coat well with sauce. Cover
and cool, then chill. Re-coat pears
with sauce from time to time.
  Decorate each pear with a 'leaf'
of angelica and a strip of orange
rind. Serve well chilled with
plenty of whipped cream.
Serves 6.

Note
Pears cook extremely well in the
microwave. When poaching pears,
always undercook slightly as they
will continue to cook while
standing. Overcooked pears
become pulpy and lose their shape.

Clockwise from left: Maple Syrup and Pecan Ice Cream, Coconut Ice Cream and Grapefruit Sorbet

Maple Syrup and Pecan Ice Cream

100%, 50% .... 9 minutes

500 ml (16 fl oz) single cream
250 ml (8 fl oz) milk
2 egg yolks
200 ml (6½ fl oz) maple syrup
30 g (1 oz) butter
60 g (2 oz) pecan nuts, chopped

Place cream and milk in a jug and microwave on 100% for 3 minutes until very hot. Beat yolks until pale in colour and add hot cream. Beat again. Then microwave on 50% for 3 minutes, whisking every minute. Stir in maple syrup and leave to cool.

In a shallow dish, microwave butter on 100% for 1 minute. Add nuts, stir to coat, then microwave for 2 minutes more, stirring after 1 minute. Stir into cooled ice cream mixture. Freeze in an ice cream tray and beat mixture at least twice while it is freezing.
Serves 6-8.

Coconut Ice Cream

100%, 50% .... 6 minutes

300 ml (10 fl oz) milk
150 ml (5 fl oz) double cream
30 g (1 oz) butter
100 g (3½ oz) desiccated coconut
3 egg yolks
45 ml (3 tbsp) golden syrup
few drops of vanilla extract

Combine milk, cream, butter and coconut in a jug. Microwave on 100% for 3 minutes. Meanwhile, beat egg yolks and syrup well. Pour hot liquid on to egg mixture and beat. Return to jug and microwave on 50% for 3 minutes, whisking every minute. Add vanilla extract and leave to cool. Pour into a container and freeze.

When frozen, cut into blocks and leave to soften slightly. Drop a few blocks at a time on to the moving blades of a food processor. Process until a 'band' forms on the base, then refreeze.
Serves 4.

Grapefruit Sorbet

A tangy and refreshing sorbet, it is good served either as a palate cleanser or as a light dessert after a rich meal.

100% .... 10 minutes

5 grapefruit
350 g (12 oz) caster sugar
600 ml (19 fl oz) water
thinly pared rind of 1 lemon
15 ml (1 tbsp) Pernod
125 ml (4 fl oz) semi-sweet
   white wine
2 egg whites
selection of fruit in season
   to decorate

Squeeze grapefruit and reserve juice. Place sugar, water and lemon rind in a large bowl and microwave on 100% for 10 minutes, stirring at least twice during cooking time. Add grapefruit juice, Pernod and wine. Leave to cool, then remove rind. Pour into a freezer tray and freeze overnight.

Whisk egg whites to a peaking consistency. Cut frozen grapefruit ice into blocks and, using a food processor, reduce to a smooth slush by dropping one-third of the blocks through the feed tube on to the moving blades. When smooth, drop in about one-third of the egg white. Continue processing until combined. Repeat with remaining two-thirds. Return sorbet to freezer for at least 2 hours.

To serve: Scoop into small balls and serve either on plates, garnished with colourful fruits, or in small glass bowls.
Serves 6-8.

Variations
To change the flavour of the sorbet, simply change the juice. Use orange juice or lemon juice for a sorbet with a tang. Alternatively, try mixing 90 ml (3 fl oz) puréed kiwi fruit with the citrus juice of your choice and continue as above.

Apricot Cream

100%, 50% .... 8 minutes

8 fresh apricots
60 ml (4 tbsp) water
sugar to taste
250 ml (8 fl oz) milk
2 eggs, separated
75 ml (2¹/₂ fl oz) cold water
25 ml (5 tsp) powdered gelatine
100 ml (3¹/₂ fl oz) whipping cream
whipped cream and apricots to
  decorate

Wash apricots, cut in half and remove stones. Place in a shallow casserole dish with 60 ml (4 tbsp) water and a little sugar. Cover and microwave on 100% for 4 minutes. Purée apricots and sweeten to taste. Pour milk into a jug and microwave, uncovered, for 3 minutes. Beat egg yolks well, pour on to hot milk and beat again. Combine custard and apricot purée. Leave to cool.

Pour 75 ml (2¹/₂ fl oz) water into a jug and add gelatine. Leave to stand for a few minutes, then microwave on 50% for 1 minute. Meanwhile, whip cream until thick. Stir gelatine into apricot custard and chill over ice until mixture begins to thicken. Whisk egg whites until soft peaks form. Carefully fold cream, then egg whites into custard mixture. Pour into a rinsed mould and refrigerate for at least 3 hours.

To turn out mould: Dip mould into hot water for 3 seconds, then carefully draw a small area of pudding away from the side of the mould. (This will introduce an air bubble.) Turn over on to a plate and wait for a few seconds before removing mould. Decorate with whipped cream and a few apricot slices, if desired.
Serves 6.

Nutty Chocolate Pie

100%, 50% .... 8 minutes

75 g (2¹/₂ oz) butter
100 g (3¹/₂ oz) pecan nuts, chopped
18 Nice biscuits, crushed
45 ml (3 tbsp) soft brown sugar

FILLING
30 ml (2 tbsp) cold water
15 ml (1 tbsp) powdered gelatine
150 g (5 oz) plain chocolate, broken
  into pieces
100 ml (3¹/₂ fl oz) water, boiling
2 eggs, separated
45 ml (3 tbsp) caster sugar
few drops of vanilla extract
125 ml (4 fl oz) whipping cream,
  whipped

DECORATION
45 ml (3 tbsp) whipping cream,
  whipped
chocolate shavings

Place butter in a bowl and microwave on 100% for 1 minute. Stir in nuts, biscuits and sugar.

Press mixture into base and sides of a 23-cm (9-in) pie plate and microwave for 1¹/₂ minutes. Remove from microwave and allow to cool.

To make filling: Combine water and gelatine and leave to stand for 5 minutes. Place chocolate in a large glass bowl and microwave for 3-4 minutes, stirring once or twice during this time. Add boiling water and stir to combine.

Beat egg yolks and sugar until thick and pale, add vanilla extract and stir into chocolate mixture. Microwave gelatine on 50% for 45 seconds. Stir and add to chocolate mixture, then whisk egg whites to a peaking consistency and fold into mixture. Finally, whip cream until soft peaks form and fold into mixture.

Pour filling into prepared crust and chill until set. Just before serving, decorate with whipped cream and chocolate shavings.
Serves 8.

Chocolate Trifle

Chocolate Trifle

100%, 70%, 50% ..... 17 minutes

3 eggs
100 g (3½ oz) caster sugar
few drops of vanilla extract
100 g (3½ oz) plain flour
30 ml (2 tbsp) cocoa powder
pinch of salt
2.5 ml (½ tsp) baking powder
1 orange, peeled, pith removed, and sliced
100 ml (3½ fl oz) rum
60 g (2 oz) caster sugar
100 ml (3½ fl oz) water, warmed

CHOCOLATE SAUCE
60 g (2 oz) plain chocolate, broken into pieces
250 ml (8 fl oz) milk
60 g (2 oz) caster sugar
1 egg
1 egg yolk
20 ml (4 tsp) cornflour

TOPPING
250 ml (8 fl oz) whipping cream
60 g (2 oz) caster sugar (optional)

60 g (2 oz) pecan nuts or hazelnuts, chopped
chocolate rolls to decorate (page 136)

Beat eggs, sugar and vanilla together until very light and fluffy. Sift flour with cocoa powder, salt and baking powder and gradually fold into egg mixture. Pour into a greased and lined 23-cm (9-in) round glass baking dish and microwave on 100% for 4-4½ minutes. Remove from oven and leave to stand in the dish for 5 minutes, then turn out and cool.

Cut cake into two layers. Fit one layer into an attractive serving dish and top with orange slices, then cover with remaining layer of cake. Pour rum over. Next, combine caster sugar and hot water in a bowl and microwave on 100% for 2 minutes. Stir well until all sugar has dissolved, then spoon over cake and set aside.

To make chocolate sauce: Microwave chocolate in a bowl on 50% for 2-3 minutes, or until

melted and smooth. Set aside. Microwave milk on 70% for about 3 minutes. Meanwhile, in a large bowl, beat together sugar, egg, egg yolk and cornflour until creamy, then gradually add hot milk, beating constantly. Microwave on 50% for about 4 minutes, or until mixture is thick enough to coat the back of a spoon, stirring well after each minute. Stir in melted chocolate. Strain sauce into another bowl, then cover and cool. When sauce is cool, spoon over cake base.

To make topping: Whip cream to stiff peaks, sweeten with caster sugar, if desired, and pipe over sauce. Sprinkle with chopped nuts and decorate with chocolate rolls.
Serves 6.

Grand Marnier Custard

100%, 30% .... 7 minutes

4 egg yolks
30 ml (2 tbsp) caster sugar
150 ml (5 fl oz) milk
75 ml (2½ fl oz) single cream
30 ml (2 tbsp) Grand Marnier

Beat egg yolks and sugar until pale. Combine milk and cream in a large jug and microwave on 100% for 2-3 minutes until very hot. Pour on to yolk mixture, little by little, beating well. Microwave on 30% for 3-4 minutes, stirring every minute. Stir in liqueur, then set over ice to cool quickly. Cover top of custard with greaseproof paper to prevent a skin from forming. Refrigerate until required. Ideal with fruit desserts, such as poached pears, caramelized oranges and fruit compote.
Makes about 300 ml (10 fl oz).

Poached Pears with Passion Fruit Sauce

100% .... 15 minutes

500 ml (16 fl oz) white wine
250 ml (8 fl oz) water
100 ml (3½ fl oz) medium sherry
100 g (3½ oz) caster sugar
rind of ½ lemon
4 firm pears

SAUCE
pulp from 8-10 fresh passion fruit or
   125 g (4 oz) canned passion
   fruit pulp
75 ml (2½ fl oz) water
45 g (1½ oz) caster sugar
5 ml (1 tsp) cornflour
15 ml (1 tbsp) kirsch

DECORATION
8 rose-scented geranium leaves
45 ml (3 tbsp) whipping cream,
   lightly whipped

Combine wine, water, sherry, sugar and lemon rind in a large bowl and microwave on 100% for 5 minutes, stirring twice during cooking time. Pour syrup into a large shallow casserole dish.

Peel pears, halve and remove cores, leaving stalk intact on one side of each pear half. Arrange pears in syrup, thickest side outwards, and cover with vented plastic wrap. Microwave for 3-7 minutes. (The cooking time for pears can vary greatly and depends on the size and type of pear used. The pears should still be firm when removed from the microwave and they are best when cooled in the syrup.) Chill well.

To make sauce: Combine passion fruit pulp, water, sugar and cornflour in a jug and microwave for 2-3 minutes. Stir once during cooking time. Cool, then flavour with kirsch.

To serve: Cut each pear half into about eight slices, leaving stem end intact, and fan pear out with your fingers. Spoon a little of the sauce on to eight plates. Set a fanned pear half in each pool of sauce and finish with a geranium leaf. For a final touch, pipe a zig-zag of cream to one side and drag a cocktail stick through this to give a feathery appearance. Serves 6-8.

Brownie Pizza

A scrumptious combination of chocolate brownie base topped with ice cream, fruit, nuts and chocolate sauce.

100%, 70% .... 12 minutes

185ml (6 fl oz) golden syrup
75 ml (2¹/₂ fl oz) single cream
250 g (9 oz) chocolate chips or plain chocolate, broken into pieces
120 g (4 oz) butter
100 g (3¹/₂ oz) caster sugar
2 eggs
few drops of vanilla extract
90 g (3 oz) plain flour
2.5 ml (¹/₂ tsp) salt
60 g (2 oz) walnuts or pecan nuts, chopped

TO SERVE
sliced strawberries
sliced kiwi fruit
sliced bananas
sliced peaches
chopped walnuts or pecan nuts
vanilla ice cream

Combine syrup and cream in a large glass bowl. Microwave on 100% for 3-4 minutes, stirring twice. Add chocolate and stir to melt.

Set aside 150 ml (5 fl oz) of the chocolate sauce and add butter and sugar to remaining sauce. Mix well. Leave to cool for a few minutes, then beat in eggs and vanilla. Gradually blend in sifted flour, salt and nuts. Pour into a greased and lined 23-cm (9-in) round glass baking dish and microwave on 70% for 4-5 minutes. Check if cooked and microwave for 1-3 minutes more if necessary. Cool in the dish for 5 minutes, then turn out and cool on a rack.

To serve: Cut into wedges and top with fruits, chopped nuts and scoops of ice cream. Drizzle a little of the remaining chocolate sauce over each portion.
Serves 8-10.

Chocolate Slice

This very rich dessert improves with time. Serve very small slices with strong coffee.

70%, 30% .... 7 minutes

1 piece glacé pineapple, roughly chopped
2 glacé apricots, roughly chopped
2 pieces of preserved melon, roughly chopped
125 g (4 oz) glacé cherries, halved
100 ml (3¹/₂ fl oz) dark rum
250 g (9 oz) plain chocolate, broken into pieces
60 ml (4 tbsp) water
2 eggs
60 g (2 oz) caster sugar
125 g (4 oz) butter
250 g (9 oz) shortbread biscuits, broken into pieces
100 g (3¹/₂ oz) mixed nuts, roughly chopped

DECORATION
100 ml (3¹/₂ fl oz) whipping cream, whipped
glacé cherries
nuts

Soak fruit in rum for at least 1 hour. Place chocolate and water in a bowl and microwave for 4-5 minutes on 70%, stirring from time to time. In another bowl, beat eggs well, then beat in sugar.

Microwave butter on 30% for about 2 minutes. (The butter should be very soft but not melted.) Beat butter and chocolate into egg mixture, then stir in remaining ingredients. Spoon mixture into a greased 20-cm (8-in) spring-form pan. Chill for at least 12 hours.

To serve: Remove from pan and decorate with cream rosettes, cherries and nuts.
Serves 10.

Lemon and Strawberry Snow

100%, 50% .... 9 minutes

45 ml (3 tbsp) water
20 ml (4 tsp) powdered gelatine
325 ml (10½ fl oz) water
60 ml (4 tbsp) lemon juice
thinly pared rind of 1 lemon
75 g (2½ oz) caster sugar
20 ml (4 tsp) white wine
2 egg whites
300 g (10 oz) strawberries, washed, hulled and halved

SAUCE
2 egg yolks
75 g (2½ oz) caster sugar
5 ml (1 tsp) cornflour
300 ml (10 fl oz) milk
10 ml (2 tsp) vanilla extract
15 ml (1 tbsp) brandy

Combine 45 ml (3 tbsp) water and gelatine in a small jug. Leave to stand for a few minutes, then microwave on 50% for 45 seconds. Combine 325 ml (10½ fl oz) water, lemon juice, lemon rind and half the sugar in a bowl and microwave on 100% for 2 minutes. Stir in gelatine and strain. Add wine, then refrigerate until liquid becomes consistency of unbeaten egg white. (Stir frequently while chilling.)

Whisk egg whites until just forming soft peaks, then whisk in remaining sugar. (Do not whisk too stiffly.) Fold into gelatine mixture and pour into a rinsed 15-cm (6-in) square cake pan. Spoon strawberries evenly into mixture. Chill until set.

To make sauce: Combine egg yolks, sugar and cornflour in a bowl. Microwave milk on 100% for 2-3 minutes until just boiling, then whisk into yolks. Microwave on 50% for 2-3 minutes, whisking every 30 seconds. Finally, whisk in vanilla and brandy. Chill well.

To serve: Dip pan into hot water for 3 seconds, loosen edges and turn out 'snow' on to a board. Cut into squares. Lift portions on to flat plates, spoon a little sauce over and around and serve.
Serves 4-6.

Milk Tart

100%, 70% .... 13 minutes

1 x 23-cm (9-in) pastry shell, cooked (page 157)
cinnamon sugar to decorate

FILLING
500 ml (16 fl oz) milk
1 small piece of cinnamon stick
30 g (1 oz) butter
75 g (2½ oz) caster sugar
2 eggs, separated
30 ml (2 tbsp) plain flour
30 ml (2 tbsp) cornflour
pinch of salt

Pour milk into a large jug, add cinnamon stick and microwave on 100% for 3-4 minutes until very hot. Using an electric mixer, beat together butter and sugar until pale in colour. Add egg yolks and beat again. Then beat in flour, cornflour and salt.

Remove cinnamon stick from very hot milk and pour milk, little by little, on to egg mixture, stirring well to combine. When combined, pour mixture back into jug or into a large glass bowl and microwave on 70% for 6-7 minutes until well thickened, stirring every 2 minutes.

Whisk egg whites to a soft peaking consistency and fold into mixture. Pour filling into pastry shell and microwave on 70% for about 2 minutes. Leave to cool completely before sprinkling tart with cinnamon sugar.
Serves 6-8.

Hints

• Before adding a moist or juicy filling to an uncooked pastry shell, seal the pastry by brushing it with beaten egg yolk.
• One-crust pies are best for microwave baking. A double-crust pie does not bake properly and the bottom tends to become soggy.

Chocolate Boxes filled with Lemon Mousse

This is a most elegant dessert for a formal dinner party and not as difficult to prepare as it might seem. The chocolate panels are very easy to make but it is essential that cooking chocolate be used as it sets more firmly than dessert chocolate.

100%, 70%, 50%, 30% .... 15 minutes

600 g (1 lb 5 oz) plain cooking chocolate, broken into pieces
45 ml (3 tbsp) whipping cream, whipped, to decorate

MOUSSE
4 eggs, separated
125 g (4 oz) caster sugar
rind of 1 lemon, finely grated
juice of 2 lemons
60 ml (4 tbsp) water
10 ml (2 tsp) powdered gelatine
250 ml (8 fl oz) whipping cream

Place chocolate in a large bowl and microwave on 70% for 8-10 minutes, stirring every 2 minutes. Using a metal spatula, spread chocolate evenly on to waxed paper which has been secured to a tray. (This prevents the paper from curling as the chocolate sets.) When set, but not hard, cut enough 5-cm (2-in) squares to make eight boxes. (You will need five squares per box.)

Return all left-over chocolate to bowl and microwave on 70% to melt again. Then make a paper cone, fill it with melted chocolate and pipe a small decoration on to 32 of the squares. (Make sure the chocolate is completely set before lifting the squares off the paper.)

To assemble: Take five squares, place one square on waxed paper and, using a paint brush, paint melted chocolate along the edges. Secure the other four pieces to the 'base' and paint up the sides to make a perfect box shape. Neaten edges and dry completely. Repeat with the other squares.

Finally, using remaining chocolate and a paper icing bag,

pipe some pieces of chocolate lace on to greaseproof paper as decorations for the finished dessert. Allow 'lace' to dry before peeling off.

To make mousse: Beat egg yolks well, then gradually add sugar. Beat until very thick and pale in colour. Microwave lemon rind and juice on 100% for 45 seconds. Beat into yolk mixture, then microwave on 30% for 3 minutes, beating thoroughly after every minute. Combine water and gelatine and leave to stand for 2 minutes. Microwave on 50% for 45 seconds and beat into yolk mixture.

Half-whip cream and whisk egg whites until of a soft peaking consistency. First fold cream into mixture, then gently fold in egg whites. When well combined, carefully divide mixture between the eight chocolate boxes. Leave mousse to set in refrigerator for at least 2 hours.

Before serving, decorate tops with a swirl of whipped cream and a few pieces of chocolate lace Serves 8.

Hints
• When melting chocolate for use in a cake or dessert, microwave on 100%. When melting chocolate for decorative work or sweet-making, it is best to microwave on a lower power level.
• Chocolate holds its shape even when melted, so stir often during the microwaving time to prevent overheating.
• It does not matter how often chocolate is melted provided it is never overheated. If overheating should occur, the oil in the chocolate will separate out and the chocolate will be unusable.
• Chocolate should be worked at blood temperature. If you do not possess a sugar thermometer to test the temperature, simply dip a finger into the warming chocolate and press a little to your lip. If it feels neither hot nor cold, then it is ready to use.

Almond Cream

Almond Cream

100% .... 5 minutes

250 g (9 oz) blanched almonds
125 g (4 oz) caster sugar
250 ml (8 fl oz) milk
20 ml (4 tsp) powdered gelatine
30 ml (2 tbsp) water
185 ml (6 fl oz) whipping cream
140 ml (14½ fl oz) soured cream
fresh fruit to serve

Place almonds and sugar in a blender and blend until fairly fine. Microwave milk on 100% for 2 minutes, add to almonds and blend again to combine. Cool, then refrigerate overnight.

Next day, strain through a fine sieve, discard almond pulp and microwave almond-flavoured milk for 2½-3 minutes until boiling. Meanwhile, sprinkle gelatine on to water and leave to stand for 2 minutes.

Add boiling milk to gelatine and stir to dissolve. Whip whipping cream until soft peaks form, then fold both fresh and soured cream

into almond mixture. Pour into eight individual moulds or one ring mould. Refrigerate for at least 4 hours.

To serve: Dip each mould into very hot water for 3 seconds, loosen the edge to introduce an air bubble, then turn on to a serving plate or, in the case of individual moulds, on to a fish plate. Serve with fresh fruit, such as slices of mango and strawberries.
Serves 8.

Hint

To blanch almonds: Microwave 250 ml (8 fl oz) water for about 2½ minutes on 100%, or until boiling. Add the almonds and microwave for 30 seconds. Drain, then slip off the skins.

Summer Pudding

For this classic dessert use any of the juicy, soft, berried fruits of summer.

70% .... 7 minutes

2 eggs
60 g (2 oz) caster sugar
few drops of vanilla extract
few drops of almond essence
60 g (2 oz) plain flour
generous pinch of baking powder
5 ml (1 tsp) grated lemon rind
cream to serve

FRUIT MIXTURE
675 g (1½ lb) soft red fruit, such as strawberries, raspberries, red-currants or loganberries
60 g (2 oz) caster sugar
30 ml (2 tbsp) fruit-flavoured liqueur

Beat eggs and sugar with vanilla extract and almond essence until a very pale cream in colour. Sift together flour and baking powder, stir in lemon rind and

fold into egg mixture. Gently turn into a deep, greased and lined 18-cm (7-in) microwave cake dish and microwave on 70% for 3-4 minutes, or until just firm. Leave to stand until cool, then turn out and slice cake horizontally to form three layers.

Take two layers and cut pieces to fit the bottom and sides of a pudding basin. Combine fruits, sugar and liqueur in a dish, cover and microwave on 70% for 3 minutes.

Using a slotted spoon to strain off juice, transfer fruit mixture to prepared basin. Cover with third layer of cake to form a lid and pour fruit juices over pudding. Cover with plastic wrap, then weight the top and refrigerate overnight. Turn out, cut into wedges and serve with cream.
Serves 6.

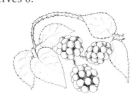

Pineapple Cheesecake

100%, 50%, 30% .... 8 minutes

150 g (5 oz) Nice biscuits, crushed
5 ml (1 tsp) ground cinnamon
75 g (2½ oz) butter

FILLING
400 g (14 oz) canned pineapple
 pieces, drained
30 ml (2 tbsp) kirsch
100 ml (3½ fl oz) canned
 pineapple juice
30 ml (2 tbsp) powdered gelatine
3 egg yolks
125 g (4 oz) caster sugar
125 ml (4 fl oz) water, heated
500 g (18 oz) cream cheese
grated rind of 1 lemon
5 ml (1 tsp) lemon juice
250 ml (8 fl oz) whipping cream
4 egg whites

DECORATION
75 ml (2½ fl oz) whipping cream,
 whipped
pineapple pieces
angelica

Place biscuit crumbs in a bowl and add cinnamon. Microwave butter on 100% for 1-1½ minutes and stir into crumbs. Press biscuit mixture on to base of a spring-form pan.

To make filling: Combine pineapple pieces and kirsch and set aside for 30 minutes. Meanwhile, mix pineapple juice and gelatine in a jug and allow to stand for a few minutes. Place egg yolks in a bowl, beat well, then slowly add sugar and beat continuously for about 5 minutes. Then microwave yolk mixture on 30% for 5 minutes, beating well after every minute. Finally, beat in hot water.

Microwave gelatine on 50% for 1 minute. Stir well and beat into yolk mixture. In a separate bowl, combine cream cheese, lemon rind and juice. Beat thoroughly and add to yolk mixture, combining about one-third at a time. Stir in pineapple pieces.

Whip cream to a soft peaking consistency and fold into cheesecake filling. Whisk egg whites to a peaking consistency and also fold in. Then pour into prepared pan and chill for at least 4 hours.

To remove cheesecake, run a metal spatula around inside edge of pan to loosen sides. Release and remove ring, then, using a large cake or fish slice, lift cake off base. Decorate top with swirls of cream, pieces of pineapple and angelica.
Serves 8-10.

Variation

STRAWBERRY CHEESECAKE
Substitute 300 g (11 oz) strawberries, hulled, washed and halved, for 400 g (14 oz) canned pineapple pieces, and 100 ml (3½ fl oz) strawberry fruit juice for 100 ml (3½ fl oz) water. Decorate with a few whole or halved strawberries.

Note

This cheesecake freezes well for up to one month. Freeze after pouring mixture into the pan. Once frozen, remove cheesecake from pan and wrap carefully in plastic wrap. To thaw, leave cheesecake to stand at room temperature for 4 hours. Decorate with cream and fruit before serving.

Hints

• Using the microwave to dissolve gelatine is so easy, and it is time-saving. Just measure the required liquid in a jug or bowl, sprinkle the gelatine over and leave to stand for a few minutes until softened. Microwave, uncovered, on 50%. The timing will depend on the amount of liquid and gelatine used, but 45-60 seconds is sufficient for 45-90 ml (3-6 tbsp).
• Gelatine mixtures with a high fat content but a low egg white content can be frozen.

Orange Cream Caramel

100%, 50%, 30% ..... 23 minutes

4 eggs
60 g (2 oz) caster sugar
few drops of vanilla extract
500 ml (16 fl oz) milk
100 ml (3½ fl oz) orange-flavoured
liqueur
cream to serve

CARAMEL
45 ml (3 tbsp) sugar
30 ml (2 tbsp) water

In a liquidizer, blend together eggs, caster sugar, vanilla, milk and 60 ml (4 tbsp) of the liqueur. Strain into a jug.

To make caramel: Combine sugar and water in a glass ring dish and microwave on 100% for 3 minutes. Check for colour, then, if necessary, microwave for 2-3 minutes more, or until golden brown.

Then pour egg mixture over caramel and cover with vented plastic wrap. Microwave on 100% for 2 minutes, on 50% for 3 minutes and then on 30% for 8-12 minutes, or until custard begins to set. Remove plastic and cool, then chill well. Turn out on to a plate and pour remaining liqueur over. Serve with cream. Serves 6-8.

Variation
Use a coffee-flavoured liqueur or brandy instead of the orange liqueur.

Floating Islands

100%, 50% .... 21 minutes

250 ml (8 fl oz) milk
1 vanilla pod
3 eggs, separated
pinch of salt
75 g (2½ oz) caster sugar
100 ml (3½ fl oz) single cream
30 ml (2 tbsp) Amaretto liqueur

CARAMEL SYRUP
150 g (5 oz) granulated sugar
100 ml (3½ fl oz) water

Microwave milk and vanilla pod in a shallow casserole on 100% for 3 minutes. Leave to stand for 5 minutes, then remove vanilla pod.

Whisk egg whites with salt until stiff, then gradually whisk in half the sugar. Drop four or five spoonfuls of mixture into milk and microwave for about 1 minute until set. Using a slotted spoon, lift off egg white puffs and drain on absorbent kitchen paper. Repeat until all egg white mixture has been used up (about four batches in all). Strain milk.

Beat egg yolks with remaining sugar until thick and pale in colour. Add strained milk, cream and Amaretto and beat to combine. Pour mixture into a jug and microwave on 50% for 3-4 minutes, whisking every 30 seconds. Place a piece of greaseproof paper directly on top of custard to prevent a skin forming, then chill.

To make caramel syrup: Combine sugar and water in a medium-sized bowl and microwave on 100% for 2 minutes. Stir and brush sides of bowl with a little water to remove sugar crystals. Microwave for a further 6-8 minutes until syrup turns a good, deep caramel colour.

To serve: Pour custard into an attractive shallow dish, float 'islands' on top of custard, drizzle liberally with caramel and sprinkle with nuts. Serve as soon as possible.
Serves 6.

Fresh Fruit Savarin

100% .... 19 minutes

150 ml (5 fl oz) milk
10 g (¼ oz) compressed yeast
30 ml (2 tbsp) caster sugar
250 g (9 oz) plain flour
pinch of salt
100 g (3½ oz) butter
2 eggs, lightly beaten

SYRUP
300 ml (10 fl oz) water
200 g (7 oz) granulated sugar
60 ml (4 tbsp) dark rum or orange-
flavoured liqueur

TO SERVE
125 g (4 oz) apricot jam
500 g (18 oz) fresh fruit, such as
strawberries, grapes or orange
slices
250 ml (8 fl oz) whipping cream,
whipped

Pour milk into a jug and
microwave on 100% for about
15 seconds until it reaches blood-
heat. Add yeast and 5 ml (1 tsp) of
the sugar and stir to combine.
Sprinkle 30 ml (2 tbsp) of the flour
on top of the milk and cover with
plastic wrap. Microwave for
10 seconds, then leave to stand
for 5 minutes. Repeat microwaving and standing times.

Sift remaining flour and salt into
a mixing bowl or work bowl of a
food processor and add
remaining sugar. Microwave
butter for 30 seconds to soften (it
should not be melted) and add to
eggs. Beat lightly and stir in yeast
mixture. Add to flour mixture and
beat thoroughly until a smooth,
soft batter forms. Generously
grease or spray a 23-cm (9-in)
microwave ring mould, turn
batter into mould and cover with
plastic wrap.

Prove mixture by microwaving
for 10 seconds, then leave to stand
for 10 minutes. Repeat this
procedure twice more. (The
mixture should rise to the top of
the mould.) Remove plastic wrap
and microwave savarin dough for
4½-6 minutes until just dry on
top. Leave to stand for 10
minutes, then turn out to cool.

To make syrup: Combine water
and sugar in a jug and microwave
for 10 minutes, stirring after
5 minutes. Cool slightly and add
rum or liqueur. Place a plate
under the warm savarin, spoon
syrup over until it is completely
absorbed. Transfer to a serving
plate and chill.

To serve: Spoon jam into a small
bowl and microwave for
1-2 minutes until warm. Brush top
and sides of savarin with jam,
then arrange fruit around edge
and fill centre with cream.
Serves 8.

Variation

RUM BABA
This is a typical French dessert
using the identical dough to that
used for a savarin but with the
addition of dried fruit. Babas may
be made in small ring moulds,
ramekin dishes or custard cups.
Follow directions for making
a savarin but add to dough: 45 g
(1½ oz) currants and 45 g (1½ oz)
sultanas, soaked in 60 ml (4 tbsp)
rum.

Almond Pastry Cream

Beat together 45 g (1½ oz) well-
softened butter, 30 ml (2 tbsp)
plain flour, 2 egg yolks and 20 ml
(4 tsp) caster sugar. In a jug,
microwave 150 ml (5 fl oz) milk
and 100 ml (3½ fl oz) single
cream on 100% for 2 minutes.
Pour on to yolk mixture, beating
continuously until smooth. Add
45 g (1½ oz) crumbled almond
paste and microwave on 50% for
2-3 minutes, whisking every
minute until well thickened and
smooth. Stir in 30 g (1 oz)
chopped toasted almonds (page
36) just before serving. (If this
cream is to be served cold, cover
the surface with greaseproof
paper once it is cooked to prevent
a skin from forming.)

This pastry cream is an excellent
accompaniment to savarin and an
alternative to fresh fruit. Makes
about 450 ml (15 fl oz).

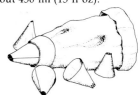

Pumpkin and Mincemeat Cheesecake

100%, 70%, 50% ..... 33 minutes

125 g (4 oz) Marie biscuit crumbs
30 g (1 oz) soft brown sugar
2.5 ml (¹/₂ tsp) ground cinnamon
60 g (2 oz) butter
whipped cream to decorate

APPLE FRUIT MINCEMEAT
4 cooking apples, peeled and cored
75 g (2¹/₂ oz) raisins
125 g (4 oz) soft brown sugar
250 ml (8 fl oz) dry white wine
2.5 ml (¹/₂ tsp) ground cinnamon
2.5 ml (¹/₂ tsp) ground cloves
2.5 ml (¹/₂ tsp) grated nutmeg
2.5 ml (¹/₂ tsp) ground ginger
60 g (2 oz) butter
60 ml (4 tbsp) brandy

FILLING
500 g (18 oz) cream cheese
100 g (3¹/₂ oz) caster sugar
2 eggs
2 egg yolks
30 ml (2 tbsp) plain flour

2.5 ml (¹/₂ tsp) ground cinnamon
2.5 ml (¹/₂ tsp) ground ginger
generous pinch of ground cloves
generous pinch of grated nutmeg
125 ml (4 fl oz) single cream
few drops of vanilla extract
250 g (9 oz) pumpkin, cooked
   and mashed

Combine biscuit crumbs, sugar
and cinnamon. Microwave butter
in a bowl on 100% for 1 minute,
then add to crumb mixture,
stirring well to combine. Press
into the base of a 25-cm (10-in)
round glass baking dish and chill.
   To make apple mincemeat:
Chop apples and combine with
raisins, sugar and wine.
Microwave on 100% for
3 minutes. Stir in spices, butter
and brandy, then microwave on
50% for 12-15 minutes, or until
apples are tender and liquid has
been reduced by about half. Cool
mixture to room temperature.
   To make filling: In a large bowl,
combine cream cheese, sugar,
eggs and egg yolks and beat until
smooth. Add flour sifted with
cinnamon, ginger, cloves and

nutmeg, then add cream, vanilla
and mashed pumpkin. Mix
thoroughly. Microwave filling on
70% for about 8 minutes, stirring
every 2 minutes.
   Drain mincemeat and spread
over crust. Pour cheesecake filling
over mincemeat and microwave
on 50% for 4-6 minutes, or until
mixture begins to set. Cool to
room temperature, then chill
well. Top with whipped cream,
if desired.
Serves 12.

Syrups and Sauces for Fruit Salads

RED WINE SYRUP
Combine 45 ml (3 tbsp) soft
brown sugar with 90 ml (3 fl oz)
red wine and microwave on 50%
for 1¹/₂ minutes. Stir to dissolve
sugar, then cool. Pour over sliced
strawberries and kiwi fruit.
Makes about 125 ml (4 fl oz).

MINTY CITRUS SAUCE
Combine 250 ml (8 fl oz) orange
juice, 45 ml (3 tbsp) lemon juice,
45 ml (3 tbsp) sugar and 15 ml
(1 tbsp) chopped mint. Microwave on 50% for 2 minutes. Cool,
strain and pour over melon balls.
Makes about 350 ml (11 fl oz).

ORANGE AND RUM SAUCE
Combine 250 ml (8 fl oz) orange
juice, 45 ml (3 tbsp) light rum and
10 ml (2 tsp) orange zest. Microwave on 50% for 2 minutes. Cool,
then pour over blueberries,
grapes and melon balls. Makes
about 300 ml (10 fl oz).

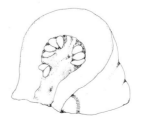

Sherry Cream Soufflé

50% .... 1 minute

30 ml (2 tbsp) powdered gelatine
125 ml (4 fl oz) water
375 ml (12 fl oz) medium sherry
6 eggs, separated
175 g (6 oz) caster sugar
15 ml (1 tbsp) lemon juice
250 ml (8 fl oz) whipping cream

DECORATION
whipped cream
chopped nuts
1 crystallized flower

Sprinkle gelatine over water in a glass measuring jug and leave to stand for 5 minutes. Microwave for 1 minute on 50% to dissolve gelatine. Add sherry, mixing well, then leave mixture to cool until it is the consistency of unbeaten egg white.

Whisk egg whites until frothy, then gradually whisk in 125 g (4 oz) of the sugar. Add lemon juice and continue whisking until egg whites are stiff.

Beat egg yolks until frothy. Add remaining sugar and beat until thick. Add slightly thickened sherry mixture to yolk mixture. Whip cream and fold into yolk mixture. Fold in a quarter of the egg whites, then fold in the remainder. Spoon mixture into a 23-cm (9-in) soufflé dish with a deep waxed paper collar attached. Chill for 3-4 hours.

To serve: Pipe whipped cream stars around top of soufflé, remove collar and pat chopped nuts around sides. Place a crystallized flower in the centre. Keep refrigerated until required. Serves 10-12.

Hint

To prepare a soufflé dish: Cut a piece of waxed paper long enough to wrap around the dish. Fold it in half, waxed side outwards, and wrap the paper around the outside of the dish. Tie with string just under the lip of the dish and smooth the edges of the paper before filling with soufflé mixture.

Fresh Fruit Mousse

50% .... 1 minute

45 ml (3 tbsp) water
10 ml (2 tsp) powdered gelatine
200 ml (6½ fl oz) fresh fruit purée, such as mango, plum or nectarine
45 ml (3 tbsp) sweet white wine
60 g (2 oz) caster sugar
250 ml (8 fl oz) whipping cream
3 egg whites

DECORATION
75 ml (2½ fl oz) whipping cream, whipped
fresh fruit slices

Pour water into a jug and add gelatine. Stir and allow to stand for 1-2 minutes, then microwave on 50% for 1 minute, stirring once. Combine purée, wine and half the sugar. Stir in hot gelatine.

Whip cream until soft peaks form and set aside. Whisk egg whites to a soft peaking consistency, add remaining sugar and whisk again. Then carefully fold cream into fruit mixture, followed by egg whites.

Pour mousse into a glass serving dish or individual bowls and refrigerate for at least 2 hours. Before serving, decorate with swirls of stiffly whipped cream and slices of fresh fruit.
Serves 6-8.

Hints

• Do not use fresh pineapple or paw paw in a gelatine dish without cooking the fruit first.
• When microwaving over-ripe fruits, do not use any additional liquid as these fruits are easily puréed to make delicious toppings or bases for ice cream.

Rich Bread Pudding

100%, 70%, 50% ..... 19 minutes

60 g (2 oz) butter
300 g (11 oz) bread, broken into
  pieces, or mixture of cake
  and bread, broken into pieces
250 ml (8 fl oz) single cream
300 ml (10 fl oz) milk
45 ml (3 tbsp) peach-flavoured
  liqueur
125 g (4 oz) caster sugar
2-3 eggs, beaten
45 g (1½ oz) raisins or sultanas
60 ml (4 tbsp) desiccated coconut
45 g (1½ oz) pecan nuts or
  walnuts, chopped
2.5 ml (½ tsp) ground cinnamon
pinch of grated nutmeg

SAUCE
60 g (2 oz) butter
60 g (2 oz) icing sugar
1 small egg yolk
60 ml (4 tbsp) brandy

Place butter in a large bowl and
microwave on 100% for 1 minute.
Add all ingredients and mix well
to combine. (The mixture should
be very moist, but not sloppy.)
Turn into a greased baking dish
and microwave on 70% for
5 minutes. Stir mixture gently
and microwave for 3 minutes
more. Leave to stand for 10
minutes, then microwave on 50%
for a further 6-8 minutes, or until
just set. Leave to stand for
another 10 minutes.
  To make sauce: Beat together
butter and icing sugar and
microwave for about 2 minutes on
70%, stirring every 30 seconds.
Beat well, then gradually beat in
egg yolk. Stir in brandy and set
aside to cool.
  To serve: Sprinkle pudding with
icing sugar and brown under a
hot grill. Serve sauce separately.
Serves 8.

Hint
**To add extra flavour to a quick
bread pudding, include left-over
cake, chopped up biscuits and even
chopped up chocolate, or try fruit-
flavoured liqueurs such as banana
or apricot.**

Baked Apples with Fig Filling

70% .... 15 minutes

75 g (2½ oz) dried figs
75 g (2½ oz) whole blanched
  almonds, toasted (page 36)
45 g (1½ oz) raisins
30 ml (2 tbsp) aniseed-flavoured
  liqueur
5 ml (1 tsp) aniseed
5 ml (1 tsp) grated orange rind
5 ml (1 tsp) ground cinnamon
2.5 ml (½ tsp) ground cloves
6 firm ripe apples
125 ml (4 fl oz) maple syrup
60 ml (4 tbsp) aniseed-flavoured
  liqueur
125 ml (4 fl oz) water
60 ml (4 tbsp) lemon juice
whipped cream to serve

Soak figs in water to cover for
30 minutes, then drain. Place figs
in a food processor. Set aside
12 almonds and add remainder to
processor. Add raisins, 30 ml
(2 tbsp) liqueur, aniseed, orange
rind, cinnamon and cloves.
Process to a paste.
  Core apples, remove top 2.5 cm
(½-in) of the skin and pierce
several times with a skewer. Fill
apples with fig mixture and place
in a deep baking dish. Top each
with two reserved almonds,
pressing them into the filling.
  Combine maple syrup,
remaining 60 ml (4 tbsp) liqueur,
water and lemon juice and pour
into dish. Spoon sauce over
apples and microwave on 70% for
about 15 minutes, or until tender,
basting occasionally. Allow to
cool before serving either warm or
at room temperature with
whipped cream.
Serves 6.

Baked Stuffed Peaches

70% .... 5 minutes

800 g (1 lb 14 oz) canned peach
  halves
100 g (3½ oz) mincemeat
45 ml (3 tbsp) Cointreau or brandy
45 ml (3 tbsp) finely grated orange
  rind
2.5 ml (½ tsp) ground cinnamon
45 ml (3 tbsp) toasted almonds
  (page 36), chopped
200 ml (6½ fl oz) orange juice
ice cream to serve (optional)

Drain peach halves, reserving
juice. Arrange peaches in a
shallow, microwaveproof serving
dish. Combine mincemeat,
liqueur or brandy, orange rind,
cinnamon and almonds,
moistened slightly with a little
orange juice. Spoon a generous
amount into each peach half.
  Mix remaining orange juice with
about 200 ml (6½ fl oz) of the
reserved peach juice. Pour into
dish. Cover and microwave on
70% for 4-5 minutes until piping
hot. Serve with ice cream if
desired.
Serves 4-6.

Wine-poached Mangoes

100%, 50% .... 25 minutes

750 ml (1¼ pints) dry white wine
150 g (5 oz) caster sugar
2.5-cm (½-in) piece of cinnamon
  stick
2.5 ml (½ tsp) whole black
  peppercorns
2.5 ml (½ tsp) grated orange rind
2.5 ml (½ tsp) grated lemon rind
4 half-ripe, medium-sized
  mangoes, peeled
15 ml (1 tbsp) fresh basil leaves,
  cut into strips

In a large casserole, combine
wine, sugar, cinnamon stick,
peppercorns, orange and lemon
rind and microwave on 100% for
5 minutes. Stir to dissolve sugar
and microwave for 5 minutes
more. Add mangoes, reduce
power to 50% and microwave for
3-5 minutes, or until tender.
Transfer mangoes to shallow
serving bowls.
  Microwave poaching syrup on
100% for 10 minutes. Discard
cinnamon stick. Spoon syrup over
mangoes. Serve warm, decorated
with strips of basil.
Serves 4.

Hot Fruit Salad Sauce

Fruity Rice Pudding

100%, 30% .... 35 minutes

60 g (2 oz) short-grain or
 pudding rice
400 ml (13 fl oz) water, boiling
generous pinch of grated nutmeg
1 strip of lemon rind
10 ml (2 tsp) lemon juice
45 ml (3 tbsp) caster sugar
185 ml (6 fl oz) evaporated milk
few drops of vanilla extract
15 g (¹/₂ oz) butter
45 g (1¹/₂ oz) raisins
45 g (1¹/₂ oz) sultanas
15 g (¹/₂ oz) dried apricots,
 chopped
125 ml (4 fl oz) whipping cream,
 whipped

Place rice, water, nutmeg, lemon
rind and juice in a large, deep jug.
Cover with vented plastic wrap
and microwave on 100% for
10 minutes. Leave to stand for
about 10 minutes, then remove
lemon rind.
 Add sugar, evaporated milk and
vanilla extract. Microwave on
defrost or 30% for 20 minutes,
stirring occasionally. Add butter,
raisins, sultanas and apricots.
Microwave for a further
5 minutes. Leave to cool for about
5 minutes, then fold in whipped
cream and serve while still warm.
Serves 4.

Hints
• Perk up a plain rice pudding by
adding 75 g (2¹/₂ oz) chopped,
stoned dates or 150 g (5 oz) chopped
pineapple to the mixture.
• To give a thicker consistency to a
plain rice pudding and to enhance
the flavour, stir 45 ml (3 tbsp)
instant caramel pudding mixture
into the liquid.

Hot Fruit Salad Sauce

100% .... 18 minutes

400 g (14 oz) canned apricot halves
400 g (14 oz) canned peach halves
400 g (14 oz) canned pineapple
 chunks
400 g (14 oz) canned, stoned black
 cherries
small piece of cinnamon stick
100 ml (3¹/₂ fl oz) orange-
 flavoured liqueur
60 ml (4 tbsp) cornflour

Pour undrained fruit into a large
casserole dish. Add cinnamon
stick, cover and microwave on
100% for 12 minutes. Remove
cinnamon stick.
 Combine liqueur and cornflour.
Stir a little hot liquid into
cornflour mixture, then pour
cornflour mixture on to fruit and
stir well. Microwave, covered, on
100% for 6 minutes, stirring fruit
mixture every 2 minutes. Serve
hot over ice cream or squares of
plain cake.
Serves 10-12.

Bananas Foster

100% .... 5 minutes

60 g (2 oz) butter
200 g (7 oz) soft brown sugar
2.5 ml (¹/₂ tsp) ground cinnamon
60 ml (4 tbsp) banana-flavoured
 liqueur
30 ml (2 tbsp) orange juice
4 bananas, cut in half lengthways
 and halved
60 ml (4 tbsp) rum
vanilla ice cream to serve

In an attractive bowl or casserole
dish, microwave butter on 100%
for 45 seconds. Add sugar,
cinnamon, liqueur and orange
juice. Stir to mix, then microwave
for 2-3 minutes, stirring
frequently. Add bananas and
spoon sauce over. Microwave for
1 minute more, then remove from
oven. Pour rum over bananas and
flame. Serve over vanilla ice
cream.
Serves 4.

Hot Strawberry Crêpes

100%, 50% .... 11 minutes

125 ml (4 fl oz) water
60 g (2 oz) caster sugar
600 g (1 lb 5 oz) strawberries, washed and hulled
60 ml (4 tbsp) orange-flavoured liqueur
12-14 crêpes (page 132)
thinly pared orange rind, cut in julienne, to decorate

FILLING
250 g (9 oz) cream cheese
5 ml (1 tsp) finely grated orange rind
100 ml (3½ fl oz) cream
30 ml (2 tbsp) caster sugar

Combine water and 60 g (2 oz) caster sugar in a large jug and microwave on 100% for 5 minutes, stirring at least twice during this time. Cool slightly, then pour into a blender. Add about half the strawberries and all the liqueur. Blend until smooth. Set aside.

To make filling: Beat cream cheese, orange rind, cream and 30 ml (2 tbsp) caster sugar together. Reserving a few strawberries for decoration, slice or quarter remaining strawberries and stir into cream cheese mixture.

Place a good spoonful of filling on one side of each crêpe. Roll up and place in a shallow microwave-proof serving dish. Cover and microwave on 50% for 3-4 minutes. Reheat sauce on 100% for 1-2 minutes and pour over the top. Decorate with a few strawberries and strips of orange rind.
Serves 6.

Date Dessert

70%, 50% .... 12 minutes

90 g (3 oz) plain flour
2.5 ml (½ tsp) bicarbonate of soda
pinch of salt
100 g (3½ oz) soft brown sugar
60 g (2 oz) butter, softened
2 eggs
few drops of vanilla extract
125 ml (4 fl oz) soured cream
125 g (4 oz) dates, stoned and chopped
60 ml (4 tbsp) chopped pecan nuts

TOPPING
125 ml (4 fl oz) soured cream
45 ml (3 tbsp) double cream
45 ml (3 tbsp) soft brown sugar

Sift flour, bicarbonate of soda and salt into the bowl of an electric mixer or food processor. Add sugar, butter, eggs, vanilla extract and soured cream and mix well, then stir in dates and pecans.

Pour mixture into a deep, greased 25-cm (10-in) pie plate.

Place pie plate on top of an inverted saucer and microwave on 50% for 6 minutes, then on 70% for a further 5 minutes. Remove from microwave and leave to cool for 10 minutes before pouring cream topping over.

Make topping by combining all ingredients in a bowl and microwaving on 50% for 30 seconds. When dessert has cooled sufficiently, pour topping over and serve warm.
Serves 6-8.

Variation
As an alternative to the soured cream topping, serve this dessert with:

BUTTERMILK SAUCE
In a large jug, combine 200 g (7 oz) sugar, 2.5 ml (½ tsp) bicarbonate of soda, 25 ml (5 tsp) maple syrup, 100 ml (3½ fl oz) buttermilk and 100 g (3½ oz) butter. Microwave on 100% for 3-4 minutes. Pour a little of the hot sauce over each portion and serve remaining sauce separately.

Date and Brandy Tart

70% .... 18 minutes

250 g (9 oz) dates, stoned and
  chopped
75 g (2¹/₂ oz) sultanas
5 ml (1 tsp) bicarbonate of soda
250 ml (8 fl oz) water, boiling
2 eggs
200 g (7 oz) caster sugar
60 g (2 oz) butter
200 g (7 oz) plain flour
75 g (2¹/₂ oz) pecan nuts, chopped

SAUCE
175 g (2¹/₂ oz) soft brown sugar
15 g (¹/₂ oz) butter
250 ml (8 fl oz) water, boiling
few drops of vanilla extract
125 ml (4 fl oz) brandy

Place dates, sultanas, bicarbonate
of soda and boiling water in a
bowl. Stir to mix and set aside to
cool. Beat eggs well, add half the
sugar and beat again until thick
and creamy. In a separate bowl,
cream butter and remaining sugar
until light and fluffy. Stir in egg
mixture and beat to combine, then
add date mixture and stir well.
  Next, sift flour and add to
mixture, about one-third at a
time, mixing well after each
addition. Finally, stir in nuts.
Pour mixture into a greased 23-cm
(9-in) dish or pie plate and
microwave on 70% for
13-15 minutes. Leave to stand for
10 minutes before pouring sauce
over.
  To make sauce: Place all
ingredients in a jug and microwave on 70% for 2-3 minutes,
stirring at least once to dissolve
sugar. Carefully pour sauce over
hot tart. (All the sauce should be
absorbed.) Serve warm with
cream.
Serves 6-8.

Basic Custard

Pour 500 ml (16 fl oz) milk into a
large jug, saving a little to mix
with the custard powder.
Microwave milk, uncovered, on
100% for 4 minutes. Combine
remaining milk with 30 ml
(2 tbsp) custard powder and
30 ml (2 tbsp) sugar. Mix well.
Pour a little hot milk into custard
mixture, mix again, then pour
into hot milk, stirring constantly.
Microwave for a further
3 minutes, stirring every minute.
Makes about 500 ml (16 fl oz).

Shortcrust Pastry

100% .... 6 minutes

125 g (4 oz) plain flour
2.5 ml (½ tsp) salt
5 ml (1 tsp) caster sugar
60 g (2 oz) butter
1 egg yolk
45 ml (3 tbsp) water, ice cold

Combine flour, salt and sugar. Rub in butter until mixture resembles fine crumbs. Combine egg yolk and water and add enough to dry ingredients to form a dough. Turn pastry on to a lightly floured surface and knead gently, then roll out and use as desired.

To microwave pastry shells: Line pie plate with pastry and trim edges. Cut a long foil strip, about 3 cm (1¼ in) wide, and cover edge of pastry shell to prevent overcooking. Prick pastry with a fork if it is to be used with a chilled filling. Place a double layer of absorbent kitchen paper in the base of the shell, pressing gently into the edges. Scatter a layer of dry beans on top to prevent pastry from rising as it cooks. Microwave on 100% for 3½-4 minutes.

Remove beans, foil and absorbent kitchen paper and microwave pastry for 1½-2 minutes more. Cool pie shell before using. Use cooked pastry shells for pies and tarts with cold or uncooked fillings.
Makes 1 x 23-cm (9-in) pie crust.

Variations

HERB PASTRY
Omit sugar and add 5 ml (1 tsp) dried mixed herbs, or herbs of your choice.

CHEESE PASTRY
Omit sugar, add a generous pinch of dry mustard to dry ingredients and stir in 45 ml (3 tbsp) grated cheese after rubbing in butter.

SWEET PASTRY
Increase sugar to 45 ml (3 tbsp), add a few drops of vanilla extract and proceed as for shortcrust pastry.

Butterscotch Meringue

100%, 70% .... 9 minutes

1 x 20-cm (8-in) shortcrust pastry
shell
200 g (7 oz) soft brown sugar
30 g (1 oz) plain flour
45 ml (3 tbsp) cornflour
200 ml (6½ fl oz) milk
3 eggs, separated
45 g (1½ oz) butter
few drops of vanilla extract
75 g (2½ oz) chocolate chips
1 extra egg white
generous pinch of cream of tartar
60 ml (4 tbsp) caster sugar

First, prepare and pre-cook pastry shell. Then, combine soft brown sugar, plain flour, cornflour and milk in a large jug. Stir well to combine and microwave on 100% for 4 minutes, stirring every minute. (The mixture should be thick when cooked.)

Beat in egg yolks, butter and vanilla extract. Cover mixture with a piece of greaseproof paper to prevent lumps from forming.

Stir from time to time until mixture is cool, then stir in chocolate chips and turn into pie shell.

Whisk all 4 egg whites with cream of tartar until of a peaking consistency, then gradually whisk in sugar. Spoon on top of filling and microwave on 70% for 5 minutes. Brown very quickly under a preheated grill. Serve warm.
Serves 6-8.

Hint

Shortcrust pastry is tender and flaky when baked in the microwave but it does not brown. To give a good appearance, brush the pastry before baking with a little egg yolk or vanilla extract mixed with water, or add a few drops of yellow food colouring to the liquid when making the dough.

Peach and Cinnamon Crumble

70% .... 16 minutes

125 g (4 oz) butter
125 g (4 oz) soft brown sugar
grated rind of 1 lemon
4 egg yolks
100 g (3½ oz) plain flour
75 g (2½ oz) wholemeal flour
2.5 ml (½ tsp) salt
7.5 ml (1½ tsp) baking powder
800 g (1 lb 14 oz) canned peach
  slices, drained

TOPPING
100 g (3½ oz) plain flour
75 g (2½ oz) wholemeal flour
2.5 ml (½ tsp) ground cinnamon
generous pinch of grated nutmeg
pinch of ground cloves
90 g (3 oz) soft brown sugar
125 g (4 oz) butter, cubed

Cream butter and sugar with
lemon rind until light and fluffy.
Beat in egg yolks, one at a time.
Sift together dry ingredients and

gently fold into creamed mixture.
Spread in the base of a greased
23-cm (9-in) baking dish. Arrange
peach slices on top of mixture.
  To make topping: Combine
flours and spices and stir in sugar.
Rub in butter until mixture is
crumbly, then sprinkle evenly
over peaches. Microwave on 70%
for 14-16 minutes. Leave to stand
for a few minutes before cutting
into wedges. Serve warm.
Serves 6-8.

Variation
APPLE CRUMBLE
Combine 400 g (14 oz) canned pie
apples with 60 g (2 oz) sultanas,
30 g (1 oz) chopped nuts, 5 ml
(1 tsp) grated lemon rind, 15 ml
(1 tbsp) lemon juice and 30 ml
(2 tbsp) brandy. Use this mixture
as the base of the recipe and
proceed as above.

Chocolate and Cherry Baked Pudding

100%, 70% .... 14 minutes

400 g (14 oz) canned, stoned black
  cherries, drained
100 g (3½ oz) butter
75 g (2½ oz) caster sugar
2 eggs
few drops of vanilla extract
90 g (3 oz) plain flour
30 ml (2 tbsp) cocoa powder
5 ml (1 tsp) baking powder
salt
60 ml (4 tbsp) milk

SAUCE
125 g (4 oz) soft brown sugar
345 ml (11 fl oz) water
30 ml (2 tbsp) cocoa powder
2.5 ml (½ tsp) grated orange rind
30 ml (2 tbsp) kirsch or brandy

Grease a 1.5-litre (2¾-pint)
straight-sided casserole or soufflé
dish and pour in cherries. Cream
butter and sugar together until
light and fluffy. Add eggs and

vanilla extract and beat again. Sift
together dry ingredients and add
to creamed mixture alternately
with the milk. Spoon over
cherries.
  To make sauce: Combine all
ingredients in a jug and
microwave on 100% for
2 minutes. Stir to dissolve sugar,
then pour over pudding mixture.
Microwave on 70% for
10-12 minutes. Leave to stand for
10 minutes before serving hot
with cream or ice cream.
Serves 6-8.

Hot Plum Topping

100% .... 11 minutes

1 small piece of cinnamon stick
250 ml (8 fl oz) water
75 ml (2½ fl oz) white muscatel
100 g (3½ oz) caster sugar
4 cloves
1 strip of orange rind
6-8 red or yellow plums,
  quartered and stoned
10 ml (2 tsp) cornflour
30 ml (2 tbsp) rum or brandy
30 ml (2 tbsp) water
ice cream to serve

Combine cinnamon stick, water, muscatel, sugar, cloves and orange rind in a casserole dish. Microwave on 100% for 4 minutes, then add plums and cover with vented plastic wrap. Microwave for 4-5 minutes more. (The plums should be tender but not soft.) Remove plums from syrup and set aside. Remove cinnamon stick and cloves and discard.

Combine cornflour, rum and water. Stir into syrup and microwave for 1-2 minutes until bubbly and slightly thickened. Return plums to sauce and microwave for 1-2 minutes until heated through. Serve spooned over ice cream.
Serves 4.

Hot Strawberries

100% .... 11 minutes

125 g (4 oz) caster sugar
60 ml (4 tbsp) water
45 ml (3 tbsp) brandy
60 ml (4 tbsp) lemon juice
200 ml (6½ fl oz) orange juice
12 black peppercorns, cracked
600 g (1 lb 5 oz) strawberries,
  washed and hulled
vanilla ice cream to serve

Combine sugar and water in a bowl and microwave on 100% for 1 minute. Stir to dissolve sugar, then microwave for 3-4 minutes more until syrup is a good golden colour. Carefully remove bowl from microwave as it will be very hot. Then add brandy, fruit juice and peppercorns. Stir to combine. (The mixture may be a bit stringy at this point.)

Microwave for 3-4 minutes, stirring every minute, until sugar re-dissolves. Stir in strawberries and microwave for 2 minutes. Serve hot over ice cream.
Serves 4.

Layered Fruit Christmas Pudding

100%, 50% .... 22 minutes

175 g (6 oz) butter
175 g (6 oz) soft brown sugar
2 eggs
15 ml (1 tbsp) golden syrup
30 ml (2 tbsp) orange juice
few drops of rum essence or
  10 ml (2 tsp) dark rum
250 g (9 oz) plain flour
15 ml (1 tbsp) baking powder
2.5 ml (¹/₂ tsp) salt
30 ml (2 tbsp) grated orange rind

FRUIT FILLING
60 g (2 oz) butter
60 g (2 oz) soft brown sugar
2 apples, peeled, cored and grated
100 g (3¹/₂ oz) raisins or sultanas
30 ml (2 tbsp) chopped glacé
  cherries
45 g (1¹/₂ oz) pecan nuts or
  hazelnuts, chopped
45 ml (3 tbsp) chopped mixed peel
4 eggs, separated
5 ml (1 tsp) mixed spice

2.5 ml (¹/₂ tsp) ground cinnamon
2.5 ml (¹/₂ tsp) grated nutmeg
generous pinch of ground cloves
generous pinch of ground allspice

Cream butter and sugar until light and fluffy. Combine eggs, golden syrup, orange juice and rum and beat into creamed mixture. Combine flour, baking powder and salt. Sift and fold into mixture together with grated orange rind.

To make filling: Combine butter and sugar in a large bowl and microwave on 100% for 2 minutes. Stir to dissolve sugar. Add remaining ingredients and mix well.

To assemble: Grease a deep pudding basin or glass bowl and line with plastic wrap. Grease the plastic wrap. Spread a little sponge mixture in the bottom of the bowl, then top with a little of the fruit mixture, spreading evenly. Repeat layers, ending with sponge, making four layers of sponge mixture and three layers of fruit filling.

Cover loosely with plastic wrap and microwave on 100% for

12-15 minutes. (If the top is done before the bottom, cover with foil and microwave for 1 minute more.) Cool for about 20 minutes in the bowl before turning out on to a serving plate. Reheat when required on 50% for 3-4 minutes. To serve, cut in wedges and top with Rum and Orange Sauce. Serves 8-10.

Hint

Traditional Christmas pudding cooks well in the microwave and in a fraction of the time taken to cook it conventionally. The microwave is also the ideal medium for reheating Christmas pudding. Just sprinkle with a little brandy and cover the bowl with vented plastic wrap, then microwave on 50% for 10 minutes. Leave to stand for 3-4 minutes before turning out.

Remember not to include anything metallic in the pudding, such as foil-wrapped charms or coins, until the pudding is ready to serve.

Rum and Orange Sauce

100% .... 3 minutes

150 ml (5 fl oz) orange juice
30 ml (2 tbsp) lemon juice
grated rind of 1 orange
5 ml (1 tsp) cornflour
30 ml (2 tbsp) golden syrup
30 ml (2 tbsp) soft brown sugar
15-30 ml (1-2 tbsp) dark rum

Combine orange juice, lemon juice and orange rind in a bowl or jug. Blend a little of the liquid into the cornflour, then pour cornflour mixture into remaining liquid. Mix in golden syrup, soft brown sugar and rum. Microwave, covered, on 100% for 3 minutes, stirring every 30 seconds. Makes about 250 ml (8 fl oz).

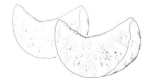

Honeyed Pear Cake

Honeyed Pear Cake

100% .... 7 minutes
Plus combination baking

60 ml (4 tbsp) thin honey
30 g (1 oz) butter
generous pinch of ground
 cinnamon
pinch of ground cloves
5 ml (1 tsp) grated lemon rind
15 ml (1 tbsp) lemon juice
15 ml (1 tbsp) brandy
4 large pears, peeled, cored and
 sliced

TOPPING
100 g (3½ oz) butter
75 g (2½ oz) caster sugar
2 eggs
100 g (3½ oz) ground almonds
few drops of vanilla extract
30 ml (2 tbsp) plain flour

Place honey and butter in a 23-cm
(9-in) pie plate. Microwave on
100% for 2 minutes. Stir well and
add cinnamon, cloves, lemon rind
and lemon juice. Microwave for a
further 2 minutes. Stir in brandy

and pears and microwave for 3
minutes.
   To make topping: Cream butter
and sugar thoroughly. Add eggs
one at a time, beating well after
each addition. Carefully fold in
ground almonds, vanilla extract
and plain flour. Spread mixture
over pears and bake according to
instructions below. Serve warm
with cream or custard.

BROTHER
Hi-Speed at 160 °C for 10 minutes,
then on Convection for 3-4
minutes.

Serves 6-8.

Apricot and Almond Crumble

100% .... 6 minutes

250 g (9 oz) dried apricots,
 quartered
1 small piece of cinnamon stick
1 strip of lemon rind
250 ml (8 fl oz) water
30 ml (2 tbsp) orange-flavoured
 liqueur
60 ml (4 tbsp) caster sugar,
 or to taste
60 g (2 oz) stale cake crumbs
cream to serve

TOPPING
75 g (2½ oz) soft brown sugar
45 ml (3 tbsp) rolled oats
60 g (2 oz) plain flour
45 g (1½ oz) ground almonds
75 g (2½ oz) butter

Place apricots, cinnamon stick,
lemon rind, water, liqueur and
sugar in a bowl. Cover with
vented plastic wrap and
microwave on 100% for

2 minutes. Leave to stand for
10 minutes, then remove
cinnamon stick and lemon rind.
Divide cake crumbs between six
ramekins and spoon some of the
apricot mixture into each.
   To make topping: Combine all
ingredients, mix until crumbly,
then sprinkle over apricots.
Arrange ramekins in a circle in
microwave oven and microwave
on 100% for 4 minutes. Leave to
stand for a few minutes, then
serve warm with cream.
Serves 6.

Sherry Cream Sauce

Mix 30 ml (2 tbsp) cornflour and
60 ml (4 tbsp) sugar in a large
bowl. Stir in 250 ml (8 fl oz)
sherry and 500 ml (16 fl oz) single
cream. Microwave on 70% for 5-6
minutes, stirring every minute
until mixture thickens and begins
to bubble. Remove from heat and
stir in a few drops of vanilla
extract. Serve warm or chilled.
(This sauce is delicious with
baked fruit, such as apples, and
other warm puddings.) Makes
about 750 ml (1¼ pints).

Rich Devil's Food Cake

100%, 30% .... 16 minutes

125 g (4 oz) butter
400 g (14 oz) caster sugar
3 eggs, separated
125 ml (4 fl oz) soured cream
5 ml (1 tsp) bicarbonate of soda
60 ml (4 tbsp) cocoa powder
185 ml (6 fl oz) water, boiling
15 ml (1 tbsp) vanilla extract
250 g (9 oz) plain flour
pinch of salt

ICING
300 g (11 oz) icing sugar
45 g (1½ oz) cocoa powder
pinch of salt
60 g (2 oz) butter
few drops of vanilla extract
30 ml (2 tbsp) milk

Cream butter and sugar together, then add egg yolks and beat well. Combine soured cream and bicarbonate of soda, stir until soda is dissolved and mix into butter mixture. Dissolve cocoa powder in boiling water and add to butter mixture. Stir in vanilla, then add sifted flour and salt. Mix well. Finally, whisk egg whites to stiff peaks and fold into batter.

Pour batter into a greased 25-cm (10-in) microwave ring pan and microwave on 30% for 7 minutes, then on 100% for 5-8 minutes. Leave to stand in pan for 10 minutes before turning out to cool on a wire rack.

To make icing: Sift icing sugar, cocoa powder and salt and combine with butter and vanilla. Mix thoroughly. Microwave milk for 30 seconds on 100% and add to mixture. Beat until smooth and spread over cooled cake.
Makes 1 x 25-cm (10-in) ring cake.

Hints
• Greasing and flouring containers for microwave baking will result in a doughy, sticky coating on the outside of the cake. Prepare containers by spraying or lightly greasing only.
• Line cake containers with waxed paper or absorbent kitchen paper and sprinkle greased containers with finely chopped nuts or finely crushed sweet biscuit crumbs so that the cakes will turn out easily.

Pineapple Upside-down Cake

100% .... 12 minutes

150 g (5 oz) plain flour
150 g (5 oz) caster sugar
10 ml (2 tsp) baking powder
2.5 ml (½ tsp) salt
1 egg
60 g (2 oz) butter, softened
reserved pineapple syrup plus milk
  to make up 125 ml (4 fl oz)
few drops of vanilla extract
generous pinch of mixed spice
pinch of grated nutmeg

TOPPING
60 g (2 oz) butter
75 g (2½ oz) soft brown sugar
400 g (14 oz) canned pineapple rings
6 maraschino cherries, halved

First make the topping: Place butter in a 20-cm (8-in) round, glass baking dish and microwave on 100% for 1 minute. Tilt dish to coat base evenly. Sprinkle soft brown sugar evenly over base.

Drain pineapple, reserving syrup, and arrange on base of dish, with a cherry in the middle of each ring.

Place all ingredients for cake in the bowl of a food processor and beat on low speed for about 3 minutes until mixture is smooth. Spread mixture evenly over fruit. Place dish on an inverted saucer and microwave on 100% for 9-11 minutes, or until a cocktail stick inserted near the centre comes out clean.

Invert cake on to a serving plate and leave dish to stand over cake for a few minutes before removing. Serve warm or cool.
Makes 1 x 20-cm (8-in) round cake.

Variation

PEACH UPSIDE-DOWN CAKE
Substitute 400 g (14 oz) canned, sliced peaches and peach juice for the pineapple rings and syrup. Add a few drops of almond essence to the cake mixture.

Crazy Chocolate Cake

100% .... 9 minutes

175 g (6 oz) plain flour
200 g (7 oz) caster sugar
45 g (1½ oz) cocoa powder
5 ml (1 tsp) bicarbonate of soda
5 ml (1 tsp) salt
250 ml (8 fl oz) water, warmed
few drops of vanilla extract
75 ml (2½ fl oz) oil
5 ml (1 tsp) white vinegar

GLAZE
100 g (3½ oz) caster sugar
60 g (2 oz) butter
30 ml (2 tbsp) milk
30 ml (2 tbsp) cocoa powder
few drops of vanilla extract
60 ml (4 tbsp) chopped nuts
  (optional)

Sift flour, sugar, cocoa powder, bicarbonate of soda and salt into a 23-cm (9-in) square microwave baking pan. Make three 4-cm (1½-in) holes in the flour mixture with a fork. Pour warm water and a few drops of vanilla extract into one hole. Pour oil into another. Pour vinegar into the third. Stir until well mixed.

Microwave on 100% for 5 minutes, check to see if nearly cooked, then microwave for 1½-2 minutes more, or until a skewer inserted near the centre comes out clean. Cool completely in pan.

To make glaze: Combine sugar, butter, milk and cocoa powder and microwave on 100% for 1 minute. Mix well, then microwave for 1 minute more. Mix well again and leave to cool. Stir in a few drops of vanilla extract, spread mixture over cake and sprinkle with nuts, if desired. Leave until set, then cut into squares.
Makes about 18 squares.

Strawberry Yogurt Cake

100% .... 10 minutes

125 g (4 oz) butter
200 g (7 oz) caster sugar
2 eggs
200 g (7 oz) plain flour
10 ml (2 tsp) baking powder
pinch of salt
5 ml (1 tsp) bicarbonate of soda
250 ml (8 fl oz) strawberry-
  flavoured yogurt
15 ml (1 tbsp) brandy

DECORATION
icing sugar
blanched almonds
glacé cherries

First beat butter until pale in colour. Add sugar and cream together until light and fluffy. Beat in eggs, one at a time. Into a separate bowl, sift flour, baking powder and salt. Add bicarbonate of soda to yogurt and stir well. Then add flour and yogurt mixtures alternately to creamed mixture, starting and ending with flour. Beat in brandy.

Turn batter into a greased 25-cm (10-in) microwave ring pan and microwave on 100% for 7-10 minutes, or until surface is almost dry. Leave to stand for 10 minutes before turning out to cool on a wire rack. When cold, sift a little icing sugar over cake and decorate with whole almonds and cherries.
Makes 1 x 25-cm (10-in) ring cake.

Hints
• Cake batter containing baking powder may be left to stand for 3-4 minutes before microwaving in order to start the reaction between baking powder and liquid. This results in better volume.
• Because cakes rise higher in the microwave than in the conventional oven, only fill containers half full. Any left-over batter can be baked as cup cakes.

Pumpkin Bread

70% .... 15 minutes

125 g (4 oz) butter
75 g (2½ oz) soft brown sugar
60 ml (4 tbsp) caster sugar
2 eggs
45 ml (3 tbsp) molasses
15 ml (1 tbsp) grated orange rind
150 g (5 oz) cooked pumpkin,
  mashed
300 g (11 oz) plain flour
7.5 ml (1½ tsp) bicarbonate of
  soda
2.5 ml (½ tsp) ground cinnamon
2.5 ml (½ tsp) ground ginger
250 ml (8 fl oz) buttermilk
icing sugar

Lightly oil a deep 25-cm (10-in) microwave ring pan. Cream butter and sugars thoroughly until light and fluffy. Beat in eggs, one at a time. Add molasses, orange rind and pumpkin and beat again. Sift together dry ingredients and add about one-third to the creamed mixture, then add one-third of the buttermilk. Repeat until both dry ingredients and buttermilk have been used up.

Pour mixture into prepared pan and microwave on 70% for 13-15 minutes. Leave to stand for 20 minutes before turning out on to a rack to cool completely. Serve sprinkled with a little sifted icing sugar.
Makes 1 x 25-cm (10-in) ring cake.

Hint
In microwave baking, ring-shaped cake dishes allow the centre of a cake to bake at the same rate as the outer edges. If you do not have a ring dish, improvise by using an ordinary glass casserole and placing an upright glass in the centre.

Banana Cake

50%, 100% .... 22 minutes

125 g (4 oz) butter, softened
275 g (10 oz) caster sugar
2 eggs
3 small ripe bananas, mashed
few drops of almond essence
275 g (10 oz) plain flour
2.5 ml ($^1/_2$ tsp) baking powder
2.5 ml ($^1/_2$ tsp) bicarbonate of soda
pinch of salt
60 ml (4 tbsp) plain yogurt
1 sliced banana and a little
   lemon juice to decorate

BANANA FUDGE ICING
30 g (1 oz) butter
175 g (6 oz) soft brown sugar
45 ml (3 tbsp) milk
150 g (5 oz) icing sugar, sifted
15 ml (1 tbsp) single cream

Grease a 25-cm (10-in) microwave ring pan. Cream butter and sugar until light and fluffy. Beat in eggs, one at a time, then add banana and almond essence. Sift dry ingredients together and fold about one-third into banana mixture. Add a third of the yogurt and mix well to combine. Continue until all ingredients have been combined.

Pour mixture into ring pan and microwave on 50% for 12 minutes. Increase power to 100% and microwave for a further 1-2 minutes. Leave cake to stand in pan for about 15 minutes before turning out on to a rack. Cool completely before icing.

To make icing: Place butter, sugar and milk in a bowl and microwave on 50% for 5 minutes. Stir well, then increase power to 100% and microwave for 3 minutes. Pour into a cold bowl and cool slightly. Beat icing sugar and cream into butter mixture (the mixture should be of a 'drizzling' consistency) and pour carefully over banana cake. While icing is still soft, decorate cake with banana slices dipped in a little lemon juice.

Makes 1 x 25-cm (10-in) ring cake.

Carrot Cake

100%, 30% .... 9 minutes

125 ml (4 fl oz) oil
150 g (5 oz) soft brown sugar
2 eggs
2.5 ml ($^1/_2$ tsp) bicarbonate of soda
2.5 ml ($^1/_2$ tsp) almond essence
150 g (5 oz) self-raising flour
5 ml (1 tsp) mixed spice
5 ml (1 tsp) ground cinnamon
60 g (2 oz) unblanched almonds,
   chopped
6 medium-sized carrots, grated
60 g (2 oz) desiccated coconut
5 ml (1 tsp) finely grated orange
   rind
30 ml (2 tbsp) orange juice
grated orange rind or chopped
   unblanched almonds to decorate

CREAM CHEESE ICING
60 g (2 oz) butter
125 g (4 oz) cream cheese
125 g (4 oz) caster sugar
125 g (4 oz) icing sugar, sifted
few drops of vanilla extract

Beat oil, sugar and eggs thoroughly. Add bicarbonate of soda and almond essence and beat again. Sift together flour and spices and beat into mixture, about one-third at a time. Add almonds, carrot, coconut, orange rind and juice and beat to combine. (The mixture will be very thick.)

Pour batter into a sprayed or greased 23-cm (9-in) microwave ring pan and microwave on 100% for 6-7 minutes. Leave cake to cool in pan for at least 10 minutes before turning out on to a rack.

To make icing: Soften butter in microwave on 30% for 1-2 minutes, depending on hardness of butter. Using an electric mixer, beat butter and cream cheese together. Add caster sugar and beat well, then add sifted icing sugar, a little at a time, beating well after each addition. Finally, add vanilla extract. Spread icing over cake and decorate with grated orange rind or chopped almonds.

Makes 1 x 23-cm (9-in) ring cake.

Wholemeal Fig Cake

70% .... 11 minutes

150 g (5 oz) butter
125 g (4 oz) soft brown sugar
3 eggs
90 g (3 oz) wholemeal flour
45 g (1½ oz) digestive bran
60 g (2 oz) self-raising flour
10 ml (2 tsp) baking powder
1 lemon
200 g (7 oz) dried figs, chopped
60 g (2 oz) carrot, finely grated
100 g (3½ oz) coffee crystals and
   lemon zest to decorate

Cream butter and sugar until light
and fluffy. Add eggs, one at a
time, beating well after each
addition. Mix in wholemeal flour
and bran, then add sifted self-
raising flour and baking powder.
Grate rind of lemon and add to
mixture. Peel lemon. Remove
skin from segments, chop flesh
and add to mixture. Stir in figs
and grated carrot.
   Turn mixture into a greased,
20-cm (8-in) round cake dish
and microwave on 70% for
9-11 minutes. Leave to cool for
15 minutes on a flat surface before
removing from dish. Sprinkle
with coffee crystals and lemon
zest.
Makes 1 x 20-cm (8-in) round
cake.

Hints
• Standing time is very important in
microwave baking. Cakes continue
to cook for some time after being
removed from the microwave, so
the tops should still be slightly
moist at the end of the microwaving
time. As a general rule, leave cakes
to stand for about 10 minutes
before turning out to cool.
• Always place cakes on a solid,
heat-resistant surface during
standing time so that the maximum
amount of heat will be retained by
the container and the bottom of the
cake will continue to cook.
• If the moist surface of a cake does
not firm up during standing time,
try covering the cake loosely with
waxed paper to keep in the heat.

Tropical Carrot Cake

70% .... 9 minutes

125 g (4 oz) plain flour
7.5 ml (1½ tsp) bicarbonate of
   soda
5 ml (1 tsp) ground cinnamon
2.5 ml (½ tsp) salt
125 ml (4 fl oz) oil
200 g (7 oz) caster sugar
1 extra large egg
90 g (3 oz) canned crushed
   pineapple, with juice
150 g (5 oz) carrots, grated
45 g (1½ oz) desiccated coconut
60 ml (4 tbsp) chopped walnuts

ICING
60 g (2 oz) low-fat soft cheese
30 g (1 oz) butter
200 g (7 oz) icing sugar, sifted
10 ml (2 tsp) milk
few drops of vanilla extract
60 ml (4 tbsp) desiccated coconut

Combine and sift flour,
bicarbonate of soda, cinnamon
and salt. Beat together oil, sugar
and egg thoroughly. Add flour
mixture and beat until smooth.
Add pineapple, carrot, coconut
and walnuts and mix well. Pour
into a greased and lined 23-cm
(9-in) square baking dish and
microwave on 70% for
7-9 minutes, or until top is almost
dry. Leave to cool in dish.
   To make icing: Beat together
low-fat cheese and butter until
smooth. Add icing sugar
alternately with milk and vanilla.
Stir in coconut, then spread icing
over cake. Cut into squares to
serve.
Makes 16 large or 25 small
squares.

Hint
The centre of a heavy or very rich
cake, such as a carrot or fruit cake,
may be hollowed out slightly
before baking to prevent the
finished cake doming or cracking.

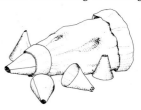

Streusel Coffee Cake

100% .... 8 minutes

150 g (5 oz) caster sugar
60 g (2 oz) butter
few drops of vanilla extract
1 egg
125 ml (4 fl oz) milk
175 g (6 oz) plain flour
10 ml (2 tsp) baking powder
2.5 ml (½ tsp) salt

STREUSEL TOPPING
100 g (3½ oz) soft brown sugar
30 ml (2 tbsp) plain flour
10 ml (2 tsp) ground cinnamon
30 g (1 oz) butter
45 g (1½ oz) hazelnuts or pecan
  nuts

Beat together sugar, butter, vanilla and egg until light and fluffy. Stir in milk. Sift dry ingredients together and add to mixture. Stir until smooth. Make streusel topping by combining all ingredients thoroughly.

Spread half the batter in a greased 23-cm (9-in) square or round baking dish and sprinkle with half the streusel mixture. Cover with remaining batter and top with remaining streusel mixture.

Microwave on 100% for 7-8 minutes, rotating dish a quarter turn every 3 minutes if necessary. Remove from oven and leave to stand for 10 minutes before serving. Serve warm – with cream if desired.
Makes 1 x 23-cm (9-in) square or round cake.

Variations

APPLE COFFEE CAKE
Chop 400 g (14 oz) canned apple pie filling and spread half over the first layer of cake batter. Sprinkle with half the streusel mixture, then repeat cake, apple and streusel layers.

JAM COFFEE CAKE
In a measuring jug, microwave 125 g (4 oz) fruit jam or marmalade on 100% for 45-60 seconds to soften. Drizzle half the warmed jam over the first layer of cake batter. Sprinkle with half the streusel mixture, then repeat cake, jam and streusel layers.

SOUTHERN PEACH COFFEE CAKE
Drain 425 g (15 oz) canned peach slices thoroughly and marinate in 30 ml (2 tbsp) brandy for 20 minutes. Drain. Arrange half the peach slices on the first layer of cake batter. Sprinkle with half the streusel mixture, then repeat cake, peach and streusel layers.

STRAWBERRY COFFEE CAKE
Slice 200 g (7 oz) fresh strawberries and sprinkle with 30 ml (2 tbsp) caster sugar and 30 ml (2 tbsp) kirsch. Leave strawberries to marinate for 10 minutes, then drain. Arrange half of them on the first layer of cake batter, sprinkle with streusel mixture, then repeat cake, strawberry and streusel layers.

Hint
The corners of square baking dishes may be shielded with small pieces of foil during baking. This will prevent overcooking of the corners.

Spicy Maple Cake (left) and Apple Cake

Apple Cake

100%, 70% .... 14 minutes

**60 ml (4 tbsp) finely chopped nuts,
  such as walnuts or pecan nuts
3 eggs
90 g (3 oz) caster sugar
150 g (5 oz) butter
90 g (3 oz) plain flour
15 ml (1 tbsp) baking powder
2.5 ml (^{1}/$_2$ tsp) ground cinnamon
4 large apples, peeled and diced
30 ml (2 tbsp) rum
icing sugar**

Grease a deep 25-cm (10-in) microwave ring pan and sprinkle with chopped nuts. Beat eggs and sugar until thick and creamy. Microwave butter on 70% for l minute, then beat into egg mixture. Sift together flour, baking powder and cinnamon and add to egg mixture, blending just until flour is moistened. Stir in apples and rum and turn into prepared pan.

Microwave batter on 70% for 7 minutes, then increase power to 100% and microwave for 4-6 minutes more. Remove cake from microwave and leave to stand for 10 minutes before turning out to cool on a wire rack. Dust with icing sugar if desired and serve with cream or ice cream.
Makes 1 x 25-cm (10-in) ring cake.

Hints

• To check whether a cake is ready to be removed from the microwave, insert a skewer or wooden cocktail stick near, but not in, the centre. If the skewer comes out clean, the cake is ready.
• Always check a cake after the minimum time and microwave longer only if necessary. Overcooking by even 1^1/$_2$ or 2 minutes will result in a cake with hard, dry outer edges. Remember, you can check the progress of a cake often. Unlike conventional baking, a cake will not sink if the door is opened briefly.

Spicy Maple Cake

100%, 50% .... 22 minutes

**450 g (1 lb) plain flour
10 ml (2 tsp) baking powder
5 ml (1 tsp) bicarbonate of soda
5 ml (1 tsp) ground ginger
5 ml (1 tsp) ground cinnamon
2.5 ml (^{1}/$_2$ tsp) ground cardamom
2.5 ml (^{1}/$_2$ tsp) ground allspice
2.5 ml (^{1}/$_2$ tsp) ground cloves
generous pinch of salt
200 g (7 oz) soft brown sugar
2 eggs
250 g (9 oz) butter
185 ml (6 fl oz) buttermilk
185 ml (6 fl oz) maple syrup
30 ml (2 tbsp) dark rum**

GLAZE
**400 g (14 oz) icing sugar, sifted
90 g (3 oz) butter, softened
90 ml (3 fl oz) maple syrup
30 ml (2 tbsp) dark rum**

Combine and sift flour, baking powder, bicarbonate of soda, spices and salt. Set aside. Beat sugar and eggs together thoroughly. Add butter and continue to beat well. Combine buttermilk, maple syrup and rum and beat into egg mixture. Add dry ingredients and mix well.

Turn batter into a deep 25-cm (10-in) microwave ring pan and microwave on 50% for 15 minutes, then on 100% for 4-7 minutes, or until top springs back when lightly touched. Leave to stand for 10 minutes before turning out on to a wire rack to cool.

To make glaze: Blend together all ingredients and thin with a little water if necessary. Place a baking sheet under the cooling rack and spoon glaze over cake. Scrape up glaze from baking sheet and spoon over cake again.
Makes 1 x 25-cm (10-in) ring cake.

Citrus and Ginger Cheesecake

100% .... 1 minute
Plus combination baking

10 Marie biscuits, crushed
6 gingernut biscuits, crushed
30 ml (2 tbsp) soft brown sugar
2.5 ml (½ tsp) ground cinnamon
60 g (2 oz) butter
30 ml (2 tbsp) single cream

FILLING
250 g (9 oz) cream cheese, softened
125 ml (4 fl oz) mayonnaise
  (any type)
100 g (3½ oz) caster sugar
3 large eggs
15 ml (1 tbsp) grated orange rind
15 ml (1 tbsp) lemon juice
few drops of vanilla extract

DECORATION
whipped cream
lemon or orange slices

Combine finely crushed biscuit crumbs with sugar and cinnamon.

Microwave butter for 30-45 seconds on 100%, add to crumbs and mix in. Then stir in cream and press mixture into base and sides of a 5-cm (2-in) deep x 20-cm (8-in) round baking dish. Set aside.
  To make filling: Beat cream cheese and mayonnaise until smooth. Mix in sugar, then eggs, one at a time. Add grated orange rind, lemon juice and vanilla and beat well. Turn into prepared crust and bake according to instructions below until just set. Cool on a wire rack, then chill. Serve topped with whipped cream and lemon or orange slices.

BROTHER
Hi-Speed at 200 °C for 10 minutes, then at 180 °C for 6-8 minutes.

Serves 8-10.

Chocolate Surprise Cake

100% .... 8 minutes

125 g (4 oz) plain flour
150 g (5 oz) caster sugar
60 ml (4 tbsp) cocoa powder
2.5 ml (½ tsp) bicarbonate of soda
generous pinch of salt
few drops of vanilla extract
60 g (2 oz) butter
185 ml (6 fl oz) buttermilk
1 egg

FILLING
75 g (2½ oz) desiccated coconut
60 ml (4 tbsp) golden syrup
15 ml (1 tbsp) plain flour
few drops of almond essence
30 ml (2 tbsp) single cream

ICING
250 g (9 oz) icing sugar
30 ml (2 tbsp) cocoa powder
45 g (2½ oz) butter, softened
few drops of vanilla extract
45 ml (3 tbsp) single cream
toasted coconut (page 174)

Combine all cake ingredients in a large bowl, then, using an electric beater on medium speed, mix for about 3 minutes until batter is smooth. Turn into a greased 23-cm (9-in) square baking dish and smooth the top.
  Combine all ingredients for filling, mix well and drop by the spoonful into chocolate batter. Microwave on 100% for 5 minutes. Check to see if cake is nearly cooked, then microwave for 1½-2½ minutes more, or until a skewer inserted near the centre comes out clean. (The top of the cake should still be moist.) Cool.
  To make icing: Sift icing sugar and cocoa powder into a large bowl. Mix in butter and vanilla, then beat in cream, a little at a time, until mixture is of a spreading consistency. Spread over cake and sprinkle with toasted coconut.
Makes 16 large or 25 small squares.

Strawberry and Hazelnut Galette

100%, 50% .... 25 minutes

60 g (2 oz) hazelnuts
100 g (3¹/₂ oz) plain flour
small pinch of salt
45 g (1¹/₂ oz) caster sugar
100 g (3¹/₂ oz) butter

FILLING
300 ml (10 fl oz) whipping cream
45 ml (3 tbsp) icing sugar
30-45 ml (2-3 tbsp) Cointreau
300-600 g (11 oz-1 lb 5 oz) strawberries, washed and hulled
icing sugar
30 g (1 oz) plain chocolate (optional)

Place nuts on a plate and microwave on 100% for 2-3 minutes until hot. Rub off skins with the palms of your hands. Microwave a browning dish for 6 minutes, add nuts and microwave for 3-4 minutes, stirring every minute to prevent over-browning. When nuts have cooled, finely grind about two-thirds and chop remainder.

Sift flour and salt into a bowl, add sugar and ground hazelnuts and stir to combine. Next, rub in butter, mix to a pastry dough and cut in two. Set a 23-cm (9-in) flan ring on a microwave baking sheet and line it with baking parchment. Press one-half of the pastry into the ring, then remove ring and microwave pastry for 3-5 minutes. Leave to cool slightly before lifting on to a rack to cool completely.

Repeat with second portion but, after pressing into shape, sprinkle with chopped hazelnuts. Press nuts into pastry and continue as above. While still warm, divide pastry into eight wedges.

To fill: Whip cream until thick. Add sugar and liqueur to taste, beat again and spread most of the cream over the base layer. Then, reserving a few for decoration, chop up strawberries and arrange on top of cream. Place the eight triangles on top of the strawberries and dust lightly with sifted icing sugar.

To decorate: In a bowl, micro-wave chocolate for 1-2 minutes on 50%. Dip ends of reserved whole strawberries into chocolate and leave to dry on a small piece of foil. Pipe swirls of remaining cream on to the triangles and top with chocolate-tipped straw-berries.
Serves 8.

Praline Ring

100%, 70% .... 25 minutes

100 g (3¹/₂ oz) butter, softened
100 g (3¹/₂ oz) soft brown sugar
100 g (3¹/₂ oz) caster sugar
3 eggs
few drops of vanilla extract
125 g (4 oz) self-raising flour
generous pinch of baking powder
small pinch of salt
100 ml (3¹/₂ fl oz) plain yogurt
100 ml (3¹/₂ fl oz) whipping cream,
  whipped, and maraschino
  cherries to decorate

PRALINE
150 g (5 oz) caster sugar
100 ml (3¹/₂ fl oz) water
pinch of cream of tartar
45 g (1¹/₂ oz) almonds

BUTTER CREAM FILLING
300 ml (10 fl oz) milk
45 g (1¹/₂ oz) cornflour
175 g (6 oz) butter, softened
175 g (6 oz) caster sugar
few drops of vanilla extract

First make the praline: Mix sugar and water together in a medium-sized bowl and microwave on 100% for 2 minutes. Stir in cream of tartar and microwave for a further 8-10 minutes until syrup turns a deep golden colour.

Place nuts on a well-greased baking sheet and pour caramel over. Leave to cool completely, then remove praline from baking sheet and break into pieces. To crush, drop a few pieces at a time on to moving blades of a food processor. Process until finely chopped.*

To make cake: Cream butter and sugars until light and fluffy. Add eggs and vanilla and beat well. Sift flour with baking powder and salt and add about one-third to creamed mixture. Beat well. Then add about one-third of the yogurt and beat well. Repeat until dry ingredients and yogurt have been used up.

Turn mixture into a greased 23-cm (9-in) microwave ring pan and microwave on 70% for 7 minutes, then increase power level to 100% for 2-3 minutes.

Leave to stand for 10 minutes before turning out on to a rack to cool.

To make butter cream filling: Microwave 280 ml (9 fl oz) of the milk on 100% for 2 minutes. In a bowl, combine remaining milk and cornflour, then pour boiling milk into cornflour mixture and stir well. Microwave for 1 minute until very thick. Beat well and leave to cool until just warm.

Meanwhile, cream together butter and sugar until light and fluffy. Add vanilla, then beat in cornflour mixture, about a quarter at a time, until thoroughly combined.**

When cake is completely cold, slice in half, or in three, and fill with butter cream filling. Sandwich layers together again and cover cake completely with remaining butter cream. Sprinkle liberally with praline. Pipe swirls of cream on top and decorate with cherries.
Makes 1 x 23-cm (9-in) ring.

*Praline may be stored in an airtight container for several weeks.

**This is an ideal filling or icing for any sponge-type cake.

Hints
• To convert conventional baking recipes: The best recipes for microwave baking are those rich in butter or margarine and eggs. If the recipe you want to convert is not rich, add an extra egg and about 30 g (1 oz) butter or margarine to the mixture. If the recipe contains three or more eggs, you may wish to decrease the liquid called for by about a quarter.
• Be sure to select the correct container sizes, but remember that these will need to be deeper than those used for conventional baking. Check if ready at one quarter of the conventional time and add more time if necessary.

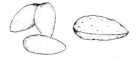

Caramel-glazed Coffee Cake

100%, 70% .... 13 minutes

60 g (2 oz) butter, softened
125 g (4 oz) caster sugar
1 egg
few drops of almond essence
125 g (4 oz) plain flour
2.5 ml (½ tsp) baking powder
2.5 ml (½ tsp) bicarbonate of soda
185 ml (6 fl oz) soured cream

FILLING
45 ml (3 tbsp) soft brown sugar
45 ml (3 tbsp) chopped nuts
45 ml (3 tbsp) toasted coconut
  (page 174)
2.5 ml (½ tsp) ground cinnamon

GLAZE
30 g (1 oz) butter
200 g (7 oz) caster sugar
few drops of vanilla extract
30-45 ml (2-3 tbsp) soured cream

First, combine all filling
ingredients in a bowl and set
aside.
  Next, place butter in a mixing
bowl and beat well. Add sugar,
egg and almond essence. Beat
thoroughly to combine. Sift dry
ingredients and beat into mixture,
about one-third at a time,
alternating with the soured
cream.
  Then spread half the cake
mixture into a well-greased 20-cm
(8-in) baking dish and cover with
half the filling. Repeat layers.
Microwave on 70% for
8-10 minutes and leave to cool for
10 minutes.
  To make glaze: Place butter in a
large jug and microwave on 100%
for 2-3 minutes until it turns a
deep golden colour. Mix in castor
sugar and vanilla extract and add
sufficient soured cream to give a
drizzling consistency. When cake
is sufficiently cool, drizzle glaze
over the top.
Makes 1 x 20-cm (8-in) cake.

Chocolate and Coconut Biscuits

100%, 50% .... 35 minutes

250 g (9 oz) butter
200 g (7 oz) caster sugar
250 g (9 oz) self-raising flour
60 ml (4 tbsp) cocoa powder
pinch of salt
150 g (5 oz) desiccated coconut
125 ml (4 fl oz) water, boiling
5 ml (1 tsp) instant coffee granules
**100 g (3½ oz) plain chocolate,
  broken into pieces**
icing sugar for dusting

CHOCOLATE ICING
**60 g (2 oz) plain chocolate,
  broken into pieces**
45 g (1½ oz) butter
200 g (7 oz) icing sugar, sifted
pinch of salt
1 small egg, lightly beaten
185 ml (6 fl oz) single cream
few drops of vanilla extract

Cream together butter and sugar until light and fluffy. Sift dry ingredients into a bowl and add coconut. Combine water and instant coffee and stir to dissolve. Add one-third of the dry ingredients to the butter mixture and beat to combine. Then add one-third of the dissolved coffee and beat thoroughly. Repeat until all ingredients have been combined.

Line a microwave baking sheet with greaseproof paper, or just grease the baking sheet. Roll dough into walnut-sized balls and arrange on baking sheet in a circle, leaving 6 cm (2½ in) between each ball. Microwave on 100% for 4-5 minutes, then lift biscuits off paper with a spatula and cool on a rack. Repeat until all dough has been used (about five more batches).

To make chocolate icing: Place chocolate and butter in a large bowl and microwave on 50% for 1-2 minutes, or until melted. Beat in icing sugar, salt and egg until smooth. Chill mixture well, then beat in cream and vanilla and continue to beat for 3-4 minutes, or until thick.

When biscuits are cool, microwave 100 g (3½ oz) chocolate on 50% for 2½-3 minutes, stirring at least once during cooking time. Spread chocolate on flat side of half the biscuits and top with a plain biscuit as you go. When all the biscuits have been sandwiched together, spread tops with chocolate icing. Dust with a little sifted icing sugar.
Makes about 18 double biscuits.

Choconut Squares

100% .... 6 minutes

75 g (2½ oz) butter
**100 g (3½ oz) Marie biscuit
  crumbs**
**100 g (3½ oz) plain chocolate,
  grated**
60 g (2 oz) desiccated coconut
100 g (3½ oz) walnuts, chopped
150 ml (5 fl oz) condensed milk

Place butter in a 23-cm (9-in) square glass baking dish and microwave on 100% for 1 minute. Stir in crumbs, mixing well to combine, and press evenly to cover bottom of dish. Microwave for 1-1½ minutes.

Sprinkle base with grated chocolate, then coconut and chopped nuts. Pour condensed milk evenly over surface and microwave for 3-4 minutes until mixture is bubbling all over surface. Cool, then cut into squares or bars.
Makes 64 bite-sized squares or, if preferred, 18 bars.

Spicy Peanut Butter Biscuits

50% .... 15 minutes

125 g (4 oz) butter
125 g (4 oz) crunchy peanut butter
250 g (9 oz) soft brown sugar
1 egg
few drops of vanilla extract
200 g (7 oz) plain flour
pinch of salt
2.5 ml (½ tsp) ground cinnamon
generous pinch of grated nutmeg
pinch of ground cloves
2.5 ml (½ tsp) baking powder

Cream together butter, peanut butter and sugar. Add egg and vanilla, beat well, then sift in dry ingredients. Combine well. Chill mixture for 15 minutes.
  Line a microwave baking sheet or turntable with greased greaseproof paper. Shape peanut butter mixture into small balls and place six in a circle on the sheet, flattening each with the prongs of a fork. Microwave on 50% for 2-3 minutes, leave to stand for 5 minutes, then cool on a wire rack. Repeat with remaining dough.
Makes about 30 biscuits.

Note
Large batches of biscuits or cookies take longer to microwave than to bake conventionally as only a few can be baked at a time.
  It is important to note, too, that because many biscuits and bars need hot, dry air to form their characteristic crisp crust, not all recipes designed for conventional baking convert successfully to microwaving.

Pineapple and Coconut Squares

70%, 100% .... 20 minutes

1 x 400 g (14 oz) pkt vanilla cake mix
2.5 ml (½ tsp) baking powder
400 g (14 oz) canned crushed pineapple
3 eggs
60 ml (4 tbsp) oil
45 ml (3 tbsp) water
30 ml (2 tbsp) dark rum
100 g (3½ oz) desiccated coconut

ICING
100 g (3½ oz) butter
300 g (11 oz) icing sugar, sifted
45 ml (3 tbsp) dark rum
45 g (1½ oz) toasted coconut (see *Hint*)

Place cake mix, baking powder, pineapple, eggs, oil, water and rum in a large bowl. Beat with an electric mixer for about 4 minutes until smooth. Add coconut and mix well.
  Grease or spray two 23-cm (9-in) square baking dishes and pour half the cake mixture into each. Microwave the first dish on 70% for 5-6 minutes, then increase power level to 100% for 3-4 minutes. Allow to cool in dish. Repeat with second dish. Meanwhile, make the icing.
  Cream butter thoroughly, then gradually add sifted icing sugar. Add rum and beat again. Spread icing on top of both cakes and sprinkle with toasted coconut. Cut into squares to serve.
Makes 32 large or 50 small squares.

Hint
To toast coconut: Spread 45 g (1½ oz) desiccated coconut evenly on to a paper plate. Microwave on 100% for 5-6 minutes, stirring every minute.

Butter Pecan Squares

100%, 50% .... 15 minutes

125 g (4 oz) butter
150 g (5 oz) plain flour
75 g (2½ oz) caster sugar

FILLING
150 g (5 oz) caster sugar
125 ml (4 fl oz) clear honey
2 eggs, beaten
30 g (1 oz) butter, softened
30 g (1 oz) plain flour
few drops of vanilla extract
5 ml (1 tsp) lemon juice
generous pinch of salt
75 g (2½ oz) pecan nuts

Soften butter on 50% for about 45 seconds. Combine with flour and sugar and beat well. Press into the bottom of a 23-cm (9-in) square baking dish and microwave on 100% for 3-4 minutes.

To make filling: Combine sugar, honey, eggs, butter, flour, vanilla, lemon juice and salt in a bowl and beat well. Microwave on 50% for 3 minutes, stirring well

every minute. Pour over crust and arrange pecan nuts on top. Microwave on 100% for about 5-7 minutes, or until filling is set. Cool on a wire rack, then cut into squares to serve.
Makes 16 large or 25 small squares.

Hint
To shell nuts: Place 125 g (4 oz) unshelled nuts in a jug and cover with cold water. Microwave on 100% for 2-3 minutes, then drain and crack open shells immediately. If the kernels are slightly damp, place them on a plate and microwave them for 1 minute on 100%, then leave to stand for 5 minutes before using.

Peanut and Raisin Bars

These bars are sticky and chewy and full of goodness.

100% .... 7 minutes

20 g (¾ oz) butter
200 g (7 oz) soft brown sugar
100 g (3½ oz) unsalted peanuts, coarsely chopped
75 g (2½ oz) seedless raisins
75 g (2½ oz) plain flour
45 ml (3 tbsp) porridge oats
pinch of bicarbonate of soda
pinch of salt
2 large eggs
few drops of vanilla extract
icing sugar

Place butter in a 23-cm (9-in) square baking dish and microwave on 100% for 45 seconds. Tilt dish to coat base. Combine sugar, peanuts, raisins, flour, oats, bicarbonate of soda and salt in a bowl. Mix well, then beat in eggs and vanilla. Spoon mixture over melted butter in baking dish. Spread to edges but do not stir.

Microwave on 100% for 5½-6 minutes. (The mixture should still be moist in the centre.) Allow to stand for 5 minutes, then sprinkle with icing sugar. Place a wire rack on a tray and turn out baked mixture. Leave to cool, then sprinkle with more icing sugar and cut into bars. Store in a single layer in an airtight tin.
Makes 12-18 bars.

Chocolate-topped Peanut Butter Bars

100%, 50% .... 8 minutes

60 ml (4 tbsp) smooth peanut butter
60 ml (4 tbsp) caster sugar
60 ml (4 tbsp) soft brown sugar
45 ml (3 tbsp) butter
1 egg
few drops of vanilla extract
60 g (2 oz) plain flour
45 g (1½ oz) porridge oats
2.5 ml (½ tsp) bicarbonate of soda
pinch of salt

TOPPING
30 ml (2 tbsp) smooth peanut butter
90 g (3 oz) plain chocolate,
  broken into pieces
30 ml (2 tbsp) chopped peanuts
  (optional)

Beat together peanut butter, sugars, butter, egg and vanilla extract until light and fluffy. Combine dry ingredients and add to peanut butter mixture. Mix well and spread in a 23-cm (9-in) square baking dish. Shield corners of dish with foil and microwave on 100% for 3-5 minutes, or until top is no longer moist. Cool before spreading with topping.

To make topping: Place peanut butter and chocolate in a small bowl and microwave on 50% for 1½-3 minutes, or until melted. Stir, then spread over baked mixture. Sprinkle with peanuts and cut into squares.
Makes 16 large or 25 small squares.

Chocolate Chip Squares

100% .... 7 minutes

125 g (4 oz) butter
150 g (5 oz) soft brown sugar
1 egg
15 ml (1 tbsp) milk
few drops of vanilla extract
150 g (5 oz) plain flour
2.5 ml (½ tsp) baking powder
generous pinch of ground
  cinnamon
pinch of salt
100 g (3½ oz) chocolate chips
45 g (1½ oz) nuts, chopped
  (optional)

Cream butter and sugar together until light and fluffy. Add egg and beat well. Stir in milk and vanilla. Combine flour, baking powder, cinnamon and salt and sift into butter mixture. Mix well, then stir in chocolate chips and nuts.

Turn mixture into a greased 23-cm (9-in) square baking dish. Shield corners with small pieces of foil and microwave on 100% for 5-6½ minutes, rotating dish a quarter turn every 2 minutes if necessary. Cool baked mixture in dish before cutting into squares. Makes 16 large or 25 small squares.

Hint
Because biscuits and bars baked in the microwave do not brown as they do in the conventional oven, they are usually iced before serving so that the difference in appearance is not noticeable. If no icing is used, there are several toppings that improve the appearance.

A mixture of cinnamon and sugar, toasted coconut or chopped nuts, or a blend of soft brown sugar and nuts can be sprinkled on top before microwaving. Sifted icing sugar can also be most effective when sprinkled over microwaved bars.

Lemon-layered Brownies

70% .... 13 minutes

125 g (4 oz) plain flour
60 ml (4 tbsp) icing sugar
45 ml (3 tbsp) cocoa powder
125 g (4 oz) butter, softened
60 ml (4 tbsp) chopped walnuts

LEMON LAYER
2 eggs
175 g (6 oz) caster sugar
30 ml (2 tbsp) lemon juice
2.5 ml ($1/2$ tsp) grated lemon rind
2.5 ml ($1/2$ tsp) baking powder
30 g (1 oz) plain flour, sifted
icing sugar

Sift flour, icing sugar and cocoa powder into a bowl, add butter and walnuts and work until mixture becomes moist. Press into a greased 23-cm (9-in) square dish and microwave on 70% for 3-4 minutes until mixture begins to bubble.

To make lemon layer: Beat eggs thoroughly, add sugar and continue beating until mixture is thick and pale in colour, then beat in lemon juice and rind. Sift together baking powder and flour, fold into mixture and pour over chocolate layer. Microwave for 7-9 minutes until almost set. When completely cool, sprinkle with sifted icing sugar and cut into squares.
Makes 16 large or 25 small squares.

Orange and Ginger Bars

100%, 50% .... 9 minutes

60 g (2 oz) butter, softened
75 g (2½ oz) soft brown sugar
2 eggs
100 g (3½ oz) plain flour
2.5 ml (½ tsp) bicarbonate of soda
pinch of salt
2.5 ml (½ tsp) ground ginger
2.5 ml (½ tsp) ground cinnamon
60 ml (4 tbsp) golden syrup
30 ml (2 tbsp) water, boiling

ICING
45 g (1½ oz) butter
15 ml (1 tbsp) single cream
5 ml (1 tsp) grated orange rind
15 ml (1 tbsp) orange juice
300 g (11 oz) icing sugar, sifted

Place all ingredients, except syrup and water, in a large mixing bowl. Combine syrup and water and add to mixture, beating thoroughly with an electric mixer until smooth. Grease or spray a 30 x 20-cm (12 x 8-in) dish. Turn mixture into dish and microwave on 100% for 5-7 minutes. Leave to cool before icing.

To make icing: Place butter, cream, orange rind and juice in a bowl and microwave at 50% for 1-2 minutes until very soft. Gradually beat in icing sugar until a spreading consistency forms. Spread on top of cooled cake and cut into bars.
Makes about 24 bars.

Hint
To soften brown sugar which has hardened: Place 200 g (7 oz) brown sugar in a microwave dish or bowl and add a slice of bread or a wedge of apple. Cover and microwave for 25 seconds on 100%. Leave to stand for a few minutes before using.

Date Bars

100% .... 18 minutes

250 g (9 oz) dates, stoned and chopped
300 ml (10 fl oz) water
25 ml (5 tsp) lemon juice

CRUMBLE
125 g (4 oz) plain flour
2.5 ml (½ tsp) bicarbonate of soda
60 g (2 oz) porridge oats
generous pinch of ground cinnamon
125 g (4 oz) soft brown sugar
45 g (1½ oz) pecan nuts, chopped
125 g (4 oz) butter

Place dates, water and lemon juice in a bowl. Cover with vented plastic wrap and microwave on 100% for 5 minutes. Uncover and cool slightly.

To make crumble: Sift flour and bicarbonate of soda into a bowl. Stir in oats, cinnamon, sugar and pecans. Microwave butter on 100% for 3-4 minutes to melt. Mix into dry ingredients.

Press half the crumble mixture into a greased 23-cm (9-in) square glass dish. Cover with date mixture and top with remaining crumble. Press down well. Shield corners of dish with foil and microwave on 100% for 9 minutes. Leave to cool, then cut into squares.
Makes 16 large or 25 small squares.

Hints
• The best biscuits for microwaving are those made from a stiff, crumbly mixture containing more flour than butter.
• Sugar biscuits also bake well in the microwave but biscuits made from a soft mixture tend to become hard and dry.

Chocolate Nut Biscuits

50% .... 12 minutes

125 g (4 oz) butter
90 g (3 oz) soft brown sugar
175 g (6 oz) plain flour
30 ml (2 tbsp) cocoa powder
pinch of salt
generous pinch of baking powder
10 ml (2 tsp) water
few drops of vanilla extract
about 24 pecan nut halves

Cream butter and sugar until light and fluffy. Sift together flour, cocoa powder, salt and baking powder and add to butter mixture. Add water and vanilla and mix to a stiff dough. Chill for 15 minutes, then form into small balls.

Line a microwave baking sheet or turntable with greased greaseproof paper. Place six balls in a circle on the sheet and flatten with the bottom of a glass. Press a pecan half into each biscuit. Microwave on 50% for 2-3 minutes, leave to stand for 5 minutes, then cool on a wire rack. Repeat with remaining dough. Makes about 24 biscuits.

Hint

EDIBLE GLITTER
For a sparkling finish to cakes and cookies at Christmas time, combine 125 ml (4 fl oz) water with 60 ml (4 tbsp) gum arabic in a bowl and microwave on 50% for 1½-2 minutes. Strain through a fine sieve, then colour gum mixture with food colouring.

Paint a thick layer of mixture on an ungreased metal baking sheet and stand it in a sunny or warm place. As the glitter dries, it flakes off the tray.

Turn dried glitter on to a piece of brown paper, fold paper over and crush glitter with a rolling pin. Store in an air-tight container. (The mixture may be kept in liquid form in the refrigerator for up to 2 years.)

Coconut and Almond Macaroons

Take care not to overcook these delicate biscuits.

100%, 70% .... 6 minutes

125 g (4 oz) desiccated coconut
75 g (2½ oz) caster sugar
2 egg whites (from large eggs)
few drops of almond essence
few drops of vanilla extract
2.5 ml (½ tsp) finely grated lemon rind
45 ml (3 tbsp) plain flour
generous pinch of baking powder
maraschino cherries or pecan nuts to decorate

Combine coconut, half of the sugar and 1 egg white in a bowl. Mix well and microwave on 100% for 2 minutes, stirring twice. Stir in almond essence and vanilla extract, lemon rind and sifted flour and baking powder. Whisk remaining egg white to soft peaks, then gradually whisk in remaining sugar. Fold into coconut mixture.

Spoon into twelve paper baking cases and bake six at a time in a microwave muffin pan, microwaving on 70% for 1½-2 minutes. Cool in paper cups on a wire rack. Top with a quarter maraschino cherry or half a pecan nut, if desired.
Makes 12 macaroons.

Lemon Bars

100% .... 12 minutes

400 g (14 oz) canned sweetened
    condensed milk
125 ml (4 fl oz) lemon juice
5 ml (1 tsp) grated lemon rind
75 g (2½ oz) butter, melted
150 g (5 oz) Marie biscuit crumbs
75 g (2½ oz) soft brown sugar
45 g (1½ oz) walnuts, chopped

Beat together condensed milk,
lemon juice and lemon rind until
thick and smooth. Set aside.
Microwave butter on 100% for
1-1½ minutes and pour on to
combined biscuit crumbs and
sugar. Mix well, then press about
two-thirds of mixture into the
bottom of a 23-cm (9-in) square
baking dish.
   Pour lemon mixture over biscuit
base and spread evenly. Sprinkle
remaining crumb mixture and
nuts over the top and pat down
gently. Shield corners of dish
with foil and microwave on 100%
for 8-10 minutes. Leave to cool in
dish, then cut into bars.
Makes about 18 bars.

Oatmeal Fruit Bars

100% .... 8 minutes

175 g (6 oz) rolled oats
300 g (11 oz) plain flour
150 g (5 oz) soft brown sugar
7.5 ml (1½ tsp) ground cinnamon
2.5 ml (½ tsp) bicarbonate of soda
250 g (9 oz) butter
300 g (11 oz) whole apricot jam

Combine oats, flour, sugar,
cinnamon and bicarbonate of
soda, then rub in butter until
mixture is crumbly. Set aside half
the mixture and press remainder
into a greased 30 x 20-cm
(12 x 8-in) baking dish. Spread
with apricot jam and sprinkle
reserved mixture over.
   Microwave on 100% for
6-8 minutes, then leave to stand
for at least 15 minutes before
cutting.
Makes about 24 bars.

Oatmeal Fruit Bars, (left) and Lemon
Bars

Orange Tea Bread

100%, 70% .... 13 minutes

225 g (8 oz) plain flour
7.5 ml (1½ tsp) baking powder
pinch of salt
2.5 ml (½ tsp) ground cinnamon
125 g (4 oz) caster sugar
60 ml (4 tbsp) currants
30 g (1 oz) butter
100 g (3½ oz) orange marmalade
1 egg
125 ml (4 fl oz) milk

TOPPING
60 ml (4 tbsp) soft brown sugar
30 ml (2 tbsp) orange juice
45 ml (3 tbsp) orange-flavoured
  liqueur

Sift flour, baking powder, salt and cinnamon into a large bowl. Mix in sugar and currants. Place butter in a bowl and microwave on 100% for 30-40 seconds until melted. Add remaining ingredients, mix well, then stir into flour.

Turn into a 23 x 9-cm (9 x 3½-in) microwave loaf dish and microwave on 70% for 8-10 minutes. (The top of the loaf should still be a little moist.) Leave to cool for 10 minutes.

Meanwhile, prepare topping by combining all ingredients in a jug and microwaving for 1-2 minutes until sugar has dissolved. When bread has cooled for 10 minutes, prick top with a skewer and pour topping over. Once liquid has been absorbed, turn loaf out to cool completely. Slice and serve with butter.
Makes one 23 x 9-cm (9 x 3½-in) loaf.

Mexican Corn Bread

100%, 50% .... 14 minutes

3 bacon rashers, rinds removed,
  diced
1 onion, finely chopped
150 g (5 oz) cornmeal
60 g (2 oz) plain flour
15 ml (1 tbsp) baking powder
5 ml (1 tsp) salt
2 eggs, beaten
300 ml (10 fl oz) milk
75 g (2½ oz) Cheddar cheese,
  grated
125 ml (4 fl oz) oil
125 g (4 oz) creamed sweetcorn
10-20 ml (2-4 tsp) finely chopped
  chilli pepper, or to taste

Place bacon in a bowl and microwave on 100% for 1 minute. Stir in onion and microwave for 2 minutes more. Drain. Combine cornmeal, flour, baking powder and salt. Mix together remaining ingredients, including bacon and onion, and stir into dry ingredients until just blended.

Turn into a greased 23-cm (9-in) baking dish and microwave on 50% for 7 minutes, then on 100% for 2-4 minutes, or until a skewer inserted in the centre comes out clean. Leave to stand for about 10 minutes before cutting into wedges to serve.
Makes 1 x 23-cm (9-in) round loaf.

Hint
When converting quick bread recipes for microwave use it may be necessary to:
• decrease the liquid content of a moist batter by about 30 ml (2 tbsp)
• increase the fat content of a low fat batter by 30 g (1 oz).

Strawberry and Date Loaf

70% .... 10 minutes

2 eggs
60 ml (4 tbsp) oil
150 g (5 oz) soft brown sugar
45 g (1½ oz) dates, stoned
  and chopped
60 ml (4 tbsp) strawberry jam
5 ml (1 tsp) finely grated lemon rind
125 g (4 oz) plain flour
generous pinch of salt
2.5 ml (½ tsp) bicarbonate of soda
2.5 ml (½ tsp) mixed spice
2.5 ml (½ tsp) ground cinnamon
100 ml (3½ fl oz) buttermilk

Combine eggs, oil and sugar in a large bowl and beat well. Add dates, strawberry jam and lemon rind and mix to combine. Sift dry ingredients into a bowl, then add about one-third to egg mixture, mixing to combine. Now add one-third of the buttermilk and mix. Repeat this twice more.
  Grease a 25 x 13-cm (10 x 5-in) microwave loaf dish. Turn batter into dish and microwave on 70% for 8-10 minutes. Leave to stand for at least 10 minutes before removing from dish.
Makes one 25 x 13-cm (10 x 5-in) loaf.

Lemon and Hazelnut Tea Loaf

70% .... 10 minutes

125 g (4 oz) butter
200 g (7 oz) caster sugar
2 eggs
175 g (6 oz) plain flour
7.5 ml (1½ tsp) baking powder
2.5 ml (½ tsp) salt
125 ml (4 fl oz) milk
60 g (2 oz) hazelnuts, chopped
45 ml (3 tbsp) finely grated lemon
  rind

Cream together butter and sugar until light and fluffy, then beat in eggs, one at a time. Sift in flour, baking powder and salt and beat until smooth. Blend in milk and fold in hazelnuts and rind.
  Pour batter into a greased microwave loaf or ring dish, lined with plastic wrap, and microwave on 70% for 8-10 minutes. Leave to stand for 10 minutes before turning out to cool on a wire rack. Makes 1 loaf.

Bran Knobs

100%, 70%, 15% ..... 64 minutes

125 g (4 oz) sunflower seeds
400 g (14 oz) plain flour
60 g (2 oz) All-Bran
150 g (5 oz) soft brown sugar
20 ml (4 tsp) baking powder
2.5 ml (½ tsp) salt
250 g (9 oz) butter
2 eggs
185 ml (6 fl oz) milk

Microwave a browning dish on 100% for 5 minutes, sprinkle sunflower seeds on to dish and stir. Microwave for 1-2 minutes more, stirring every 30 seconds.

Sift flour into a large bowl, add sunflower seeds, All-Bran, sugar, baking powder and salt. Cut butter into small cubes, add to mixture and rub in. Lightly beat together eggs and milk and add to mixture to form a soft, workable dough. Grease or spray a 30 x 20-cm (12 x 8-in) dish and line base with absorbent kitchen paper or plastic wrap.

Greasing hands with a little butter, roll walnut-sized pieces of dough into finger shapes. Arrange in rows, leaving space between each ball to allow for spreading. Microwave on 100% for 7 minutes, then reduce power to 70% and bake for a further 20-25 minutes. Leave to stand for 5 minutes, then break into 'knobs'. (The 'knobs' will still be slightly soft when they come out of the microwave but will become crisp as they cool.)

To dry baked 'knobs', place them on a microwave baking sheet, cover with waxed paper and microwave on 15% for 20-25 minutes, rearranging them every 5 minutes. Cool and store. Makes about 20 'knobs'.

Banana and Macadamia Nut Bread

100% .... 14 minutes

3 large, ripe bananas
10 ml (2 tsp) lemon juice
200 g (7 oz) caster sugar
125 g (4 oz) butter
250 g (9 oz) plain flour
5 ml (1 tsp) baking powder
5 ml (1 tsp) salt
2 eggs, beaten
5 ml (1 tsp) bicarbonate of soda
15 ml (1 tbsp) water
60 g (2 oz) salted macadamia nuts, chopped

Mash bananas, stir in lemon juice and sugar and set aside for 15 minutes. Microwave butter in a bowl on 100% for 1 minute, then beat into bananas. Sift together flour, baking powder and salt and blend into banana mixture a little at a time. Add eggs to mixture, stirring well to combine.

Dissolve bicarbonate of soda in the water and add to banana mixture. Mix well, then stir in nuts. Spoon into a greased and lined microwave loaf or ring dish and microwave on 100% for 10-13 minutes. Leave to stand in pan for 5 minutes before turning out to cool on a wire rack. Makes 1 loaf.

Fluffy Orange Spread
Beat together 100 g (3½ oz) cream cheese and 60 g (2 oz) softened butter until smooth. Gradually beat in 60 ml (4 tbsp) orange juice, then add 15 ml (1 tbsp) caster sugar and 15 ml (1 tbsp) orange rind and mix until well blended. (This spread is excellent on fruit and nut quick breads.) Makes about 200 g (7 oz).

Brown Batter Bread

50% .... 18 minutes

60 g (2 oz) plain flour
60 g (2 oz) wholemeal flour
5 ml (1 tsp) bicarbonate of soda
2.5 ml (^{1}/$_2$ tsp) salt
60 ml (4 tbsp) cornmeal
45 ml (3 tbsp) crushed wheat flakes
45 ml (3 tbsp) wheatgerm
75 ml (2^1/$_2$ fl oz) molasses
250 ml (8 fl oz) buttermilk
90 g (3 oz) raisins (optional)

Combine all ingredients in a large mixing bowl and beat with an electric mixer for about 3 minutes. Grease two 500 ml (16 fl oz) measuring jugs, divide mixture in half and spoon into jugs. Cover with vented plastic wrap and microwave, one at a time, on 50% for 8-9 minutes. Leave loaves to stand for at least 10 minutes before removing from jugs. Makes 2 small loaves.

Mixed Fruit Bread

70% .... 10 minutes

60 ml (4 tbsp) finely chopped nuts
150 g (5 oz) plain flour
90 g (3 oz) dried mixed fruit
100 g (3^1/$_2$ oz) dates, stoned and chopped
60 ml (4 tbsp) caster sugar
60 ml (4 tbsp) clear honey
1 egg
10 ml (2 tsp) grated orange rind
7.5 ml (1^1/$_2$ tsp) baking powder
generous pinch of salt
60 ml (4 tbsp) milk
60 ml (4 tbsp) orange juice

Grease a 23-cm (9-in) ring dish and sprinkle base and sides with nuts. Sift flour into a bowl and add remaining ingredients. Using an electric mixer, beat for 1 minute, then pour into ring dish.
   Microwave on 70% for 8-10 minutes. Leave to cool for at least 10 minutes before removing from dish. Slice when cold.
Makes 1 x 23-cm (9-in) ring-shaped loaf.

Poppy Seed Wedges

100%, 70% .... 14 minutes

250 g (9 oz) plain flour
15 ml (1 tbsp) finely snipped chives
10 ml (2 tsp) poppy seeds
10 ml (2 tsp) unbleached sesame seeds
10 ml (2 tsp) caster sugar
7.5 ml (1^1/$_2$ tsp) baking powder
2.5 ml (^{1}/$_2$ tsp) bicarbonate of soda
2.5 ml (^{1}/$_2$ tsp) salt
60 g (2 oz) Cheddar cheese, grated
1 egg
90 ml (3 fl oz) oil
150 ml (5 fl oz) milk
15 ml (1 tbsp) vinegar

TOPPING
15 g (1 oz) butter
30 ml (2 tbsp) dried breadcrumbs
30 ml (2 tbsp) grated Parmesan cheese
5 ml (1 tsp) poppy seeds
5 ml (1 tsp) unbleached sesame seeds

Sift flour into a large bowl and add chives, seeds, sugar, baking powder, bicarbonate of soda, salt and Cheddar cheese. Mix together lightly. Combine egg, oil, milk, and vinegar. Beat lightly and add to dry ingredients. Mix to combine. Turn mixture into a greased 23-cm (9-in) pie plate or baking dish and shape into a slightly domed loaf.
   To make topping: Place butter in a bowl and microwave on 100% for 30-40 seconds. Add remaining ingredients and work together until crumbly. Sprinkle evenly over loaf.
   Make a few deep criss-cross cuts in dough and microwave on 70% for 10-13 minutes. Leave to stand for about 10 minutes before slicing. Serve warm with butter. Makes 1 round loaf (about 16 wedges).

Gingerbread Square

Wholemeal Oatmeal Bread

100%, 70% .... 13 minutes

185 ml (6 fl oz) buttermilk
1 egg, beaten
15 g (¹/₂ oz) butter
250 g (9 oz) wholemeal flour
90 g (3 oz) rolled oats
100 g (3¹/₂ oz) seedless raisins
75 g (2¹/₂ oz) soft brown sugar
7.5 ml (1¹/₂ tsp) baking powder
2.5 ml (¹/₂ tsp) bicarbonate of soda
2.5 ml (¹/₂ tsp) salt

Combine buttermilk and egg, mixing well. Place butter in a bowl, microwave for 30 seconds on 100% and stir into buttermilk mixture. Combine remaining ingredients in a large bowl, make a well in the centre and pour in buttermilk mixture.
  Mix well, then turn dough on to a lightly floured board and knead gently for about 3 minutes. Shape into a round and place on a greased microwave baking sheet.

Make a criss-cross slash in the top with a sharp knife.
  Microwave on 70% for 10-13 minutes, or until a skewer inserted in the centre comes out clean. Transfer to a wire rack to cool.
Makes 1 round loaf.

Hints
• Assemble all ingredients before starting to mix quick breads. These mixtures should be combined quickly and baked immediately for best results.
• Measure ingredients accurately and only fill containers half full as the mixtures will rise high when baked.

Gingerbread Square

70% .... 13 minutes

75 ml (2¹/₂ fl oz) oil
75 ml (2¹/₂ fl oz) water
45 ml (3 tbsp) molasses
75 g (2¹/₂ oz) caster sugar
125 g (4 oz) wholemeal flour
generous pinch of bicarbonate of soda
5 ml (1 tsp) baking powder
5 ml (1 tsp) ground ginger
2.5 ml (¹/₂ tsp) ground cinnamon
2 egg whites

Beat together oil, water, molasses and sugar. Mix in dry ingredients. Beat egg whites to a peaking consistency and fold into mixture. Pour into a greased 20-cm (8-in) square dish or microwave pan and microwave on 70% for 10-13 minutes. Leave to cool in pan for at least 10 minutes. Remove and cut into squares. Dust with icing sugar, if desired.
Makes 25 squares.

Apricot Pecan Bread

70% .... 10 minutes

100 g (3¹/₂ oz) pecan nuts, finely chopped
150 g (5 oz) wholemeal flour
125 ml (4 fl oz) milk
60 g (2 oz) dried apricots, chopped
75 ml (2¹/₂ fl oz) oil
60 g (2 oz) sugar
60 ml (2 tbsp) honey
1 egg
10 ml (2 tsp) grated orange peel
2.5 ml (¹/₂ tsp) ground cinnamon
10 ml (2 tsp) baking powder
2.5 ml (¹/₂ tsp) salt

Grease a 1.5-litre (2³/₄-pint) microwave ring dish and coat with half the chopped nuts. Combine remaining ingredients and mix well. Spoon into dish and microwave on 70% for 8-10 minutes, or until a skewer inserted near the centre comes out clean. Leave to stand for 8-10 minutes before turning out.
Makes 1 ring-shaped loaf.

Welsh Tea Loaf

100%, 70% .... 12 minutes

200 ml (6¹/₂ fl oz) water
250 g (9 oz) seedless raisins
10 ml (2 tsp) bicarbonate of soda
175 g (6 oz) butter, softened
150 g (5 oz) caster sugar
1 extra-large egg
15 ml (1 tbsp) molasses or treacle
few drops of vanilla extract
pinch of salt
250 g (9 oz) plain flour

Combine water and raisins and microwave on 100% for 4 minutes. Stir in bicarbonate of soda and set aside to cool. Cream butter and sugar, then beat in egg. Add molasses or treacle, vanilla extract and salt and beat well. Stir in flour and add raisin mixture, mixing until well blended.

Spoon batter into a greased 25-cm (10-in) microwave ring dish, lined with plastic wrap, and microwave on 70% for 6-8 minutes. Leave to stand for 10 minutes, before turning out to cool on a wire rack. When cool, drizzle with confectioner's glaze. Makes 1 x 25-cm (10-in) ring loaf.

Confectioner's Glaze
Combine 125 g (4 oz) sifted icing sugar and 30-45 ml (2-3 tbsp) milk. Blend until smooth, using just enough milk to give a drizzling consistency.

Variations
MOCHA GLAZE
Add 15 ml (1 tbsp) cocoa powder and 2.5 ml (¹/₂ tsp) instant coffee powder to icing sugar.

SPICY GLAZE
Add 2.5 ml (¹/₂ tsp) ground cinnamon and a pinch of grated nutmeg to icing sugar.

CITRUS GLAZE
Substitute 30 ml (2 tbsp) lemon or orange juice for 30 ml (2 tbsp) of the milk in the basic glaze.

American Bran and Carrot Muffins

100% .... 10 minutes

90 g (3 oz) bran flakes, crushed
125 g (4 oz) plain flour
60 ml (4 tbsp) soft brown sugar
10 ml (2 tsp) baking powder
2.5 ml (¹/₂ tsp) bicarbonate of soda
2.5 ml (¹/₂ tsp) salt
2.5 ml (¹/₂ tsp) ground cinnamon
generous pinch of grated nutmeg
250 ml (8 fl oz) milk
1 egg
45 ml (3 tbsp) oil
150 g (5 oz) carrot, grated
60 ml (4 tbsp) chopped nuts,
  such as hazelnuts or walnuts
60 ml (4 tbsp) sultanas

Combine bran flakes, flour, sugar, baking powder, bicarbonate of soda, salt, cinnamon and nutmeg in a large bowl. Mix together milk, egg and oil and stir into dry ingredients. Add carrot, nuts and sultanas, stirring well to combine.

Spoon batter into six paper baking cases and place in a microwave muffin dish. Microwave on 100% for 3-5 minutes. Cool on a wire rack. Repeat with remaining batter.
Makes 10-12 muffins.

Hint
Try the following muffin toppings:

STREUSEL TOPPING
Combine 100 g (3¹/₂ oz) soft brown sugar, 30 ml (2 tbsp) plain flour, 10 ml (2 tsp) ground cinnamon, 30 g (1 oz) butter and 45 g (1¹/₂ oz) chopped nuts.

NUT CRUNCH TOPPING
Combine 45 g (1¹/₂ oz) plain flour, 30 ml (2 tbsp) soft brown sugar, 30 g (1 oz) butter, 45 ml (3 tbsp) chopped nuts and 30 ml (2 tbsp) cornflake crumbs.

CINNAMON SUGAR TOPPING
Combine 45 ml (3 tbsp) soft brown sugar and 2.5-5 ml (¹/₂-1 tsp) ground cinnamon.

American Lemon, Date and Nut Muffins

100% .... 12 minutes

100 g (3¹/₂ oz) soft brown sugar
90 g (3 oz) butter
75 ml (2¹/₂ fl oz) lemon juice
60 ml (4 tbsp) clear honey
125 ml (4 fl oz) soured cream
1 egg
10 ml (2 tsp) grated lemon rind
200 g (7 oz) plain flour
7.5 ml (1¹/₂ tsp) baking powder
2.5 ml (¹/₂ tsp) salt
2.5 ml (¹/₂ tsp) bicarbonate of soda
150 g (5 oz) dates, stoned and chopped
60 g (2 oz) nuts, such as pecan nuts or walnuts, coarsely chopped
60 ml (4 tbsp) hot water

Combine sugar, butter, lemon juice and honey in a jug and microwave on 100% for 2 minutes. Stir well and leave to cool to room temperature. In a large mixing bowl, combine soured cream, egg and lemon rind. Beat well, then add sugar mixture.

Sift together flour, baking powder, salt and bicarbonate of soda and add to liquid ingredients. Stir until just blended, then add dates, nuts and hot water. Mix for 10 seconds.

Spoon half the mixture into six paper baking cases, place in a microwave muffin dish and microwave on 100% for 3-5 minutes. Cool on a wire rack. Repeat with remaining batter. Makes 12 muffins.

Hint
When converting your own muffin recipe to microwave baking, add 15-30 g (¹/₂-1 oz) more butter for every 125 g (4 oz) flour used.

Savoury Cheese Muffins

Combination baking

90 g (3 oz) All-Bran
300 ml (10 fl oz) milk
100 ml (3¹/₂ fl oz) oil
2 eggs
2.5 ml (¹/₂ tsp) dried oregano
2.5 ml (¹/₂ tsp) dried thyme
15 ml (1 tbsp) snipped chives
15 ml (1 tbsp) chopped fresh parsley
30 ml (2 tbsp) grated Parmesan cheese
2.5 ml (¹/₂ tsp) paprika
2.5 ml (¹/₂ tsp) salt
250 g (9 oz) plain flour
60 g (2 oz) Cheddar cheese, grated
paprika

Soak All-Bran in milk for about 10 minutes. Lightly beat together oil, eggs and dried herbs. Add bran mixture to oil mixture and beat well, then stir in chives, parsley and Parmesan cheese. Finally, sift in dry ingredients and beat to combine.

Grease two microwave muffin dishes and spoon about 45 ml (3 tbsp) of the mixture into each muffin cup. Sprinkle with Cheddar cheese and dust with paprika. Bake one dish at a time according to directions below. Cool muffins slightly, then split and serve with butter.

BROTHER
Preheat for 7 minutes on 250 °C. Bake on Hi-Speed for 3¹/₂ minutes, then Turbo for 5 minutes.

Makes 12 large muffins.

Thirty-day Muffins

70% .... 4 minutes

2 eggs
300 g (11 oz) soft brown sugar
75 ml (2¹/₂ fl oz) oil
300 g (11 oz) plain flour
2.5 ml (¹/₂ tsp) salt
7.5 ml (1¹/₂ tsp) bicarbonate of soda
175 g (6 oz) bran
500 ml (16 fl oz) milk
few drops of vanilla extract
125 g (4 oz) sultanas

Beat together eggs and soft brown sugar thoroughly. Add oil and beat again. Sift flour, salt and bicarbonate of soda and add. Mix in remaining ingredients and refrigerate in an air-tight container for up to one month. Use as required.

To use, spoon about 20 ml (4 tsp) into paper baking cases and place either on a plate or in a microwave muffin dish. Microwave on 70% for 3-3¹/₂ minutes.
Makes about 50 muffins.

Variations
Add the following ingredients just before microwaving.

BANANA MUFFINS
Add two mashed bananas and a little cinnamon.

SPICY APPLE MUFFINS
Omit the sultanas and add 200 g (7 oz) fresh or canned pie apples, chopped, and a little mixed spice.

MARMALADE MUFFINS
Add 45 ml (3 tbsp) marmalade.

Savoury Celery and Onion Loaf

70% .... 7 minutes

250 g (9 oz) self-raising flour
2.5 ml (¹/₂ tsp) salt
2.5 ml (¹/₂ tsp) baking powder
45 g (1¹/₂ oz) sultanas
1 celery stick
2 eggs
15 ml (1 tbsp) finely chopped onion
125 g (4 oz) low-fat soft cheese
45 g (1¹/₂ oz) butter, softened

Sift flour, salt and baking powder into a mixing bowl and add sultanas. Cut celery into 1-cm (¹/₂-in) lengths and place in container of a blender or food processor. Add eggs, onion, soft cheese and butter. Blend until smooth, then add to dry ingredients. Mix thoroughly. (The dough should be of a fairly stiff consistency.)

Spoon into a greased 20-cm (8-in) microwave ring dish and microwave on 70% for 5¹/₂-6¹/₂ minutes, or until well risen and a cocktail stick inserted near the centre comes out clean. Leave to stand in ring dish for 10 minutes before turning out on to a wire rack to cool.
Makes 1 ring-shaped loaf.

Hints
• To prepare baking containers for quick breads, grease or spray and then line with waxed paper or absorbent kitchen paper. Do not flour the containers.
• Add brown sugar, treacle, spices, nuts and dried fruit to the ingredients, or use wholemeal flour to make quick breads, scones and muffins look more appealing.

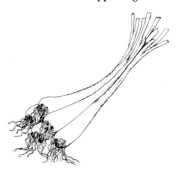

Quick Scone-based Pizza

Scones

100% .... 6 minutes

250 g (9 oz) plain flour
15 ml (1 tbsp) baking powder
2.5 ml (½ tsp) salt
90 g (3 oz) butter
30 ml (2 tbsp) caster sugar
   (for sweet scones only)
1 egg
185 ml (6 fl oz) milk

TOPPING FOR SWEET SCONES
melted butter
30 ml (2 tbsp) caster sugar
5 ml (1 tsp) ground cinnamon

TOPPING FOR SAVOURY SCONES
15 ml (1 tbsp) melted butter
generous pinch of paprika

Sift flour, baking powder and salt into a bowl. Rub in butter until mixture resembles fine crumbs. Stir in sugar if making sweet scones. Combine egg and milk and add to crumbed mixture with enough liquid to form a stiff dough.

Roll or pat out dough to a thickness of 1 cm (½ in). Cut into rounds and arrange six scones at a time on a plate lined with a double thickness of absorbent kitchen paper.

For sweet scones, brush tops with melted butter and sprinkle with a combination of sugar and cinnamon. For savoury scones, combine melted butter and paprika and brush over scone tops.

Microwave on 100% for 2-3 minutes, or until no longer doughy. Leave to stand for 1 minute, then remove to a wire rack. Repeat with remaining scones.

If desired, omit toppings and brush tops of microwaved scones with a little melted butter. Place under a hot grill to brown. Makes 12 scones.

Variations

FRUIT SCONES
Add 45 g (1½ oz) raisins or sultanas to dry ingredients before adding liquid. Proceed as above.

WHEATGERM SCONES
Substitute 60 ml (4 tbsp) wheatgerm for 60 ml (4 tbsp) of the flour and proceed as above.

SAVOURY SCONES
Add 60 g (2 oz) grated Cheddar cheese and 5 ml (1 tsp) dried mixed herbs to dry ingredients before adding liquid. Proceed as above.

WHOLEMEAL SCONES
Substitute 125 g (4 oz) wholemeal flour for 125 g (4 oz) of the plain flour and proceed as above.

Note

To microwave scones in a browning dish, prepare scone mixture as above. Preheat a browning dish for 4 minutes on 100%, grease with a little oil and heat for 30 seconds more. Place six scones in a circle on the dish and microwave on 100% for 2-3 minutes.

QUICK SCONE-BASED PIZZA
Sift 125 g (4 oz) plain flour, 2.5 ml (1½ tsp) cream of tartar and a generous pinch of bicarbonate of soda into a bowl. Add a generous pinch of dried oregano and rub in 30 g (1 oz) butter. Mix to a scone dough consistency with 60 ml (4 tbsp) milk. Grease a 20-cm (8-in) pie plate and press in dough. Microwave on 100% for 2 minutes.

Spread 345 ml (11 fl oz) seasoned tomato sauce (page 204) over dough, sprinkle with 100 g (3½ oz) grated Cheddar cheese and dot with a few black olives and a few anchovy fillets. Microwave for 3 minutes. Leave to stand for 2 minutes before serving.
Serves 4-6.

Healthy Brown Bread

100%, 50% .... 14 minutes

125 g (4 oz) plain flour
125 g (4 oz) wholemeal flour
10 g (^{1}/$_4$ oz) instant dried yeast
5 ml (1 tsp) salt
15 ml (1 tbsp) sugar
45 ml (3 tbsp) rolled oats
15 ml (1 tbsp) wheatgerm
15 ml (1 tbsp) sesame seeds
60 g (2 oz) butter
250 ml (8 fl oz) milk
cracked wheat

Combine plain flour, wholemeal flour, yeast, salt, sugar, oats, wheatgerm and sesame seeds in a mixing bowl and rub in 45 g (1^1/$_2$ oz) of the butter. Microwave milk in a jug on 100% for 1^1/$_2$ minutes and add to dry ingredients. Mix to form a soft but not sticky dough.

Knead dough until smooth and elastic. Shape into a smooth ball, place in a well-greased 18-cm (7-in) soufflé dish and cover with absorbent kitchen paper.

Prove dough by microwaving it on 100% for 15 seconds, then leaving it to stand for 10 minutes. Repeat process at least once more, or until dough has doubled in bulk. Microwave remaining butter for 30 seconds to melt, then brush over top of dough and sprinkle with cracked wheat. Microwave on 50% for 6 minutes, then on 100% for 3-4 minutes.

Gently remove loaf from dish and place on absorbent kitchen paper on base or turntable of microwave oven and microwave for 1 minute more. Leave to stand for 5 minutes, then cool on a wire rack. Eat within 2 days.
Makes 1 large loaf.

Variations

SAVOURY ONION LOAF
Add 5 ml (1 tsp) dried mixed herbs to dry ingredients and knead in 30 ml (2 tbsp) finely chopped onion and 90 g (3 oz) grated Cheddar cheese, then proceed as above.

HAM AND CHEESE LOAF
Follow above recipe, working in 60 ml (4 tbsp) finely chopped cooked ham and 90 g (3 oz) grated Cheddar cheese during kneading.

GARLIC HERB LOAF
Add 10 ml (2 tsp) chopped fresh parsley and 1 finely chopped garlic clove to dry ingredients. Proceed as above.

Classic Rye Bread

100% .... 7 minutes

10 ml (2 tsp) soft brown sugar
125 g (4 oz) strong white flour
300 g (11 oz) rye flour
7.5 ml (1½ tsp) salt
10 g (¼ oz) instant dried yeast
345-375 ml (11-12 fl oz) water,
    warmed
10 ml (2 tsp) molasses
oil
caraway seeds

Combine sugar, flours, salt and yeast. Combine warm water and molasses and add enough to dry ingredients to make a soft dough. Knead until smooth and elastic.

Oil a large bowl, place dough in bowl and turn to coat with oil. Cover loosely with plastic wrap. Microwave dough on 100% for 15 seconds, then leave to stand for 8-10 minutes. Repeat process twice more, or until dough has doubled in bulk. Knock down dough, knead for 2 minutes, then shape into a ball.

Make a slash across top of dough with a sharp knife. Place dough in a large, round, greased casserole dish, brush with oil and sprinkle with caraway seeds. Cover loosely with plastic wrap and prove again as above until dough has doubled in volume. Microwave on 100% for 5-6 minutes. Leave to stand for 10 minutes, then turn out and cool on a wire rack.
Makes 1 large loaf.

Hint
The appearance of yeast breads baked in the microwave can be improved by adding a variety of ingredients to the top of the bread. Brush the oven-ready loaf with a little melted butter and sprinkle with one of the following: crushed wheat, uncooked oatmeal, savoury biscuit crumbs, wheatgerm, sesame or poppy seeds, seasoned cornflake crumbs or finely chopped nuts.

Casserole Bread with Herbs

100%, 70% .... 13 minutes

350 g (13 oz) plain flour
10 ml (2 tsp) salt
5 ml (1 tsp) caster sugar
10 g (¼ oz) instant dried yeast
250 ml (8 fl oz) water, warmed
60 ml (4 tbsp) molasses or treacle
30 ml (2 tbsp) oil
1 egg
100 g (3½ oz) wheatgerm
10 ml (2 tsp) chopped fresh parsley
15 ml (1 tbsp) snipped fresh chives
5 ml (1 tsp) dried mixed herbs
1 large carrot, finely grated

Combine 250 g (9 oz) of the flour with salt, sugar and yeast. Add half the warm water and mix for about 3 minutes. Add remaining water, molasses, oil and egg and beat well. Then stir in wheatgerm, parsley, chives, herbs, carrot and enough of the remaining flour to make a soft batter.

Turn into a well-greased 2-litre (3½-pint) casserole dish, cover with plastic wrap and microwave on 100% for 15 seconds. Leave to stand for 8 minutes, then repeat microwaving and standing procedure at least twice more, or until dough has doubled in bulk. Remove plastic wrap and microwave on 70% for 8-12 minutes. Leave to stand in dish for 10 minutes before turning out to cool on a wire rack.
Makes 1 large loaf.

Wholemeal American Muffin Loaf

100% .... 16 minutes

500 ml (16 fl oz) milk
125 ml (4 fl oz) water
30 g (1 oz) fresh yeast
15 ml (1 tbsp) soft brown sugar
400 g (14 oz) plain flour
5 ml (1 tsp) salt
2.5 ml ($^1\!/_2$ tsp) bicarbonate of soda
200 g (7 oz) wholemeal flour
extra wholemeal flour

Place milk and water in a jug and microwave on 100% for 1-1$^1\!/_2$ minutes until warm. Add yeast and sugar and stir to combine. Sprinkle mixture with 30 ml (2 tbsp) of the weighed plain flour and cover with vented plastic wrap. Microwave for 10 seconds, leave to stand for 3 minutes, then repeat once more. (The top will begin to foam.)

Meanwhile, sift remaining plain flour, salt and bicarbonate of soda into a large mixing bowl. Add wholemeal flour, stir to combine, then pour in yeast mixture. Using an electric mixer, beat for about 4 minutes, or knead by hand till dough is smooth and elastic.

Grease two 25 x 12-cm (10 x 5-in) microwave loaf dishes and divide mixture between them. Dust tops of loaves with a little extra wholemeal flour. Cover with plastic wrap and microwave both for 15 seconds, then leave to stand for 10 minutes. Repeat two or three times until dough has doubled in size.

Microwave each loaf separately for 5-6 minutes. (The surface of the cooked loaves will be pale in colour.) Leave to cool for 10 minutes before removing from dishes. Serve sliced and toasted with butter and honey or syrup. Makes 2 large loaves.

Walnut Bread

This bread goes well with cheese, chilled grapes and a white or rosé wine.

100% .... 3 minutes
Plus combination baking

10 g ($^1\!/_4$ oz) instant dried yeast
5 ml (1 tsp) salt
60 g (2 oz) wholemeal flour
480 g (14 oz) plain flour
250 ml (8 fl oz) milk
75 ml (2$^1\!/_2$ fl oz) water
100 g (3$^1\!/_2$ oz) walnuts, coarsely chopped
100 g (3$^1\!/_2$ oz) onion, finely chopped
120 g (4 oz) butter, softened

Combine yeast, salt, wholemeal flour and half the plain flour in a large mixing bowl. In a jug, microwave milk and water on 100% for 1-2 minutes until very warm and add to dry ingredients. Using an electric mixer, mix to moisten, then beat on medium speed for 3 minutes. Stir in nuts, onion and butter and mix well. Finally, blend in enough of the remaining flour to make a stiff dough.

Cover loosely with plastic wrap and microwave for 15 seconds, then leave to stand for 10 minutes. Repeat this process twice more, or until mixture has doubled in bulk.

Knock down dough and knead for 2-3 minutes. Then shape into a round and place on a greased microwave baking sheet. Leave to rise, uncovered, for about 15 minutes, then bake according to instructions below until loaf is nicely browned and sounds hollow when tapped. Cool on a wire rack.

BROTHER
Hi-Speed at 220 °C for 10 minutes, then bake on convection at 180 °C for about 25-30 minutes.

Makes 1 large loaf.

Pineapple Knots

100% .... 4 minutes
Plus combination baking

250-300 g (9-11 oz) plain flour
2.5 ml (½ tsp) salt
45 ml (3 tbsp) sugar
10 g (¼ oz) instant dried yeast
150 ml (5 fl oz) milk and
  water mixed
1 egg
45 g (1½ oz) butter, cut into cubes

FILLING
30 g (1 oz) butter
150 g (5 oz) caster sugar
45 g (1½ oz) mixed nuts, chopped
1 glacé pineapple ring, chopped
3 glacé apricots, chopped

GLAZE
45 ml (3 tbsp) pineapple juice
45 g (1½ oz) caster sugar

ICING
75 g (2½ oz) icing sugar
pineapple juice

Sift about half the flour with the
salt into a large mixing bowl. Add
sugar and yeast and stir to
combine. Microwave milk and
water in a jug on 100% for
45 seconds to 1 minute until
warm. Add to dry ingredients.
Then, using an electric mixer
fitted with a dough hook, mix to a
smooth dough. Add egg and
butter and mix well. Gradually
add remaining flour (the dough
should be firm and moist) and
continue mixing for about
4 minutes, or 10 minutes by hand.

Turn dough into a large, well-
greased plastic bag and prove by
microwaving dough on 100% for
15 seconds and then leaving it to
stand for 10 minutes. Repeat this
procedure twice more, or until
dough has doubled in bulk.

Meanwhile, prepare filling by
creaming butter and sugar
together and stirring in nuts and
fruit.

Roll out dough to a 50 x 22-cm
(20 x 9-in) rectangle. Working
lengthways, spread filling over
half the dough, fold remaining
half back over filling and press

down lightly to seal. Cut into
twelve strips. Tie each strip
loosely into a knot and arrange six
on a baking sheet with the ends
tucked underneath. Cover loosely
with plastic wrap and allow to rise
for 10-15 minutes. Bake according
to instructions below, repeating
with second batch.

To make glaze: Combine
pineapple juice and sugar in a jug
and microwave for 1-2 minutes
until sugar has dissolved and
mixture has become slightly
sticky. Brush knots and bake on
convection for a further
3 minutes.

To make icing: Sift icing sugar
into a bowl and add sufficient
pineapple juice to give a thick
pouring consistency. When knots
are cool, drizzle a little icing over
each.

BROTHER
Preheat 7 minutes at 180 °C. Bake
on Hi-Speed for 4 minutes, then
on Turbo for 8.

Makes 12 knots.

Honey Butter

Beat together thoroughly until
light and fluffy: 125 g (4 oz)
softened butter, 175 g (6 oz) clear
honey and 15 ml (1 tbsp) grated
orange or lemon rind. (This
spread is ideal for tea breads and
is especially tasty on toasted
American muffin bread.) Makes
about 275 g (10 oz).

Seed Loaves

Bake the bread in four small soufflé dishes or in two clay flower-pots for an unusual effect.

100% .... 2 minutes
Plus combination baking

10 g (¹/₄ oz) instant dried yeast
30 ml (2 tbsp) sugar
10 ml (2 tsp) salt
750 g (1³/₄ lb) plain flour
500 ml (16 fl oz) milk, warmed
45 ml (3 tbsp) grated Parmesan cheese
60 ml (4 tbsp) soured cream
1 egg yolk, beaten
sesame seeds

Combine yeast, sugar, salt and half the flour in the bowl of an electric mixer. Add warmed milk, mix to combine, then beat for 3 minutes on medium speed. Add Parmesan cheese and soured cream, mixing well. Add enough of the remaining flour, a little at a time, to give a stiff dough. Knead until smooth and elastic.

Transfer dough to a well-oiled bowl, turning to coat, and cover loosely with plastic wrap. Prove dough by microwaving on 100% for 15 seconds, then leaving to stand for 10 minutes. Repeat process twice until dough has doubled in bulk.

Knock down dough and divide into four portions. Shape each into a round and place in four small, greased soufflé dishes. Cover and prove again.

Brush tops with beaten egg yolk and sprinkle with sesame seeds. Place loaves in a circular pattern in microwave and bake as directed below, or until loaves are golden brown and sound hollow when tapped. Remove bread from dishes and cool on wire racks.

BROTHER
Hi-Speed at 190 °C for 16-20 minutes.

Makes 4 small loaves.

Wholemeal Beer Bread

100% .... 2 minutes
Plus combination baking

10 g (¹/₄ oz) instant dried yeast
15 ml (1 tbsp) soft brown sugar
60 ml (4 tbsp) water, warmed
175 g (6 oz) strong white flour
175 g (6 oz) wholemeal flour
30 ml (2 tbsp) non-fat dried milk powder
30 ml (2 tbsp) oil
7.5 ml (1¹/₂ tsp) salt
250 ml (8 fl oz) beer, at room temperature
15 ml (1 tbsp) sesame seeds

Sprinkle yeast and sugar on to water and stir to dissolve. Leave to stand in a warm place until foamy (about 10 minutes). Combine strong white flour, wholemeal flour, milk powder, oil, salt and yeast mixture in a bowl. Slowly add beer, beating constantly until dough leaves sides of bowl clean. Knead until smooth and elastic.

Place dough in a large oiled bowl and turn to coat. Cover loosely with plastic wrap and microwave on 100% for 15 seconds, then leave to stand for 10 minutes. Repeat this proving process at least twice more, or until dough has doubled in bulk.

Knock down dough and knead into a ball. Place on a lightly oiled baking sheet and prove again as above until dough has doubled in bulk. Sprinkle top of dough with sesame seeds and bake on combination baking, as directed below.

BROTHER
Hi-Speed at 190 °C for 18-24 minutes.

Makes 1 round loaf.

Apple Coffee Cake

Apple Coffee Cake

100%, 50% .... 12 minutes

350 g (12 oz) plain flour
2.5 ml (¹/₂ tsp) salt
30 ml (2 tbsp) sugar
7.5 ml (1¹/₂ tsp) instant dried yeast
60 ml (4 tbsp) water
125 ml (4 fl oz) milk
60 g (2 oz) butter
1 egg

FILLING
45 g (1¹/₂ oz) butter
75 g (2¹/₂ oz) sugar
60 g (2 oz) soft brown sugar
6 Marie biscuits, crushed
10 ml (2 tsp) ground cinnamon
generous pinch of grated nutmeg
2.5 ml (¹/₂ tsp) finely grated lemon rind
2 Granny Smith apples
10 ml (2 tsp) lemon juice

Sift flour and salt into a large mixing bowl, then add sugar and yeast. Combine water and milk in a jug and microwave on 100% for 30 seconds, or until the tempera-

ture of the milk reaches blood heat. Microwave butter for 1 minute, add to liquid, then mix in egg. Add liquids to flour to give a soft dough. Knead until a smooth, pliable dough forms (about 1 minute in a food processor, 4 minutes in a large electric mixer or 10 minutes by hand).

Turn dough into a plastic bag, microwave for 15 seconds, then leave to stand for 10 minutes. Repeat this process at least twice more, or until dough has doubled in bulk. Knock down dough, knead, cover and set aside.

To make filling: Microwave butter in a small bowl for 45 seconds to melt, then cool slightly. In a separate bowl, combine sugars, biscuit crumbs, spices and rind. Peel, core and slice apples into about 12 wedges each. Sprinkle with lemon juice.

To assemble: Divide dough into quarters, then divide each quarter into six and shape into balls. Dip each ball into the melted butter and then into the crumb mixture, coating evenly. Arrange in a well-greased 25-cm (10-in) microwave

ring dish, alternating with apple slices. Repeat with a second layer of dough and apple. Cover and microwave for 15 seconds, leave to stand for 10 minutes and repeat if necessary. (The dough is ready to microwave when it is springy to the touch – that is, when the 'dent' made by a finger disappears after a few seconds.)

Remove cover, sprinkle dough with any remaining crumbs and microwave on 50% for 6 minutes. Increase power to 100% and microwave for a further 1¹/₂-2 minutes. Leave to stand for 5 minutes before turning out. Makes 1 x 25-cm (10-in) ring-shaped bun.

Hint
To reheat bread rolls: Wrap one roll in a paper napkin and microwave on 100% for 10-15 seconds. For several rolls, place in a wicker basket and cover, then microwave for about 10 seconds per roll.

Bread Rolls

To make bread rolls, use any yeast bread recipe and follow the directions for mixing and for the first proving of the dough. The number of rolls made will depend on the size of the recipe but, as a guideline, a one-loaf recipe makes about 16 rolls.

For a one-loaf recipe, grease two 20-cm (8-in) cake dishes. Divide dough into equal-sized pieces (about 16) and shape each piece into a smooth ball. Place seven balls in a circle in each dish, with one ball in the centre. Cover and prove as for bread until dough doubles in bulk. Uncover, brush with a little milk and sprinkle with seeds.

Stand one dish at a time on a microwaveproof rack and microwave on 100% for 4-6 minutes, or until well-risen and firm to the touch. Leave to stand for 10 minutes, then turn out on to a rack to cool. Pull rolls apart to serve.

Chocolate Croissant Plait

Think of a large croissant – cut into slices! Prepare this dough and keep it refrigerated overnight, then simply roll out and finish off just before breakfast.

100% .... 40 seconds
Plus combination baking

225 g (8 oz) plain flour
2.5 ml (¹/₂ tsp) salt
30 ml (2 tbsp) sugar
5 ml (1 tsp) instant dried yeast
45 ml (3 tbsp) warm water
125 ml (4 fl oz) buttermilk
30 ml (2 tbsp) oil
175 g (6 oz) butter, coarsely grated and frozen
100 g (3¹/₂ oz) chocolate chips
egg for brushing
60 ml (4 tbsp) flaked almonds

Sift flour and salt into a large bowl. Add sugar and yeast and stir to combine. In a jug, combine water and buttermilk. Microwave on 100% for 30-40 seconds to make sure it is warm, then stir in oil. Add to flour. Now, using a mixer fitted with a dough attachment, knead until smooth and elastic (about 4 minutes). Add butter and work only until combined.

Turn dough out on to a lightly floured board and roll out to a 35 x 15-cm (14 x 6-in) rectangle. Fold both ends to the middle, then fold dough in half. Repeat this rolling and folding process twice more. Wrap in foil and chill for at least one hour.

When ready, roll out dough to a 30 x 22-cm (12 x 9-in) rectangle and lift on to a greased microwave baking sheet. Using the back of a knife, mark off a rectangle down centre of dough, but do not cut through. Sprinkle this area with chocolate chips and press in lightly.

Next, using a sharp knife, cut through dough at 2.5-cm (1-in) intervals from indented line to outer edge. Repeat on the other side. Brush ends lightly with water and fold in the cut pieces, alternating from left to right. Cover loosely with absorbent kitchen paper and leave to rise in a warm place for about 20 minutes. Brush top with beaten egg and sprinkle with almonds. Bake as directed below. Serve warm or cold.

BROTHER
Preheat at 180 °C for 7 minutes. Bake on Hi-Speed at 180 °C for 18-22 minutes.

Makes 1 x 30-cm (12-in) plait.

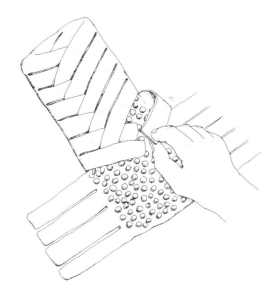

Healthy Wholemeal Bread

100% .... 45 seconds
Plus combination baking

150 g (5 oz) strong white flour
200 g (7 oz) wholemeal flour
100 g (3¹/₂ oz) crushed wheat
45 g (1¹/₂ oz) bran
10 g (¹/₄ oz) instant dried yeast
5 ml (1 tsp) salt
60 ml (4 tbsp) sunflower seeds
60 ml (4 tbsp) linseed
60 ml (4 tbsp) cider vinegar
30 ml (2 tbsp) molasses
60 ml (4 tbsp) oil
hot water
few extra seeds for sprinkling

In a large bowl, combine flours, crushed wheat, bran, yeast, salt and seeds. Mix together vinegar molasses, oil and a little hot water and pour on to dry ingredients. Then, using an electric mixer fitted with a dough hook, mix to a sticky dough. Continue mixing for at least 2 minutes.

Divide mixture in half and turn into two well-greased 23 x 9-cm (9 x 3¹/₂-in) microwave loaf dishes. Sprinkle tops with a few extra seeds and cover loosely with plastic wrap. Microwave on 100% for 15 seconds, then leave to stand for 10 minutes. Repeat this proving procedure twice more until mixture has risen almost to top of dishes.

Bake each loaf separately as directed below. Remove from microwave and allow to cool for 10 minutes before turning out on to a wire rack to cool completely.

BROTHER
Hi-Speed at 190 °C for 18-24 minutes.

Makes 2 medium-sized loaves.

Rosemary and Ricotta Loaf

100% .... 45 seconds
Plus combination baking

300 g (11 oz) plain flour
30 ml (2 tbsp) caster sugar
5 ml (1 tsp) salt
10 ml (2 tsp) chopped fresh rosemary
10 g (¹/₄ oz) instant dried yeast
30 ml (2 tbsp) chopped spring onions
1 carrot, finely grated
250 g (9 oz) Ricotta cheese
30 ml (2 tbsp) oil, preferably Italian olive
125 ml (4 fl oz) water, warmed
1 egg

Place about half the flour in the work bowl of a food processor fitted with a metal blade. Pulse to aerate. Add sugar, salt, rosemary, yeast, onions and carrot. Pulse to combine. Add cheese and process for about 10 seconds.

Mix oil, water and egg together and add to flour mixture. Process to mix completely. Add remaining flour, about 60 ml (4 tbsp) at a time, through feed tube, processing for about 5 seconds after each addition.

Turn mixture into a greased or sprayed 1.5-litre (2³/₄-pint) casserole dish and cover loosely with plastic wrap. Microwave on 100% for 15 seconds, then leave to stand for 10 minutes. Repeat this proving process at least twice more until mixture has risen almost to top of dish. Bake according to instructions below. Leave to stand for 10 minutes in dish before turning out to cool on a wire rack.

BROTHER
Hi-Speed at 190 °C for 11-22 minutes.

Makes 1 loaf.

Friandises

100%, 70% .... 13 minutes

**fruits such as tangerine segments,
 grapes, strawberries and cherries
stoned dates
selection of nuts**

SUGAR CARAMEL
**200 g (7 oz) caster sugar
150 ml (5 fl oz) water**

Remove pith from tangerine
segments. Leave stems on grapes,
strawberries and cherries. Wash
and dry thoroughly.

   To make caramel: Mix sugar and
water together in a medium-sized
bowl and microwave on 100% for
2 minutes. Stir, then microwave
for a further 8-10 minutes,
depending on how dark a caramel
is required, but do not allow
caramel to become too brown as
cooking will continue after bowl
has been removed from
microwave.

   Have ready two oiled forks and
a well-oiled baking sheet. Dip
fruit sections, one at a time, into
caramel. Remove and allow
excess caramel to drip off, then
place on baking sheet. Continue
in this way until all fruit has been
used up. Should caramel become
too thick to work with, microwave
for 1 minute on 100%, then
continue as before.

   When caramelized fruits are
hard, lift off baking sheet, trim off
any excess caramel and serve in
tiny paper cups.
This quantity of caramel is
enough for 50 friandises.

Hint
**When making friandises, dip the
nuts and fruit with firm skins, such
as grapes and cherries, before the
fruit with soft skins, such as
strawberries, as the sugar tends to
start crystallizing once the soft
fruits have been dipped.**

Chocolate, Ginger and Macadamia Bark

100%, 50% .... 11 minutes

6 small pieces of crystallized ginger
250 ml (8 fl oz) water, boiling
300 g (11 oz) white chocolate,
  broken into pieces
250 g (9 oz) plain chocolate,
  broken into pieces
100 g (3½ oz) macadamia nuts,
  roughly chopped
30 ml (2 tbsp) finely chopped
  orange rind

Place ginger in a jug, add boiling water and microwave on 100% for 1 minute. Drain well and pat dry. Mince ginger finely. Line a baking sheet with waxed paper.

Place white chocolate in a bowl and microwave for about 5 minutes on 50%, stirring every minute until melted and smooth. Microwave plain chocolate for about 4 minutes on 50%, stirring every minute until melted and smooth.

To white chocolate add 15 ml (1 tbsp) of the minced ginger, half the nuts and half the orange rind. Pour in three strips down waxed paper, about 2.5 cm (1-in) apart. Add remaining ingredients to plain chocolate and pour down length of pan between white chocolate lines. Spread until plain and white chocolate meet, then draw the tip of a knife through both chocolates to form a swirl pattern.

Chill until set, then break into large pieces. Place in an airtight container and refrigerate until needed.

Makes about 600 g (1 lb 5 oz).

Chocolate Caramels

These are rich and good! Always take care when working with white chocolate as it overheats and burns very easily.

100%, 70% .... 43 minutes

375 ml (12 fl oz) single cream
125 g (4 oz) butter
450 g (1 lb) soft brown sugar
60 ml (4 tbsp) maple syrup
few drops of vanilla extract
100 g (3½ oz) walnuts, chopped
300 g (11 oz) plain cooking
  chocolate, broken into pieces
90 g (3 oz) white chocolate,
  broken into pieces

In a large bowl, combine cream and butter and microwave on 100% for 2-3 minutes until butter has melted. Add brown sugar and maple syrup and beat well. Microwave for 6 minutes, stirring every 2 minutes. Then stir in vanilla and microwave for 20-25 minutes until 'hard ball' stage is reached (page 201).

Prepare a 25 x 20-cm (10 x 8-in) pan by lining base and sides with greaseproof paper. Sprinkle walnuts on base, then pour boiled mixture over nuts and refrigerate for at least 30 minutes. Cut into 4 x 2.5-cm (1-in) rectangles. Chill well.

To dip caramels: Microwave plain cooking chocolate on 70% for 4-6 minutes, stirring every minute. Dip each caramel individually, allowing excess chocolate to drip off before placing on a sheet of foil. Refrigerate until set. Microwave white chocolate for 2-3 minutes, stirring every 50 seconds. Spoon chocolate into a paper piping bag made from greaseproof paper and cut off tip. Pipe a zig-zag over each coated caramel.

If covered, these sweets will keep for up to 4 days in the refrigerator.

Makes about 40 caramels.

Clockwise from top left: Almond Fudge, Quick Double-layer Fudge and Deluxe Truffles

Almond Fudge

100%, 70% .... 31 minutes

90 g (3 oz) unsalted butter
150 g (5 oz) blanched almonds
500 ml (16 fl oz) milk
200 g (7 oz) caster sugar
2.5 ml (¹/₂ tsp) ground cardamom
 or pinch of ground cloves
almond halves

Place 30 g (1 oz) of the butter in a casserole dish and microwave on 100% for 45 seconds. Add blanched almonds, stir and microwave for about 3-5 minutes, stirring frequently until lightly browned. Drain on paper towels and transfer to a bowl. Microwave milk for 3 minutes, then pour on to almonds and leave to stand for 2 hours.

Purée almond and milk mixture in a blender until smooth and thick. Pour into a dish and microwave for about 10 minutes, or until most of the milk has evaporated and remaining paste mounds in a spoon. Add sugar and stir well. Microwave for 2-3 minutes to melt sugar. Add remaining butter and microwave on 70% for about 9 minutes, or until mixture is consistency of fudge. Stir in cardamom and turn into a greased baking dish.

Cool slightly, then pat into an even layer and leave to cool completely. Cut into squares and top each with half an almond. Store in a tightly covered container for up to two weeks. Makes about 500 g (1 lb 2 oz).

Quick Double-layer Fudge

100%, 50% .... 5 minutes

225 g (8 oz) smooth peanut butter
125 g (4 oz) butter
375 g (13 oz) icing sugar
175 g (6 oz) chocolate chips
15 g (¹/₂ oz) butter

Combine peanut butter and 125 g (4 oz) butter in a large bowl. Microwave on 100% for 1¹/₂ minutes. Mix in icing sugar and spread in a 23-cm (9-in) square dish.

Microwave chocolate chips on 50% for about 3 minutes, or until melted and smooth. Stir in 15 ml (1 tbsp) butter and spread over peanut butter mixture. Chill for at least 1 hour, then cut into squares. Makes 36 or 49 squares.

Deluxe Truffles

70% .... 4 minutes

125 g (4 oz) plain chocolate,
 broken into pieces
45 g (1¹/₂ oz) butter
30 ml (2 tbsp) honey
30 ml (2 tbsp) whisky
60 g (2 oz) cake crumbs or finely
 crushed wafer biscuits
chocolate vermicelli

Place chocolate in a bowl and microwave on 70% for 3-3¹/₂ minutes, stirring from time to time. Stir in butter, honey and whisky. If not sufficiently melted, microwave for 30 seconds more. Add cake crumbs or crushed biscuits and stir until completely mixed. Chill in refrigerator for about 2 hours.

Scoop out small spoonfuls and roll into balls. Roll in chocolate vermicelli and place in paper cases to serve.
Makes about 30 truffles.

Clockwise from top left: Marshmallows, Chocolate Nut Fudge and Marshmallow and Date Squares

Marshmallows

100% .... 16 minutes

400 g (14 oz) caster sugar
15 ml (1 tbsp) golden syrup
345 ml (11 fl oz) water
35 ml (7 tsp) powdered gelatine
2 egg whites
few drops of vanilla extract
45 ml (3 tbsp) cornflour
45 ml (3 tbsp) icing sugar

Combine sugar, golden syrup and 250 ml (8 fl oz) of the water in a large bowl and microwave on 100% for 4 minutes. Stir well. Microwave for about 12 minutes more until mixture reaches 'soft ball' stage. Meanwhile, soak gelatine in remaining water for 2 minutes. Add to boiling syrup and stir to dissolve.

Whisk egg whites until stiff, then gradually pour in syrup. Continue whisking until mixture hold its shape. Add vanilla extract. Pour into a well-greased 25 x 20-cm (10 x 8-in) pan and place in refrigerator to set. When firm, cut into squares with a hot knife. Sift cornflour and icing sugar together and roll each square in this mixture. Alternatively, roll in toasted coconut.
Makes about 48 squares.

Hint
To test for the 'soft ball' stage: Pour 60 ml (4 tbsp) cold water into a small bowl, then add about 2.5 ml (½ tsp) of the boiled sugar mixture. When worked between two fingers, this sugar should form into a soft ball. The same method applies to the 'hard ball' and 'crack' stages, with the sugar being that much harder in each instance.

Chocolate Nut Fudge

100% .... 18 minutes

500 g (18 oz) caster sugar
250 ml (8 fl oz) buttermilk
90 g (3 oz) plain cooking
  chocolate, broken in pieces
45 g (1½ oz) butter
few drops of vanilla extract
100 g (3½ oz) hazelnuts or pecan
  nuts, roughly chopped

In a large bowl, combine sugar, buttermilk and chocolate. Microwave mixture on 100% for 6 minutes, stirring every 2 minutes. Then microwave without stirring for 10-12 minutes until 'soft ball' stage is reached (see *Hint* opposite). Drop in butter and vanilla. Do not stir.

When mixture has cooled, stir in nuts and beat slowly with a wooden spoon. As fudge thickens and loses its gloss, turn it into a 23-cm (9-in) square pan lined with greaseproof paper. Cool before cutting into 2.5-cm (1-in) squares. Makes 64 squares.

Marshmallow and Date Squares

100% .... 3 minutes

250 g (9 oz) marshmallows
  (page 201), quartered
60 g (2 oz) butter
250 g (9 oz) dates, stoned
  and chopped
125 g (4 oz) Rice Krispies
60 g (2 oz) desiccated coconut
icing sugar (optional)

Place marshmallows and butter in a shallow casserole dish and microwave on 100% for 2-3 minutes until melted. Stir in remaining ingredients.

Press mixture into a greased 33 x 23-cm (13 x 9-in) pan and chill on bottom shelf of refrigerator for about 2 hours. Cut into squares. For a lighter colour, toss squares in a little icing sugar before serving.
Makes about 40 squares.

Coconut Ice

100% .... 8 minutes

150 ml (5 fl oz) milk
450 g (1 lb) caster sugar
pinch of tartaric acid
few drops of pink food colouring
125 g (4 oz) desiccated coconut

Combine milk, sugar and tartaric acid in a large bowl. Microwave on 100% for 6-8 minutes, stirring every 2 minutes. The mixture should now be at the 'soft ball' stage (page 201).

Divide mixture into two bowls, adding a few drops of pink colouring to one of the bowls. Mix half the coconut into each bowl and beat well. Turn one half into a greased 20-cm (8-in) square pan and press down with the back of a spoon. Spoon remaining half on top, press down firmly and leave until well set. Cut into squares. Makes about 36 squares.

Coffee Twists

100% .... 14 minutes

250 g (9 oz) caster sugar
125 ml (4 fl oz) water
10 ml (2 tsp) instant coffee granules
10 ml (2 tsp) water, boiling
5 ml (1 tsp) orange oil*

Combine sugar and water in a large bowl and microwave on 100% for 4 minutes, stirring every minute. Now microwave for 8-10 minutes until pale golden, or at the 'crack' stage (page 201). Meanwhile, combine instant coffee, boiling water and orange oil. Leave to stand for a few minutes, then strain through a fine sieve.

Leave sugar mixture to stand until bubbles subside, then carefully stir in coffee mixture. Pour syrup on to a well-oiled marble surface or baking sheet. Allow to stand until edges are cool enough to be handled. Lift edges with oiled hands and stretch toffee thinly. Cut off pieces with well-oiled scissors and bend or twist into required shapes. If toffee becomes too stiff to work with, rewarm on 100% in 5-second bursts.
Makes about 250 g (9 oz).

* Available from speciality stores and some supermarkets.

Coconut Ice, (top) and Peanut Brittle

Clockwise from left: Boiled Sweet Drops, Coffee Twists and Three-nut Candy

Peanut Brittle

100% .... 10 minutes

200 g (7 oz) caster sugar
75 ml (2½ fl oz) golden syrup
45 ml (3 tbsp) water
30 g (1 oz) butter
175 g (6 oz) salted peanuts
few drops of vanilla extract
5 ml (1 tsp) baking powder

Place sugar, golden syrup and water in a large bowl. Microwave on 100% for 4 minutes, stirring after 2 minutes. Add butter and peanuts and microwave, without stirring, for 5-6 minutes until mixture turns a light golden colour. Carefully stir in vanilla extract and baking powder. Turn on to a greased or sprayed baking sheet. Leave to cool, then break into pieces and store in an airtight container.
Makes about 425 g (15 oz).

Boiled Sweet Drops

100% .... 14 minutes

250 g (9 oz) caster sugar
125 ml (4 fl oz) water
few drops of red, green and
  yellow colouring
few drops flavouring oils of
  your choice*

Combine sugar and water in a large bowl and microwave on 100% for 4 minutes, stirring twice during this time to dissolve sugar. Microwave for a further 8-10 minutes until pale golden, or at the 'crack' stage (page 201).
  Divide sugar mixture into three small bowls. Add colouring and flavouring to each bowl. Drop small spoonfuls of each flavour on to greaseproof paper that has been greased or sprayed. When set, peel sweets off paper.
Makes about 250 g (9 oz).

* Available from speciality stores and some supermarkets.

Three-nut Candy

100%, 50% .... 25 minutes

150 g (5 oz) caster sugar
185 ml (6 fl oz) water
5 ml (1 tsp) butter
185 ml (6 fl oz) milk
60 g (2 oz) unsalted cashew nuts
60 g (2 oz) flaked almonds
60 g (2 oz) shelled pistachio nuts
few drops of green food colouring

Microwave sugar, water and butter on 50% for 5-7 minutes, stirring every 2 minutes until sugar is melted. Microwave on 100% for 5 minutes, or until mixture boils. Add milk and microwave for 10-13 minutes, or until mixture is thick. (A drop placed on a greased plate, cooled and pinched, should feel thick and tacky.) Blend nuts in a processor until mixture resembles coarse meal.
  Remove milk mixture from microwave and blend in food colouring to make it a pale green. Add nuts and mix until mixture stiffens slightly. Pour into a greased 23-cm (9-in) square dish, spreading evenly. With a greased knife edge, mark into squares, then cool completely before cutting. Store in an airtight container.
Makes 36 or 49 squares.

Hint
To clean a bowl after boiling sugar in it: Fill the bowl with hot water and microwave on 100% for 4 minutes. The hard, sticky caramel will soften and the bowl will be easy to wash.

Seasoned Tomato Sauce (top left), Barbecue Sauce (right) and Marmalade Sauce (front)

Seasoned Tomato Sauce

100% .... 15 minutes

30 ml (2 tbsp) oil
1 onion, chopped
1-2 garlic cloves, crushed
4-5 tomatoes, skinned and chopped
30 ml (2 tbsp) bottled tomato sauce
2.5 ml (½ tsp) sugar
salt and black pepper
10 ml (2 tsp) chopped fresh basil
   or 5 ml (1 tsp) dried
1 bay leaf
15 ml (1 tbsp) Italian olive oil

Place oil in a large casserole and microwave on 100% for 1 minute. Add onion and garlic, toss to coat with oil and microwave for 4 minutes, stirring twice. Add tomatoes, tomato sauce, sugar, seasoning, herbs and bay leaf. Stir well. Cover and microwave for 8-10 minutes, stirring once. Remove bay leaf, stir in olive oil and serve with pasta or as required.
Makes about 300 ml (10 fl oz).

Marmalade Sauce

Excellent to serve with ham or sausages.

100% .... 6 minutes

2.5 ml (½ tsp) dry mustard
10 ml (2 tsp) soft brown sugar
generous pinch of ground ginger
pinch of cayenne pepper
pinch of ground cloves
pinch of salt
150 ml (5 fl oz) red wine
45 ml (3 tbsp) sweet sherry
60 ml (4 tbsp) raisins
30 ml (2 tbsp) redcurrant jelly
30 ml (2 tbsp) orange juice
7.5 ml (1½ tsp) grated orange rind
15 ml (1 tbsp) lemon juice
15 ml (1 tbsp) cornflour

In a large measuring jug, combine mustard, sugar, spices, salt, wine, sherry and raisins. Microwave on 100% for 3 minutes. In another jug, mix together remaining ingredients.
   Add a little of the hot liquid to the cold. Stir well, then pour cold liquid into hot liquid. Stir well to combine and microwave for 2-3 minutes until sauce has become clear and has boiled thoroughly.
Makes about 250 ml (8 fl oz).

Hints
• Sauces thickened with flour need no changes to the ingredients when converting conventional recipes to microwave use.
• Sauces using cornflour thicken more rapidly and need even less stirring than flour-based sauces.
• Sauces thickened with egg yolk need careful preparation. About half the hot liquid should always be carefully stirred into the beaten egg yolks first and only then should the egg yolk mixture be stirred into the remaining sauce. This prevents the egg yolk from being cooked before it is properly incorporated into the sauce.

Barbecue Sauce

100% .... 19 minutes

45 ml (3 tbsp) oil
1 large onion, chopped
1 garlic clove, crushed
400 g (14 oz) canned tomatoes, liquidized
60 ml (4 tbsp) brown vinegar
15 ml (1 tbsp) Worcestershire sauce
45 ml (3 tbsp) sugar
10 ml (2 tsp) dry mustard
salt and black pepper
pinch of cayenne
1 bay leaf
5 ml (1 tsp) soy sauce

Pour oil into a large bowl and microwave on 100% for 1 minute. Add onion and garlic, stir to coat with oil and microwave for 3 minutes. Add remaining ingredients and stir well. Microwave for 15 minutes, stirring every 5 minutes. Remove bay leaf. Serve with grilled meats, hamburgers or hot dogs.
Makes about 500 ml (16 fl oz).

Cranberry Orange Sauce with crumbed Camembert

Béarnaise

100%, 30% .... 11 minutes

45 ml (3 tbsp) dry white wine
15 ml (1 tbsp) tarragon vinegar
2 spring onions, chopped
2.5 ml (½ tsp) dried tarragon
black peppercorns
3 egg yolks
125 g (4 oz) butter
salt

Place white wine, tarragon vinegar, spring onions, dried tarragon and a few peppercorns in a flat dish. Microwave, uncovered, on 100% for 4 minutes until liquid has reduced to at least half. Strain and set aside.

Using a food processor fitted with a metal blade, process egg yolks until light in colour. Microwave butter for 3 minutes until very hot. With machine running, pour hot butter on to yolks. Process for about 45 seconds. Add strained liquid and a little salt. Process to combine. Serve hot.

To reheat: Cover and microwave on 30% for 2-4 minutes, or until hot. Whisk well and serve with beef, lamb, chicken or fish. Makes about 170 ml (5½ fl oz).

Variations
AVOCADO BEARNAISE
Follow directions for making traditional Béarnaise, substituting wine vinegar for tarragon vinegar. Finally, fold in 1 puréed avocado. Serve with beef, chicken or fish.

PINEAPPLE BEARNAISE
Follow directions for making traditional Béarnaise, substituting pineapple juice for dry white wine. Finally, stir in 60 ml (4 tbsp) crushed pineapple. Serve with beef or chicken.

Note
Microwaved sauces can be made well in advance and reheated at the last moment without the texture or flavour being affected.

Cranberry Orange Sauce

Traditionally served with turkey, this sauce is also excellent with pork and veal.

70% .... 6 minutes

400 g (14 oz) canned whole cranberry sauce
90 ml (3 fl oz) orange juice
45 ml (3 tbsp) white vinegar
45 ml (3 tbsp) Crème de Cassis
60 g (2 oz) sultanas
15 ml (1 tbsp) grated orange rind
whole segments from 1 orange, skinned
2.5 ml (½ tsp) ground cinnamon
pinch of ground cloves

Combine all ingredients in a deep 2-litre (3½-pint) casserole dish. Cover with waxed paper and microwave on 70% for 5-6 minutes, or until heated through. Stir once or twice during cooking. Serve warm or cold. Makes about 600 ml (19 fl oz).

Cucumber Sauce

50% .... 3 minutes

125 ml (4 fl oz) soured cream
60 g (2 oz) cucumber, peeled, seeded and chopped
5 ml (1 tsp) chopped fresh parsley
2.5 ml (½ tsp) chopped fresh dill or generous pinch of dried dill
2.5 ml (½ tsp) snipped fresh chives
5 ml (1 tsp) lemon juice
pinch of salt

Combine all ingredients in a jug and microwave on 50% for 3 minutes, or until warmed through. Serve with poached fish, such as salmon or sole. Makes about 250 ml (8 fl oz).

Cherry Sauce

Loganberry Sauce

Cherry Sauce

100% .... 7 minutes

45 g (1½ oz) caster sugar
30 ml (2 tbsp) cornflour
250 ml (9 fl oz) raspberry juice
400 g (14 oz) canned red cherries,
    stoned
5 ml (1 tsp) grated lemon rind
few drops of vanilla extract
30 ml (2 tbsp) brandy

In a deep glass bowl, combine
sugar and cornflour. Stir in
raspberry juice, cherries with
liquid and lemon rind. Microwave
on 100% for 5-7 minutes until
thickened and bubbling, stirring
after every minute. Stir in vanilla
extract and brandy. Serve over ice
cream or pancakes filled with
natural yogurt sweetened with
sugar and flavoured with
cinnamon.
Makes about 750 ml (1¼ pints).

Sabayon Alexander

50% .... 5 minutes

2 eggs
2 egg yolks
60 ml (4 tbsp) caster sugar
7.5 ml (1½ tsp) cornflour
125 ml (4 fl oz) brandy
45 ml (3 tbsp) Crème de Cacao
125 ml (4 fl oz) whipping cream

Beat eggs and yolks together well.
Add sugar and beat thoroughly,
then beat in cornflour, half the
brandy and all the Crème de
Cacao. Microwave on 50% for
4-5 minutes, whisking every
30 seconds. Beat until cool. Whip
cream with remaining brandy
until soft peaks form. Carefully
fold in sabayon mixture.
  Serve sauce at room
temperature over vanilla ice
cream or rich puddings, such as
Christmas pudding or mince tart.
(It may be made up to 12 hours in
advance.)
Makes about 600 ml (19 fl oz).

Loganberry Sauce

100% .... 2 minutes

400 g (14 oz) canned loganberries
30 ml (2 tbsp) sugar
10 ml (2 tsp) lemon juice
30 ml (2 tbsp) kirsch

Drain off about half the syrup
from the canned loganberries.
Pour loganberries, remaining
syrup and sugar into a jug and
microwave on 100% for
2 minutes. Pour into a blender,
add lemon juice and kirsch and
blend. Strain through a sieve and
chill before using. Ideal with ice
cream.
Makes about 375 ml (12 fl oz).

Note
**If frozen, this sauce will keep for
up to three weeks.**

Syrup of Rose Petals

100% .... 11 minutes

petals from 12 fully-opened red
    and pink roses
juice of 2 lemons
600 g (1 lb 5 oz) granulated sugar
400 ml (13 fl oz) water, boiling
few drops of wine-red colouring

Separate petals and rinse well.
Place in a large bowl, add half the
lemon juice and leave to stand
overnight. Combine sugar and
water and microwave on 100% for
4 minutes, stirring twice. Add
remaining lemon juice and
microwave for 4 minutes longer.
  Chop rose petals in batches in a
food processor and add to syrup.
Microwave for 3 minutes. Cover
and allow to cool. Strain through
muslin and add a few drops of
colouring to give a good colour.
Pour into a jar and store in a cool
place. Use over ice cream or to
add colour and flavour to milk
shakes.
Makes about 750 ml (1¼ pints).

Chocolate Fudge Sauce

Hot Orange Sauce

100% .... 12 minutes

60 g (2 oz) butter
60 g (2 oz) caster sugar
200 g (7 oz) canned frozen orange
  juice, thawed
100 ml (3½ fl oz) water
30 ml (2 tbsp) cornflour
grated orange rind
30 ml (2 tbsp) Cointreau

Place butter in a bowl and microwave on 100% for 2 minutes. Stir
in sugar. Microwave for 2
minutes, then add orange juice.
Stir to combine. (Any lumps will
disappear when the sauce is
heated.) Microwave, uncovered,
for 3 minutes.
   Combine water and cornflour.
Stir a little hot liquid into
cornflour mixture, then pour back
into hot orange juice. Stir well.
Microwave, uncovered, for
5 minutes, stirring every minute.
Add orange rind and liqueur.
Serve over ice cream.
Makes about 300 ml (10 fl oz).

Hot Ice Cream Sauce

100% .... 7 minutes

100 g (3½ oz) mixed dried fruit
150 g (5 oz) bottled maraschino
  cherries, chopped, and their juice
60 g (2 oz) butter
15 ml (1 tbsp) soft brown sugar
1 small piece of cinnamon stick
grated rind and juice of 1 orange
  and 1 lemon
juice from 400 g (14 oz) can of
  cherries
125 ml (4 fl oz) brandy
100 ml (3½ fl oz) medium sherry
30 ml (2 tbsp) Cointreau
60 ml (4 tbsp) water
10-15 ml (2-3 tsp) cornflour

Combine all ingredients up to and
including juice from cherries.
Microwave, covered, on 100% for
5 minutes. Cool for 5 minutes.
Add brandy, sherry and liqueur.
Combine water and cornflour,
add to hot liquid and stir well.
Microwave for 2 minutes more,
stirring once.
Makes about 750 ml (1¼ pints).

Chocolate Fudge Sauce

Vary the flavour of this sauce by
using different liqueurs, such as
orange, coffee, cherry, even brandy
or rum.

100% .... 4 minutes

30 ml (2 tbsp) thin honey
125 ml (4 fl oz) single cream
100 g (3½ oz) plain chocolate
100 g (3½ oz) milk chocolate
few drops of vanilla extract
15-30 ml (1-2 tbsp) liqueur

Place honey, cream and chocolate
in a 1-litre (1¾-pint) casserole
dish or measuring jug and
microwave on 100% for 2½-3½
minutes. Stir until completely
smooth. Add vanilla and liqueur
and mix well. Serve warm over ice
cream.
Makes about 375 ml (12 fl oz).

Butterscotch Sauce

100%, 70% .... 7 minutes

175 g (6 oz) golden syrup
125 g (4 oz) caster sugar
125 ml (4 fl oz) single cream
30 g (1 oz) butter
few drops of vanilla extract

Combine all ingredients in a large
jug. Microwave on 100% for
2 minutes, stir well, then microwave on 70% for 4-5 minutes
more. Stir well and pour over ice
cream.
Makes about 400 ml (13 fl oz).

Pear, Date and Pecan Chutney

100%, 70%, 50% ..... 45 minutes
Conventional cooking 10 minutes

375 ml (12 fl oz) cider vinegar
250 ml (8 fl oz) orange juice
200 g (7 oz) caster sugar
100 g (3½ oz) soft brown sugar
15 ml (1 tbsp) grated orange rind
2 garlic cloves, finely chopped
1 x 4-cm (1½-in) cinnamon stick
15 ml (1 tbsp) freshly grated
  ginger root
2.5 ml (½ tsp) salt
2.5 ml (½ tsp) crumbled dried
  red chilli
generous pinch of crushed
  cardamom seeds
2 kg (4½ lb) pears, peeled
150 g (5 oz) dates, stoned
  and chopped
60 g (2 oz) pecan nuts, roughly
  chopped

Place vinegar, orange juice and
sugars in a large casserole dish
and microwave on 100% for
4 minutes, stirring twice. Stir to
dissolve sugar, then add orange
rind, garlic, cinnamon, ginger,
salt, chilli flakes and cardamom.
Microwave for 3 minutes. Reduce
power to 70% and microwave for
8 minutes more.

Quarter and core pears and cut
into thick slices. Add to spice
mixture together with dates and
nuts and microwave for
5 minutes. Reduce power to 50%
and microwave for 20-25 minutes,
or until mixture is syrupy, stirring
often. Discard cinnamon stick and
spoon chutney into two hot,
sterilized 500 ml (16 fl oz)
preserving jars.

Clean rims, seal with lids and
place jars in a deep saucepan.
Pour in enough boiling water to
cover jars by at least 2.5 cm (1 in).
Place lid on pot and boil on stove
for 10 minutes. Remove jars from
water bath. Cool to room
temperature.

When jars are cold, press centre
of each lid. If centre of lid stays
down, jar is sealed. Store in a cool
dry place. If lid pops up, store
chutney in the refrigerator. Keep
chutney refrigerated after
opening.
Fills 2 x 500 ml (16 fl oz) jars.

Clockwise from left: Sweet Onion Relish, Banana Chutney and Chilli, Cucumber and Pepper Relish

Sweet Onion Relish

Delicious with beef dishes and barbecued meats.

100% .... 8 minutes

6 onions, peeled and sliced
7.5 ml (1½ tsp) salt
1 Granny Smith apple, chopped
1 red pepper, diced
1 green pepper, diced
125 ml (4 fl oz) cider vinegar
100 g (3½ oz) sugar
10 ml (2 tsp) chopped fresh tarragon
  or 2.5 ml (½ tsp) dried tarragon
2.5 ml (½ tsp) white pepper
2.5 ml (½ tsp) ground mace

Combine all ingredients in a large casserole dish and microwave on 100% for 6-8 minutes, or until onions are just tender. Turn into hot sterilized jars and seal. Store in refrigerator.
Fills 2 x 400 ml (13 fl oz) jars.

Banana Chutney

100% .... 20 minutes

10 ripe bananas, diced or sliced
400 ml (13 fl oz) white vinegar
75 g (2½ oz) seedless raisins
1 onion, finely chopped
150 g (5 oz) soft brown sugar
1 green pepper, seeded and
  chopped
2.5 ml (½ tsp) salt
2.5 ml (½ tsp) ground ginger
generous pinch of cayenne pepper
2 garlic cloves, crushed
10 ml (2 tsp) dry mustard

Combine all ingredients in a large bowl. Cover with vented plastic wrap and microwave on 100% for 20 minutes. Stir twice during cooking time. Pour into clean, dry jars and cool before sealing. Store in a cool, dry place.
Fills 2 x 400 ml (13 fl oz) jars.

Chilli, Cucumber and Pepper Relish

100% .... 2 minutes

2 small garlic cloves
1 small red chilli, split and seeded
75 ml (2½ fl oz) oil
45 ml (3 tbsp) white wine vinegar
10 ml (2 tsp) sugar
7.5 ml (1½ tsp) salt
5 ml (1 tsp) ground cumin
3 red peppers
1 green or yellow pepper
1 large cucumber, peeled
1 small onion, peeled

Chop garlic and chilli in a food processor. Add oil, vinegar, sugar, salt and cumin. Process to mix. Pour into a bowl and microwave on 100% for 1½ minutes.
  Cut peppers into thin strips. Slice cucumber and onion. Place vegetables in a casserole, add chilli mixture and toss to mix. Refrigerate for a minimum of 12 hours before serving.
Makes 6 servings.

Cucumbers with Dill

100% .... 2 minutes

2 cucumbers
10 ml (2 tsp) salt
10 ml (2 tsp) caster sugar
150 ml (5 fl oz) cider vinegar
10 ml (2 tsp) chopped fresh dill or
  5 ml (1 tsp) dried dill

Wash cucumbers well, slice thinly and place in a deep bowl, sprinkling each layer with a little salt. Cover and refrigerate for 2 hours, then drain well and press out excess juice.
  Combine sugar and vinegar in a jug and microwave on 100% for 2 minutes. Cool and pour over cucumbers. Gently stir in dill and refrigerate for several hours before using. (These pickled cucumbers will store for several months.)
Fills 1 x 600 ml (19 fl oz) jar.

Pickled Courgettes

100% .... 4 minutes

**500 g (18 oz) courgettes, thinly
  sliced
salt
5 ml (1 tsp) ground turmeric
5 ml (1 tsp) salt
30 ml (2 tbsp) honey
10 ml (2 tsp) white mustard seeds
black peppercorns
300 ml (10 fl oz) cider vinegar
30 ml (2 tbsp) dry sherry
2 onions, sliced**

Sprinkle courgettes with salt. Set
aside for 45 minutes. Combine
turmeric, 5 ml (1 tsp) salt, honey,
mustard seeds, peppercorns and
vinegar and microwave on 100%
for 4 minutes. Add sherry, then
leave to cool.

Drain courgettes, wash and pat
dry. Pack with onion rings into
warmed, cleaned jars and cover
with spiced vinegar. Seal well and
store in refrigerator for about
3 days before using.
Fills 2 x 400 ml (13 fl oz) jars.

Sweet-and-sour
Vegetable Relish

100%, 50%, 30% ..... 37 minutes

**45 ml (3 tbsp) caster sugar
20 ml (4 tsp) water
75 ml (2½ fl oz) cider vinegar
45 ml (3 tbsp) oil
2 garlic cloves, finely chopped
2 onions, sliced
250 g (9 oz) pickling onions,
  skinned
l red pepper, seeded and thinly
  sliced
185 ml (6 fl oz) dry white wine
75 g (2½ oz) currants
2.5 ml (½ tsp) salt
pinch of cayenne pepper
500 ml (16 fl oz) water
125 g (4 oz) cooked sweetcorn
  kernels**

Combine sugar and 20 ml (4 tsp)
water in a heavy glass bowl and
microwave on 100% for about
4 minutes to caramelize. Add
vinegar. Microwave for 1 minute
to dissolve caramel. Set aside.

Microwave oil for 1 minute. Add
garlic, onions and pickling onions
and microwave for 4 minutes,
stirring twice. Add pepper,
reserved vinegar mixture, wine,
currants, salt, cayenne and 250 ml
(8 fl oz) of the water. Microwave
on 50% until vegetables are very
soft (about 10-12 minutes),
stirring occasionally.

Add sweetcorn and more water
if needed and microwave on 30%
for about 15 minutes. (The
mixture should be thick and
syrupy.) Stir occasionally. Cool to
room temperature, cover and
store in refrigerator for up to four
weeks.
Fills 2 x 500 ml (16 fl oz) jars.

Note
**Relishes and chutneys are made
most successfully in the
microwave. In addition, not only is
the cooking time more than halved,
but the foods retain their true
colours and shapes, and the kitchen
is not filled with the usual
overpowering odours.**

Cauliflower and
Cabbage Pickle

100% .... 5 minutes

**500 g (18 oz) cauliflower, broken
  into florets
250 g (9 oz) red cabbage, cored
  and chopped
2 dried red chillies
6 black peppercorns
45 g (1½ oz) salt
300 ml (10 fl oz) white wine vinegar
500 ml (16 fl oz) water**

Layer cauliflower and cabbage in
a clean jar and slide in chillies and
peppercorns. Combine salt,
vinegar and water in a jug and
microwave on 100% for
5 minutes. Set aside to cool, then
pour over vegetables, making
sure they are completely covered.
Seal well and store in refrigerator
for at least three days before
serving.
Fills 2 x 400 ml (13 fl oz) jars.

Lemon Marmalade

100% .... 110 minutes

1 kg (2 lb 2 oz) lemons
250 ml (8 fl oz) water, boiling
1.5 litres (2½ pints) cold water
1.25 kg (2 lb 10 oz) sugar

Using a zester, remove zest from lemons, or peel very thinly and cut into fine julienne shreds. Cover zest with 250 ml (8 fl oz) boiling water and leave to stand for 10 minutes. Drain off water and reserve zest.

Squeeze juice from lemons and set aside. Then cut up pulp roughly and place in a large bowl with the pips. Add 1 litre (1¾ pints) of the cold water, cover with vented plastic wrap and microwave on 100% for 20 minutes. Strain pulp through a jelly cloth. Reserve liquid and set pulp aside.

Meanwhile, place reserved zest in a bowl, pour over remaining 500 ml (16 fl oz) cold water and microwave for 10 minutes. Strain off liquid and add to pulp. Reserve zest. Cover pulp mixture and microwave for 15 minutes. Strain off liquid and set aside. Discard pulp.

In a very large bowl, combine sugar, lemon juice and reserved liquids. Microwave for 20 minutes, stirring from time to time, then add zest and microwave for 40-45 minutes until setting stage is reached. (Stir every 5 minutes during this period and remove scum as it forms.)

Leave marmalade to cool slightly before pouring into sterilized jars. Cover loosely. When completely cool, top up with a little more marmalade. Cover tightly, label and store. Fills 3 x 400 ml (13 fl oz) jars.

Hint
If you have a slow cooker, use the pottery insert for preserving. It is large and has straight sides which help prevent the contents from boiling over.

Tropical Marmalade

100% .... 55 minutes

1 grapefruit, sliced
1 orange, sliced
1 lime or lemon, sliced
1 pineapple, peeled, cored and diced
1.75 litres (2 pints) water
1.8 kg (3¾ lb) preserving sugar
60 ml (4 tbsp) treacle
10 ml (2 tsp) finely chopped fresh ginger

Combine fruit and water in a non-metallic bowl and leave to soak overnight. Place pips in a small muslin bag and add to mixture. Microwave on 100%, uncovered, for 15 minutes, then leave to stand for 2 hours.

Stir in sugar, treacle and ginger and microwave for 35-40 minutes until setting point is reached. (Stir every 5 minutes during this period and remove any scum that may form.) Allow to cool slightly before pouring into sterilized jars. Cover loosely. When cool, top up with a little more marmalade. Cover tightly, label and store. Fills 3 x 400 ml (13 fl oz) jars.

Hint
To sterilize jars: Pour a little water into two or three jars. Microwave on 100% for up to 5 minutes, depending on the size of the jars, then pour the water out and stand the jars upside down to drain. (Do not microwave more than three jars at a time.)

Similarly, plastic lids, each containing a little water, may be sterilized in the microwave, too, but never sterilize metal lids using this method.

Fig Preserve

100% .... 57 minutes

500 g (18 oz) small green figs
1 litre (1³/₄ pints) cold water
5 ml (1 tsp) calcium hydroxide
750 ml (1¹/₄ pints) water, boiling

SYRUP
600 g (1 lb 5 oz) granulated sugar
750 ml (1¹/₄ pints) water, boiling
10 ml (2 tsp) lemon juice

Wash figs well and remove stems. Cut a small cross in rounded end and place figs in a bowl. Combine cold water and calcium hydroxide. Pour over figs and leave to stand for 12 hours.

Rinse figs well, then stand in fresh cold water for about 15 minutes. Drain and add 750 ml (1¹/₄ pints) boiling water to figs. Cover with vented plastic wrap and microwave on 100% for 7 minutes. Drain well.

To make syrup: Combine sugar, water and lemon juice in a large bowl. Cover and microwave for 10 minutes, stirring twice during cooking time. Add fruit to boiling syrup, then microwave, uncovered, for 30 minutes, stirring from time to time.

Drain figs from syrup and pack into warmed, dry jars. Microwave syrup, uncovered, for 10 minutes. Pour over figs and cover loosely with lid. When cool, tighten lid and store.
Fills 2 x 400 ml (13 fl oz) jars.

Brandied or Sherried Prunes

Fill a 1-litre jar with about 350 g (12 oz) prunes, 45 g (1¹/₂ oz) seedless raisins and half a lemon, thinly sliced. In a large jug, combine 185 ml (6 fl oz) brandy or sherry with 185 ml (6 fl oz) apple juice and microwave on 100% for 3 minutes. Pour over fruit and leave to stand overnight. Store in the refrigerator and serve with meat or in a fruit salad.
Makes about 675 g (1¹/₂ lbs).

Grapefruit Curd

A tasty variation on the favourite traditional lemon flavour.

100%, 70%, 50% .... 7 minutes

4 eggs
finely grated rind of 1 grapefruit
finely grated rind of 1 lemon
juice of 1 grapefruit
45 ml (3 tbsp) lemon juice
450 g (1 lb) caster sugar
100 g (3¹/₂ oz) butter,
  cut into cubes
5 ml (1 tsp) cornflour

Place eggs in a large bowl and beat well. Stir in rinds and fruit juices, sugar, butter and cornflour. Microwave on 100% for 2 minutes, whisking every 30 seconds. Reduce power to 70% and microwave for a further 2 minutes, stirring once during cooking time. Beat well.

Then reduce power to 50% and microwave for 2-3 minutes until mixture is thick enough to coat the back of a wooden spoon. Cool slightly and pour into two 300 ml (10 fl oz) jars. Top with paper discs brushed with brandy. Cover when cold. Label and store in refrigerator for up to six months. Fills 2 x 300 ml (10 fl oz) jars.

Hint

To soften jams and jellies to a spreading consistency, microwave on 100% for 3 seconds for every 300 g (11 oz).

Candied Peel Strips

100%, 70% .... 42 minutes

1 orange
1 grapefruit
water
200 g (7 oz) caster sugar
75 ml (2¹/₂ fl oz) water
15 ml (1 tbsp) golden syrup
30 ml (2 tbsp) Cointreau
extra sugar
60 g (2 oz) plain cooking chocolate, broken into pieces

Cut fruit into quarters, carefully remove flesh and set aside for another purpose. Slice peel thinly into strips, either by hand or using a food processor, then place in a large bowl. Add water to cover. Microwave, covered, on 100% for 7 minutes. Drain off water and repeat this process twice more, then set aside.

In a large bowl, combine sugar, water, golden syrup and liqueur. Microwave for 2 minutes, stir well and brush sides of bowl with water to remove crystals. Micro-

wave for 3 minutes more. Then add peel and liqueur and microwave for 10-12 minutes until peel is glossy. Drain well and spread on a wire rack overnight.

Next day, toss peel in sugar. Microwave chocolate on 70% for 3-4 minutes and stir to melt completely. Dip ends of peel in chocolate and lay on a piece of foil to dry.

Makes about 250 g (9 oz).

Cherries in Brandy

100% .... 7 minutes

500 g (18 oz) cherries, stems removed
1 cinnamon stick, broken in half
225 g (8 oz) sugar
125 ml (4 fl oz) water
15 ml (1 tbsp) lemon juice
150 ml (5 fl oz) brandy

Wash and dry cherries. Pack into two warmed, sterilized 400 ml (13 fl oz) glass jars together with half a cinnamon stick. Combine sugar, water and lemon juice in a bowl and microwave on 100% for 3 minutes, stirring every minute during cooking time. Then microwave without stirring for 4 minutes. Leave to cool slightly and add brandy.

Pour syrup over cherries, seal, label and store in a dark place. Keep for at least one month before using. Serve cherries over ice cream. The liquid can also be strained and drunk as a liqueur.
Fills 2 x 400 ml (13 fl oz) jars.

Strawberry Jam with Kirsch

100% .... 29 minutes

500 g (18 oz) strawberries, hulled
30 ml (2 tbsp) lemon juice
350 g (12 oz) preserving sugar
1 strip of lemon rind
1 small piece of cinnamon stick
2.5 ml (¹/₂ tsp) black peppercorns
15-30 ml (1-2 tbsp) kirsch

Wash strawberries and drain well. Combine fruit and lemon juice in a large bowl and microwave on 100% for 7 minutes. Add sugar and stir well.

Tie lemon rind, cinnamon and peppercorns in a muslin bag and add to jam. Microwave for 18-22 minutes until setting point is reached, stirring every 5 minutes and removing any scum that forms. Remove muslin bag. Cool slightly before adding kirsch, then pour into a warmed, dry sterilized jar.
Fills 1 x 400 ml (13 fl oz) jar.

Fruit Punch with Brandy

100%, 50% .... 57 minutes

5 litres (9 pints) pineapple juice
750 ml (1¹/₄ pints) brandy
500 ml (16 fl oz) guava juice*
¹/₂ small pineapple, peeled and
 cubed
3 oranges, peeled and quartered,
 peel reserved
100 g (3¹/₂ oz) soft brown sugar
10 large prunes
100 g (3¹/₂ oz) sultanas
60 ml (4 tbsp) tamarind pulp*
90 ml (3 fl oz) clear honey
5-cm (2-in) cinnamon stick to
 decorate

CANDIED PEEL
water
100 g (3¹/₂ oz) caster sugar
45 ml (3 tbsp) water
10 ml (2 tsp) golden syrup

Combine all ingredients for
punch in a very large bowl, except
reserved orange peel. Microwave
on 100% for 10 minutes, stirring
to dissolve sugar. Reduce power
to 50% and microwave for
15 minutes more. Cool
completely and chill overnight.

 To make candied peel: Cut
reserved orange peel into narrow
strips, place in a small bowl with
enough water to cover. Microwave on 100% for 4 minutes, then
drain and repeat twice more.
Drain and set aside.

 Combine sugar, 45 ml (3 tbsp)
water and golden syrup.
Microwave for 2 minutes, stirring
well. Brush sides of bowl with
water to remove crystals and
microwave for a further
2 minutes, then add peel.
Microwave for 4-6 minutes more
until peel is glossy. Drain well
and spread on a wire rack
overnight.

 Strain punch, pressing solids to
release liquid. Serve cold or
reheat by microwaving on 50%
for 15-20 minutes. Decorate with
candied peel and cinnamon stick.
Serves 24.

*** Available from speciality food
shops.**

From left: Iced Coffee, Hot Coffee Crème, Mocha Cappuccino and Chocolate Rum Coffee

Iced Coffee

100% .... 4 minutes

500 ml (16 fl oz) cold, strong coffee
345 ml (11 fl oz) water
20 ml (4 tsp) instant coffee granules
2.5 ml (½ tsp) Angostura bitters
few drops of vanilla extract
30 ml (2 tbsp) caster sugar
100 ml (3½ fl oz) whipping cream, whipped
15 ml (1 tbsp) grated chocolate

Pour cold coffee into an ice-cube tray and freeze until solid. Microwave water in a large jug for 4 minutes until boiling vigorously. Stir in coffee granules, bitters, vanilla extract and sugar.
  Fill three or four long glasses with frozen coffee cubes. Place a long-handled spoon into each glass to prevent glass from cracking and pour in hot coffee mixture. Stir and top each serving generously with whipped cream and grated chocolate.
Serves 3-4.

Hot Coffee Crème

100% .... 10 minutes

1 litre (1¾ pints) chocolate ice cream
1 litre (1¾ pints) vanilla ice cream
3 litres (5 pints) freshly brewed coffee
125 ml (4 fl oz) coffee-flavoured liqueur
60 ml (4 tbsp) light rum
few drops of vanilla extract
ground cinnamon

Make ice cream into balls and freeze until hard. In a large bowl, microwave coffee on 100% for 10 minutes, then stir in coffee-flavoured liqueur, rum and vanilla extract. Place ice cream balls in a heatproof punch bowl and pour coffee mixture over ice cream. Swirl to mix. Sprinkle with a little cinnamon and ladle into punch cups.
Serves 15.

Mocha Cappuccino

100%, 50% .... 4 minutes

30 ml (2 tbsp) drinking chocolate powder
250 ml (8 fl oz) hot, strong coffee
generous pinch of ground cinnamon
500 ml (16 fl oz) milk
4 marshmallows (page 201)

Place drinking chocolate powder, coffee and cinnamon in a blender and whizz until frothy. Measure milk in a jug and microwave on 100% for 2-3 minutes until just boiling. Add to coffee in blender and whizz until foamy. Divide equally between 4 mugs or cups, top with marshmallows and microwave on 50% for 30 seconds. Serve immediately.
Serves 4.

Chocolate Rum Coffee

100%, 70% .... 4 minutes

125 ml (4 fl oz) hot, strong coffee
10 ml (2 tsp) caster sugar
60 g (2 oz) plain chocolate, broken into pieces
pinch of ground cinnamon
250 ml (8 fl oz) milk
30 ml (2 tbsp) light rum
60 ml (4 tbsp) whipped cream
ground cinnamon

Pour coffee into a jug, add sugar and microwave on 100% for 2 minutes. Stir well, then add chocolate and cinnamon. Stir to melt chocolate.
  Microwave milk for 2 minutes on 70%, add to coffee and whisk until frothy. Divide between two mugs. Add 15 ml (1 tbsp) rum to each, top with whipped cream and dust with a little cinnamon.
Serves 2.

Spiced Apple Tea

Loganberry Liqueur

Spiced Apple Tea

100% .... 6 minutes

600 ml (19 fl oz) apple juice
500 ml (16 fl oz) double-strength tea
pinch of ground ginger
pinch of ground cloves
generous pinch of ground
  cinnamon
thin apple slices to decorate

In a very large jug, combine all ingredients except apple slices and microwave on 100% for 5-6 minutes. Strain and pour into cups. Decorate with apple slices. Serves 4.

Note
This tea is also very good served cold over ice.

Hot Bloody Mary

100%, 50% .... 23 minutes

1.25 litres (2¼ pints) tomato juice
250 ml (8 fl oz) orange juice
juice of 3 lemons
45 ml (3 tbsp) dried tarragon
30 ml (2 tbsp) caster sugar
5 ml (1 tsp) salt
10 ml (2 tsp) ground black pepper
few drops of Tabasco
125 ml (4 fl oz) vodka, or to taste
  (optional)
celery and chives to garnish

Combine all ingredients, except vodka, in a large bowl and microwave on 100% for 8 minutes, then reduce power to 50% and microwave for 15 minutes longer. Add vodka, if desired, then pour into mugs and garnish with celery and chopped chives.
Serves 8.

Mulled Apple Juice

100%, 50% .... 21 minutes

9 cloves
9 whole allspice
2 x 5-cm (2-in) cinnamon sticks
4 litres (6½ pints) apple juice
200 g (7 oz) soft brown sugar
250 ml (8 fl oz) brandy (optional)
2 lemons, thinly sliced

Tie spices in a muslin bag and place in a very large casserole dish with the apple juice and sugar. Microwave on 100% for 6 minutes, then stir well. Reduce power to 50% and microwave for 15 minutes longer. Remove spices, add brandy, if desired, and ladle into mugs. Float a lemon slice on top of each.
Serves 16.

Loganberry Liqueur

100% .... 3 minutes

250 g (9 oz) fresh loganberries
200 g (7 oz) caster sugar
750 ml (1¼ pints) gin

Wash loganberries and drain. Place sugar and 125 ml (4 fl oz) of the gin in a measuring jug and microwave on 100% for 2 minutes. Stir and microwave for 1 minute. Pour sugar mixture over berries in a bowl, stir gently, then cool to room temperature.

When cool, place mixture in a large jar with a tight-fitting lid. Add remaining gin. Close tightly and keep in a cool place. Turn jar every few days. The liqueur is ready to drink after about 3 weeks, but it is better if left for about 2 months before using. Makes about 750 ml (1¼ pints).

Hot Rum Nog

Hot Rum Nog

70% .... 4 minutes

4 eggs, separated
30 ml (2 tbsp) icing sugar
60 ml (4 tbsp) brandy
125 ml (4 fl oz) rum
500 ml (16 fl oz) milk
grated nutmeg

Whisk egg whites until frothy, then whisk in icing sugar. Whisk egg yolks into whites and divide mixture equally between four mugs. Pour measured brandy, rum and milk into a large jug and microwave on 70% for about 4 minutes, then pour into mugs, beating well. Sprinkle with grated nutmeg.
Serves 4.

Liqueur Coffee de Luxe

50% .... 1 minute

45 ml (3 tbsp) Grand Marnier
10 ml (2 tsp) soft brown sugar
250 ml (8 fl oz) hot, strong,
  black coffee
45 ml (3 tbsp) whipped cream
few shreds of orange zest

Pour liqueur and brown sugar into a glass, microwave on 50% for 1 minute, then stir well. Fill glass three-quarters full with hot coffee and stir to make sure that the sugar has dissolved. Top with cream, pouring it carefully over the back of a spoon to ensure that it floats on the surface. Sprinkle with orange zest.
Serves 1.

Mulled Wine

100% .... 12 minutes

1 large piece of cinnamon stick
12 allspice berries
6 cloves
1 small piece of whole nutmeg
750 ml (1¼ pints) light red wine
100 ml (3½ fl oz) sweet sherry
30 ml (2 tbsp) caster sugar
1 strip of lemon rind
30 ml (2 tbsp) Curaçao

Tie spices in a muslin bag and combine with wine, sherry, sugar and lemon rind in a large bowl. Microwave on 100% for 10-12 minutes until piping hot, then remove spices and stir in Curaçao. Pour into small, heatproof glasses and drink very hot.
Serves 8.

Strawberry Party Punch

A popular treat for a children's party.

100% .... 2 minutes

90 g (3 oz) packet strawberry jelly
250 ml (8 fl oz) water
200 g (7 oz) frozen lemon
  concentrate, thawed
1 litre (1¾ pints) pineapple juice
1 litre (1¾ pints) ginger ale
ice cubes
sliced strawberries to decorate

Separate strawberry jelly cubes, place in a large bowl and set aside. Microwave water on 100% for 2 minutes, then stir into jelly, mixing well to dissolve. Add lemon concentrate and stir well. Pour in pineapple juice and chill well. Just before serving, add ginger ale and ice cubes. Decorate with sliced strawberries.
Serves about 20.

Using your microwave

All the recipes in this book have been tested in microwaves with an output of 600 and 650 watts. If you have a microwave with a lower wattage output – for example, 500 watts – you may need to add approximately 15 seconds per minute of cooking time to the recipes. If your microwave has an output of 700 watts, decrease the cooking times by a few seconds per minute.

All the microwaves used for testing had variable power levels and each power level served a definite purpose. It is therefore important that the power levels recommended in the recipes be used wherever possible. Consult your own microwave's instruction book for similar power levels.

If your microwave does not have corresponding power levels, some foods can be microwaved at a higher power level than recommended if additional attention is given to stirring, turning or rotating the food. Delicate egg dishes or foods that require slow simmering should not be attempted at high power levels.

The cooking times given for all recipes are intended as a guide, since the amount of microwave energy required will differ according to the make of microwave used, the size and type of container, the food load, temperature of food before cooking, depth of food in the container and personal preference where foods such as meats, poultry, casseroles or vegetables are concerned. The times given above each recipe are the total cooking times and do not include preparation time.

Combination cooking

The recipes for combination microwave and convection cooking have been tested in several popular brands of microwave, including the Brother, which is available in most countries.

Please note that instructions for combination cooking differ from manufacturer to manufacturer and from model to model, each having its own power levels and programmes. Therefore, although our recipes give the suggested programme for the Brother combination microwave, it is vital that you consult your own manual for a recipe similar to the one you wish to follow from this book, in order to obtain specific cooking instructions. It is a good practice, too, always to check your dish at the minimum recommended time and add more time if necessary.

MEAT DEFROSTING AND COOKING CHART

MEAT	DEFROST TIME Per 500 g (18 oz) (30%)	COOKING TIME Per 500 g (18 oz) (100%)	METHOD
BEEF			
Steak, sirloin and rump	3-4 minutes, stand 5-10 minutes	for 3 medium steaks: 5 minutes on 1st side, 3-3½ minutes on 2nd side	Separate pieces as soon as possible. Microwave in browning dish.
Boned and rolled	8-12 minutes, stand 1 hour	*rare* 8-10 minutes *medium* 9-12 minutes *well done* 10-13 minutes	Defrost wrapped for half the time. Unwrap, shield warm sections, and lie meat on its side.
Large joints on the bone	10-14 minutes, stand 1 hour	*rare* 8-10 minutes *medium* 9-12 minutes *well done* 10-13 minutes stand 10 minutes	Defrost wrapped for half the time, then shield bone. Turn meat over after half the defrosting time, then again after half the cooking time.
Minced beef, lamb or pork	9-12 minutes stand 5 minutes	use as required	Break up during defrosting. Remove thawed pieces.
Stewing beef, lamb or pork	10-12 minutes, stand 15 minutes	use as required	Separate pieces during defrosting. Remove thawed sections.
LAMB OR VEAL			
Leg	8-10 minutes, Stand 30 minutes	8-11 minutes, stand 15 minutes	Shield bone-end during defrosting and halfway through cooking.
Shoulder or loin	7-8 minutes, stand 30 minutes	8-11 minutes	Shield thin portion during defrosting and three quarters of the way through cooking time.
Chops	3-5 minutes, stand 5-10 minutes	8-10 minutes, stand 1 minute	Separate chops during defrosting. Microwave in browning dish. Turn after 2½ minutes.
PORK			
Leg	8-9 minutes, stand 1-1½ hours	11-14 minutes, stand 20 minutes	Select a joint with a uniform shape. Tie into shape if necessary.
Loin	6-8 minutes, stand 30 minutes	8-11 minutes, stand 10 minutes	Shield bone-end during defrosting and halfway through cooking time.
Chops	3-5 minutes, stand 10-15 minutes	10-12 minutes, stand 2 minutes	Separate chops during defrosting. Microwave in browning dish. Turn after 3 minutes.
OFFAL			
Liver and kidney	8-10 minutes, stand 5 minutes	3-5 minutes, stand 1 minute	Separate pieces during defrosting. Use browning dish for cooking. Turn after 2 minutes.
SAUSAGES			
Sausages	6-8 minutes, stand 10 minutes	8-10 minutes, stand 3-4 minutes	Prick skins before cooking. Using browning dish if desired. For added colour, brush with a browning agent.

POULTRY DEFROSTING AND COOKING CHART

POULTRY	DEFROST TIME Per 500 g (18 oz) (30%)	COOKING TIME Per 500 g (18 oz) (100%)	METHOD
Chicken (whole)	9-10 minutes, stand 30 minutes	10-12 minutes	Shield drumsticks for first half of cooking time. Use a cooking bag or covered casserole. Stand 10 minutes after cooking.
Chicken (portions)	6-8 minutes, stand 10 minutes	8-10 minutes	Separate during defrosting. Rearrange during cooking.
Duck	10-12 minutes, stand 30 minutes	10-12 minutes	Shield drumsticks for first half of cooking time. Place duck in microwave, breast-side down, and turn over half-way through cooking time. Stand 10-15 minutes after cooking.
Turkey	10-12 minutes, stand 1 hour	11-13 minutes	Turn over 3-4 times during cooking. Shield drumstick and wings for first half of cooking time. Stand 15 minutes after cooking.

Note: When cooking poultry, the power used may be decreased to 70%, and the cooking time increased by approximately a third. Allow 5-8 minutes' extra cooking time for stuffed chicken or duck. For stuffed turkey, allow 8-11 minutes' additional cooking time.

FISH DEFROSTING AND COOKING CHART

FISH	DEFROST TIME (30%)	COOKING TIME (100%)
Fillets of hake, cod, sea bass, etc., 500g (18 oz)	5-7 minutes, stand 5 minutes	5-6 minutes
Haddock, 500 g (18 oz)	5 minutes, stand 5 minutes	4-5 minutes
Salmon steaks, 500 g (18 oz)	5 minutes, stand 5 minutes	5-7 minutes
Trout, 2 medium	5-7 minutes, stand 5 minutes	5-6 minutes
Sole, 2 large	5-6 minutes, stand 5 minutes	4-5 minutes
Kipper fillets and 'boil in the bag' fish, 300 g (11 oz)	3-4 minutes, stand 5 minutes	3-4 minutes
Prawns, 500 g (18 oz)		
large, with shells and heads	7-8 minutes, stand 5 minutes	4-5 minutes
small, peeled and deveined	4-5 minutes, stand 5 minutes	2-4 minutes

DEFROSTING OF BREADS AND CAKES

FOOD	QUANTITY	APPROXIMATE TIME (30%)	METHOD
Bread, whole or sliced	1 kg (2¼ lb)	6-8 minutes	Unwrap. Place on paper towel. Turn over during defrosting. Stand 5 minutes.
Bread	26 × 12 cm	4-6 minutes	Unwrap. Place on paper towel. Turn over during defrosting. Stand 5 minutes.
Bread	1 slice	10-15 seconds	Unwrap. Place on paper towel. Stand 1-2 minutes. Time accurately.
Bread rolls	2 4	20-25 seconds 30-40 seconds	Unwrap. Place on paper towel. Stand 1-2 minutes. Time accurately.
Cup cakes or muffins	4	1-1½ minutes	Unwrap. Place on paper towel. Stand 5 minutes.
Sponge cake	22 cm	2-3 minutes	Unwrap. Place on paper towel. Turn over after 1 minute. Stand 5 minutes.
Doughnuts or sweet buns	4	1½-2 minutes	Unwrap. Place on paper towel. Turn over after 1 minute. Stand 5 minutes.
Loaf cakes or ring cakes	26 × 12 cm or 22-25 cm diameter	5-7 minutes	Unwrap. Place on paper towel. Turn over after 3 minutes. Stand 10 minutes.
Bars	20-22 cm square	4-6 minutes	Unwrap. Place on paper towel. Stand 5-10 minutes.
Crumpets	4	25-30 seconds	Unwrap. Place on paper towel. Stand 3-4 minutes. Time accurately.
Pancakes or crêpes	10	3-4 minutes	Unwrap. Place on plate. Cover with plastic wrap.
Pies or tarts	20-23 cm	4-6 minutes	Unwrap. Stand 10 minutes.
Pies, cooked (small individual, to thaw only)	1 4	25-30 seconds 2-3 minutes	Unwrap. Place upside down on paper towel. Stand 2 minutes.

FRESH VEGETABLE COOKING CHART

VEGETABLE	QUANTITY	WATER ADDED	COOKING TIME (100%)	PREPARATION
Artichokes, globe	4	150 ml (5 fl oz)	15-20 minutes	Wash and trim lower leaves.
Asparagus, green	250 g (9 oz)	45 ml (3 tablespoons)	6-8 minutes	Trim ends, leave whole
Asparagus, white	250 g (9 oz)	45 ml (3 tablespoons)	8-10 minutes	Trim ends, leave whole
Aubergine	2 medium-sized	45 ml (3 tablespoons)	8-10 minutes	Slice, sprinkle with salt Stand for 30 minutes, rinse and dry
Beans, broad	450 g (1 lb)	45 ml (3 tablespoons)	9-11 minutes	Remove from pods
Beans, green	450 g (1 lb)	45 ml (3 tablespoons)	8-10 minutes	String and slice, or cut
Beetroot	6 medium	150 ml (5 fl oz)	28-32 minutes	Trim tops, prick
Brinjal	2 medium	45 ml (3 tablespoons)	8-10 minutes	Slice, sprinkle with salt. Stand 30 minutes, rinse and dry
Broccoli	450 g (1 lb)	45 ml (3 tablespoons)	8-12 minutes	Trim ends, cut into even-sized lengths
Brussels sprouts	450 g (1 lb)	45 ml (3 tablespoons)	12-15 minutes	Remove outer leaves, trim
Butternut	1 medium	45 ml (3 tablespoons)	12-15 minutes	Cut in half, remove membranes and seeds. Cook cut side down. Turn halfway through cooking
Cabbage	450 g (1 lb)	15 ml	7-9 minutes	Shred or chop
Carrots, whole new	450 g (1 lb)	45 ml (3 tablespoons)	7-9 minutes	Scrape
Carrots, sliced large	450 g (1 lb)	45 ml (3 tablespoons)	8-10 minutes	Peel, slice in rings or long strips
Cauliflower, whole	1 medium	45 ml (3 tablespoons)	9-11 minutes	Trim outside leaves and stem
Cauliflower, cut into florets	1 medium	45 ml (3 tablespoons)	7-9 minutes	Cut into medium-sized florets
Celery	450 g (1 lb)	45 ml (3 tablespoons)	10-12 minutes	Trim and slice
Courgettes	450 g (1 lb)	30 ml (2 tablespoons) water or stock	6-8 minutes	Trim ends and slice
Leeks	4 medium	45 ml (3 tablespoons)	7-11 minutes	Trim and slice or cook whole if small
Marrow	450 g (1 lb)	15 ml	8-10 minutes	Cut into slices and quarter. Add 30 ml butter with water
Mushrooms	250 g (9 oz)	30 ml water or stock or 30 ml butter	4-6 minutes	Wipe and slice or cook whole
Onions, whole	4-6	30 ml butter or oil	8-10 minutes	Peel
Onions, sliced	4-6	30 ml butter or oil	7-9 minutes	Peel and slice
Parsnips	450 g (1 lb)	45 ml (3 tablespoons)	9-11 minutes	Peel and slice
Peas, shelled	250 g (9 oz)	30 ml	8-10 minutes	Add a sprig of mint
Potatoes, new	450 g (1 lb)	30 ml	12-13 minutes	Scrub well and prick
Potatoes, baked	4 medium	–	12-16 minutes	Scrub well and prick
Potatoes, mashed	4 medium	m5 ml	16-18 minutes	Peel and cut into cubes
Pumpkin	450 g (1 lb)	45 ml (3 tablespoons)	8-10 minutes	Peel and dice
Spinach	450 g (1 lb)	–	6-9 minutes	Cook with water that clings to the leaves. Remove thick stalks
Squash, hubbard	450 g (1 lb)	45 ml (3 tablespoons)	8-10 minutes	Peel and dice
Squash, patty pan	4 medium-sized	45 ml (3 tablespoons)	5-7 minutes	Wash well and prick
Sweetcorn	4 ears	–	7-8 minutes	Rotate half-way through cooking time
Sweet potatoes	4 medium	45 ml (3 tablespoons)	12-15 minutes	Peel and slice
Tomatoes, sliced	4 medium	–	4-5 minutes	Slice, dot with butter
Tomatoes, stewed	4 medium	15 ml (1 tablespoon)	6-8 minutes	Peel and chop roughly
Turnips	3 medium	30 ml (2 tablespoons)	10-12 minutes	Peel and dice

PASTA AND RICE COOKING CHART

PASTA/RICE	COOKING TIME (100%)	PREPARATION
Egg noodles and tagliatelle, 250 g (9 oz)	7-9 minutes, stand 5 minutes	Add 600 ml (19 fl oz) boiling water, 2.5 ml (½ tsp) salt, 10 ml (2 tsp) oil
Spaghetti, 250 g (9 oz)	14-16 minutes, stand 5 minutes	Add 900 ml (29 fl oz) boiling water, 2.5 ml (½ tsp) salt, 10 ml (2 tsp) oil
Macaroni, 250 g (9 oz)	10-12 minutes, stand 5 minutes	Add 600 ml (19 fl oz) boiling water, 2.5 ml (½ tsp) salt, 10 ml (2 tsp) oil
Lasagne, 250 g (9 oz)	14-16 minutes	Add 1 ℓ (1¾ pints) boiling water, 2.5 ml (½ tsp) salt, 10 ml (2 tsp) oil
Pasta shells, 250 g (9 oz)	18-20 minutes, stand 5 minutes	Add 1 ℓ (1¾ pints) boiling water, 2.5 ml (½ tsp) salt, 10 ml (2 tsp) oil
Rice, 200 g (7 oz)	12-15 minutes, stand 20 minutes	Add 500 ml (16 fl oz) boiling water, 2.5 ml (½ tsp) salt, 10 ml (2 tsp) oil. Keep rice sealed during standing time
Brown rice, 200 g (7 oz)	25-30 minutes, stand 20 minutes	Add 600 ml (19 fl oz) boiling water, 2.5 ml (½ tsp) salt, 5 ml (1 tsp) oil. Keep rice sealed during standing time

General index

Index to hints